MASCULINITY, MILITARISM AND EIGHTEENTH-CENTURY CULTURE, 1689–1815

JULIA BANISTER
Leeds Beckett University

CAMBRIDGE
UNIVERSITY PRESS

University Printing House, Cambridge CB2 8BS, United Kingdom

One Liberty Plaza, 20th Floor, New York, NY 10006, USA

477 Williamstown Road, Port Melbourne, VIC 3207, Australia

314–321, 3rd Floor, Plot 3, Splendor Forum, Jasola District Centre,
New Delhi – 110025, India

79 Anson Road, #06-04/06, Singapore 079906

Cambridge University Press is part of the University of Cambridge.

It furthers the University's mission by disseminating knowledge in the pursuit of
education, learning, and research at the highest international levels of excellence.

www.cambridge.org
Information on this title: www.cambridge.org/9781107195196
DOI: 10.1017/9781108163927

© Julia Banister 2018

This publication is in copyright. Subject to statutory exception
and to the provisions of relevant collective licensing agreements,
no reproduction of any part may take place without the written
permission of Cambridge University Press.

First published 2018

Printed in the United Kingdom by Clays, St Ives plc

A catalogue record for this publication is available from the British Library.

ISBN 978-1-107-19519-6 Hardback

Cambridge University Press has no responsibility for the persistence or accuracy of URLs
for external or third-party internet websites referred to in this publication and does not
guarantee that any content on such websites is, or will remain, accurate or appropriate

Contents

Acknowledgments		*page* vii
	Introduction: Debating Military Masculinity	1
1	The Military Man and Augustan Anxieties: Trenchard, Steele, Boswell	14
2	Performing Military Professionalism: The Trials of Admirals Thomas Mathews and Richard Lestock, 1744–1746	44
3	The New Old Military Hero: The Trial of Admiral John Byng, 1756–1757	72
4	The Military Man and the Return to the Gothic Past: Hume, Hurd, Walpole	97
5	The Military Man and the Culture of Sensibility: Smith, Ferguson, Mackenzie	123
6	The Making of Military Celebrity: The Trials of Admirals Augustus Keppel and Hugh Palliser, 1778–1779	151
7	(De)Romanticizing Military Heroism: Clarke, Southey, Austen	185
	Conclusion: Rethinking Military Masculinity	218
Bibliography		227
Index		253

Acknowledgments

These acknowledgements must begin at the beginning by thanking those to whom I owe the oldest debts of gratitude: thank you to Stephen Bending, and also Stephen Bygrave, Emma Clery and Markman Ellis. The beginning was some time ago and I'm grateful to everyone who has offered encouragement since. The following chapter on Admiral Byng's court martial develops and expands my contribution to *Masculinity and the Other: Historical Perspectives* (Cambridge Scholars Press). That publication resulted from one of many conferences from which I have benefited and my thanks to all those conferences' organizers. In recent years I have been lucky enough to be working alongside two exceptionally collegial colleagues, Sue Chaplin and Nick Cox, and also to find excellent scholarship and fellowship at the Eighteenth Century and Romantic Research Seminar, University of Leeds. These acknowledgements ought to end at the end, with my thanks to Linda Bree, the two rigorous and insightful anonymous readers, and all at Cambridge University Press. But the last line before the first line belongs to Jeremy Davies – 'for that and more' – and to Lynda Banister and Miles Banister.

Introduction
Debating Military Masculinity

> We talked of war. JOHNSON. "Every man thinks meanly of himself for not having been a soldier, or not having been at sea." BOSWELL. "Lord Mansfield does not." JOHNSON. "Sir, if Lord Mansfield were in a company of General Officers and Admirals who have been in service, he would shrink; he'd wish to creep under the table." BOSWELL. "No; he'd think he could *try* them all." JOHNSON. "Yes, if he could catch them: but they'd try him much sooner."[1]
>
> *The Life of Samuel Johnson* (1791)

In this fragment of conversation, James Boswell records an exchange of views with Samuel Johnson about the relationship between eighteenth-century masculinity and eighteenth-century militarism. Johnson's opinion, that every civilian man 'thinks meanly of himself', permits the military man, whether solider or sailor, to hold himself in high regard. The man who has experienced military service, whether on land or at sea, is entitled to feel that he is more than adequate as a man, Johnson suggests, whereas the civilian knows that he is lacking, that he is somehow insufficient. With this, Johnson generalizes both military service and masculinity. As Boswell goes on to note, when Johnson pronounced on the lives of soldiers and sailors in their separate services, he could cast praise and censure on either, but 'when warmed and animated by the presence of company, he, like other philosophers, whose minds are impregnated with poetical fancy, caught the common enthusiasm for splendid renown.'[2] Of course, Johnson's confident assertion that every non-military man feels inadequate is coupled with his recognition that military service was, to many men, insufficiently tempting. Johnson's everyman had every opportunity to experience military service in the long eighteenth century; with each of the wars fought

---

[1] James Boswell, *The Life of Samuel Johnson*, 2 vols. (London: Charles Dilly, 1791), II, p. 211.
[2] Boswell, *The Life of Johnson*, II, p. 212.

during this period, the ranks and decks of the nation's services required ever greater numbers. The practical demands of assembling and equipping, directing and sustaining ever-expanding military forces weighed heavily upon often fractious and factional parliaments.³ Little wonder, then, that Boswell counters Johnson's opinion by invoking Lord Mansfield, the Lord Chief Justice and a conspicuous political figure. With his swift rejoinder, Boswell asserts that a modern professional man, a man in a position of authority and influence, has no reason to be embarrassed for not having seen military service. Whereas Johnson maintains that militarism and manliness are interconnected in a way every man necessarily understands, however reluctantly, Boswell dismisses any such connection as idealistic and outdated.

It has been some time since David Morgan, in what was a pioneering collection of essays for the emerging field of masculinity studies, asked scholars to pay greater attention to masculinities formed in relation to military service: 'of all the sites where masculinities are constructed, reproduced and deployed, those associated with war and the military are some of the most direct.'⁴ In recent years, valuable work on the social and cultural history of military service in the eighteenth century has been undertaken, notably by Margarette Lincoln, Matthew McCormack and Catriona Kennedy.⁵ However, the history of men and war can all too easily become, as McCormack puts it, 'an assumption rather than a subject for gender history in its own right.'⁶ The assumption may well be rooted in the fact that military service was for centuries an exclusively (at least in theory) male occupation, but it may well be nourished by the way that, as

---

³ Jeremy Black weighs the significance of government administration in creating British military power in *Britain as a Military Power: 1688–1815* (London: UCL Press, 1999). See also John Brewer, *The Sinews of Power: War, Money and the English State, 1689–1783* (London: Unwin Hyman, 1989).
⁴ David H. J. Morgan, 'Theatre of War: Combat, the Military, and Masculinities', in *Theorizing Masculinities*, ed. by Harry Brod and Michael Kauffman (Thousand Oaks, CA: SAGE, 1994), pp. 165–82 (at p. 165).
⁵ Margarette Lincoln, *Representing the Royal Navy: British Sea Power, 1750–1815* (Aldershot: Ashgate, 2002); Matthew McCormack and Catriona Kennedy, *Soldiering in Britain and Ireland, 1750–1850: Men at Arms* (Basingstoke: Palgrave Macmillan, 2012); Catriona Kennedy, *Narratives of the Revolutionary and Napoleonic Wars: Military and Civilian Experience in Britain and Ireland* (Basingstoke: Palgrave Macmillan, 2013).
⁶ *Public Men: Masculinity and Politics in Modern Britain*, ed. by Matthew McCormack (Basingstoke: Palgrave MacMillan, 2007), p. 3. See also Karen Harvey, 'The History of Masculinity, circa 1650–1800', *Journal of British Studies*, 44 (2005), 296–311. Mention must also be made of Karen Hagemann's work on masculinity and European militarism: 'The Military and Masculinity: Gendering the History of the Revolutionary and Napoleonic Wars, 1792–1815', in *War in an Age of Revolution*, ed. by Roger Chickering and Stig Förster (Cambridge: Cambridge University Press, 2010), pp. 331–52; *Masculinities in Politics and War: Gendering Modern History*, ed. by Stefan Dudink, Karen Hagemann and John Tosh (Manchester: Manchester University Press, 2004).

Paul Higate observes, 'the archetypal warrior figure tends to be constructed in opposition to a range of others, marginal masculinities, femininities, and civilians.'[7] Higate's point is that gender historians tend to idenfity the military man as the bearer of a distinct, clearly-defined masculinity, albeit one that jostles for hegemonic status with other masculinities and femininities in any historical period. This study takes a different approach. Rather than focus on the military man's relationships with 'others', the following chapters identify competing versions of the military 'self' and argue that these versions can reveal the currency of different conceptualizations of masculinity during the long eighteenth century. In other words, this study takes as its starting point the notion that ideas about militarism, like those forwarded by Johnson and Boswell, are predicated upon, and so become vehicles for, ideas about masculinity, and more specifically about whether masculinity can and should be understood as an essence, lodged within and made manifest by a 'naturally' sexed body, or as a contingent, malleable and commodifiable construction. In practice, this entails mapping accounts of militarism forwarded by critics and commentators who conceptualize gender as a 'natural', in the sense of essential, product of the apparently timelessly sexed body, and those who are able to see gender as something acquired and enacted, that is, arguments that can be termed proto-constructionist.

To study a century in which Britain was so often at war is to find an abundance of representations of and discussions about military men, but the following chapters are primarily concerned with those representations and discussions that can be positioned in relation to two narratives that are long-standing within eighteenth-century studies. The first of these is the late seventeenth and early eighteenth-century investment in civic humanism. In his classic work *The Machiavellian Moment*, J. G. A. Pocock argues that at the time of the Restoration, and for much of the century that followed, civic humanist thought was a powerful weapon in the hands of those anxious to arrest the spread of what they considered to be the new and dangerous forms of corruption that had emerged with the return of monarchical power and the emboldening of courtier politicians. Throughout this period, Pocock argues, the self-consciously civic-minded saw themselves as 'a classical *populus*, a community of virtue, ... their virtue as consisting in their freeholds.'[8] To these civic thinkers, property

---

[7] *Military Masculinities: Identity and the State*, ed. by Paul R. Higate (Westport, CT: Praeger, 2003), p. 201.
[8] J. G. A. Pocock, *The Machiavellian Moment: Florentine Political Thought and the Atlantic Republican Tradition*, 2nd ed. (Princeton, NJ: Princeton University Press, 1975; repr. 2003), p. 408.

ensured liberty, for the freeholder was protected from dependence and so secured against all forms of tyranny, but with the status of the independent citizen came the responsibility to defend the nation from other kinds of attack. Machiavelli's seventeenth-century predecessors clung to the idea that the purest way to discharge that responsibility was, as it had been in the classical past, through participation in a national militia, and in the years after the Revolution of 1688, when the issue of the relationship between power and the people was pressing, 'the myth of the English militia became potent'.[9] The efforts to revive the militia throughout the century that followed have been documented by J. R. Western and, more recently, Matthew McCormack, but it might be fair to say that the eighteenth-century's civic thinkers are better known to eighteenth-century studies as the Jeremiahs who railed against 'luxury', for as Emma Clery has shown, eighteenth-century anxiety about the increasing importance of urbane sociability and leisured consumption was also anxiety about the growing acceptability of the feminization of male manners.[10]

Drawing on Pocock's account of civic thinking, my discussion begins with the argument that the civic investment in the militiaman was also an investment in the essential 'nature' of masculinity. Pocock observes that the civic thinkers of the late seventeenth and eighteenth century did not see, or perhaps more accurately did not acknowledge, any anachronism in appealing to the classical past for models that might serve to reform the present. In Pocock's words, 'the civic or participatory ideal … acknowledged to exist mainly in the past … employed a theory of social personality in which virtue was held to be civic and was grounded on material bases which could not be bartered away without the loss of virtue itself.'[11] The fundamental importance of 'material bases' for the 'participatory ideal' can be extended from the materiality of property to the materiality of the body. As Pocock states, in the classical republic each propertied citizen was a 'participant in the authority by which he was ruled; this entailed relations of equality which made in fact extremely stern demands on upon him, but by premising that he was *kata phūsin* [according to nature] formed to participate in such citizenship it could be said that it was his 'nature',

---

[9] Pocock, *Machiavellian Moment*, p. 414.
[10] J. R. Western, *The English Militia in the Eighteenth Century: The Story of a Political Issue, 1660–1802* (London: Routledge, 1965); Matthew McCormack, *Embodying the Militia in Georgian England* (Oxford: Oxford University Press, 2015). For the 'luxury debate' see John Sekora, *Luxury: The Concept in Western Thought, Eden to Smollett* (Baltimore: Johns Hopkins University Press, 1977) and Emma Clery, *The Feminization Debate in Eighteenth-Century England: Literature, Commerce and Luxury* (Basingstoke: Palgrave Macmillan, 2004).
[11] Pocock, *Machiavellian Moment*, p. 436.

'essence' or 'virtue' to do so.'[12] In other words, the civic citizen-soldier who acts militarily in accordance with his responsibility to do so is virtuous in the sense that he does what he ought, but also in the sense that he, and specifically 'he', does what he is 'formed' to do. This reading of Pocock's argument can be reinforced by turning to McCormack's history of the 'New Militia'. According to McCormack, efforts to revive the militia in the mid-century were motivated by fears for the nation's masculinity as much as its safety. Thus, the desire to embody the militia reveals the mid-century's enthusiasm for embodying a notion of masculinity that could combat the ever-present threat of national decline via the slippery slope of 'politeness' into the abject abyss of effeminacy.[13] Beginning with the importance of virtuous-because-amateur citizen-soldier as a idealized model for masculinity and militarism, then, this study tracks the argument that the military man does what he is formed to do by positioning the militiaman as one of several models for militarism that are equally invested in the timelessness of men's essential 'nature', models I gather together with the term 'old hero'.

Historians of eighteenth-century gender have long held the view that the century saw a hardening of attitudes with regard to the relationship between gender and the sexed (and sexual) body.[14] The most significant work on eighteenth-century understandings of the body is still to be found in Lacqueur's study of the epistemological shift from the 'one-sex' to the 'two-sex' model, that is, from the idea that male and female bodies were inverted versions of each other to the idea that they were differently formed and opposite in nature.[15] Lacqueur's thesis underpins Dror Wahrman argument that the 1770s and 1780s saw the transition from an *ancien régime* of gender', in which gender was understood to be 'learned, imitated, performed, donned, and doffed at will', to a 'new sex-gender regime' in which gender was understood to be 'innate, essential, and pre-determined by sex.' For Warhman, the *ancién regime* is characterized by

---

[12] J. G. A. Pocock, 'Virtues, Rights, Manners: A Model for Historians of Political Thought', in *Virtue, Commerce, and History: Essays on Political Thought, Chiefly in the Eighteenth Century* (Cambridge: Cambridge University Press, 1985), pp. 37–50 (at p. 43).
[13] McCormack, *Embodying the Militia in Georgian England*, esp. pp. 13–32.
[14] For an overview of this argument see Robert B. Shoemaker, *Gender in English Society, 1650–1850: The Emergence of Separate Spheres?* (London: Longman, 1998). For the argument that the eighteenth century saw the naturalization of heterosexuality, see Randolph Trumbach, *Sex and the Gender Revolution*: Vol. 1: *Heterosexuality and the Third Gender in Enlightenment London* (Chicago: University of Chicago Press, 1998); Tim Hitchcock, *English Sexualities, 1700–1800* (Basingstoke: Macmillan, 1997).
[15] Thomas Lacqueur, *Making Sex: Body and Gender from the Greeks to Freud* (Cambridge, MA: Harvard University Press, 1990).

'gender play' and the arrival of the modern moment by 'gender panic'.[16] And yet, Lacqueur's history of the body can equally be read, not as a linear narrative of transition, but as a single history told in two stages. Lacqueur asserts that the 'one-sex' model, the belief that male and female sex organs were the same but inverted, sustained a hierarchy in which women were lesser. In the 'two-sex' model, the idea of fundamental difference between male and female sex organs sustained a hierarchy in which women were 'other'.[17] In both cases, gender positions are prescribed and inequality justified on the basis of binary oppositions 'read into a body that did not itself mark these distinctions clearly', a body 'burdened with the cultural work done by these propositions.'[18] In both stages, then, the physical body is made into meaning, or to put it another way, neither the 'one-sex' nor the 'two-sex' model offers a narrative in which meaning is not contrived from the physicality of the body.

Whereas Wahrman takes Lacqueur's argument to mean that gender was able to float freely until it was netted and pinned to the body at the end of the century as part of the new 'identity regime', this study appeals to Lacqueur's narrative in order to suggest that the body was available as a foundation for conceptualizations of gender throughout the eighteenth century. Given that the connection between matter and meaning is far from 'natural', as the shift from the 'one-sex' to the 'two-sex' model indicates, this study also encounters the inescapable tension within arguments that extract gender from the body. The argument that bodily matter can and should be understood to be the basis for gender is simultaneously an appeal to the physicality of body – that which is, apparently, 'real' – and an assertion that there is something that exceeds the mere physicality of human flesh and blood – that is, the qualities and characteristics that are said belong to, or are produced by a specifically male or a specifically female body. In other words, an argument for 'natural' gender relies on the tangible 'truth' of bodily matter to give substance to that which must be more than just a mass of tangible material. Such an argument is inevitably an exercise in high-wire rhetoric, ever prone to wobbling and, ultimately, falling in on itself.

As mentioned at the start of this introduction, this study is concerned with competing versions of the military man. Though eighteenth-century

---

[16] Dror Wahrman, *The Making of the Modern Self: Identity and Culture in Eighteenth-Century England* (New Haven, CT: Yale University Press, 2004), pp. 48, 41.
[17] Lacqueur, *Making Sex*, esp. pp. 148–54.
[18] Ibid., pp. 61–2, 153.

civic thinkers denied the anachronism of returning to classical models, their appeal to the virtuous citizen-soldier was to come under pressure from the rise of the 'modern' soldier. The idea that a 'military revolution' occurred in Europe between 1500 and 1800 was proposed by Michael Roberts and established as a master narrative for military history by Geoffrey Parker.[19] The military revolution thesis holds that over the course of three centuries the technologies and tactics, the funding and administration and the social and cultural significance of military service, on land and at sea, changed such that by the end of the eighteenth century all that was 'old' had been replaced by that which was 'new'. As Azar Gat argues, the military revolution, made possible by the revolution in European trade and commerce, 'paralleled ... Europe's wider, sweeping transformation during those same centuries: indeed, ... it formed an "aspect" of early modernization.'[20] As such, the narrative of the military revolution is also an account of the modernization of the men who served in the increasingly permanent, professionalized armies and navies. Certainly, the introduction of new weapons, designed to be wielded in newly structured battles, whether on land or at sea, required the increasing numbers of soldiers and sailors, deployed in the service of global imperial ambition, to be moulded by new kinds of discipline and training. Following Parker, Michael Duffy asserts that the growth in the size of countries' permanent military establishments is the crucial marker of the change from pre-modern to modern, since higher numbers prompted the development of state machinery able to finance, equip and sustain the increase, as well as authorities to manage these modernized military men.[21]

When Roberts introduced the idea of the military revolution he forwarded it as the 'great divide separating medieval society from the modern world', one aspect of which was to replace military men who were 'individualist[s]' with those who were standardized.[22] With this, Roberts

---

[19] Michael Roberts, 'The Military Revolution, 1500–1660', in *The Military Revolution Debate: Readings on the Military Transformation of Early Modern Europe*, ed. by Clifford J. Rogers (Boulder, CA: Westview Press, 1995), pp. 13–35 (first publ. (Belfast, 1956)); Geoffrey Parker, 'The Military Revolution 1560–1660 – A Myth?', in *The Military Revolution Debate*, pp. 37–54 (first publ. *Journal of Modern History*, 48.2 (1976), 195–214.

[20] Azar Gat, 'What Constituted the Military Revolution of the Early Modern Period?', in *War in an Age of Revolution*, pp. 21–48 (at p. 23).

[21] Geoffrey Parker, *The Military Revolution: Military Innovation and the Rise of the West, 1500–1800* (Cambridge: Cambridge University Press, 1988); *The Military Revolution and the State, 1500–1800* (Exeter: University of Exeter Press, 1980), ed. by Michael Duffy, pp. 1–9.

[22] Roberts, 'The Military Revolution', pp. 13, 29.

pre-empted Michel Foucault's account of the emergence of the modern soldier during the eighteenth century:

> Let us take the ideal figure of the soldier as it was still seen in the early seventeenth century ... he bore certain signs: the natural signs of his strength and courage, the marks, too, of his pride; his body was the blazon of his strength and valour ... By the late eighteenth century, the soldier has become something that can be made; out of formless clay, an inapt body, the machine required can be constructed.[23]

Foucault's argument that the modern soldier was pressed into being, like clay in a mould, concurs with military historians' view that the 'submergence of the individual', as Roberts puts it, occurred during what Martin van Creveld terms the 'Age of Machines', the period in which technological advances in weaponry meant that 'the ability to kill ... was no longer directly related to an individual's physical prowess, but tended to become a question of trained, professional skill.'[24] That said, Foucault's description of the standardized modern soldier as a product of what he terms the 'military dream of society' draws out the implications of the phrase 'age of machines', for Foucault holds that whereas the *ancien régime* subjected bodies to power using corporeal punishment, the modern regime understood bodies to be formless clay until inscribed/impressed by power and so exercised power by producing bodies.[25] The modern soul is not trapped within the inscribed body, Foucault asserts, for 'the [illusion of the] soul is the prison of the body.'[26] It is the immateriality of the Foucauldian body, the fact that the "body' in Foucault's discourse does not function as a name of some thing, as a linguistic symbol representing a real object out there somewhere obediently sitting still while it is referred to', that underpins Judith Butler's seminal account of the social construction of gender through performativity.[27] With this in mind, it is possible to see that, whereas the civic militiaman acts because he is formed by nature to do so, the military revolution's modern military man performs, in a Butlerian sense, that which is not supposed or required to be 'natural'. The modern military man is, in Foucault's words, 'above all a fragment of mobile space, before he is courage or honour'.[28]

---

[23] Michel Foucault, *Discipline and Punish: The Birth of the Prison*, trans. by Alan Sheridan (London: Penguin, 1975; repr. 1991), p. 135.
[24] Roberts, 'The Military Revolution', p. 29; Martin van Creveld, *Technology and War, from 2000BC to the Present* (New York: Macmillan 1989), pp. 81–149 (at p. 82).
[25] Foucault, *Discipline and Punish*, p. 169.
[26] Ibid., p. 30.
[27] Ladelle McWhorter, 'Culture of Nature? The Function of the Term 'Body' in the Work of Michel Foucault', *The Journal of Philosophy*, 86.11 (1989), 608–14 (at p. 613).
[28] Foucault, *Discipline and Punish*, p. 164.

Although this study absorbs and combines Foucault's account of the modern military man and Butler's theory of performativity, it does so with due regard to Butler's reservations about 'formless clay.' Butler takes issues with Foucault, and by extension with his historicizing of performativity, for in her view, Foucault's narrative of the emergence of the socially constructed body figures history as a 'writing instrument' and so turns the body into 'a ready surface or blank page available for inscription, awaiting the "imprint" of history itself.'[29] For Butler, the body does not precede performance: performance produces the illusion of 'true' materiality, and with it 'natural' sex/gender. This study historicizes performativity by identifying arguments that treat the illusion as 'real' or 'true', that is, arguments that defend the bodily 'nature' of militarism and masculinity. However, this study also historicizes performativity by exploring how far representations of and discussion about the modern military man were able to conceive of a space between gender and the body. The Lockean turn towards empirical observation by the beginning of the eighteenth century introduced the idea of the blank mind, the *tabula rasa*, waiting to be inscribed by experience; an appropriate corollary to this would be a blank body, a *corpus rasa*, waiting for inscription, perhaps, but no longer pre-inscribed. One way to historicize performativity, then, is to recognize that an awareness of the blank body – a body that is not yet illusion, but is no longer the source of meaning – is the precursor to the Foucauldian/Butlerian mobile, empty space. Such proto-constructionism may not be robust from every angle; some of the texts I examine seem to have difficulty conceptualizing femininity as a construction, for example. However, this approach to historicizing performativity is able to identify arguments that in some way 'trouble' the interiority and naturalness of militarism, and with this, the interiority and naturalness of masculinity.

Of course, to follow competing versions of the military man is also to be alert to the conflicts and tensions that are internal to them. The essentialized citizen-soldier and his decedents are unstable, but the 'truth' of antiquity helps conceals contradictions; in comparison, the constructed modern military man is even less secure, for lacking the rhetorical ballast provided by the sexed body, proto-constructionist arguments are inherently vulnerable to attack. That said, it might be though that this study of civic militiamen, in their many forms, and modern military men will resolve itself into

---

[29] Judith Butler, 'Foucault and the Paradox of Bodily Inscriptions', *The Journal of Philosophy*, 86.11 (1989), 601–7 (at p. 603).

a single narrative of 'change'. Pocock argues that civic thinking was particularly potent in the late seventeenth and early eighteenth century but that it declined from this point. His chronology seems to tally with the military historians' view that the military revolution that began in the sixteenth century was completed by the end of the eighteenth. Historian of masculinity, John Tosh, can be drawn in to this, for in a survey of the period 1750–1850 Tosh notes of the 'bearing of arms', a term that leans towards the civic ideal of citizen-soldiering, not least because he defines this as 'the central attribute of manhood since feudal times', declined in importance: 'Military manliness was still at a premium during the Napoleonic Wars, but it rapidly lost ground after 1815.' Tosh's overarching argument is that change happens slowly, but this is one transition, he argues, that 'bears the unmistakable imprint of bourgeois values in the ascendant.'[30] And yet, Jeremy Black's account of the military revolution raises a note of caution. Black argues that the accepted span of the military revolution could well be narrowed to highlight the late seventeenth and early eighteenth centuries as the critical period of transition, particularly for Britain and its old enemy, France, but he is equally interested in the fact that all military innovation was subject to constraints, from impassably muddy roads and rotting wooden hulls to poor harvests, making for poor supplies and exacerbating outbreaks of epidemics.[31] Rather than try to forge a neatly linear narrative for modernization in both attitudes to militarism and masculinity, this study examines parallel, or rather seemingly parallel, lines of argument that were shaped by their inherent tensions, by contact with each other and by wider cultural forces. Having stated that this is a study of competing versions of the ideal military man, it must be said that the following chapters are concerned to follow ideals that clashed against, rather than conquered or displaced each other.

The following paragraphs are intended to clarify the structure of this book. The opening chapter offers a close study of the standing army debate which took place in England in the final years of the seventeenth century. The standing army debate was a response to the call for the modernization of the nation's military services and in this first chapter I tease out the ways in which each side in that debate forwarded a model military man and an

---

[30] John Tosh, 'The Old Adam and the New Man: Emerging Themes in the History of English Masculinities, 1750–1850', in *English Masculinities 1660–1800*, ed. by Tim Hitchcock and Michèle Cohen (Harlow, Essex: Addison Wesley Longman, 1999), pp. 217–38 (at p. 222).
[31] Jeremy Black, *A Military Revolution? Military Change and European Society, 1550–1800* (Basingstoke: Macmillan, 1991), pp. 35–52. See also Christopher Duffy, *The Military Experience in the Age of Reason* (London: Routledge and Kegan Paul, 1987), pp. 313–8.

account of masculinity. Subsequent chapters focus on debate about the military man as conducted in a range of literary texts and in concert with major eighteenth-century cultural concerns: politeness, the gothic, sensibility and celebrity. But although this is a study of representations and arguments, this book also pays heed to Karen Harvey and Alexandra Shepard's warning that historians of masculinity 'need to deal not just in free-floating cultural attributes, but in grounded social or psychic contexts of experience that interact with representations.'[32] To that end, three of the following chapters focus on case studies of naval courts martial: the trials of Admirals Thomas Mathews and Richard Lestock, 1744–6; the trial of Admiral John Byng, 1756–7; and the trials of Admirals Augustus Keppel and Sir Hugh Palliser, 1778–9. The notion of the military revolution is as relevant to the navy as to the army; indeed, for Black, 'navies provide some of the best indicators of change.'[33] By following five naval trials, these chapters are able to bring the cases into dialogue with each other. Furthermore, each case study has been chosen on the basis of the strength of popular interest shown in it, for the navy was the last line of defence against invasion and news of naval failure generated widespread interest in those deemed to be responsible. As Daniel Baugh notes, courts martial 'directed a searchlight of publicity on the conduct of sea officers', and so in focusing on these five trials, I highlight moments in the eighteenth century when a man was called to describe and justify his military actions to a court composed of his peers but also to the public at large.[34]

While some of the texts studied in the following chapters might have had comparatively small readerships, the five naval trials concluded with formal verdicts passed by the court and informal verdicts that circulated in the popular public sphere. My sense of the public sphere derives from Jürgen Habermas' account of the rise and fall of the bourgeois public sphere. By the end of the eighteenth century, Habermas argues, 'the reign of public opinion appeared as the reign of the many and the mediocre' as

---

[32] Karen Harvey and Alexandra Shepard, 'What Have Historians done with Masculinity? Reflections on Five Centuries of British History, circa 1500–1950', *Journal of British Studies*, 44 (2005), 274–80 (at p. 280).

[33] Jeremy Black, 'A Military Revolution? A 1660–1792 Perspective', in *The Military Revolution Debate*, pp. 95–114 (at p. 97). See also Parker, *The Military Revolution*, pp. 82–114; Michael Duffy, 'The Foundations of Naval Power', in *The Military Revolution and the State*, pp. 49–90; Laurent Henninger, 'Military Revolutions and Military History', *Palgrave Advances in Modern Military History*, ed. by Matthew Hughes and William J. Philpott (Basingstoke: Palgrave Macmillan, 2006), pp. 8–22 (at pp. 13–15).

[34] Daniel Baugh, *British Naval Administration in the Age of Walpole* (Princeton, NJ: Princeton University Press, 1965), p. 144.

'private persons came to be the private persons of a public rather than a public of private persons.'[35] My willingness to employ Habermas' distinction between a public of private persons – the bourgeois public sphere – and the private persons of the public – the popular public sphere – takes note of more recent work on extra-parliamentary politics. Though Habermas recognizes that 'the "sense of the people", "the common voice", "the general cry of the people", and finally "the public spirit"' are terms that were used from the beginning of the eighteenth century, he warns that 'such occurrences, of course, must not be construed prematurely as a sign of a kind of rule of public opinion.'[36] In contrast, historians of the public, building on the foundations laid by E. P. Thompson's rehabilitation of the eighteenth-century crowd, have sought to document a tradition of eighteenth-century extra-parliamentary protest which reveals, as Black puts it, that 'those who … did not possess the vote, could seek to influence political decisions'. This may not constitute the 'rule' of public opinion, but in recovering the 'sense of the people', the term Kathleen Wilson prefers, scholars have gone some way to identify what Nicholas Rogers terms 'the creative possibilities of the common people in class struggle.'[37] The fact that this public was intensely interested in military as well as party-political matters is indicated by Linda Colley, whose thesis, that British identity was 'an invention formed above all by war', stresses that, by the end of the century, the nation wholeheartedly embraced its military men as heroes.[38]

Of course, this book makes no claim to have comprehensively documented eighteenth-century understandings of militarism or conceptualizations of masculinity. In particular, I am conscious that my approach does not specifically highlight women's views. For some feminist scholars, a Habermasian distinction between types of public sphere fails to take into account women's exclusion from public life: in Johanna Meehan's words, 'Habermas's account suffers from a gender blindness that occludes the differential social and political status of men and women.'[39] That said, it has

---

[35] Jürgen Habermas, *The Structural Transformation of the Public Sphere*, trans. by Thomas Burger (Cambridge: Polity Press, 2006; repr. 1989) pp. 133, 128–9.
[36] Habermas, *Structural Transformation*, p. 64.
[37] Jeremy Black, *Robert Walpole and the Nature of Politics in Early Eighteenth-Century Britain* (Basingstoke: Macmillan, 1990), p. 65; Kathleen Wilson, *The Sense of the People: Politics, Culture, and Imperialism in England, 1715–1785* (Cambridge: Cambridge University Press, 1998; repr. 1995); Nicholas Rogers, *Crowds, Culture, and Politics in Georgian Britain* (Oxford: Clarendon Press, 1998), p. 7.
[38] Linda Colley, *Britons: Forging the Nation, 1707–1837*, 2nd ed. (New Haven, CT: Yale University Press, 2005), p. 5.
[39] *Feminists Read Habermas: Gendering the Subject of Discourse*, ed. by Johanna Meehan (New York: Routledge, 1995), p. 7.

Introduction: Debating Military Masculinity 13

been some time since Amanda Vickery observed approvingly that, 'doubts now circulate within women's history about the conceptual usefulness of the separate spheres framework.'[40] With this in mind, the final chapter considers how proto-feminism responded to accounts of militarism that essentialized masculinity and so reinforced the gender binary. Rather than aim for as wide a survey of attitudes to masculinity and militarism as possible, then, I have narrowed the focus of these chapters to follow seemingly parallel lines of argument: the civic argument that all men are essentially military men and the counter-argument that modern men perform militarism and masculinity. In so doing, I have sought to map the cultural function of the military man, or rather, versions of the military man, as vehicles for ideas about the 'nature' of masculinity in the long eighteenth century.

---

[40] Amanda Vickery, 'Golden Age to Separate Spheres? A Review of the Categories and Chronology of English Women's History', *The Historical Journal*, 36.2 (1993), 383–414 (at p. 393).

CHAPTER I

The Military Man and Augustan Anxieties
Trenchard, Steele, Boswell

> It is the Fashion of the F[rench] K[ing] to have a STANDING ARMY, and it is the Fashion of his Subjects to be Slaves under that STANDING ARMY ... And I am afraid we shall never think our selves compleatly in the Fashion till we have got Wooden Shoes too.[1]
>
> John Trenchard (1697)

During the brief period of peace between the end of the Nine Years' War in 1697 and the beginning of the War of the Spanish Succession in 1701, a pitched pamphlet war was fought in England over whether the king should, and indeed could, constitutionally, maintain a standing army during peace-time. This debate had been threatening to erupt for some time. By the mid-seventeenth century, other monarchs in western Europe had relinquished the still recognizably feudal system of raising troops for specific conflicts and had begun to maintain bodies of soldiers as standing armies. On his return from the continent in 1660, Charles II had instituted a permanent establishment of royal guards, and during the tense 1680s James II had quietly increased their number, but neither had attempted to create a permanent army, and so when William III became king in 1689 he did not acquire a standing force.[2] While England was at war with France (1689–97), discussion of the army's standing had to be curtailed; but on the outbreak of peace, William requested leave to retain some of those who had served in the conflict, and thereby create a standing army. As precedent decreed that during peace-time the army should be reduced to guards and garrisons, William's petition unleashed

---

[1] [John Trenchard], *A Letter from the Author of the Argument Against a Standing Army, to the Author of the Balancing Letter* (London, 1697), p. 6.
[2] John Childs, *Armies and Warfare in Europe, 1648–1789* (Manchester: Manchester University Press, 1982) and *The British Army of William III, 1689–1702* (Manchester: Manchester University Press, 1987); Craig Rose, *England in the 1690s: Revolution, Religion and War* (Oxford: Blackwell, 1999).

a storm of impassioned argument. Those opposed to the creation of a standing army argued that allowing men to be permanently embodied placed too much trust in William abiding by the limits imposed upon a monarch within a mixed constitution and so rendered the nation vulnerable. With so many men, it was argued, the king might turn against the very people who had accepted him as monarch. Those in favour of the king's petition argued that not sanctioning a standing army placed too much trust in another king, Louis XIV, abiding by the recently negotiated peace treaty and so left the nation just as vulnerable. There could be no danger from England's own monarch, so the argument went, as the Bill of Rights (1689) had enshrined Parliament's right to refuse to finance military campaigns, and this checked the king's power.

To read the standing army debate is to see that the Glorious Revolution had not brought stability to what was, to borrow Julian Hoppit's phrase, 'an anxious age'.[3] So divisive was the issue that it forged strange political alliances; a new Junto of court Whigs supported William's petition, while the possibility of a standing army horrified those in opposition who otherwise had good reason to oppose each other: Tories who still mourned the deposition of James II and 'old' Whigs who kept faith with commonwealth principles.[4] My reading of the standing army debate emphasizes that the contributors voiced their anxieties, not just about the balance of power between the king and the people, but also about the 'nature' of the nation's military men, for while the anti-standing army authors, most prominently John Trenchard, sought to revive the national militia – the body of citizens-turned-soldiers who could be marshalled when required for the defence of the realm – those who supported the proposal to establish a standing army demanded the introduction of 'professional, controlled, relatively homogenous' soldiers who would fight as required in return for a regular wage.[5] The second and third parts of the chapter trace the latter, the argument for modernizing militarism, into the first half of the eighteenth century to explore the tension between that argument and the culture of politeness. As Paul Langford makes plain, politeness developed in concert with the growth of a metropolitan culture of consumption, and the spaces

---

[3] Julian Hoppit, *A Land of Liberty? England 1689–1727* (Oxford: Clarendon, 2000).
[4] Lois G. Schwoerer, *"No Standing Armies!": The Antimilitary Ideology in Seventeenth-Century England* (Baltimore: Johns Hopkins University Press, 1974). See also J. A. Downie, 'Chronology and Authorship of the Standing Army Tracts: A Supplement', *Notes and Queries*, 23.8 (1976), 342–6; Laurence Kennedy, 'Standing Armies Revisited (1697–1700): Authorship, Chronology and Public Perception', *Notes and Queries*, 43.3 (1996), 287–92.
[5] Childs, *Armies and Warfare*, p. 28.

of polite society were first and foremost places of social exchange in which the ability to please others was the primary commodity.[6] In other words, to be polite, an individual had to acquire the social skills valued by polite society. In this milieu, Philip Carter argues, masculinity became 'a social category, created, maintained or undermined by men's social … performance.'[7] By turning to the quintessential 'polite' periodical, *The Spectator* (1711–14), and to James Boswell's *London Journal* (1762–3), this chapter argues that proponents of politeness acknowledged the modern military man as a fellow performer, but also that this point of connection was a shared weakness. To its critics, performance was necessarily hollow, unstable, lacking in substance. Thus, while advocates for politeness sought to defend the virtue of the modern military man, they were also anxiously aware that the alliance highlighted that which was inherently and unresolvedly problematic with regard to their and the modern military man's masculinity.

'A Pen and Ink War': The Standing Army Debate

'Soldiers by Instinct': The Anti-Standing Army Argument

As Lois Schwoerer observes, the civic republican politics of the mid-seventeenth century played a significant part in the opposition to William's proposal to establish a standing army.[8] The anti-standing army authors, most notably the one-time lawyer John Trenchard, but also the Irish scholar John Toland and the landed Scotsman Andrew Fletcher, argued against the creation of a permanently embodied army on the basis that such a force had the potential to become an instrument of absolutist tyranny and so threatened the liberty of the people. However, to call this argument 'anti-military', as Schwoerer does, is somewhat misleading. The anti-standing army argument was concerned with strengthening the nation's military might, for as Trenchard put it, '[the] Nation is surest to live in Peace, that is most capable of making War; and a Man that hath a Sword by his side, shall have least occasion to make use of it.'[9] For the anti-standing army

---

[6] Paul Langford, *A Polite and Commercial People, England 1727–1783* (Oxford: Clarendon, 1989). See also Michèle Cohen, *Fashioning Masculinity: National Identity and Language in the Eighteenth Century* (London: Routledge, 1996).
[7] Philip Carter, *Men and the Emergence of Polite Society: Britain, 1660–1800* (Harlow, Essex: Pearson, 2001), p. 209.
[8] Schwoerer, *"No Standing Armies!"*
[9] [John Trenchard], *An Argument Shewing That a Standing Army Is Inconsistent with a Free Government and Absolutely Destructive to the Constitution of English Monarchy* (London, 1697), p. 12.

authors, the answer to England's military needs lay in maintaining a strong navy to deter invaders and, crucially, in reviving the long-lapsed militia and thereby creating a force that could protect the nation in the event of an invasion. Rather than take an 'antimilitary' stance, then, the anti-standing army authors wanted as many men as possible to participate, at sea or on land, in military activity. Those who did not become sailors would be liable to be balloted for the militia, and though they were to be enrolled for a limited time only, repeated cycles of balloting would ensure that, at any point in time, all men would have served, be serving or be liable to give service in the future. Furthermore, for Toland and Fletcher, who forwarded detailed and ambitious plans for militia reform, the fact that every man would be liable to serve meant that men of all stations would be equal before the ballot. Fletcher states that 'no Bodies of Military Men can be of any force or value, unless many Persons of Quality or Education be among them', and though he refuses to arm 'slaves' on the basis that their loyalty cannot be guaranteed, Toland goes so far as to argue that it is essential to include servants to ensure that 'every Person in the Kingdom becomes a Soldier.'[10] There can be no danger, Toland adds, because servants would have only supervised access to arms.

The argument that men could protect their right to liberty only by providing service as militiamen was reinforced by the civic appeal to history.[11] For Trenchard in particular, the nation's militiamen were the descendants of classical citizen-soldiers:

> In those days there was no difference between the Citizen, the Souldier, and the Husbandman, for all promiscuously took Arms when the publick Safety required it, and afterwards laid them down with more Alacrity than they took them up: So that we find amongst the *Romans* the best and bravest of their Generals came from the Plough, contentedly returning when the Work was over, and never demanded their Triumphs till they had laid down their Commands, and reduced themselves to the state of private Men.[12]

Here, Trenchard employs an idea that would have been very familiar to those with a classical education, that the acts of taking up of military arms and agricultural tools were once interchangeable; in another of his

---

[10] [Andrew Fletcher], *A Discourse of Government with Relation to Militia's* (Edinburgh, 1698), pp. 48, 47; [John Toland], *The Militia Reform'd: Or, An Easy Scheme of Furnishing England with a Constant Land-Force Capable to Prevent or to Subdue any Forein Power, and to Maintain Perpetual Quiet at Home Without Endangering the Public Liberty*, 2nd ed. (London: Daniel Brown; Andrew Bell, 1699), p. 30.
[11] Pocock, *Machiavellian Moment*, pp. 427–61.
[12] [Trenchard], *An Argument Shewing*, p. 7.

pamphlets 'peace' is defined as 'a Cessation of the Exercise of the use of Arms, that we may with Safety turn our Swords into Plough-shares, and Spears into Pruning-hooks.'[13] Trenchard borrows the argument that arms were once easily exchanged for tools in order to argue that they might be again. In other words, his recourse to the classical past strengthens the argument that every modern male citizen can be militarized by indicating that their military capacity is rooted in a timeless male 'nature' shared by citizen, soldier and husbandman, past and present.

In returning to the classical citizen-soldier, then, Trenchard and the other 'Roman Whigs' appealed to the past to confirm that the capacity for militarism is essential to men. Trenchard's assertion that using military arms was once no different from using agricultural tools construes both as exercises of physical, bodily labour and with this he indicates that men's bodies are necessarily capable of militarism. The same argument can be found in the staunch 'old' Whig Samuel Johnson's calculation that it could make no sense to pay twenty thousand men to be standing soldiers at the real cost of potentially enslaving the nation when England could field its population of seven million adult men as militiamen. In Johnson's opinion, such a mass of English bodies would be more than a match for an army of standing soldiers, who,

> if they did …but seriously reflected, that they venture their Lives to support an unnatural and wicked Power of Oppression, as good Soldiers as many of them be, it would make their Swords drop out of their Hands. On the other side, when Men fight for a Country and Constitution that there is no out-living, and Death its self is the less damage of the two, they are ready to sacrifice themselves for it … [W]here there is sheer Courage in a Nation, Men are Soldiers by instinct.[14]

For Johnson, the fact that every man has the capacity to be a military man means that foreign invaders should never be able to get the better of English liberty: 'the Keepers of it are too many to be kill'd.'[15] As Johnson argues elsewhere, militiamen will defend English liberty by 'manfully fight[ing] it out to the separation of their Souls from their Bodies'.[16] Like Trenchard's appeal to the classical past, Johnson's assertion that any one

---

[13] [Trenchard], *A Letter from the Author*, p. 4.
[14] [Samuel Johnson], *A Confutation of a Late Pamphlet Intituled, A Letter Ballancing the Necessity of Keeping a Land Force in Times of Peace with the Dangers that may Follow on It* (London: A. Baldwin, 1698), pp. 19–20.
[15] [Samuel Johnson], *The Second Part of the Confutation of the Ballancing Letter. Containing an Occasional Discourse in Vindication of Magna Charta* (London: A. Baldwin, 1700), p. 78.
[16] [Johnson], *The Second Part of the Confutation of the Ballancing Letter*, p. 22.

of the nation's men could become a militiaman is a contention that male bodies are necessarily, in the sense of essentially, capable of militarism, and thus a vehicle for essentializing masculinity. That said, the instability of this essentialist argument can be glimpsed in Johnson's praise for 'sheer Courage ... by instinct'. In the anti-standing army account of it, courage is a quality that inheres within, but one that can be confirmed only by physical expressions without. The anti-standing army argument invests heavily in what is natural, innate and essential, but if that which is external guarantees that which is internal, the physical is also more than physical. As a result, the 'truth' of essential militarism, like that of masculinity, is everywhere and nowhere at once.

Though overtly concerned with developing the nation's military forces, the anti-standing army argument that men are soldiers by instinct contains within it the argument that both militarism and masculinity are natural to and so products of the properly male body. After all, to say that seven million Englishmen could serve as militiamen is not to argue that they could become military men with adequate training, but that they already are. Trenchard does acknowledge the counter-argument, that, in his words, 'War is become more a Mystery, and therefore more Experience is necessary to make good Souldiers', but though he recognizes that modern soldiering might require some specialist skills, he maintains that military exercise is merely 'obeying a few words of Command; these are Mysteries that the dullest Noddle will comprehend in a few Weeks.' He concedes that fortification and gunnery might be more complex, for 'these are Arts not to be learned without much Labour, and Experience', but states that even these 'are as much gained in the Closet as in the Field; and I suppose no Man will say, that the keeping standing Forces is necessary to make a good Ingineer.'[17] Of course, Trenchard plays down any kind of difficulty in order to protect the anti-standing army claim that every male body has the potential to be a military body. When he states that 'Nature hath armed all Creatures with Weapons to oppose those that assault them, and the Policy of Man hath found out several Artificial ones for himself', he naturalizes the capacity for military service and presents man-made weapons as mere adjuncts to the body.[18]

In comparison, Toland and Fletcher are less hostile to the value of military training. Unlike Trenchard, who makes plain that actual experience of war 'is not essential either to a Standing Army or a Militia', Toland states,

[17] [Trenchard], *An Argument Shewing*, pp. 24–5.
[18] [Trenchard], *A Letter from the Author*, p. 7.

'I readily own that the MILITIA, as now regulated, is burdensom and useless; but it follows not that all are necessarily so … In a word, when our Men are better train'd, they will not make such a ridiculous Figure under their Arms.'[19] Fletcher goes further in arguing that militiamen must be trained in order to 'strengthen and dispose the Body for fight':

> Beginning with them early, when like wax they may be moulded into any shape, would dispose them to place their greatest Honour in the performance of those Exercises, and inspire them with the Fires of Military Glory, to which that Age is so enclined; which Impression being made upon their youth, would last as long as life. Such a Camp would be as great a School of Vertue as of military Discipline.[20]

Such enthusiasm can be explained by R. Claire Snyder's argument that the citizen-soldier in the civic tradition 'performs' in a Butlerian sense: 'individuals *become* republican citizens *only* as they engage together in civic and martial practices … Hence the process of becoming a citizen is never finished.'[21] True enough, Toland and Fletcher offer schemes for training the militia that emphasize repetitive enactments. Toland calls for militia meetings to be held every Saturday or Sunday afternoon on every village plain or green and for militia camps to be established quarterly in London for larger militia exercises. Fletcher presents an even more comprehensive plan, in which all men at the age of twenty-two spend at least a year in a camp, constantly exposed to 'a good Model of Militia' – physical exercises, horsemanship, foraging, the wearing of plain clothes and reading military histories – after which they should participate in regular meetings in their villages in order to sharpen their skills.[22] The precision of their plans, plans which stress the importance of men gathering together regularly and in public spaces, betrays some anxiety, some recognition that the modern man must *become* a militiaman, as Synder argues, through practice. However, to identify performativity in the past is not the same as to enquire how far past arguments anticipate the notion of performativity in their conceptualizations of gender. On this basis, to focus on what Toland and Fletcher's plans for meetings and camps disclose is to miss that both schemes are predicated on the idea that men should participate because they are, timelessly and universally, male, not because they hope to become

---

[19] [Trenchard] *An Argument Shewing*, p. 25; [Toland], *The Militia Reform'd*, pp. 12–13.
[20] [Fletcher], *A Discourse of Government*, pp. 59, 60.
[21] R. Claire Snyder, *Citizen Soldiers and Manly Warriors: Military Service and Gender in the Civic Republican Tradition* (Lanham, MD: Rowman & Littlefield, 1999), p. 3.
[22] [Fletcher], *A Discourse of Government*, p. 50.

soldiers. Fletcher may argue that young men can be shaped like wax, just as Foucault argues that the modern soldier is made from 'formless clay', but he also assumes that these randomly balloted men have a pre-existing attachment to militarism such that they are already 'enclined' towards it. For Toland and Fletcher, the benefit to be had from learning how to use swords and spears is less important than the latent capacity that inheres within and precedes any such instruction and thus that which can be read as a plan to produce gender through repeated acts must also be read on its own terms as a denial of performativity.

'Men ... set Apart': The Pro-Standing Army Position

Whereas the anti-standing army authors argued against the proposal to establish a permanent army by appealing to timeless 'truth', those sympathetic to the cause of the standing army, notably the Williamite politician John Somers and, in his guise as a writer-for-hire, Daniel Defoe, asserted the reality of change. Somers objected to the anti-standing army argument for reviving the militia on the basis that 'it is a wrong way of arguing, to apply the Precedent of any one Time to another, unless all Things in both Times agree', and as Defoe put it, 'in order to state the Case [regarding the standing army] right, we are to distinguish first between *England* formerly, and *England* now.'[23] Trenchard may have looked back to the classical past, but the pro-standing army authors argued for a change in the composition of the nation's soldiery on the basis that such a change had already occurred on the continent as a response to changes in the nature of warfare. Thus Defoe writes,

> War is no longer an Accident, but a Trade, and they that will be any thing in it, must serve a long Apprenticeship to it: Human Wit and Industry has rais'd it to such a perfection; and it is grown such a piece of Manage, that it requires People to make it their whole Employment; the War is now like the Gospel, Men must be set apart for it.[24]

Trenchard and the anti-standing army authors had called for the militarization of the nation's seven million men; here, Defoe highlights the increasing complexity of modern warfare in order to argue that men must be 'set

---

[23] [John Somers], *A Letter Ballancing the Necessity of Keeping a Land-Force in Times of Peace: With the Dangers that May Follow On It* (London[?], 1697), p. 9; [Daniel Defoe], *An Argument Shewing, That a Standing Army with Consent of Parliament is not Inconsistent with a Free Government* (London: E. Whitlock, 1698), p. 3.

[24] [Daniel Defoe], *A Brief Reply to the History of Standing Armies in England with Some Account of the Authors* (London, 1698), p. 14.

apart' in order to master the skills required. In other words, the argument in favour of the standing army held that the nation required standing soldiers because it required trained soldiers. As an anonymous pro-standing army author put it, 'tis most certain that Experience and Discipline makes an Army serviceable: And if the Security of the Nation requires a Martial Strength, 'tis ridiculously impolitick to disband the Learned, only to teach the Ignorant.'[25]

Rather than concede that, in Johnson's words, 'men are Soldiers by instinct', the pro-standing army authors took the position that military men must be produced. For Trenchard, the history of citizen-soldiering provided ample evidence to suggest that a body of militiamen could overpower even a larger number of trained enemy soldiers. In contrast, Somers, who was prepared to concede that the call for a militia was not without some merit, asked his opponents to consider seriously the notion that amateurs could match trained professionals. 'Great Bodies may be brought together', he writes,

> but you and I have seen Armies too much not to know the difference that is between Troops that have been long trained, who have learned the Art and are accustomed to the Discipline of War, and the best Bodies of raw and undisciplined Multitudes. The whole Method of War is now such, that undisciplined Troops must prove a very unequal Match, to much greater Numbers of Men, who yet perhaps, upon half their Practice, might prove too hard for them.

With this, he questions both the 'truth' of the historical record – he later states that it is apparent 'from the Histories of all Nations, that regular and disciplined Troops will be far superior to the best and strongest Militia in the *World*' – and the 'truth' of the male body.[26] For Somers, male bodies that have not been trained are always inferior to those that have been shaped and hardened by service. Defoe rehearses this point when he considers the armies raised by Charles II for the Dutch Wars and even more recently by William for the Nine Years' War:

> I saw them both and they were composed of as jolly, brave, young Fellows as ever were seen; but being raw, and not us'd to hardship, the first Army lay, and rotted in *Flanders* with Agues and Fluxes… and so 'twill always fare with any Army of English men, 'till they have been abroad, and inur'd to

---

[25] *Remarks Upon a Scurrilous Libel called An Argument, Shewing that a Standing Army is Inconsistent with a Free Government* (London, 1697), p. 20.
[26] [Somers], *A Letter Ballancing*, p. 7, 12.

the Service. I appeal to any Man, who knows the Nature of our Men; they are the worst raw Men in the World, and the best when once got over it.[27]

Here, Defoe counters the anti-standing army account of the male body by suggesting that it is the very bodiliness of the soldier – the susceptibility of flesh to disease – that makes him vulnerable rather than invincible. For Defoe as for Somers, male bodies are not imbued with latent military capacity; rather, they are simply raw matter that must be moulded by exterior forces. Given that this challenges the essence of masculinity as much as militarism, it is fitting that, in asking any 'Man' who knows the 'Nature of our Men' to corroborate his account, Defoe employs the terms man and men to refer to those with knowledge of military affairs rather than men in general.

In raising the argument that men must be 'set apart' in order to acquire military skills, the pro-standing army authors indicate that masculinity, like militarism, is acquired rather than innate. Certainly, those who supported the proposal for a standing army recognized the importance of 'nature' in the anti-standing army argument: as one pro-standing army author announced in response to Trenchard: 'I am no more a Friend to Armies than the Author; but the Law of Nature teaches every Man to Embrace his own Security, and that Point alone makes me a Friend to an Army.'[28] For the anti-standing army authors, training is of less importance than courage, for the former is artificial and the latter natural. According to one pro-standing army author, however, even courage needs to be acquired, for 'there is something in the bravest Nature that will not secure it self against Surprizes: "tis therefore necessary in a Souldier to know the face of an Enemy, to feel the Hardships of a Camp, and grow familiar with dangers.'[29] Defoe had made the same point earlier in the 1690s when he borrowed a pithy phrase from Lord Rochester's 'A Satyr against Reason and Mankind' – '*all Men would be Cowards if they Durst*' – for a pamphlet in support of Williamite Whiggery. The sentiment reappears in his attack on the mythicization of 'natural' courage: 'the Gentlemen of the Club may say what they please, and talk fine things at home of the natural Courage of the *English*, but I must tell them, Courage is now grown less a

---

[27] [Defoe], *A Brief Reply to the History*, p. 11.
[28] *Some Remarks Upon a Late Paper, Entituled, An Argument, Shewing, that a Standing Army is Inconsistent with a Free Government, and Absolutely Destructive to the Constitution of the English Monarchy* (London[?], 1697), p. 9.
[29] *A Letter to a Foreigner, on the Present Debates about a Standing Army* (London: Dan Brown, 1698), p. 6.

Qualification of a Soldier than formerly; not but that 'tis necessary too, but Management is the principle Art of War.'[30]

In maintaining that military skill is learned rather than latent, and that courage is acquired rather than natural, Defoe and the other pro-standing army authors counter anti-standing army essentialism with what can be termed proto-constructionism; their arguments overtly reject the reliance on bodily nature in ways that anticipate Butlerian performativity. But whereas the anti-standing army authors inadvertently undermine the timeless truth of men's nature with their differing views on training, the pro-standing army position in favour of performance was inherently vulnerable to the charge that their military man could not be relied on because he lacked substance. The anti-standing army authors were keen to highlight that the king had asked the country to pay for a standing army during a period of peace following an expensive war.[31] In reply, Defoe turned the cost of maintaining an army into an advantage: the King could not carry on a war without finances granted by Parliament; that is, that the nation's sword and the nation's purse would be held safely because held in different hands.[32] Nevertheless, the problem of money bedevilled the pro-standing army position, for the anti-standing army authors could argue that the amateur English militiaman, who fights for his and others' liberty, fights because he can, not because he must. In contrast, so the anti-standing army argument goes, the soldier who fights for payment does so in response to what is offered to him, not in accordance with that which is within him. The nation cannot rely on this standing soldier because he simply responds to external forces; taking payment confirms that he has no inner courage nor fixed morality to draw on. For Trenchard, 'Souldiers of Fortune' are nothing more than 'Men of dissolute and debauched Principles … who make Murder their Profession, and enquire no farther into the Justice of the Cause, than how they shall be paid; who must be false, rapacious and cruel in their own Defence.'[33] Thomas Orme, who had been a captain in the army before the Revolution, paints the professional soldier in similarly lurid terms by claiming to have overheard a veteran officer swear that he would kill any man if asked, 'subservient to his Pay.'[34]

The friends of the standing army tried to use their conceptualization of the nature of the body – of its raw materiality, akin to the raw materials

---

[30] [Daniel Defoe], *A dialogue betwixt Whig and Tory, aliàs Williamite and Jacobite* (London, 1693), p. x; [Defoe], *A Brief Reply to the History*, p. 14.
[31] Hoppit, *Land of Liberty*, pp. 123–31.
[32] [Defoe], *An Argument Shewing*, p. 17.
[33] [Trenchard], *An Argument Shewing*, p. 28.
[34] [Thomas Orme], *The Late Prints for a Standing Army and in Vindication of the Militia Consider'd, are in Some Parts Reconcil'd* (London, 1698), p. 20.

so vital to the mercantile and commercial world – to undermine the anti-standing army authors' connection between 'nature' and virtue. One anonymous pro-standing army author took issue with Trenchard for suggesting that 'Inconstancy, Levity, Infidelity, and indeed every dangerous Vice, every Insult of Arbitrary Oppression and Tyranny, and all the Natural Tendencies to a Universal Slavery, run in the very Veins of a Standing Army, when all the shining Vertues imaginable are the unquestion'd Graces of a Militia.'[35] But if the anti-standing army argument was over-invested in the body, the pro-standing army position was weakened by both the ease with which their opponents could levy the charge that the standing soldier lacked (moral) substance and their own discomfort with, as one supporter of the standing army put it, 'the Necessity of an Army'.[36] Somers, Defoe and their allies sought to replace the timeless and universal everyman of the militia with the man who must be dedicated to modern war, but in arguing that all men have to learn how to be military men, they indicate that only some should be expected to do so. In a reformulation of Trenchard's assertion that the nation must keep its sword by its side, one anonymous contributor to the debate pointed out that 'several true sensible *Englishmen* are of the opinion, that the longer we maintain a *Standing Armed Force*, we shall be the longer from having Occasion to make use of them.'[37] At heart, the pro-standing army argument advocated that any fighting should be done by 'them'. The desire to keep the professional military man at arm's length is made apparent in the argument that warfare should be kept out of sight, or as Defoe put it, 'if there be a war to keep it abroad.'[38] As a fellow hired-hand, Defoe might have been kindly disposed towards the standing soldier, but his refusal to allow that 'there is an intrinsick Value in a *Red Coat*' questions the intrinsic value to the male body and also the intrinsic value to the modern military man. Defoe certainly champions modern militarism, but he is also critical of the modern military man, and this combination leads to an uneasy accord rather than fulsome friendship: 'I am no Soldier, nor ever was, but I am sensible we enjoy the present Liberty, the King his Crown, and the Nation their Peace, bought with the Price of the Blood of these *Ragamuffins*, as he calls them, and I am for being civil to them at least.'[39] As

---

[35] *Remarks Upon a Scurrilous Libel*, p. 4.
[36] *Some Remarks Upon a Late Paper*, p. 12.
[37] *The Case of a Standing Army Army* [sic] *Fairly and Impartially Stated. In Answer to the Late History of Standing Armies in England: and Other Pamphlets Writ on That Subject* (London, 1698), p. 14.
[38] [Defoe], *An Argument Shewing*, preface.
[39] [Daniel Defoe], *Some Reflections on a Pamphlet Lately Publish'd, Entituled, An Argument Shewing that a Standing Army is Inconsistent with a Free Government, and Absolutely Destructive to the Constitution of the English Monarchy* (London: E. Whitlock, 1697), p. 21.

this chapter goes on to discuss, for the proponents of politeness, who inherited the pro-standing army position in opposition to civic essentialism, the issue of whether to be more than passingly civil to the modern military man was even more problematic.

Being Polite: Steele and *The Spectator*

It is possible to argue that the standing army debate effectively came to a close just two years after it had begun when Parliament passed the Disbanding Bill (1699) to reduce the number of men in military service.[40] In fact, this was only a partial victory for the anti-standing army argument, as the bill did not reduce numbers as far it might, and so although the controversy seems to have kindled and cooled rapidly, the heat that was generated in just a few years lasted long into the eighteenth century. For Trenchard and his comrades, the courtier politicians' campaign for a standing army was inextricably intertwined with the emergence of the culture of politeness. This is not to say that the anti-standing army authors valued rough incivility. Trenchard protests about debating with 'Journymen Scriblers' who were unused to 'soft Language and Gentleman-like Behaviour.'[41] More significantly, Toland argues that the revival of the militia would ensure that 'Men of ARTS and ARMS will be the very same Species among us, whereas now they are extremely different in most Parts of the World; for the former are generally *Cowards*, and the latter *barbarous* and *rude*.'[42] Rather than make an absolute virtue of barbarity, Toland allows that men of arms might also be men of arts in order to indicate that militarism ought not to be treated as a specialized skill which only certain men need bother acquire. However, for the anti-standing army authors, England was in danger of becoming enslaved to a new kind of politeness, one derived from the *politesse* which, like his standing army, gilded the French king's absolutist tyranny. In Johnson's words,

> Let the more refined parts of the World brag, that their King can send for their Head, tax them high and low, send them to their Wars, or to their Gallies as they please; and let them laugh at those few Nations as borish and barbarous, uncourtly and uncivilized, who are not so entirely devoted to the Will of their Prince, as they are: provided none of these slavish Principles come hither, we fear no other Invasion. God has given us here a World by

---

[40] Schwoerer, *"No Standing Armies!"*, p. 156.
[41] [Trenchard], *A Letter from the Author*, p. 3.
[42] [Toland], *The Militia Reform'd*, pp. 74–5.

our selves, and if any Slaves from abroad can beat us out of it, we ought not to enjoy it an hour longer; for he made no part of the World for Cowards.[43]

Here, Johnson implies that those who would rather not bear arms for the nation are liable to be forced to bear arms by their king, but the ancillary point is that those who pride themselves on being courtly and civilized, like those who serve for payment, are capable only of cowardice. For the anti-standing army authors, the emergence of military service as a profession and the inflation in the currency of polite gentility posed the same threat.

Although the term 'politeness' had been absorbed into the English language in the fifteenth century as a general term of commendation, by the early eighteenth century it had started to be used for a style of civility that centred on ' "the art of pleasing in company" ' but which became, in Lawrence Klein's words, a 'unifying rubric for greatly diverse activities'.[44] A kissing-cousin to French *politesse*, English politeness established itself, as Klein has shown, in opposition to 'the ethical and political purity that country ideologues in the neo-Machiavellian tradition sought in cultural simplicity', specifically, the 'tendency for virtue to be associated with, if not restricted to, rudimentary cultural conditions.'[45] For Habermas, the rise of politeness is one manifestation of the emergence of a bourgeois public sphere, for the new culture of politeness created a new standard for virtue that broke with civic ideas of virtuous citizenship. Habermas writes,

> With the rise of the sphere of the social ... the theme of the modern (in contrast to the ancient) public sphere shifted from the properly political tasks of a citizenry acting in common (i.e. administration of law as regards internal affairs and military survival as regards external affairs) to the more properly civic tasks of a society engaged in critical public debate (i.e. the protection of a commercial economy).[46]

As Habermas indicates, the culture of politeness had little time for classical forms of social organization, but this is not to say that the polite and commercial people were completely uninterested in military matters. Indeed, I want to suggest that the culture of politeness championed the modern military man as the alternative to the civic ideal of citizen-soldiering.

---

[43] [Johnson], *A Confutation of a Late Pamphlet*, p. 14.
[44] Lawrence Klein, 'The Third Earl of Shaftesbury and the Progress of Politeness', *Eighteenth-Century Studies*, 18.2 (1984–5), 186–214 (at pp. 190, 186).
[45] Klein, 'The Third Earl of Shaftesbury', p. 213.
[46] Habermas, *Structural Transformation*, p. 52.

However, in turning to the *Spectator* papers it also becomes apparent that even those who pointedly rejected the 'humanist ethical-political lessons of the classical past' were, like Defoe, wary of being too polite to those set apart for modern military life.[47]

According to Habermas, the emergence of the bourgeois public sphere can best be mapped alongside the growth of a new literary phenomenon in the early eighteenth century: the periodical.[48] Early periodicals had the capacity to disseminate the tea-table philosophy of polite sociability and the *Spectator*, with its titular play on viewing and being viewed, is, as John Brewer notes, paradigmatic in this respect.[49] The *Spectator* papers, penned largely by Joseph Addison and Richard Steele, were published March to December 1711–12 and June to December 1714, that is, in the closing years of the War of the Spanish Succession. Although the papers make little explicit reference to the conflict, the presence of an army officer, Captain Sentry, at Mr Spectator's club, a club composed of 'the most conspicuous Classes of Mankind', is an indication that Addison and Steele are as interested in the man of arms as the middling merchant, Sir Andrew Freeport, or the landed gentleman, Sir Roger de Coverley.[50] Sentry is introduced to *Spectator* readers in an early paper by Steele, and according to Steele the captain cuts a more than acceptable figure: he is 'a Gentleman of great Courage, good Understanding, but invincible Modesty', and 'very agreeable to the Company: for he is never over-bearing, though accustomed to command Men in the utmost Degree below him: nor ever too obsequious, from a Habit of obeying Men highly above him.'[51] Here, author and character begin to blur. The young Steele had joined the King's Life Guards and participated in the Nine Years' War, notably at the battle of Steenkerque (1692), after which he had transferred to the equally prestigious Coldstream Guards as private secretary to the colonel.[52] Steele's position in the Guards enabled him to spend peace-time in London society,

---

[47] David Alvarez, '"Poetical Cash": Joseph Addison, Antiquarianism, and the Aesthetic Value', *Eighteenth-Century Studies*, 38.3 (2005), 509–31 (at p. 513). See also Brian Cowan, 'Mr Spectator and the Coffeehouse Public Sphere', *Eighteenth-Century Studies*, 37.3 (2004), 345–66 (at p. 359).

[48] Habermas, *Structural Transformation*, p. 42. On print culture, see Hoppit, *A Land of Liberty?*, pp. 167–82.

[49] John Brewer, *The Pleasures of the Imagination: English Culture in the Eighteenth Century* (Abingdon: Routledge, 1997; repr. 2013), pp. 90–6.

[50] [Addison], No. 34, *The Spectator*, 8 vols. (London: S. Buckley; J. Tonson, 1712–15), I, p. 187. Authorship attributions follow *The Spectator*, ed. by Donald F. Bond, 5 vols. (Oxford: Clarendon, 1965).

[51] [Steele], No. 2, *The Spectator*, I, pp. 11–12.

[52] Calhoun Winton, *Captain Steele: The Early Career of Richard Steele* (Baltimore: Johns Hopkins University Press, 1964).

but as the War of the Spanish Succession loomed, he found himself captain of a regiment of foot guarding a crumbling fort in Suffolk. Steele failed in his efforts to secure a place in a new regiment of dragoons to be commanded by an old patron and, lacking other useful connections and having no means with which to secure a better commission, he abandoned the military profession.[53] Give this, Steele might have been writing about himself when characterizing Sentry as one who had shown 'great gallantry' at certain battles and sieges, but 'quitted a Way of Life in which no Man can rise suitably to his Merit, who is not something of a Courtier, as well as a Soldier.' In fact, Steele's less-than-veiled, almost civic, criticism of the army purchase system draws attention to the complexity of Sentry's status as the club's 'model' military man. The fact that Sentry curtailed his military career – he 'frankly confesses that he left the World because he was not fit for it' – means that the representative military man is not actually a serving officer while a member of the club.[54] The awkwardness of Sentry's standing is compounded when Steele identifies him as Sir Roger's heir. On Roger's death, Sentry inherits a country estate and embraces his new identity, declaring 'I am become a Country Gentleman.'[55] With this, the un/military man retires from urban and urbane society.

The precariousness of Sentry's position as a model military man indicates much about Steele's defence of, but also difficulty in accommodating, the modern military man. This combination can be seen in Steele's paper on military courage, the *Spectator*'s most significant reflection on militarism. In this paper Mr Spectator asks Sentry how military men conquer the fear of death, given that 'we, the rest of mankind, arm ourselves against [it] with so much Contemplation, Reason and Philosophy.'[56] Sentry sympathizes with this as a predictable question from one ' "not Conversant in Camps" ' and explains, ' "when a Man has spent some Time in that Way of Life, he observes a certain Mechanick Courage which the ordinary Race of Men become Masters of from acting always in a Crowd." ' Courage does not, he suggests, inhere within soldiers' bodies; rather, soldiers acquire fearlessness through familiarity with military life. For Steele, the male body is not imbued with an innate capacity for militarism, and courage is a result

---

[53] For the army purchase system, see Childs, *The British Army of William III*, pp. 57–63.
[54] [Steele], No. 2, *The Spectator*, I, pp. 11–12.
[55] [Steele], No. 544, *The Spectator*, VII, p. 399.
[56] [Steele], No. 152, *The Spectator*, II, pp. 368–9. Steele may be said to include himself in Mr Spectator's 'we' given the sudden death of a friend a few weeks earlier. See James H. Averill, 'The Death of Stephen Clay and Richard Steele's *Spectators* of August 1711', *The Review of English Studies*, 28 (1977), 305–10.

of mental effort. '"Without a Resignation to the Necessity of dying,"' Steele writes, '"there can be no Capacity in Man to attempt anything [that is] glorious; but when they have once attained to that Perfection, the Pleasures of a Life spent in Martial Adventures, are as great as any of which the human Mind is capable."'[57] Steele develops this argument against 'natural' courage in a later paper on the cruelty of a French captain to an English prisoner. The former's treatment of the latter inspires Sentry to warn that 'true courage' 'manifests the force of true genius', whereas 'Courage, without Regard to Justice and Humanity, was no other than the Fierceness of a wild Beast.' 'Alas!', Steele concludes, 'it is not so easy a thing to be a brave Man as the unthinking Part of Mankind imagine.'[58]

In his paper on courage, Steele defines bravery as something that military men acquire and with this he rehearses the pro-standing army rejection of essentialism. However, Steele's defence of the modern military man is as qualified as Defoe's. Having begun with a general account of military courage, Steele's paper goes on to distinguish between the rank-and-file soldiers and the officers, identifying the former as the 'Gross of Mankind' who have a 'general way of loose thinking', such that they cope with the possibility of death in large part because they experience easy pleasures far more than they face dangers. In particular, those who '"arrive at a certain Habit of being void of Thought"', those who are driven by sensory gratification, are immune to the finer feelings of friendship: '"they lament no Man whose Capacity can be supplied by another."'[59] Although Steele defends the modern military man, then, he is prepared to vouch only for the virtue of the officer class:

> He is beloved of all that behold him: They wish him in Danger as he views their Ranks, that they may have Occasions to save him at their own Hazard. Mutual Love is the Order of the Files where he commands; every Man afraid for himself and his Neighbour, not lest their Commander should punish them, but lest he should be offended. Such is his Regiment who knows Mankind, and feels their Distresses so far as to prevent them. Just in distributing what is their Due, he would think himself below their Taylor to wear a Snip of their Cloaths in Lace upon his own; and below the most rapacious Agent, should he enjoy a Farthing above his own Pay. Go on, brave Man, immortal Glory is thy Fortune, and immortal Happiness thy Reward.[60]

[57] [Steele], No. 152, *The Spectator*, II, pp. 369, 370.
[58] [Steele], No. 350, *The Spectator*, V, pp. 176–7.
[59] [Steele], No. 152, *The Spectator*, II, pp. 369, 372.
[60] [Steele], No. 152, *The Spectator*, II, pp. 372–3.

This officer is very far from the mercenary soldier of fortune imagined by the anti-standing army authors. Here, Steele acknowledges that army officers controlled the money given to them by government for clothing their soldiers and that this system could be exploited by the greedy and callous, but he asserts that there are officers who refuse to cheat the men in order to trim their own coats and line their own pockets.[61]

As warm as Steele is prepared to be with regard to the modern military officer, though, even he struggles to allow the military paragon to be a master of politeness. The ability to converse was central to the culture of politeness and Steele begins his paper on courage by commenting favourably on the modern military man's skill in social intercourse:

> There is no sort of People whose Conversation is so pleasant as that of military Men, who derive their Courage and Magnanimity from Thought and Reflection. The many Adventures which attend their Way of Life make their Conversation so full of Incidents, and gives then so frank an Air in speaking of what they have been Witness of, that no Company can be more amiable than that of Men of Sense who are Soldiers. There is a certain irregular Way in their Narrations or Discourse, which has something more warm and pleasing than we meet with among Men, who are used to adjust and Methodize their Thoughts.[62]

With this, Steele suggests that the military man is capable of that which is most valued by polite society, but this is also cautious and, ultimately, contradictory praise. Steele commends those military men who 'derive their Courage and Magnanimity from Thought and Reflection', that is, the officer class, but he praises them for producing 'irregular' narratives that are more pleasing that those constructed by men who 'methodize their thoughts'. The combination of 'thought and reflection' with 'frank[ness]' and 'irregularity' is one that ensures that Steele's polite military man is so heavily qualified, so tightly defined, as to be tied up in knots. As a result, it is not surprising, that, in a later paper, Steele's vision of the 'warm and pleasing' military conversationalist gives way to the view, expressed by a 'correspondent', there are but 'few Soldiers whom a military Life, from the Variety of Adventures, has not rendered over-bearing, but humane, easy, and agreeable.'[63]

Given Steele's efforts to champion the modern military man, Andrew Lincoln is right to suggest that the *Spectator* tries to envision a soldier

---

[61] For discussion of army clothing, see Childs, *The British Army of William III*, pp. 167–71.
[62] [Steele], No. 152, *The Spectator*, II, p. 368.
[63] [Steele], No. 342, *The Spectator*, V, p. 128.

whose 'gentler manners' are no impediment to politeness, but for all Steele's efforts to show that the military man might be of interest to polite society, he comes to agree with Addison that politeness and militarism are incompatible.[64] According to Addison, the demands placed on the professional military man inculcate precisely those qualities that can only be impolite. Rather than manage to be an agreeable conversationalist, Addison argues, the modern, professional soldier is more likely to be a 'Military Pedant': 'every thing he speaks smells of Gunpowder; if you take away his Artillery from him, he has not a Word to say for himself.'[65] Addison's position is then clarified in a paper bearing the epigram 'Bella, horrid Bella!' which argues that the golden age of philosophical argument ended when one man used physical force to settle a dispute, thus establishing a principle for future 'argument': 'draw up a hundred thousand Disputants on each side, and convince one another by dint of Sword.'[66] That said, it is Addison's paper on 'The History of the Female Republic' that best summarizes the *Spectator*'s position on the modern military man and his relationship with polite society. On one level, the paper echoes the pro-standing army argument that military skill is acquired rather than natural to the male body. The women of the republic are Amazonians who have been trained to 'Shoot, Dart, or Sling' and though they are routed by a male republic the combatants then join forces and fight side-by-side against a common enemy.[67] Of course, Addison's proto-constructionism is undermined by the signs of discomfort with the idea of military woman. Addison returns women to their separately sexed bodies by stating that they were defeated for reasons which include the fact that 'the General was brought to Bed, or (as others say) Miscarried the very Night before the Battel.' Addison renders military femininity oxymoronic once again when he states that in the female republic 'no Woman was to be married 'till she had killed her Man.'[68] While I would question Erin Mackie's argument that, in the *Spectator*, 'sexualized gender differences serve as a new alternative ground of embodied authenticity as the older reliance on inborn status distinctions falls away', Addison's attack on the military woman does indicate that the papers promote, as she argues, 'paternalistic

[64] Andrew Lincoln, 'War and the Culture of Politeness: The Case of *The Tatler* and *The Spectator*', *Eighteenth-Century Life*, 36.2 (2012), 60–79 (at p. 67). See also Andrew Lincoln, 'The Culture of War and Civil Society in the Reigns of William III and Anne', *Eighteenth-Century Studies*, 44.4 (2011), 455–74.
[65] [Addison], No. 105, *The Spectator*, II, p. 126.
[66] [Addison], No. 239, *The Spectator*, III, p. 395.
[67] [Addison], No. 434, *The Spectator*, VI, p. 210.
[68] [Addison], No. 434, *The Spectator*, VI, pp. 212, 210.

domestic norms.'⁶⁹ Yet as limited as Addison's proto-constructionism is, he imagines an alternative to civic military virtue that has wider ramifications. As much as the paper might want to separate male and female, a more significant difference – that between militarism and politeness – emerges in the conclusion. Having defeated their common enemy, the men and women lay down their arms and engage in social interactions which give rise to architecture, painting, poetry, dancing and personal grooming. The softening of their military ways leads to a civilizing of their societies and thus to 'the most Flourishing and Polite Government in the Part of the World which they Inhabited.'⁷⁰ Though the *Spectator* papers' authors do seem to want to move beyond civic ideology, ultimately even modern militarism smells too much of gunpowder and too little of hair powder to be properly polite.

Performing Politeness: Boswell's *London Journal*

As the *Spectator* papers illustrate, the legacy of the standing army debate cannot be reduced to a simple opposition between civic advocates for militarism and those for modern politeness. The modern military man shares a fundamental similarity with the paragon of politeness, for both acquire their skills and so both can be understood to be performers, in a Butlerian sense. However, in sharing that which anticipates constructionist understandings of gender, modern militarism and modern politeness shared that which made them vulnerable to criticism. When countering the proposal to introduce a standing army, Trenchard and his allies had attacked not just corruption at the heart of government,

> Who can enough lament the wretched Degeneracy of the Age we live in? To see Persons who were formerly noted for the most vigorous Assertors of their Country's Liberty, … so infamously fall in with the arbitrary measures of the Court, [and] appear the most active Instruments for enslaving their Country …is so violent and surprizing a transition … All the stated Maxims, in relation to the nature of Mankind, which have been long ago settled and establish'd by Philosophers and observing Men, are now baffled and exploded; and we have nothing left us to contemplate, but the wild extravagancies of Romantic Fables, the sudden

---

⁶⁹ Erin Mackie, *Market à la Mode: Fashion, Commodity and Gender in* The Tatler *and* The Spectator (Baltimore: John Hopkins University Press, 1997), pp. 166, 11.
⁷⁰ [Addison], No. 434, *The Spectator*, VI, p. 214.

conveyances of nimble finger'd Jugglers, the inimitable dispatches of transubstantiating Priests, or the now more credible Metamorphoses of Men into Beasts.[71]

While this is clearly aimed at William's courtier Whigs, Toland's lament for the 'nature of Mankind', for the 'Metamorphoses of Men into Beasts', is also an attack on their account of masculinity. Here, Toland attempts to embed anti-standing army essentialism on the rational high ground, presenting his opponents as mere peddlers of fable and slight-of-hand trickery. Whereas the argument in favour of the militiaman anchored civic militarism to the 'truth' of the apparently timelessly, universally and reliably sexed body, the metamorphotic modern military man, like the master of politeness, had no such ballast and as such was vulnerable to the criticism that performance lacked substance, that it could only be unstable, unreliable and dangerous.

To advocates for polite society the nature, or lack thereof, of performance was a virtue. The culture of politeness was a culture that valued performance: to be polite was to be seen to be polite by others and since 'the polite individual was the product of cultivation', as Klein has argued, she or he was necessarily a 'social actor'.[72] For the philosopher of politeness, Anthony Ashley Cooper, Earl of Shaftesbury, performance provided the basis for a new kind of virtue. Klein states that for Shaftesbury, 'the ideal citizen was the orator, [and thus] civic virtue was not expressed simply in the capacity to bear arms for the sake of the republic.'[73] The shift from citizen-soldier to orator, from bearing arms to engaging in debate, forwards polite performance as a virtuous because similarly socially oriented endeavour. Shaftesbury had been a critic of court Whiggery in the wake of the Revolution, but he soon shifted his political affiliations and thereby consolidated his friendship with the influential pro-standing army author Somers.[74] In 'A Letter Concerning Enthusiasm' (1708), addressed to Somers, Shaftesbury defends the modern virtue of social acting. Appealing to Somers as 'the noblest actor and of the noblest part assigned to any mortal on this earthly stage', Shaftesbury argues that individuals should subject their enthusiasms to unenthusiastic scrutiny so as to be acceptable to others. Anticipating

---

[71] [John Toland], *The Danger of Mercenary Parliaments* (London[?], 1698[?]), p. 4.

[72] Lawrence Klein, 'Politeness and the Interpretation of the British Eighteenth Century', *The Historical Journal*, 45.4 (2002), 869–98 (at p. 875). See also Jenny Davidson, *Hypocrisy and the Politics of Politeness: Manners and Morals from Locke to Austen* (Cambridge: Cambridge University Press, 2004), pp. 46–75.

[73] Lawrence Klein, *Shaftesbury and the Culture of Politeness: Moral Discourse and Cultural Politics in Early Eighteenth-Century England* (Cambridge: Cambridge University Press, 1994), p. 149.

[74] Lawrence Klein, 'Liberty, Manners and Politeness in Early Eighteenth-Century England', *The Historical Journal*, 32.3 (1989), 583–605 (at p. 586).

Adam Smith's *Theory of Moral Sentiments* (1759), Shaftesbury requires the individual to shape his or her self to suit his or her audience. Even Somers, Shaftesbury argues, must feel that he can 'discover' a better self when in public.[75] In 'Soliloquy, or Advice to an Author' (1710) Shaftesbury repeats the idea that the performance of politeness is both self-creation and self-improvement. For Shaftesbury, what is 'natural' is nothing more than raw material that can be improved such that an individual might perform an even more 'natural' self: 'if a natural good taste be not already formed in us, why should we not endeavour to form it, and become natural?'[76] Shaftesbury is clear that even the physical body is not naturally natural; rather, it can be made natural, since a graceful body must 'by reflection and the assistance of art have learned to form those motions which on experience are found the easiest and most natural.'[77]

To forward the performer of politeness as a model for modern masculine virtue is to sever the civic connection between men and militarism and to cut masculinity loose from any natural, bodily anchor. Shaftesbury defends this by replacing the idea of essence within the body with the careful ordering of the body, for as Shaftesbury argues in 'An Inquiry Concerning Virtue and Merit' (1699), 'the admiration and love of order, harmony and proportion, in whatever kind, is naturally improving to the temper, advantageous to social affection and highly assistant to virtue, which is itself no other than the love of order and beauty in society.'[78] As Klein observes, Shaftesburian politeness concerns itself with 'the creation of an image, not the manifestation of the soul', but it is the centrality of the idea of order that confirms how far his exchange of civic virtue for polite virtue anticipates Foucauldian and Butlerian argument.[79] After all, Shaftesbury's conception of politeness as rooted in the 'love of order' bears an uncanny resemblance to Foucault's fixation on discipline as the 'art of the human body'.[80] And yet, as much as Shaftesbury's appeal to discipline seeks to secure the virtue of performance in ways that could apply to the modern military man as much as the polite gentleman, this is also a move that distances the modern military man. Foucault offers the modern soldier as an exemplary product of the disciplinary power that functions, as though in the centre of a

---

[75] Anthony Ashley Cooper, third Earl of Shaftesbury, 'A Letter Concerning Enthusiasm', in *Characteristics of Men, Manners, Opinions and Times*, ed. by Lawrence E. Klein (Cambridge: Cambridge University Press, 1999), pp. 4–28 (at p. 6).
[76] Shaftesbury, 'Soliloquy, or Advice to an Author', in *Characteristics*, pp. 70–162 (at p. 151).
[77] Shaftesbury, 'Soliloquy, or Advice to an Author', p. 85.
[78] Shaftesbury, 'An Inquiry Concerning Virtue and Merit', in *Characteristics*, pp. 163–230 (at p. 191).
[79] Klein, 'The Third Earl of Shaftesbury', p. 191.
[80] Foucault, *Discipline and Punish*, p. 137.

panopticon. Shaftesbury, on other hand, presents the self-disciplined polite performer as his own best critic. Of course, politeness became a disciplinary regime in a Foucauldian sense. According to Habermas, the bourgeois public sphere established itself through such 'a tough struggle with the old powers that it could not be absolved from having the character of a 'coercive power' itself.'[81] More recently, Addison has been characterized as 'the ideologue of the bourgeoisie, an agent of 'class-consolidation' or the 'disciplinary regime' of modernity.'[82] However, as James Boswell was to discover, the modern military man could not be easily accommodated within polite society, for polite individuals conceived of themselves as masters of self-discipline rather than subject to an external disciplinary force.

Boswell's *London Journal* is a record of one young man's attempt to perform politeness in the centre of polite society. Boswell set out from his parental home in Scotland having secured his father's grudging consent and, more importantly, a meagre allowance. For Boswell, the move was an opportunity to become his 'own master', in that he could live independently and make his own decisions, but also gain mastery over himself.[83] Boswell had spent three months in London two years earlier but had been forced by his father to return to Scotland, where he had allowed himself to become a 'heedless, dissipated, rattling fellow', seemingly as a form of protest. On his return to London, Boswell reflects on his intention to put an end to this looseness:

> I was now upon a plan of studying polite reserved behavior, which is the only way to keep up dignity of character ... I felt my mind regain its native dignity. I felt strong dispositions to be a Mr. Addison. Indeed, I had accustomed myself so much to laugh at everything that it required time to render my imagination solid and give me just notions of real life and of religion. But I hoped by degrees to attain some propriety. Mr Addison's character in sentiment, mixed with a little of the gaiety of Sir Richard Steele and the manners of Mr. Digges, were the ideas which I aimed to realise.[84]

Here, Boswell indicates that the pretender to politeness was required, as Carter puts it, to 'acquire, internalize, and then enact a range of social practices set out in advice guides or discernible from the conduct of [his] peers', for 'becoming a polite man required hard work and rigorous self-analysis,

---

[81] Habermas, *Structural Transformation*, p. 82.
[82] Scott Black, 'Social and Literary Form in the Spectator', *Eighteenth-Century Studies*, 33.1 (1999), 21–42 (at p. 22).
[83] James Boswell, *Boswell's London Journal 1762–63*, ed. by Frederick Pottle (London: Heinemann, 1952), p. 50.
[84] Boswell, *London Journal*, pp. 69–70.

and resulted in regular self-censure.'[85] Boswell had come to know the disciplinary regime of politeness through reading Addison and Steele, and so attentively that he finds himself unable to see London other than through 'ideas suggested by the Spectator and such as I could not explain to most people, but which I strongly feel and am ravished with', but he internalizes that regime so that its disciplinarity seems to him to be self-discipline.[86]

It is fitting that Boswell's other role model should be the actor and theatre manager West Digges. Boswell had a particular passion for the theatre, and living in London allowed him to cultivate this. Thomas Sheridan was one of Boswell's early associates, until he rejected a preface Boswell had penned for a new play, after which Boswell switched his allegiance to David Garrick, for whom Samuel Johnson expressed a preference. It was while in London that Boswell co-authored his first piece of critical writing, a review of David Mallet's tragedy *Elvira* (1763). However, it was also at this time that Boswell sought to become a military man. As Boswell remarks in a letter to Lady Northumberland, 'I want to be something, and I like nothing but the Army.'[87] Spurred on by 'military conversation' with friends – Colonel Gould, Captain Webster and his particular friend the Hon. Lieutenant Andrew Erskine – Boswell's time in London was spent in earnest pursuit of a prestigious commission to a regiment of the Guards:

> I told [Sheridan] ... [t]hat I was determined to be in London. That I wanted to be something; and that the Guards was the only scene of real life that I ever liked. I feel a surprising change to the better on myself since I came to London. I am an independent man. I think myself as good as anybody, and I act entirely on my own principles ... I now spoke to Sheridan with a manly firmness and a conscious assurance that I was in the right.[88]

Here, Boswell collapses his desire to be in London and his interest in the military life. To him, the two are equally necessary to his plan to become an 'independent man' and even formulating the plan enables him to feel that he is becoming more 'manly'. For Boswell, who recognizes that discipline is required for the performance of politeness, the life of a soldier seems to be similarly theatrical. He recalls a debate between Sheridan and one Captain Maud of the Blues, a regiment of the Guards,

---

[85] Carter, *Men and the Emergence of Polite Society*, pp. 197, 201.
[86] Boswell, *London Journal*, p. 133.
[87] Ibid., p. 113.
[88] Ibid., p. 88.

during which '[Sheridan] said that an actor ought to forget himself and the audience entirely, and be quite the real character; ... This Mr. Maud opposed as wrong; because an actor in that case would not play well, as he would not be enough master of himself. I think he was right.'[89] Here, Boswell concurs with the soldier who argues that actors must remain aware of themselves as actors when performing their parts, thus suggesting that he and his comrades do likewise.

Reflecting on his first week in London, Boswell congratulates himself on his performance thus far: 'I have discovered that we may be in some degree whatever character we choose. Besides, practice forms a man to anything.'[90] But although he had turned himself over to discipline, his plan to form himself into a soldier was to come to nothing. His early efforts to secure a commission were undermined from the start by his anxiety as to whether polite and military performances are really compatible. This anxiety is evident in his account of a well-attended rout. Boswell records that he had been awkward and isolated until acknowledged by the hostess, Lady Northumberland, after which he felt that he had been marked out as a 'favourite': 'I could observe people looking at me with envy.' The experience of escaping from social isolation leads him to liken the polite assembly to a military campaign: 'It was curious to find of how little consequence each individual was in such a crowd. I could imagine how an officer in a great army may be killed without being observed. I came home quiet, laid by my clothes and coolly went to bed.'[91] As much as Boswell might want to familiarize the unknowns of life in the army by likening it to the rout, having just avoided anonymity at the assembly his ardour for the military life is cooled rather rapidly by the thought that even an officer would be just one among the many casualties of a battle. His remaining enthusiasm for the military life is further smothered by a later conversation with one Captain Webster, who paints the dangers and hardships of military service in vivid colours for the young theatre critic:

> He told me that the fatigues of a German campaign are almost incredible. That he was fourteen nights running without being under cover, and often had scarcely any victuals. He said he never once repented his being a soldier, although he cursed the sad fatigues. "Men", said he, "are in that way

---

[89] Ibid., p. 114.
[90] Ibid., p. 56.
[91] Ibid., p. 78.

rendered desperate; and I have wished for an action, either to get out of the world altogether or to get a little rest after it."[92]

Ultimately, Boswell decides that the discipline required by polite society is not the same as that which might be imposed upon him by the military. This is apparent in what is a strangely contradictory assertion with regard to his suitability for the army: 'it vexes me a little to be put out of my regular plan, for which I have a most rooted affection. I do think love of form for its own sake is an excellent qualification for a gentleman of the Army, where there is such a deal of form and variety of attitude.'[93] Here, Boswell stresses that his love of order qualifies him for the army, but his affection for what he considers to be his own regular plan, albeit dictated by the Mr Addisons of polite society, conflicts with the discipline required by the military; a point he tries to resolve by imagining military 'form' in terms of 'variety'. Boswell abandons his plan when, lacking the kind of connections that might allow him to secure a prestigious commission in the Guards, he is forced to contemplate alternatives. When asked by Lord Eglinton if he would accept a commission to a marching regiment, that is, one that would leave London, Boswell replies, 'another commission would be a rope wherewith to hang myself; except you can get me one that is [being disbanded], and then I am not forced from London.'[94] Faced with having to accept such a regiment, Boswell's enthusiasm for the military life finally evaporates: 'I am very easily disconcerted. I could never submit with patience to the inconveniences of a marching corps. The want of my own bed and my own nightcap, and being confined to stretch myself in a small space, hurt[s] my cogitations.'[95] Though his desire to be a self-disciplined polite man pushes him towards militarism, it also pulls him back, and he eventually characterizes military men, not as fellow performers, but as 'unhappy, tired, slavish beings singled out from the rest of mankind for toil and pain.'[96] Ultimately, his willingness to follow the disciplinary regime of politeness is not a willingness to submit to what he comes to see as military servitude.

Given that Boswell changes his mind about militarism, it is possible to doubt the significance of his military enthusiasm. Boswell's independent life in London, his freedom to move in polite circles and to engage in polite activities, was effectively controlled by the allowance granted to him

[92] Ibid., pp. 103–4.
[93] Ibid., p. 131.
[94] Ibid., p. 217.
[95] Ibid., p. 212.
[96] Ibid., p. 225.

by his disapproving father and he must have been drawn to the military in part because this was as a role he would be paid to perform. And yet, his decision to give up trying to secure a commission is not the end of his interest in connecting militarism and masculinity. Boswell concludes that the disciplines of politeness and militarism are incompatible – that the hardships of the rout are not those of the battle – but this allows him to return to militarism when, as Carter argues, he seeks 'conscious abandonment of polite society' through sexual encounters.[97] To critics of politeness, the close connection between politeness and mixed gender sociability was one of its weaknesses. As Emma Clery has argued, polite sociability required the 'acquisition of certain characteristics gendered "feminine"' and this rendered the polite man extremely susceptible to the charge of effeminacy, defined by 'derogatory ideas also gendered "feminine", including corruption, weakness, cowardice, luxury, immorality and the unbridled play of passions.'[98] However, proponents of politeness were keen to stress that polite sociability tempered lewd behaviour by harmonizing masculine and feminine manners, and, as Vic Gatrell argues, polite men were supposed to practise sexual restraint.[99] Indeed, the *Spectator* argues that the military man is unsuited to polite society because he is sexually unstrained. Steele details what he terms the 'frequent, tho' invidious Behaviour of military Men' in a paper which censures an officer for making a clumsy address to a mother and daughter in a coach.[100] Similarly, in a paper produced for the continuation of the *Spectator*, the series of papers written without Steele, Eustace Budgell censures 'Gentlemen of the Blade' who, returning from the field, are 'so used to action that they know not how to lie still.' These soldiers are pilloried for assuming that 'that the Fair at home ought to reward them for their Services abroad' and 'they have a sort of Right to Quarter themselves upon the Ladies.'[101]

At first, Boswell seems to be willing to embrace the feminization required for participation in polite society. On his journey from Scotland

---

[97] Carter, *Men and the Emergence of Polite Society*, p. 194.
[98] Clery, *The Feminization Debate*, p. 10.
[99] Lawrence Klein, 'Gender, Conversation and the Public Sphere in Early Eighteenth-Century England', in *Textuality and Sexuality: Reading Theories and Practices*, ed. by Judith Still and Michael Worton (Manchester: Manchester University Press, 1993), pp. 100–15. See also Davidson, *Hypocrisy and the Politics of Politeness*, pp. 46–75; Vic Gatrell, *City of Laughter: Sex and Satire in Eighteenth-Century London* (London: Atlantic, 2006).
[100] [Steele], No. 132, *The Spectator*, II, p. 262.
[101] [Eustace Budgell], No. 566, *The Spectator*, VIII, p. 57.

to London he befriends a young man who intends to voyage to the East Indies despite being unable to endure the minor inconveniences of their travels: 'it was very cold. Stewart was as effeminate as I. I asked him how he, who shivered if a pane of glass was broke in a post-chaise, could bear the severe hardship of a sea life.'[102] Here, Boswell embraces the 'effeminacy' of refinement and ridicules his companion for pretending to be better suited to hardship. However, once in London, Boswell finds that his desire to perform polite masculinity is matched by his desire for sexual gratification. Of course, for all the proponents of politeness' efforts to stress the virtue of polite behaviour, politeness was, Anthony Fletcher suggests, as elastic as its critics feared. Given the 'sexual hypocrisy that lay behind courtesy book politeness and civility', Fletcher concludes, 'civility and politeness on the one hand and sexual power on the other begin to look like two sides of the same coin.'[103] Initially, then, Boswell is able to accommodate his desire to be polite and his appetite for 'female sport' by exercising some restraint when choosing partners: 'I picked up a girl in the Strand ... [but] had command enough of myself to go without touching her ... I resolved to wait cheerfully till I got some safe girl or was liked by some woman of fashion.'[104] However, once his polite amour with Louisa, a young actress, is tainted by venereal disease, Boswell's interest in performing the part of the somewhat self-disciplined 'Man of Pleasure' weakens and he resorts to engaging with street prostitutes. For Carter, this 'indicate[s] the opportunities men had consciously to quit polite society for an alternative community, at one and the same time psychologically distant and geographically close and readily accessible. Here we see the gap between ideal and actual behaviour as intentionally exploited and enjoyed.'[105] However, to look at one sexual encounter in which Boswell performs in the role of an officer, is to see, not just the elasticity of polite performance, but also what Karen Harvey terms the 'persistence' of 'traditional masculinity'.[106]

---

[102] Boswell, *London Journal*, p. 53.
[103] Anthony Fletcher, *Gender, Sex and Subordination in England 1500–1800* (New Haven, CT: Yale University Press, 1995), pp. 344, 346.
[104] Boswell, *London Journal*, p. 58.
[105] Carter, *Men and the Emergence of Polite Society*, p. 200. See also David M. Weed 'Sexual Positions: Men of Pleasure, Economy, and Dignity in Boswell's London Journal', *Eighteenth-Century Studies*, 31.2 (1997), 215–34.
[106] Karen Harvey, *Reading Sex in the Eighteenth Century: Bodies and Gender in English Erotic Culture* (Cambridge: Cambridge University Press, 2004), p. 74.

In the episode in question, Boswell abuses a prostitute while dressed as a disbanded officer. The use of the disguise means that he can conceive of this as a performance; on the same day, Boswell dresses as a barber and then attempts to pass as a highwayman with a woman, though she refuses to be seduced. And yet, when Boswell congratulates himself on the fact that 'not withstanding of my dress, I was always taken as a gentleman in disguise', he reveals his contradictory investment in a 'true' or authentic identity. As much as he might want to act the part of the disbanded officer, he seems to be adopting the disguise in order to be able to indulge in behaviour that he sees as legitimate because 'natural' rather than performative. After all, having 'pushed her up against the wall', he is assisted by a group of 'brother soldiers' who he attracts calling, ' "Brother soldiers", said I, "should not a half-pay officer r-g-r for sixpence?" '[107] As a dependent son on a limited income, Boswell's greatest desire is to establish himself as an independent man, but when he assaults the prostitute with the help of other men he uses his and their physicality as a way to exercise patriarchal dominance. Here, then, the young man who had once described the Guards as 'just like the woman that a man is in love with' adopts a disguise that allows him to retreat from the disciplinary regime of politeness to what he can believe to be the unrestrained pleasures of 'natural' masculinity.[108] Boswell gives up on the army when he comes to see the military man as the 'other' to his polite, feminized masculinity, but though he routinely conceptualizes masculinity as a performance, as construction rather than essence, the idea of natural, embodied masculinity, the ideal defended by the anti-standing army authors, seems to have an allure that he is unable to resist.

This chapter began with the standing army debate as a moment that brought together two conflicting conceptualizations of militarism which were also conceptualizations of the nature of masculinity. The reduction of the king's soldiers at the end of the Nine Years' War seems to have been a victory for Trenchard and the other anti-standing army authors, but the gradual introduction of professional soldiering was to be matched by the rise of politeness. As a fellow performer, the modern military man ought to have been on familiar terms with polite society, but in the formative period for the culture of politeness even Steele was unable to resolve the tension between the performances politeness and of modern militarism.

---

[107] Boswell, *London Journal*, p. 265.
[108] Ibid., p. 134.

Shaftesbury sought to show that politeness ought to be treated as more than an easy superficiality but Boswell's *London Journal* suggests that polite performers did not want to consider the discipline of politeness to be the same as the discipline required by modern militarism. Furthermore, if Boswell's aborted attempt to become a military man indicates that polite society could not be at ease with the military performer, his performance as a disbanded officer is also a reminder not to disregard the continuing cultural power of the anti-standing army authors' ideal of natural militarism, and, by extension, masculinity.

CHAPTER 2

Performing Military Professionalism
The Trials of Admirals Thomas Mathews and Richard Lestock, 1744–1746

> Now for News– I am in London; for which Reason, I suppose I must not be excused; tho' I hate it, remember very little, and am most likely to blunder in the Recital of that little. The House of Commons have addressed the King to try MATTHEWS and LESTOCK, and six captains, by a Court-Martial, and it is thought, some of them will be condemned.– Poor Garrick has been dangerously ill of a Fever this Week; but now, to my great satisfaction, there are Hopes of his Recovery; nay, it is noticed in the *Daily Advertiser*, that he will perform a Part next *Wednesday* Night.[1]
>
> Anthony Whistler to William Shenstone

This letter between two literary figures of the mid-eighteenth century, the poets Anthony Whistler and William Shenstone, brings together two pieces of information which seem not to be connected in any way other than by their contemporaneousness. Indeed, Whistler's lack of interest in one of the most noteworthy items of news – the forthcoming trials of Admirals Thomas Mathews and Richard Lestock – seems to stress this point. Whistler's swift summary of the Commons' decision to call for the courts martial of Mathews and Lestock contrasts with his concern for 'Poor Garrick' and willingness to join others in hoping that the actor might soon be well enough to perform. With this, Whistler polices the borders of what Habermas terms the bourgeois public sphere. At the time of the War of the Austrian Succession, Stephen Conway argues, British society became progressively more 'militarized', in the sense of increasingly interested in and opinionated about military matters.[2] Whistler's dash differentiates between

---

[1] Letter IX. Mr. Whistler to W. Shenstone, in *Selected Letters Between the Late Duchess of Somerset, Lady Luxborough, Miss Dolman, Mr. Whistler, Mr. R. Dodsley, William Shenstone, Esq., and Others*, ed. by Mr Hull, 2 vols. (London: J. Dodsley, 1778), II, pp. 31–2.
[2] Stephen Conway, *War, State and Society in Mid-Eighteenth-Century Britain and Ireland* (Oxford: Oxford University Press, 2006), pp. 139–42. For politics and public opinion during the war of the

the generally newsworthy cases of misbehaviour by senior military men and that which might be of interest to a more select audience, for Whistler's preference for the 'news' about Garrick attests to an imagined intimacy between cultured individuals: the poet–letter-writer, the poet–letter-reader and the actor–playwright–theatre manager. In short, Whistler's brisk account of Mathews and Lestock is far from disinterested, for with this Whistler seems to agree with Addison and Steele that even the most senior of military men ought to be kept at a discreet distance from the polite world.

Rather than follow Whistler's letter's lead, this chapter attends to the trials that he seems at pains to avoid, and in particular to the admirals' contributions to those trials, contributions that attest to the continued importance of ideas and ideals developed during the standing army debate. The standing army debate had come to a close with the disbanding of most of William's seasoned soldiers, but this was only a partial and temporary victory for Trenchard and the other anti-standing army authors, for as Defoe argued, repeatedly and accurately, military service was changing: 'War is become a Science, and Arms an Employment, and all our Neighbours keep standing Forces, Troops of *Veteran* Experienced Soldiers; and we must be strangely expos'd if we do not.'[3] The anti-standing army authors' ideas did not disappear, however. As M. S. Anderson has argued, though there is evidence that much of Europe was moving towards the standardization of military practices and the professionalization of military personnel at the time of the War of the Austrian Succession, this movement was countered by the persistence of other, older ideals.[4] To examine the trials of Admirals Thomas Mathew and Richard Lestock is to see both the march of modernization and a surge of resistance. The records for the battle of Toulon have led N. A. M. Rodger to conclude that '[Lestock] and most of his captains had refused to obey orders to come into action, and from a safe distance watched [Mathews] fight a costly and indecisive battle against heavy odds.'[5] At a parliamentary inquiry, and then again at their trials, the admirals were called to explain their behaviour, and in so doing they offered contrasting accounts of what they considered to be correct conduct to their judges within the court, but also to the wider public

---

Austrian succession, see Philip Woodfine, *Britannia's Glories: The Walpole Ministry and the 1739 War with Spain* (Woodbridge: Boydell, 1998); Richard Harding, *Amphibious Warfare in the Eighteenth-Century: The British Expedition to the West Indies, 1740–1742* (Woodbridge: Boydell, 1991).

[3] [Defoe], *Some Reflections on a Pamphlet Lately Publish'd*, p. 16.
[4] M. S. Anderson, *The War of the Austrian Succession, 1740–1748* (New York: Longman, 1995), pp. 22–9.
[5] N. A. M. Rodger, *Articles of War: The Statutes which Governed our Fighting Navies, 1661, 1749, 1866* (Havant: Kenneth Mason, 1982), p. 9.

beyond. John Almon's *A Review of the Reign of George II* (1762) records that the judges and the public came to very different conclusions as to the merits of these accounts: 'Lestock was honourably acquitted and reinstated in the service, Matthews was broke, and narrowly escaped being shot for cowardice and desertion. This decision is the astonishment of the present age, and will be the puzzle of the future.'[6] This chapter hazards a solution to the puzzle, as I argue that the courts acquitted the admiral who presented himself as a modern, 'professional' military man, whereas public opinion took against this as a mere performance of militarism, one dangerously lacking in corporeal substance.

Now for the New(s)

The trials of Mathews and Lestock followed an indecisive British naval engagement with the combined French and Spanish fleet off the coast of Toulon on the morning of the 11th of February 1744. The failure marked a low point in what had been a popular war. Robert Walpole's pacifist policies had sought to soothe tension between Britain and Spain in the 1720s and 1730s but the severing of Robert Jenkins' ear by the captain of a Spanish *guarda-costa* on board Jenkins' merchant ship in 1731 fuelled British bellicosity. The declaration of war against Spain in 1739 was welcomed by many, as it was widely assumed that this was a war which could be fought at a distance and won quickly. However, having declared against Spain, Britain was soon drawn into the War of the Austrian Succession, a major European conflict dominated by Bourbon and Hapsburg rivalry. With this, the main theatre for British militarism shifted from the West Indies to the continent, and though there were some causes for celebration – the triumph of the Anglo-Hanoverian-Hessian Pragmatic Army at Dettingen (1743) was greeted in England with the traditional signs of popular approval, window-smashing and bonfires – by the mid-1740s too many of Britain's military endeavours had met with failure, and none more dispiritingly so than the naval battle at Toulon, bookended as it was by invasion crises.[7] In September 1743, Mathews had uncovered information relating to a planned Franco-Jacobite invasion, and by February 1744, it was clear that French ships were gathering uncomfortably close to the English Channel. When the French fleet attempted an invasion, it was driven back by poor weather rather than

---

[6] [John Almon], *A Review of the Reign of George II*, 2nd ed. (London: J. Wilkie; Mr. Smith, 1762), p. 78.
[7] This failure dominated discussion of the nation's naval efforts from early 1744 until the end of 1746. See Robert Harris, *A Patriot Press: National Politics and the London Press in the 1740s* (Clarendon: Oxford University Press, 1993), p. 228.

British naval prowess. The arrival at the end of February of the news that a battle had been fought off Toulon made it all too plain that France had now openly, if not formally, entered the war, but the dire events of 1745 further heightened public alarm: in May the Confederate Army suffered a heavy defeat at Fontenoy and in August the Jacobite invasion brought war to British soil. In early 1746 a marine officer, one Captain Henry Russane, was condemned to death for failing to do his utmost to assist an attack on ships believed to be carrying the Young Pretender and when, in March 1746, Lestock took the stand before a jury of his naval peers the Jacobite invasion had yet to meet the Duke of Cumberland's army at Culloden.[8]

To suggest that Mathews and Lestock were simply unlucky in being subjected to courts martial scrutiny would be to underestimate the nation's interest in, and anxiety about, the progress of the war. In February 1744, newspapers were eagerly reporting that 'letters from Admiral Mathews's Fleet mention, that they have taken down their Hammocks, and clear'd every Thing in expectation of a Battle.'[9] Initial reports from the battle were contradictory but the British newspapers erred towards awarding a British victory, for as one commentator reasoned, 'had our insolent enemy gained any Advantage, they would not have failed to trumpet it throughout Europe.'[10] When more detailed information became available in early March, many reports sought to salvage something from the disappointment by stressing that Admiral Mathews and Rear-Admiral William Rowley had fought bravely, but there was no mention of Vice-Admiral Lestock.[11] It is possible that the newspapers were aware that an argument had already broken out between the commander and his vice-admiral. The effectiveness of the British attack had been adversely affected by the looseness of their line, the standard fighting formation for naval battles throughout the eighteenth century, and the day after the battle, Mathews had written to his second-in-command, Lestock, to ask why his section of the line had been so wayward:

> I am exceedingly sorry you did not judge proper, when I had made the Signal to engage the Enemy, to bear down yourself, or at least to have made the Signal

---

[8] Richard Harding, *The Emergence of Britain's Global Naval Supremacy: The War of 1739–1748* (Woodbridge: Boydell, 2010), pp. 161, 176, 190–2, 278. For the decline in Jacobite sympathy among the general public during this period, see Harris, *A Patriot Press*, pp. 193–217; Nicholas Rogers, *Crowds, Culture, and Politics in Georgian Britain* (Oxford: Clarendon Press, 1998), pp. 44–5.
[9] *London Daily Post and General Advertiser*, Friday 3rd February 1744.
[10] *Penny London Morning Advertiser*, Friday 24th February 1744.
[11] For example, *London Daily Post and General Advertiser*, Tuesday 6th March 1744, Thursday 8th March 1744; *Penny London Morning Advertiser*, Friday 9th March 1744, Friday 16th March 1744.

for a sufficient Number of your Squadron, to have endeavoured to have cut off the five *Spanish* Men of War, that were in the Rear of the *Spanish* Admiral. Such an extraordinary Proceeding of yours greatly surprizes me, and I hope you will be able to give me a very good Reason for such your Conduct.[12]

Lestock replied that he had been just three or four miles from the enemy and in alignment with his commander prior to the battle, and that he had, with all possible haste, obeyed the signal to close the gap. Mathews continued to assert that Lestock had allowed his ships to drift some five miles away from the line, a fact 'notorious to the whole Fleet', and that Lestock's division had made insufficient effort to join the attack.[13] On the 16th of March, Mathews formally relieved the vice-admiral of his command and sent him back to England under the charge of having not supported the engagement. Lestock's disgrace was then compounded when, in early April, a loose summary of a letter written by Mathews for the board of the Admiralty, the government body that formally controlled the navy, was printed by the *Penny London Morning Advertiser*:

> [Mathews] might have flattered himself to gain a complete Victory over the French and Spanish Squadrons, if all the Captains and Officers of his Fleet had done their duty alike: … Rear Admiral Rowley also behaved extremely well; that [Mathews] wishes he could say as much of Admiral L---; but that the Conduct of the Latter was quite the Reverse.[14]

On the surface, then, the rancorous aftermath of the battle of Toulon was little more than a public disagreement between two cantankerous rivals. The admirals had been on poor terms ever since Mathews had arrived in the Mediterranean to take charge of the ships that were stationed there, thus depriving Lestock of control. Decades later the bitterness of the relationship between the two men was still thought to have been an important factor in the unsuccessful battle. As the bombastically titled *The Field of Mars* (1781) explained, 'their being united here occasioned this miscarriage. Envy and resentment was their true characteristic … for the whole difference was, *one was superior*.'[15] However, in Tobias Smollett's assessment of the battle, the disagreement involved more than a clash of character:

> Matthews was brave, open and undisguised; but proud, imperious and precipitate. Lestock had signalized his courage on many occasions, and

---

[12] The details of their correspondence are taken from *Original Letters and Papers, Between Adm---l M---ws, and V. Adm---l L---k* (London: M. Cooper, 1744), pp. 9–10.
[13] *Original Letters and Papers*, p. 19.
[14] *Penny London Morning Advertiser*, Friday 6th April 1744.
[15] Entry for Toulon, in *The Field of Mars: Being an Alphabetical Digestion of the Principal Naval and Military Engagements, in Europe, Asia, Africa, and America, particularly of Great Britain and her Allies, from the Ninth Century to the Present Period*, 2 vols. (London: J. MacGowan, 1781), II, unnumbered pages.

perfectly understood the whole discipline of the navy; but he was cool, cunning and vindictive ... To gratify this passion, he betrayed the interest and glory of his country ... All the world knew that Lestock kept aloof, and that Matthews rushed into the hottest part of the engagement. Yet the former triumphed on his trial, and the latter narrowly escaped the sentence of death for cowardice and misconduct. Such decisions are not to be accounted for, except from prejudice and faction.[16]

Here, Smollett concurs with the view that rivalry had played a part, but his sense of what 'all the world knew' with respect to the relative seriousness of the faults on each side concludes that what had begun as a rivalry between the men became a matter of factional party politics. In fact, a survey of MP voting patterns at the parliamentary inquiry that preceded the trials indicates that this was more complicated still. True, the inquiry's recommendation that both Mathews and Lestock should be called to courts martial was made by MPs who voted along party lines – Lestock's friends were in government and Mathews' in the opposition – but as P. A. Luff observes, the older members of the governing alliance of Whigs had initially attempted to defend Mathews rather than automatically support Lestock: 'put simply, a set of younger and more zealous individuals chose to attack Mathews, while [the Prime Minister] and his senior colleagues preferred to protect [him].'[17] Luff suggests that the disagreement reveals that the leader of the Whigs was too weak to whip his party into supporting Mathews, but the division between older and younger voices also indicates that the subject matter could not be contained by, and therefore cannot now be reduced to, party politics.[18] The parliamentary inquiry had attempted to discover which of the officers concerned had failed to conduct themselves appropriately. As such, the inquiry's decision that both admirals deserved to face a court martial can be read as an indication of the strength of disagreement about the models of militarism that each admiral forwarded in order to exonerate his conduct.

To read accounts of the trials is to see that, at its centre, the disagreement between, and subsequently about, Mathews and Lestock was concerned

---

[16] T[obias] Smollett, *A Complete History of England, Deduced From the Descent of Julius Caesar, to the Treaty of Aix La Chapelle, 1748. Containing the Transactions of One Thousand Eight Hundred and Three Years*, 4 vols. (London: James Rivington and James Fletcher, 1757–58), IV, pp. 647–8.

[17] P. A. Luff, 'Mathews v. Lestock: Parliament, Politics and the Navy in Mid-Eighteenth-Century England', *Parliamentary History*, 10.1 (1991), 45–62 (at p. 58).

[18] Christine Gerrard, *The Patriot Opposition to Walpole: Politics, Poetry and National Myth, 1725–1742* (Oxford: Clarendon, 1994), pp. 19–45.

less with the superiority of either admiral or either political party than with the superiority of naval authority, in both a literal and an abstract sense. At the parliamentary inquiry, Lestock responded to the accusation that he had, effectively, refused to fight by claiming that Mathews had kept two contradictory signals flying at once: the signal to close the gap between his ship and the next ship in the line of battle and the signal to begin to engage the enemy. As a result, he argued, he had been compelled to sail to close the gap in the line rather than towards enemy ships. Had he broken away from the line in order to bear down on the enemy, he would have been justly chargeable: 'it would have been impossible for me to have sustain'd so heavy a Charge against Discipline and Order, when it was so obvious and plain that my Duty was to do my utmost to close with the Center, in Obedience to the Message sent to me, and the Signal for the Line which was kept abroad.'[19] In short, Lestock's defence rested on his claim that he had been following instructions, but this was also a claim that he had obeyed, not just an admiral's orders, but standard naval practice as determined by the naval authority that had its centre at the Admiralty. While the day-to-day running of the navy was managed by the Navy Board, which delegated duties to the Sick and Wounded and Victualling boards, overall responsibility for the navy lay with the Admiralty. In practice, the Admiralty could only guide rather than control definitively the strategy or conduct of naval operations, but it could and did attempt to exercise this authority.

At the parliamentary inquiry, Lestock took hold of the word 'Discipline' and defined it as obedience to the wishes of his superior officer and also obedience to the rules for conduct that governed them both. This argument was to appear all the more forcefully at his trial, for despite assuring his judges that he would 'not take up the Time of the Court to detect and confute the false Discipline and Conclusion of [Mathews] … It is sufficient for my Purpose, that I have read his Charge to Judges of your Knowledge and Conception of Discipline', Lestock continually drew attention to the witnesses' 'false' understanding of this term.[20] Crucially, Lestock strengthened his position by referring to key written documents: the *Articles of War* (the statement of naval law), the *Admiralty Instructions* (a guide for officers in the practical matters of naval business), and the *Fighting Instructions* (a guide

---

[19] *Vice-Admal Lestock's Recapitulation, as Spoke by Him at the Bar of the Honble House of Commons, on Tuesday the 9th of April, 1745* (London: John Millan, 1745), p. 8.
[20] *Vice Admiral Lestock's Defence to the Court-Martial, Giving a Short View of the Nature of His Evidence* (London, 1746), p. xi.

to battle tactics which was usually supplemented by additional instructions for signalling).[21] In a private reply to Mathews' first accusatory letter, Lestock had made sure to refer to one of these documents: 'I shall die in this Opinion, that no Man that is an Officer, who knows his Duty, will make the Signal for Line a-breast to steer down upon an Enemy, until the Fleet has been stretched, and extended in a Line of Battle, according to the nineteenth Article of the fighting Instructions.' At his trial, Lestock stressed his knowledge of naval practice in the same way: 'I could not have done more than I did, to have come up with the stern most Ships of the Enemy, consistent with the Discipline of the Navy, the Admiral's Commands expressed by his Signals abroad, and the fighting Instructions.'[22] By appealing to written 'rules', Lestock indicates that he had been concerned to obey his superior officer, but also the principal of centralized naval authority, authority that exceeded any individual member of the Admiralty, since those members were always subject to change. The anonymous author of the two principal 'pro-Lestock' texts, *A Particular Account of the Late Action in the Mediterranean* and *A Narrative of the Proceedings of his Majesty's Fleet in the Mediterranean*, reinforced Lestock's definition of discipline by arguing that the 'Power, Success, and Prosperity of a Fleet or an Army, … depends entirely upon the Wisdom or good Discipline, and the Conduct of the Leaders, particularly in the steady Execution of its Rules, and his own strict Observance of them.'[23] The grammatical slippage from 'the leaders' to 'its rules' identifies the authority that controls the navy, and likewise for the army, as the ultimate power, not the commanders of individual fleets or campaigns.

Whether or not Lestock deliberately calculated his ships' movements so as to avoid the battle, he certainly constructed a defence that managed both to shift the blame for his actions to his rival, Mathews, and to ingratiate himself with the very authority under which he had been arraigned. Mathews, on the other hand, managed his defence in such a way as to challenge both Lestock's version of events and the importance of any authority other than his own. At his own trial, Mathews' responded to Lestock's central claim that he had allowed two contradictory flags to fly at once:

> I do admit, that I made the Signal to engage the combined Fleet … and that the Fleet was not in a regular Line of Battle; but my Reason for acting

---

[21] *Fighting Instructions, 1530–1816*, ed. by Julian S. Corbett, Publications of the Navy Records Society, 29 (1905).
[22] *Vice Admiral Lestock's Defence*, pp. 31, 36.
[23] *A Narrative of the Proceedings of his Majesty's Fleet in the Mediterranean, and the Combined Fleets of France and Spain, from the Year 1741 to March 1744*, 3rd ed. (London: J[ohn] Millan, 1745), p. 98.

in that manner was obvious and plain, being drove to the Necessity of it by Mr. *Lestock*'s extraordinary Behaviour … I was fully convinced I had no Chance for bringing the *French* to Action, unless by making the Signal for engaging.[24]

In order to counter the accusation that he had mismanaged the flags, Mathews asserted that the expectation that naval officers should endeavour to engage the enemy was so 'obvious and plain' that no officer could be confused as to his duty during a battle. Lestock had construed military service as a matter of following what he termed 'discipline', but Mathews maintained that the military man should know that he has one purpose – fighting the enemy – to which all other considerations must give way. While Lestock carefully defined discipline as obedience to those articles and instructions that governed commander and subordinate alike, Mathews' openly challenged the significance of such documents, stating that he had conformed to the *Fighting Instructions* 'as long as it was in my Power', that is, until the necessity of bringing about a battle left him no other choice but to disregard the rule-book.[25]

The key 'pro-Mathews' publications, *Original Letters and Papers, Between Adm---l M----ws, and V. Adm---l L-----k* and *A Just, Genuine, and Impartial History of the Memorable Sea-Fight, in the Mediterranean*, reinforced his argument by labouring the point that Lestock, unlike Rear-Admiral Rowley, simply had not fought. Lestock had addressed the comparison, arguing that, as the rear-admiral's section of the fleet had been as wayward as his own during the battle, Rowley could hardly be held up as a paragon. True enough, Rowley had been too far ahead of Mathews' centre prior to the battle, but he had then sailed his division towards the engagement. As the author of *A Just, Genuine, and Impartial History* concluded, 'I believe it is demonstrable, that their Disobedience, as [Lestock] unjustly calls it, did more Good than his strictest Observance of Order and Discipline', this being 'establish'd by Rules founded on regular Orders, which … cannot foresee every Incident that may occur.'[26] Similarly, the author of *Original Letters and Papers* exclaimed:

---

[24] *The Charge Against Thomas Mathews, Esq; Also the Answer and Defence of Admiral Mathews to the Said Charge*, 2nd ed. (London: E. Cooper, 1746[?]), pp. 25–6. The appetite for information about the trial can be gauged from the fact that the charges and the answers were also printed as separate texts.
[25] *The Charge Against Thomas Mathews*, p. 27.
[26] *A Just, Genuine, and Impartial History of the Memorable Sea-Fight, in the Mediterranean: Between the Combined Fleets of France and Spain, and the Royal Fleet of England, under the Command of the Two Admirals Mathews and Lestock* (London: R. Walker, 1745), pp. 253, 141.

> The Question is, whether it is the most commendable for an Officer to lie idle in the Station allotted him by his Superior, and thereby perform no manner of Service; or by swerving a little, distress the Enemy and serve his Country? It being impossible to fix any certain Rule to the many different Occurrences that happen in Battle, and therefore something should be left to the Judgment and Experience of the Captain.[27]

Both pro-Mathews texts are adamant that rules cannot be fixed by an authority that does not actually participate in fighting. The latter text goes on to note that the Admiralty had provided plenty of 'Instructions' but little in the way of useful assistance, a deficiency which Mathews had been able to rectify due to 'his extraordinary Zeal and good Management'.[28]

Mathews' hostility to the authority of written 'rules' is hardly surprising, given his tense relationship with the Admiralty in the years preceding the battle. Mathews had been asked to serve in 1742, his first active duty for eighteen years, and he had immediately set about making demands for men and materials which the Admiralty struggled to meet.[29] To Mathews' credit, he, like Lestock, stayed in post despite extremely poor health, but Mathews not only strained Admiralty resources; he also questioned Admiralty instructions and corresponded tersely and often directly with the Secretary of State for the Southern Department rather than the Admiralty via their secretary (a practice preferred by other admirals including the most senior admiral in the fleet, Sir John Norris). Given this, it is a wonder that the Admiralty chose not to accept his resignation in June 1743.[30] And yet, Mathew's brusqueness with his superiors helps to explain why, given that he was on trial for his failure to secure a victory, he argued so strenuously and seemingly self-defeatingly that he had been in complete control of what turned out to be an unsuccessful engagement. Lestock had argued that all naval personnel were subject to the same external forces: Mathews counter-argued that a commander must be superior to those he commanded, and so the ultimate source of authority. 'If it was otherwise', he asked, 'by what Rule must it be determined when Chace ought to be given, or left off?' There would have been no battle at all, he argued, 'had I taken so imprudent a Step, as to have acted the Captain instead of the General (whose Motions are the Rule and Directions by

---

[27] *Original Letters and Papers*, p. 101.
[28] Ibid., pp. 121, 122.
[29] Harding, *The Emergence of Britain's Global Naval Supremacy*, pp. 131–2, 138–9.
[30] Baugh, *British Naval Administration* pp. 69–70. Harding, *The Emergence of Britain's Global Naval Supremacy*, pp. 163–4, 188.

which the Fleet are to govern themselves)'.[31] By terming himself a 'general', Mathews indicates that he acted as the leader of an army might be expected to act, further differentiating between those who control military operations of any kind and those who try to direct from London offices.

In conclusion, the clash between Lestock's definition of discipline and Mathews' rejection of this encapsulates what was a much broader debate about the function of authority in relation to the individual. Some years before the battle of Toulon, Mathews had been president at the court martial of one Captain Opie. Opie capitalized on the interest in military misbehaviour generated by the Toulon trials to air his grievances against his judges, whom he claimed had 'brought a strain'd Accusation against him, to fall under two Articles of War, where there is an absolute Contradiction and Incongruity, that manifestly proves want of Knowledge and Judgement in the Application.' Like Lestock, Opie defended his conduct by stressing his knowledge of and obedience to the navy's rules – he 'neither broke his Instructions, nor violated the Articles of War' – and by questioning his judges' knowledge of the same documents. He concludes:

> Discipline is an indeterminate Word, and it is no easy Talk to define the Limits of it, either where it begins or ends. Captain *Opie's* Judges have not yet learned to distinguish between Tyranny and Discipline, between Arrogance and Authority: The only Rule of their Government is their Will and Pleasure, and that is what many Captains call the Discipline of the Service.[32]

By Opie's account of it, 'discipline' is not to be determined by commanders but in accordance with the rules which govern all naval personnel. Opie, who, like Lestock, submits himself to centralized naval authority, is keen to stress that many captains have 'not yet learned' to acknowledge the function of authority which lies beyond themselves. At his own trial, Mathews cemented his opposition to this kind of naval authority by claiming that his right to command came from 'Royal Orders and Instructions', that is, from the king rather than government, but with the court's verdict the Admiralty finally impressed their importance upon him.[33] But though this seems to suggest that discipline was becoming a less 'indeterminate'

---

[31] *Admiral Mathews's Remarks on the Evidence Given, and the Proceedings Had, on his Trial, and Relative Thereto* (London, 1746), pp. 63, 58.

[32] *Captain Opie's Appeal Against the Illegal Proceedings of Vice-Admiral Mathews, to the Late Lords Commissioners for Executing the Office of Lord High Admiral of Great Britain* (London: M. Cooper, 1745), pp. ii, 31.

[33] *Admiral Mathews's Remarks*, p. 63.

word in the late 1740s, this chapter has yet to explore the ramifications of Lestock's claim to be a modern military man.

The New Professional

Though personality and party played their parts in the aftermath of the battle of Toulon, the trials were political in a broader sense, for the controversy revived the ideology, and intensity, of the standing army debate. That paper war had been fought over whether or not to replace the quasi-feudal system of raising and disbursing troops as needed with a new system of maintaining permanently embodied, highly trained soldiers. The anti-standing army argument, rooted as it was in the civic republicanism of the mid-century, had resisted the creation of a standing army on the basis that such soldiers would be little more than the puppets of a monarch who could not be trusted. Those in favour of the proposal had replied that modern war demanded that soldiers be made, and made modern. Lestock's account of himself clearly subscribes to the latter: he defines discipline as obedience to the established rules for flying and following flags, but also to the omnipotence of centralized naval authority. As such, Lestock's acquittal can be understood as a reward not only for submitting himself to the authority that sat in judgement upon him, but also for happening to be on the side of the revolution in military matters that introduced this kind of 'professionalism'. And yet, to look to Lestock's defence is to see that, just as the new professionalization was less than straightforward, so his model of military masculinity was precariously positioned.

According to Norbert Elias the origins of the navy as a 'profession' can be traced to the coming together of socially heterogeneous officers in the Restoration navy, but the navy of the eighteenth century was forged alongside the emergence of a range of new professions.[34] Like the three traditional professions of religion, law and medicine, the new professions were able to claim professional status on the basis that their practitioners were required to acquire and deploy 'specialist knowledge'.[35] Thus, the origins of professionalism in the early eighteenth-century

---

[34] Norbert Elias, 'Studies in the Genesis of the Naval Profession', *The British Journal of Sociology*, 1.4 (1950), 291–309. See also J. D. Davies, *Gentlemen and Tarpaulins: The Officers and Men of the Restoration Navy* (Oxford: Clarendon Press, 1991). For the growth of professionalism in the late seventeenth and early eighteenth centuries, see Geoffrey Holmes, *Augustan England: Professions, State and Society, 1680–1730* (Hemel Hempstead, George Allen & Unwin, 1982).

[35] Penelope J. Corfield, *Power and the Professions in Britain 1700–1850* (London: Routledge, 1995), pp. 18–37.

navy really lie with the introduction of the examination for midshipman in the 1670s. The exam ensured that young sailors had to demonstrate that they had acquired enough knowledge to become a lieutenant, the most junior commissioned officer. As a result, a variety of private establishments sprang up to satisfy the demand for naval education. The Admiralty seems to have been somewhat slow to notice that sailors were looking to be formally tutored for the exam, as it was not until 1702 that ships were provided with schoolmasters. This solution was radically augmented in 1733 by the founding of the Portsmouth Naval Academy, which offered an academic but practically orientated syllabus in writing, arithmetic, drawing, maths, French, fencing, the use of flintlocks, the science of military fortifications, and at times – though in a rather less systematic way – dancing. The founding of the Academy indicates that professionalization can be read as a move to increase standardization, for as H. W. Dickinson concludes, 'just as the lieutenant's examination had sought to control advancement, so the establishment of the Academy sought to regulate entry.'[36] Given this, it is not entirely surprising that the attempt was not entirely successful. Though the number of students enrolled rose steadily across the century, the Academy was widely disliked and never really threatened the less centralized system of ship-based instruction which had become inextricably linked to the tradition of ad hoc naval patronage, by which many young boys entered naval life. As a result, the two systems for preparing midshipmen for the examination – formal mainly on-shore education and a combination of patronage and ship-based schooling – ran concurrently throughout the eighteenth century. Despite a move to expand the Academy in 1808 by transferring its remit to the new Portsmouth Royal Naval College, the Admiralty achieved a single system for educating officers in 1837 only by closing the college and strengthening the provision of ship-based instruction. The on-shore Academy system failed, Dickinson concludes, not because it was unable to produce capable officers, but because of 'what it represented', that is, a 'quest for regulation' of the part of the Admiralty, aimed not just at future officers, but also at serving officers by denying them the right to patronise youngsters and thereby control who would become the officers of the future.[37]

---

[36] H. W. Dickinson, *Educating the Royal Navy: Eighteenth- and Nineteenth-Century Education for Officers* (London: Routledge, 2007), p. 201.
[37] Dickinson, *Educating the Royal Navy*, pp. 45, 201.

If the creation of the Naval Academy in the 1730s is one indication that the new professionalism emerged with the tightening of the Admiralty's control, so is another major development from the first half of the eighteenth century, one that came two years after the trials of Mathews and Lestock: the introduction of a naval uniform for naval officers. The fall of Robert Walpole and his supporters in 1742 had opened up a range of key political positions, including seats at the board of the Admiralty, which was usually comprised of a First Lord and six subordinates, only one of whom was expected to have any first-hand naval experience. The next board, formed under the leadership of Daniel Finch, earl of Winchilsea proved inadequate: for Daniel Baugh, the failure at Toulon was the 'crowning disaster' of Winchilsea's administration. However, by late 1744 a 'new generation' and a new spirit of reformist zeal had arrived at the Admiralty office, intent on 'centraliz[ing] authority in a naval organization that badly needed it.'[38] In Baugh's opinion, the new board, led by the duke of Bedford, the earl of Sandwich and Lord Anson, failed to bring about significant changes in naval administration, in ship design, and in the workings of the dockyards, but it succeeded in strengthening Admiralty control over naval personnel.[39] The introduction of a naval uniform seems to confirm this. In the absence of formal prescriptions for naval officers' dress during the early part of the eighteenth century, some naval officers had voluntarily adopted elements of army clothing, such as braided coats and scarlet waistcoats. The move to establish a distinct but comparable uniform began as a coffeehouse conversation between members of a naval club in the mid-1740s. Their resolution was passed to the board of the Admiralty, who took up the idea enthusiastically and encouraged officers to submit designs for their consideration. By 1748, a blue and white colour scheme had been chosen and an order was issued to inform admirals, captains, commanders, lieutenants and midshipmen that they were to be dressed in a 'Military Uniform Clothing' which would 'better distinguish the Rank of Sea Officers'.[40] Like the creation of the Academy, however, the introduction of the uniform was only partially successful. Dudley Jarrett notes that the order produced 'uniform without uniformity', and only in part because the wording of the regulations required much interpretation and the Admiralty's example garments were not easy accessible: he writes, 'it was ... captains and lieutenants, who asked for the uniform. When it was

---

[38] Baugh, *British Naval Administration*, pp. 88, 86.
[39] Ibid., pp. 503–4.
[40] Dudley Jarrett, *British Naval Dress* (London: J. M. Dent, 1960), p. 30.

forthcoming they showed little inclination to wear it.'[41] It seems that the uniform could be read as an attempt to impose a standardized, professionalized identity on those who preferred to see themselves as autonomous individuals. As Amy Miller notes, British naval uniform attracted so much francophobic criticism in the 1760s – the French navy having adopted a uniform in the mid-seventeenth century – that it had to be temporarily abandoned.[42]

Although Lestock's definition of discipline revived the argument made by the pro-standing army authors during the standing army debate – that militarism should be seen as a performance – it did so in a climate that was not necessarily warmly disposed towards the professionalized military man. To stabilize Lestock's defence, his supporters sought to align their admiral with contemporary naval figures who could be said to exemplify the virtues of the modern professionalized military man. According to the captain of Lestock's flag-ship, Captain Gascoigne, Admiral Edward Russell (1652–1727), who had been in service at the time of the Revolution of 1688, was one such figure, having been 'a General-Officer, whom all the best Judges of his own Time, and since, allow to have been as great a Master of perfect Discipline, as this, or any other Age or Nation ever produced.'[43] In another pro-Lestock pamphlet, Russell is identified as 'a true pattern of discipline and knowledge, who enlightened us.'[44] In comparison, the appeal on Lestock's behalf to Admiral Edward Vernon (1684–1757) is less straightforward. Vernon had been critical of Mathews during the parliamentary inquiry and had voted for Mathews to be included in the list of officers who should be tried, but he was well known for his 'deep hostility' to the Admiralty, particularly at the time of the Toulon trials.[45] Vernon remained extremely popular even when the navy was held in low regard, in part because of his victory at Porto Bello (1739), but also, as Gerald Jordan and Nicholas Rogers suggest, because his antagonistic attitude to

---

[41] Jarrett, *British Naval Dress*, p. 1. See also G. J. Marcus, *Hearts of Oak: A Survey of British Sea Power in the Georgian Era* (London: Oxford University Press, 1975), pp. 73–5.

[42] Amy Miller, *Dressed to Kill: British Naval Uniform, Masculinity and Contemporary Fashions 1748–1857* (Greenwich: National Maritime Museum, 2007), p. 26. For uniform as a means of unifying enemies as much as allies, see Mark Wishon, *German Forces and the British Army: Interactions and Perceptions, 1742–1815* (Basingstoke: Palgrave Macmillan, 2013), pp. 35–6.

[43] *Captain Gascoigne's Answer, to a Pamphlet Entitled Admiral Mathews's Remarks on the Evidence Given, and the Proceedings Had, on his Trial* (London: M. Cooper, 1746), p. 27.

[44] *Admiral Mathews's Charge Against Vice-Admiral Lestock Dissected* (London: John Millan, 1745), p. 12.

[45] Gerald Jordan and Nicholas Rogers, 'Admirals as Heroes: Patriotism and Liberty in Hanoverian England', *Journal of British Studies*, 28.3 (1989), 201–24; Wilson, *The Sense of the People*, pp. 142–51; Harding, *The Emergence of Britain's Global Naval Supremacy*, p. 197.

naval authority provided a model for popular protest.[46] Given this, Vernon would have been a very brave choice for Lestock's supporters, had he not also had a reputation as a modernizer.[47] The admiral who valued a 'happy education' more than 'the courage of brutes' had created an additional set of fighting instructions to clarify signalling procedures which the author of the *Narrative* describes as intended 'for the Improvement of his Brethren, who, if they take the Pains to peruse them, will receive Benefit and Instruction.'[48] In appealing to Vernon, then, Lestock's supporters appealed to a popular military man who, whatever his feelings about the board of the Admiralty, had advanced the cause of professionalized militarism.[49]

In Admirals Russell and Vernon, Lestock's supporters found templates for the modern professional military identity that Lestock modelled at the parliamentary inquiry and again at his court martial. However, the trial and its aftermath could not but parade the fundamental condition of this modern military identity: its disavowal of essence. To argue that modern militarism requires the acquisition and deployment of specialist knowledge is to allow modern militarism to be a performance and so expose the modern military man as lacking what his critics could term 'real' substance. Thus, when the author of the *Narrative* ruminates on the meaning of the term 'officer' she or he does very little to strengthen Lestock's case. The *Narrative* addresses itself to 'the unprejudiced Officers and Men of Understanding ...; as it is not every Man who bears a Commission, from the Admiral downwards, that can be called strictly an Officer; for in every Rank there are ignorant Men, perfect Strangers to Discipline and Duty.'[50] The idea that the term 'officer' should be allowed only to those who define discipline and duty in Lestockian terms is clearly intended to reinforce modern military professionalism, but the *Narrative* goes on to emphasize the generic qualities of the modern military man in ways that deliberately blur the boundaries between military and civilian officers:

> A Minister, an Admiral, a General, or any other public Officer, the Instruments of the Royal Authority, are invested with the Power to do good, but are restrained from doing ill. While they with a Disinterestedness, a Candor, and a Nobleness of Soul, use their Talents and Capacities in

---

[46] Harding, *The Emergence of Britain's Global Naval Supremacy*, p. 340.
[47] Baugh, *British Naval Administration*, p. 150.
[48] Vernon quoted in G. J. Marcus, *Heart of Oak*, p. 76; *A Narrative of the Proceedings*, p. 96.
[49] Conway, *War, State and Society*, pp. 213–4; Harding, *The Emergence of Britain's Global Naval Supremacy*, p. 231.
[50] *A Narrative of the Proceedings*, p. iv.

Pursuit of the true Interests of their Country ... and by their Prudence and Courage surmount all Obstacles and Difficulties: while pure Reason, Fortitude and Military Virtue appear to be the Rule of their Will ... they govern with Wisdom and Moderation, and unite in the same View to preserve Independence Abroad and Union at Home; ... [and] they punish Evil and reward Merit with Distinction, employ the Superiority of their Genius only to make their Masters Commands respected and to add Strength to his interest and Influence Abroad.[51]

This argument serves to neutralize the civic argument that 'power' should be held by the people, for the author asserts that all 'public officers' exist to 'do good'. However, by stressing that the navy or army officer is one and the same as other, non-military 'officers', the author merges the modern military man with a range of others, including the career bureaucrats who emerged with the expansion of the civil service in the early eighteenth century and who exemplify the new professionals of the Augustan age. In this account of things then, the modern professionalized military man is no more military, and therefore no less civil(ian), than an administrator.

As this extract from the *Narrative* indicates, the rhetoric that appealed directly to centralized naval authority was one and the same as that which exposed the weakness of the modern military man. After all, by stressing the similarity between military and public officers, the *Narrative* does little to conceal the fact that Lestock's professionalized military identity lacked the kind of definitional stability that many in an increasingly bellicose society demanded. A performance conjured from on-shore schooling, the cut of a newly uniform coat or a strict adherence to written rules was always going to be vulnerable to the criticism that it was too superficial to be of use when fighting an enemy. Given this, the *Narrative* further complicates the modern military man's case by explicitly comparing the education of French and British officers, to the detriment of the latter:

We do not trouble our Heads in training up Sea Officers, tho' the chief maritime Power; if they are Seamen, 'tis a meer Chance if they know any thing of military Discipline, or the Art of War; while the *French* are taught that Art, and to behave to one another like Gentlemen, with Complaisance and Politeness, and every Officer gives his Orders to his inferior, with the modest Manners of Equality; we *domineer* over one another with the lofty and imperious Air, which the Command of a *British* Ship of War naturally gives a Man: Thus our Spirits are broke, and reduced to that timid Submission and servile Dependence, which cannot be expected but from

[51] Ibid., pp. 1–2.

Men bred and educated in Obscurity. They command Gentlemen, we command Slaves.⁵²

In praising the French officers for their 'Complaisance and Politeness', the *Narrative* defines the ideal military man as one who acquires a set of skills more readily associated with performing in civil society. Though seemingly intended to defend the modern professionalized military man, this provided further ammunition to those who wanted to attack him. By comparing the British and French officers, the author once again reveals the vulnerability of the performer of professionalism. This criticism of the British way of educating sailors – meaning ship-based education – gives way to a broader criticism of those officers in positions of power who domineer over their subordinates. The unwritten coda to this is that all naval personnel ought to consider themselves equally subject to a higher, civil authority.

Like the comparison between military and public officers, the comparison between British and French officers did little to stabilize the modern military man. The anti-standing army authors had feared that the introduction of a permanent military establishment would reduce all Britons to clog-wearing *paysans*; civic critics of the 1740s could justifiably argue that the insubstantial modern military man had become dangerously indistinguishable from his enemies. According to Mark Wishon, it was the development of pan-European military professionalism in the eighteenth century, evident in 'structural, organizational and philosophical similarities', which enabled disparate armies to bond and fight as allies, but those similarities also bonded allies with their enemies, not least the shared language of politeness.⁵³ In the aftermath of the battle of Toulon, it was widely rumoured that Lestock had been overly civil to those he should have seen only as enemies. Lestock addressed what he termed the 'ridiculous' matter at the parliamentary inquiry; he admitted that he had spent time ashore conversing with 'a *French* Officer, who had taken me a Prisoner in the late War, and treated me nobly; … [but that] Mr. Rowley and Mr. Martin, now Admirals, bore me Company all the Time we convers'd together.'⁵⁴ The author of the *Narrative* attempted to further neutralize the damage by noting that the battle of Toulon had

---

⁵² *A Narrative of the Proceedings*, p. 115. For military academies in Europe, see Christopher Duffy, *The Military Experience in the Age of Reason* (London: Routledge and Kegan Paul, 1987), pp. 47–9, 50–7.
⁵³ Wishon, *German Forces and the British Army*, pp. 33–6. For the emergence of an 'international fraternity' of military men in the eighteenth century, see also Brewer, *The Sinews of Power*, pp. 55–9.
⁵⁴ *Vice-Admal Lestock's Recapitulation*, p. 12.

followed a long blockade of the harbour during which the French had been extremely civil: 'they kept up the Shew of Friendship, and frankly supplied us with whatever we demanded.'[55] And yet, the excuse that he had merely been conversing – and presumably in French, the international language of militarism and the mother tongue for polite society – served only to fuel others' fears.[56] Little wonder that the pro-Mathews *Original Letters and Papers* gestures to the rumour by commenting that Lestock had been 'extravagant in his Praises on the Conduct of the *French* Admiral.'[57] The author of *Just, Genuine, and Impartial History* makes even more of it, noting 'as for what he mentions concerning the Rumour of his holding a correspondence with the enemy, and the ridiculousness thereof. – I shall only observe, that the Seamen in general are so honest-hearted, as never to tax any Man of Misbehaviour, unless there is some Occasion.'[58] Lestock may have been shrewd in defining discipline in such a way as to stress his professionalism, but by admitting that he had conversed with a French officer he drew attention to the similarity between acquiring specialist knowledge and acquiring a military identity in much the way that a gentleman might acquire polite manners. Though Lestock's defence addressed itself to the court and the authority beyond, the rumour that he had been overly intimate with his enemies helps to indicate why it was, as Frederic Hervey recorded some years later, that 'the decisions on the two admirals were far from being relished by the nation, who saw the conduct of the two commanders with different eyes from those of their judges.'[59]

Performance and the *Corpus Rasa*

The extent to which the trials of Mathews and Lestock reinvigorated the debate begun by the standing army authors with regard to the modernization of military men is, perhaps, clearest in a comment made by Mathews at his own trial, which followed Lestock's acquittal. During the proceedings, Mathews accused Captain Gascoigne of sharing Lestock's attitude to naval service: 'As to [Gascoigne's] new-fangled Discipline, … Mr *Lestock* never got the Length of the [Spanish ship] *Real* any one Time of that Day.'[60] Gascoigne replied in print: 'I may venture to depend on the

---

[55] *A Narrative of the Proceedings*, p. 29.
[56] For the use of the French language, see Cohen, *Fashioning Masculinity*.
[57] *Original Letters and Papers*, p. 105.
[58] *A Just, Genuine, and Impartial History*, p. 253.
[59] Frederic Hervey, *The Naval History of Great Britain*, 2nd ed., 4 vols. (London: William Alard; J. Bew, 1780–3), IV, p. 302.
[60] *Admiral Mathews's Remarks*, p. 14.

Consent of every impartial Judge, that the Term *New-fangled Discipline*, may with much greater Propriety, be returned back to the Person (whoever he is) that has made me the Compliment of it.'[61] And yet, 'new-fangled' is more than appropriate, for Lestock's defence of the new professionalism had ramifications for older understandings of the relationship between gender and the body. William Horsley, self-ordained chronicler of the times and author of 'The Fool' papers, originally printed in the *Daily Gazetteer*, gestures towards this in a paper, written four weeks after the start of Mathews' trial, in which he turns his attention to the state of modern masculinity and femininity. Whilst belles and beaux might behave like each other, he argues, they 'are only something alike externally; but, examined, have nothing similar in them, but Dress and Giddiness.' In other words, a belle may be able to act like a man and a beau to act like a woman, but what is beneath clothes and manners – what is 'in' each of them – reveals that they are essentially and incommensurably different:

> Woman is form'd by Nature to please and be admired: To this End, she is fram'd tender, delicate, and fair ... The very Air, blowing upon her ... [will] disorder the whole Frame of her Mind, and [she] is never in perfect Repose, but when a-sleep; meditating on some agreeable Object, or in the Arms of the Man she loves ... Man is form'd by Nature for great and noble Pursuits: and his Frame of Body adapted to that of his Mind. He is made strong, nervous, robust; and his Soul soars after Honour and Renown, as the Eagle after its Prey; and is naturally so restless in the Pursuit, as never to be satisf'd with Acquisition.[62]

If the 'real' belle can be identified by looking at what is natural to her, it would stand to reason that the 'real' character of the admiral can be ascertained likewise. Indeed, Horsley seems to have a military man in mind when he characterizes the ideal man in terms of strength, desire for renown and restlessness.

As calculatedly self-serving as Lestock's defence may have been, his claim that he had merely followed signals made a radical statement about the 'nature' of masculinity, one that challenged older, essentialist understanding of the relationship between gender and the body. By arguing that the military man should act, in every sense, as and when instructed by an authority that controls even the most senior officer, Lestock indicates that the ideal

---

[61] *Captain Gascoigne's Answer*, p. 30.
[62] William Horsley, No. 5, Friday, 18th July 1746, *The Fool: Being a Collection of Essays and Epistles, Moral, Political, Humourous, and Entertaining*, 2 vols. (London: Nutt, Cooke and Kingman, et al., 1748), I, pp. 33–4.

military man is produced by a force that creates military men to its own specifications. As such, Lestock's modern military man shares much with the Foucaldian soldier, that 'fragment of mobile space', and anticipates Foucault and Butler's understanding of discipline as a means of moulding the empty, blank body. After all, given that he was on trial for the failure to fight, it is significant that Lestock continually stressed the steadiness of his character – declaring, for example, that the lengthy court proceedings could, 'warm a Man of much more even Temper than my self' – but made no attempt to argue that he had shown courage.[63] In fact, rather than stake a claim to courage, and thus corporality, Lestock took a stand against both by arguing that Mathews had been rash and that the battle had failed because of this. His position is seconded in the *Narrative*, which claims that 'Courage alone is not sufficient to supply all the Duties of an Admiral or General', since 'in Order and Discipline lie the whole Study of the military Art.'[64] The *Narrative*, a text that observes in its opening pages that 'Men whose Resolutions are not fixed and steady, who are capricious and inconstant … [are] incapable of reaching the Heights and Depths of their Profession', developed Lestock's point by stating that, 'in the Heat of Battle, an Admiral ought to be active and resolute, yet calm and present to himself', and, should the situation turn against him, use his talents without 'giving Way to an headstrong Imagination, and an ungovernable Passion, which knows no Bounds.'[65] Even in a difficult situation, the author argues elsewhere, the commander should still react without warmth, for 'should he therefore be inflamed with Rage, and all the Passions which possess a proud Spirit when fallen from its Hopes, he will then lose the Fruits of all his Talents.'[66] As another pro-Lestock author observes, an ideal officer should 'lead … with intrepidity; which is meant a cool courage in the commander.'[67] With these points, Lestock's supporters replaced the warmth of the innately militaristic male body with the steadiness of cool professionalism, masculine humoral heat with the modern *corpus rasa*.

At his trial Lestock had stressed his total submission to 'the Discipline of the Navy' in order to exculpate 'the greatest Crimes that a Military Man could commit against his King and Country', but his account of correct

---

[63] *Vice Admiral Lestock's Defence*, p. 190.
[64] *A Narrative of the Proceedings*, p. 93.
[65] Ibid., pp. 2, 92–3. The phrase 'In the Heat of Battle he ought to be active and resolute, yet calm and present to himself' also appears in *A Particular Account of the Late Action in the Mediterranean* (London: T. Tons, 1744), p. 22.
[66] *A Particular Account of the Late Action*, p. 22.
[67] *Admiral Mathews's Charge Against Vice-Admiral Lestock Dissected*, p. 5.

conduct, resting as it did on the virtue of the performance of professionalism, did not attempt to offer assurances guaranteed by the innately gendered body.[68] An identity that lacked anchorage in the physical body could easily be disregarded by its critics, and letters sent by Lestock to Thomas Corbett, secretary to the board of the Admiralty, in advance of the trial suggest that the admiral was aware of this. On receiving a copy of the charges against him, Lestock noted that Mathews had referred to him as the late Vice-Admiral and further irritated by similarly ambiguously addressed letters from the Admiralty, he wrote to Corbett asking 'whether I am a Vice-Admiral or not?' Of course, it may be that Lestock was pedantically attached to the aggrandizement of rank: he freely acknowledged his 'mortification' at seeing his juniors promoted above him while he waited for his trial. And yet, when a later letter addressed him using a flag-title which was more senior than his own, he was quick to alert Corbett to the error. Given this, Lestock's concern to be addressed correctly, even while suspended, points rather to his awareness of the importance of external markers in substantiating the 'new-fangled' military man. There is some indication that the Admiralty understood this in Corbett's reply to Lestock's question:

> As to Mr. M---ws styling you the late Vice-Admiral, you do not expect any Answer from their Lordships for the ways of other Men; and as to my Clerks directing my Letters to you without naming your Flag, it appears to be the usual Method of this Office, when Letters are sent to Flag-Officers, whose Flags are not flying: however, I make no scruple to direct to you (as I do this) with your Flag-Title; it being out of doubt that a Flag-Officer suspended does not cease to be a Flag-Officer.[69]

Here, Corbett refers to the 'usual' practice of not addressing officers by their flag-title when not in active service, but his words of reassurance seem to admit that a military identity which is actively acquired and consciously performed must be continually reasserted.

Lestock's supporters seem also to have been aware of the instability of the blank, empty body. At his trial, Lestock countered the vulnerability of the empty body by stressing that, to him, discipline was duty: 'where Obedience was my Duty I was not defective in paying it to the Commands of my Superior to the utmost of my Power, and that where Command was with me I did not fail to exercise it in the best Manner I was able for

---

[68] *Vice Admiral Lestock's Defence*, p. 203.
[69] *Vice-Adm---l L-st--k's Account of the Late Engagement, Near Toulon, Between His Majesty's Fleet, and the Fleets of France and Spain; as Presented by Him the 12th of March 1744–5. Also Letters To and From Adm---l L-st--k, Relating Thereto Since His Arrival in England* (London: M. Cooper, 1745), pp. 29, 8, 33, 31.

the Service.'[70] An anonymous pro-Lestock author agreed: 'Mr Lestock ... had learned under [Mathews] in a more singular manner than ever, that passive obedience was his only and ultimate duty.'[71] The author of the *Narrative* reinforces this by defining obedience as 'the first Habit which a military Man should learn.'[72] A 'habit' of behaviour, however, remains too much like a habit of clothing, a layer concealing all inadequacies beneath. In response to Lestock's appeal to duty, the pro-Mathews author of *A Just, Genuine, and Impartial History* criticised Lestock's supporters for painting him as 'the only consummate complete Officer in the Navy.'[73] Far from being the 'complete' officer, they argued, Lestock had been too narrowly focused on discipline. In order to explain his failure to send a written message to Lestock during the battle to command him to alter his course, Mathews argued that, 'as he is so strict a Disciplinarian, he must know it was his indispensable Duty, not only to have brought to, but also to have kept all Night as near the Enemy, as did his Admiral.'[74] The author of *A Just, Genuine, and Impartial History* refined the insult, calling Lestock 'so great a Disciplinarian', and styling him 'Mr. Discipline'.[75] Rather than hail Lestock as the complete officer, the title 'Mr Discipline', a deliberately anonymous, generic title, attacks the modern professional military man for offering only emptiness.

The arguments made against Lestock and his supporters by Mathews and his supporters indicate how controversial proto-constructionism was at this point in the eighteenth century. As Lawrence Klein argues, in the early eighteenth century the performance of politeness became synonymous with 'self-management and self-presentation' and this gave rise to the criticism that polite persons valued appearance over substance, 'social acting' over sincerity: '[politeness] appeared to break the continuity between moral and social personality, exploring the disponibility of the social self and pioneering its transformation into a role-player.'[76] An identity that was carefully performed rather than apparently innate lacked the authenticity provided by the corporeality of the body and to critics of politeness the acquired or constructed 'self' was little more than a mask worn by those who intended to manipulate and deceive others. Little wonder that the

---

[70] *Vice Admiral Lestock's Defence*, p. 1
[71] *Admiral Mathews's Charge Against Vice-Admiral Lestock Dissected*, p. 36.
[72] *A Narrative of the Proceedings*, p. 56.
[73] *A Just, Genuine, and Impartial History*, p. 236.
[74] *Admiral Mathews's Remarks*, p. 51.
[75] *A Just, Genuine, and Impartial History*, pp. 240, 139.
[76] Klein, 'The Third Earl of Shaftesbury', p. 191.

pro-Mathews author of *A Just, Genuine, and Impartial History* argued that, while '[Mathews] judged by his own Heart, and thence concluded all others brave, open, generous and gallant as himself', Lestock had concealed his true character under a 'Skreen of discipline' and that his 'Subtilty and close Designs were not easily to be seen into, by a Mind, open, gallant, and undesigning.'[77] This connection between the blank body and the intention to deceive is particularly clear in one seemingly minor facet of the Mathews and Lestock controversy: the discussion of whether military men could or should take up the pen as well as the sword. As Alison Duncan has noted, military men knew that there were benefits to being skilful in private correspondence: as a 'vehicle for self-presentation', impressive penmanship might help secure patronage.[78] Public penmanship, however, was a different matter. Although Gascoigne, the captain Mathews attacked for his 'new-fangled' discipline, committed himself to print he was very wary about being seen to want to be an author. Gascoigne accuses Mathews of employing a third party to write a pamphlet on his behalf and then circulating that pamphlet dishonestly: '[it] is not to be bought, but is said to be put into the Hands only of particular Persons, as if they, and the Multitudes of others by their means, were intended to be privately influenced thereby.' In contrast, he makes it clear that he has penned a reply to Mathews reluctantly, 'as there is no Possibility of any Chance, for this my Answer ever coming to the Hands of the reasonable Men, to whom that pamphlet has been deliver'd.'[79]

Whereas the 'new-fangled' Gascoigne was able to justify his authorial activities on the basis that he had published unwillingly and openly, Mathews' supporters vilified the pro-Lestock author of *A Particular Account* and the *Narrative* for publishing enthusiastically and dishonestly. In both texts, the author claimed to have been an eyewitness to the battle of Toulon, but in different capacities: firstly as an officer of the marines (perhaps because a marine officer was not subject to naval law and could more easily be seen as impartial in the matter of the courts martial) and secondly as a naval officer. The pro-Mathews author of *Original Letters and Papers* attacked the pro-Lestock author for changing his story, calling *A Particular Account* nothing more than 'bitter and rude Reflections' which were taken by 'every sensible and reasonable Man [to be] a sure Indication

---

[77] *A Just, Genuine, and Impartial History*, pp. 148, 152.
[78] Alison Duncan, 'The Sword and the Pen: The Role of Correspondence in the Advancement Tactics of Eighteenth-Century Military Officers', *Journal of Scottish Historical Studies*, 29.2 (2009), 106–22 (pp. 107–8).
[79] *Captain Gascoigne's Answer*, pp. 4, 5.

of the Author's Prepossession and Prejudice', such that the '*Marine* Officer was induced to throw off the Mask, and take up his own Character, that of the Sea-Officer: in which he publishes a Narrative of the Proceedings of His Majesty's Fleet.'[80] By adopting different characters, the pro-Mathews author drew attention to the weakness of Lestock's performance of professionalism: this chameleonic author moves between marine officer and sea officer in ways that undermine the authenticity of all such professional identities. The discussion of authorship reaches a climax in *A Just, Genuine and Impartial History* with a passage that attacks Lestock directly:

> Mr L–k sets out very haughtily, triumphing in his Acquaintance with Discipline; and the Use he makes of his pretended Knowledge is, only to see Errors in others, and to shelter himself from Justice, but not to serve his Country; I suppose he rather learn'd it to make him a penetrating Critick than an honest Man; … He made it his business to obey beyond Obedience, and because he would not be wanting in solid Remarks, he turn'd his Division into a Squadron of Observation, that he might be enabled, in case he was broke as an A – l, to come home and turn Author, and which he has performed with all the Artifice of a Bookseller; writing, multiplying and confounding, to the Tune of a pretty Penny.[81]

Here, the point that Lestock 'made it his business to obey beyond obedience' is turned into an argument that he treated his military identity as one of many interchangeable identities, easily adopted and easily cast aside according to how profitable any one might be at a given moment. *A Just, Genuine, and Impartial History* concludes by stating that Lestock was too much at ease with being an author rather than an admiral: 'the exerting himself here as a Writer is nothing, unless he could shew at the same Time, that he exerted himself as a Man of Honour when in his proper Station.' With this, Mathews' supporter asserts the importance of definitional stability. It only remains to note that he or she was right to remind Lestock that 'writing Encomiums on one's Self' would irritate the 'Body of the People'.[82]

To look to the official outcomes of the trials of Mathews and Lestock is to conclude that the verdicts rewarded the 'new-fangled' military man. After all, the acquittal of Lestock was followed by the introduction of a uniform for officers in 1748, as well as a further reform that indicates how far the

---

[80] *Original Letters and Papers*, pp. iv–v.
[81] *A Just, Genuine, and Impartial History*, pp. 130–1.
[82] Ibid., pp. 144, 127.

board of the Admiralty sought to formalize its control over naval officers: the revision of the navy's *Articles of War* in 1749.[83] Given that Rodger has argued that the War of the Austrian Succession exposed a serious problem with cowardice and disaffection among naval officers and that this provided the 'imperative to strengthen naval discipline', it could be argued that the revision of the *Articles of War* was a reaction against, rather than a move prefigured by the trials.[84] Indeed, Markus Eder's assessment of naval law in the mid-eighteenth century concludes that the revisions created a more bloodthirsty penal code by limiting judges' licence and introducing mandatory death sentences for a greater number of offences.[85] And yet, the revisions seem to have been intended to help standardize, as much as strengthen, naval punishment. The lack of standardization can be seen in the outcomes of other trials at this time. In January 1745, Captains Thomas Griffin and Savage Mostyn were thought to have failed to deal adequately with two French ships. Mostyn was called to account, but treated leniently by the court martial. In contrast, six months later Lieutenant Baker Philips was shot for what was said to be cowardice in the aftermath of his ship being captured by the French.[86] The new articles closed down some of the flexibility of courts martial verdicts and thereby reinforced the importance of centralized naval authority. Thus, the move to strengthen the navy's legal code can also be identified as a move to strengthen the importance of discipline in an abstract, Foucauldian sense: the revision of the *Articles* seems to have made the point that the rules precede the officer and that obedience to the rules creates the modern military man.

Of course, if the trials of Mathews and Lestock are to be seen as part of a broader movement towards modernization at the end of the 1740s, it has to be noted that, like the introduction of the uniform, the revisions of the *Articles* did not pass unchallenged. As Baugh has argued, a professional officer corps had to be a permanent officer corps, and this meant tackling the ambiguous status of the half-pay officer, which the new *Articles* did to some extent.[87] A pamphlet on the new *Articles* attacked the Admiralty for seeking to extend naval law to every person, 'in actual Service relative to the Fleet … as if the same [act] had been committed

---

[83] It can hardly be coincidental that in 1749 the Admiralty inspected the Portsmouth Naval Academy and approved of all aspects of the Academy's endeavours. See Dickinson, *Educating the Royal Navy*, p. 37.
[84] Rodger, *Articles of War*, p. 9.
[85] Markus Eder, *Crime and Punishment in the Royal Navy of the Seven Years War, 1755–1763* (Aldershot: Ashgate, 2004), pp. 156–7.
[86] Harding, *The Emergence of Britain's Global Naval Supremacy*, pp. 230, 250.
[87] Baugh, *British Naval Administration*, pp. 103–8.

at Sea.'[88] As the anonymous author recognized, the phrase 'actual service' made full and half-pay officers '*equally subject to Discipline.*' The author's central claim was that half-pay ought to be a reward for services carried out, not a retainer for services to come. Addressing naval officers en masse, the pamphlet argued that the '*Board* of those *Sea*-Gods' were using discipline as a tool for tyranny: 'I cannot help undertaking … to warn you of the perpetual Slavery you are doom'd to, by these oppressive Rivetters of those Shackles preparing for you in the forging Minds of your Rulers … unless (as uniformly as you are dress'd) you all determine to make such a stand for that Liberty your Forefathers left you.'[89] The recourse to 'Liberty' marks this as a thoroughly civic argument, but the parenthesized comment contemporizes this as anxiety about the advent of professionalism in the late 1740s.

As this chapter has shown, though the trials of Mathews and Lestock seem to mark a point at which the modern military man gained formal status, the official record can only reveal so much. Nicholas Tindal, whose account of the controversy states that Lestock 'under the pretexts of observing discipline, accused the admiral of such indistinctness of orders, that he did not know, or, to speak more properly, he was not obliged to know their meaning', records that when it became known that Mathews had been convicted, 'the public was astonished at this sentence.'[90] As much as Lestock's acquittal can be seen as a reward for identifying himself as a professional military man – 'the first Sea-Officer, nay the first Man of any Profession whatever, in this Land of Liberty, that ever had two Charges sent to him before his Trial' – the resentment directed at Lestock can be read as antipathy to his account of militarism, and also its implications for understandings of the nature of gender. Professionalized modern militarism was transparently a performance that, like the performance of politeness, lacked the definitional stability provided by the warm corporeality of the body.[91] The epigram to *Vice Admiral Lestock's Defence to the Court-Martial* applies as much to an assembly as to a court martial: 'he who either doth not see what is proper at that Time, or talks too much, or boasts of himself, or mindeth not with whom he is, that Man is said to

---

[88] Article 34 of the 'Act for amending, explaining and reducing into one Act of Parliament, the Laws relating to the Government of his Majesty's ships, Vessels and Forces by Sea' (1749), in Rodger, *Articles of War*, p. 28.

[89] *A Letter from a Friend in the Country to a Friend at Will's Coffee-House; in Relation to Three Additional Articles of War* (London: J. Bromage, 1749), pp. 12, 6–7.

[90] N[icholas] Tindal, *The Continuation of Mr. Rapin's History of England; From the Revolution to the Present Times*, 9 vols. (London: Mr. Knapton, 1759), IX, pp. 42–3, 48.

[91] *Vice-Admiral Lestock's Defence*, p. xv.

be a Fool.' Given that Horsley, an enemy of modern gender performance, introduces himself to his readers as '[not] one of those Fools, who ... prefer being bad Authors to being good Admirals' it is significant that he greeted the conclusion of the trials by pronouncing in Mathews' favour.[92] Horsley suggests that his views are 'generally agreed' upon, for this was 'an Affair which generally concerns the community, who have therefore the Right to enquire how those conduct themselves, whom they pay and support, whether as Delinquents or Judges': 'it is, and I hope always will be, in the Power of the People, to insist upon being satisfied.'[93] The official verdict may have supported the modern, professionalized military man, and with it the *corpus rasa*, but this was certainly not the final word on the nature of the ideal (military) man.

---

[92] Horsley, No. 1, Thursday, 10th July 1746, *The Fool*, I, p. 3.
[93] Horsley, No. 45, Friday, 24th October 1746, *The Fool*, I, pp. 317, 320.

CHAPTER 3

The New Old Military Hero
The Trial of Admiral John Byng, 1756–1757

[The Battle of Toulon was] the grandest scene exhibited during the whole war: a scene which for magnificence and importance hath rarely been equalled in any age, on any sea. Seventy-Four men of war in the Mediterranean, all in view, at the same time preparing to pour out their thunder, destructive of the human species, and decisive of the state of nations! The great, the anxious expectation raised by such a prospect may be easily imagined: but the vast machinery was too stupendous for human management, and the heroic virtue of former ages was wanting to produce a glorious catastrophe.[1]

Lives of the British Admirals (1779)

Looking back to the War of the Austrian Succession from the middle of the War of American Independence, John Berkenhout, author of the continuation to John Campbell's survey of British naval history, *Lives of the British Admirals*, records the battle of Toulon as a scene of rare importance. This was something of an odd choice; an offensive action in the midst of a turgid war, the battle had carried the hopes of a frustrated and anxious nation only to end with disappointment and recriminations. At the courts martial that followed, Lestock offered himself as a product of naval discipline and in defining military service as a performance of professionalism he defended a controversially 'new-fangled' military identity, one that had implications for conceptualizations of the nature of masculinity. Berkenhout's survey of the battle paints the scene in terms that are directly opposed to this. Berkenhout imagines the moments before the battle began as moments of sublimity, the 'vast machinery' of war primed to throw bolts of sulphurous 'thunder'. By glossing the battle with

---

[1] [John] Berkenhout, *Lives of the British Admirals: Containing a New and Accurate Naval History, From the Earliest Periods. Written by Dr. J Campbell. With a Continuation Down to the Year 1779*, 4 vols. (London: Alexander Donaldson, 1779), IV, p. 47.

Burkean terms, Berkenhout, who had himself served in the Prussian Army during the Seven Years' War (1756–63), seems to excuse Admirals Thomas Mathews and Richard Lestock for failing to master the sublime technology of modern war. And yet, in celebrating the moments before the battle, Berkenhout heightens the intended contrast between an idealized notion of past military heroism and the actual behaviour of both admirals in the recent present.

Berkenhout's lament for the 'heroic virtue of former ages' accords with literary scholars' long-held view that there was a decline in the cultural status of the 'heroic ideal' during the eighteenth century. Augustan poets cleaved to classical epic – in Dryden's words, 'the greatest work which the soul of man is capable to perform' – but, as Ulrich Broich notes, they honoured the epic by mocking their own age.[2] The decline of the classical epic can also be connected to the equally familiar tale of the rise of the novel as the literary genre of choice for the eighteenth century's polite, middle-class consumers: as Robert Folkenflik has observed, the literature of the eighteenth century abounds with hero-figures, but they are bourgeois heroes, modified and modernized to suit a world for which 'the concept of military or political heroism seems at best tarnished or dubious.'[3] This well-established narrative of the decline of heroism in literature has been further strengthened by Martin Myrone's account of the fate of the heroic image in the mid-eighteenth to early nineteenth century, a period in which, he argues, the market for large grand-manner paintings depicting 'classical ideals of virtuous masculine heroism' collapsed.[4] For scholars of eighteenth-century masculinity, however, the linearity of this narrative must be troubling. As Karen Harvey has argued, studies of masculinity in the eighteenth century can be limited by the failure to see beyond the rise of polite society.[5] Indeed, Philip Carter acknowledges that politeness never achieved a fully hegemonic position within the century's 'vigorous debate on standards of manhood' and that during the 1740s and 1750s critics of politeness were apt to cite the military as 'the last bastion of manliness in a degenerate society.'[6] Having focused on the performance

---

[2] Ulrich Broich, *The Eighteenth-Century Mock-Heroic Poem*, trans. by David Henry Wilson, 2nd ed. (Cambridge: Cambridge University Press, 1990 [1968]), p. 1.
[3] *The English Hero, 1660–1800*, ed. by Robert Folkenflik (London: Associated University Presses, 1982), p. 15.
[4] Martin Myrone, *Bodybuilding: Reforming Masculinities in British Art, 1750–1810* (New Haven, CT: Yale University Press, 2005), p. 193.
[5] Harvey, 'The History of Masculinity', pp. 305–11.
[6] Carter, *Men and the Emergence of Polite Society*, pp. 216, 133.

of military professionalism in both previous chapters, this chapter turns to trial of Admiral John Byng in order to explore an alternative model of military masculinity. By detailing the similarity between Lestock and Byng's defences, and by reading responses to Byng's trial for their criticism of his modern military identity, this chapter argues that, by mid-century, the alternative to the modern military man was no longer the classic civic citizen-solider, and was instead an equally timeless but more obviously 'natural' military man: the 'old hero'.

Byng's Re-Fangled Defence

The Seven Years' War, preceded as it was by years of hostility between Britain and France for trade and territory in North America and India, was a war for empire, fought, as Daniel Baugh and others have documented, on a global scale.[7] When the war concluded, it was on terms that provided the foundations for Britain's imperial and colonial future and foreshadowed British success in the French Revolutionary and Napoleonic Wars. But rather than view this war in terms of what was to come after, it is just as important, as Stephen Conway points out, to think in terms of what had come before.[8] By the end of the War of the Austrian Succession, Britain had established superiority at sea; had Britain been able to do so on land as well the terms of the Treaty of Aix-la-Chapelle (1748) might have been more definitive, not to mention favourable. As it was, the treaty left crucial matters concerning colonial territories undecided. Both Britain and France were unwilling to fight openly in the early 1750s, as this would force declarations of war, but while British and French diplomats pursued fruitless negotiations, both nations kept close watch on each other's colonial trade, efforts to strengthen their military establishments and relations with former allies – crucially Austria and Prussia – as well as possibilities for new continental and colonial allies.[9] By 1754 the enmity was palpable. Many in Britain were keen to avoid war, including the leader of the

---

[7] Daniel Baugh, *The Global Seven Years War, 1754–1763: Britain and France in a Great Power Contest* (Harlow: Pearson, 2011). See also Matt Schumann and Karl Schweizer, *The Seven Years War: A Transatlantic History* (Routledge: Abingdon, 2008); Fred Anderson, *Crucible of War: The Seven Years War and the Fate of Empire in British North America, 1754–1766* (London: Faber, 2000); Tom Pocock, *Battle for Empire: The Very First World War, 1756–63* (London: Caxton, 1998; repr. 2002).

[8] For Conway, the two wars are best viewed as 'one extended conflict'. *War, State and Society*, p. 5.

[9] The 'new' board of 1744 instigated a programme of dock yard reforms and ship-building. This prompted the French and Spanish to do likewise. See Clive Wilkinson, *The British Navy and the State in the Eighteenth Century* (Woodbridge: Boydell, 2004), pp. 90–4; Jonathan R. Dull, *The French Navy and the Seven Years War* (Lincoln: University of Nebraska, 2005), pp. 9–12.

ruling party of Whigs, Thomas Pelham-Holles, duke of Newcastle, but as in the 1730s, patriotic voices, though wary of entering into a continental war for the sake of Hanover, called for action against the French threat in North America.[10] At this point British and French forces in America started to jostle for superiority, and though there were early successes for Admirals Edward Boscawen and Edward Hawke and for Lieutenant Colonel Robert Monckton in the summer of 1755, in July of that year the French repelled Major General Edward Braddock's attack on Fort Duquesne and in so doing gained the upper hand. Fort Duquesne was successfully taken in 1758, but it was not until after the battles at Quebec and Quiberon Bay in 1759 that the war seemed to have turned decisively in Britain's favour.

The disappointing battle between Britain and France off the island of Minorca in May 1756 that led to the trial of Byng might not have been much more than a minor episode in British naval history, had it not occurred, like the battle of Toulon, during a difficult period for British military endeavours. The French attack on the British island of Minorca forced Britain and France to issue formal declarations of war, which then mobilized their European allies, principally Austria, Russia and Prussia, and brought what had been a war in America rather closer to Britain's shores. With the benefit of hindsight, it is possible to see the numerous factors that contributed to the loss of Minorca. First, the British response to the French plan to attack the island had been slowed by misleading intelligence.[11] When, in early 1756, news arrived in London that the French were preparing a naval squadron at Toulon, it was feared that the force was to be sent to invade Britain. Once it had been firmly established that the island of Minorca was the intended target, Byng was given command of a fleet and tasked to assist General William Blakeney's small garrison in holding the fort of St. Philip at Port Mahon. By the time Byng set sail it was already too late to prevent an invasion. Byng had not been able to put to sea until the 6th of April and did not reach the island until the 2nd of May; the French fleet had set sail on the 8th of April and in little more than two weeks French soldiers had landed and taken the undefended fort at Cuidadela. There was limited possibility of Byng making a successful intervention in the invasion. The British navy was lacking in ready ships

---

[10] Baugh, *The Global Seven Years War*, pp. 101–2; Conway, *War, State and Society*, pp. 144–53; Robert Harris, *Politics and the Nation: Britain in the Mid-Eighteenth Century* (Oxford: Oxford University Press, 2002), pp. 116–22, 135–47.

[11] Baugh, *The Global Seven Years War*, pp. 182–95; Dull, *The French Navy*, pp. 50–2.

and able sailors due to recent actions in North America and Byng was hampered from the beginning by Lord Anson's decision to send a relatively small fleet.[12] Byng's mission was further undermined by Lieutenant General Thomas Fowkes, who convinced Byng not to take 700 soldiers from his garrison at Gibraltar to assist with the landing at Minorca, as Byng had been ordered to do. Arriving too late and with too few ships and soldiers, Byng limited his ambitions to attempting to contact the besieged fort at Mahon in order to exchange messages with Blakeney. While attempting this, Byng's ships were drawn into a battle with the French fleet that he otherwise might not have hazarded. In fact, the encounter was not altogether disastrous: the British attack was compromised by a break in its line and some ships were badly damaged, but the French admiral broke away first. Had Byng pressed for a second engagement he might have been able to claim victory, but he chose to withdraw to Gibraltar, thus conceding control of the seas around Minorca and so the island itself to the enemy.[13]

Although numerous individuals contributed to the loss of Minorca, Byng made controversial decisions, notably in not pushing for a second engagement, and the episode could not but lead to a court martial. The charge against Byng read as follows:

> … the said John Byng … did withdraw or keep back, and did not do his utmost to take, seize and destroy the Ships of the French King, which it was his Duty to have engaged, and to assist such of his Majesty's Ships as were engaged in Fight with the French Ships, which it was his Duty to have assisted; and for that he the said John Byng did not do his utmost to relieve St. Philip's Castle, in his Majesty's island of Minorca, then besieged by the Forces of the French King, but acted contrary to, and in Breach of his Majesty's Command.[14]

As Byng would have known, the punishment for failing to 'do his utmost' was determined by the *Articles of War*, the revisions to which had strengthened the severity of punishments for the most serious offences.[15] As a

---

[12] Stephen F. Gradish, *The Manning of the British Navy During the Seven Years War* (London: Royal Historical Society, 1980); Richard Middleton, 'Naval Administration in the Age of Pitt and Anson, 1755–1763', in *The British Navy and the Uses of Naval Power in the Eighteenth Century*, ed. by Jeremy Black and Philip Woodfine (Atlantic Highlands, NJ: Humanities Press International, 1989), pp. 109–27.

[13] Dull, *The French Navy*, pp. 50–3.

[14] *The Trial of the Honourable Admiral John Byng, at a Court Martial, as Taken by Mr. Charles Fearne, Judge Advocate of his Majesty's Fleet. Published by Order of the Right Honourable the Lords Commissioners of the Admiralty, at the Desire of the Court-Martial* (London: R. Manby; J. Whiston and B. White; W. Sanby; J Newbery; W. Faden, 1757), pp. 3–4.

[15] Eder, *Crime and Punishment*, pp. 115–6; Rodger, *Articles of War*, pp. 9–10.

member of the courts that had tried Mathews and Lestock, Byng had contributed to condemning Mathews for the failure to secure a victory and after his own trial he recalled how he had supported the application of the bloodiest penalties then available: 'I thought it absolutely necessary Mr. Matthews should die ..., that others might avoid the like crime if they avoid the like punishment;... Can it then be supposed that I should be culpable of a breach of that which I had persisted should be branded with so ignominious a death?'[16] With this, Byng stresses that he, unlike Mathews, had not committed a crime, but the use of the word 'breach' also suggests that he considered Mathews' crime to have been the failure to act as Lestock had acted, that is, as a modern professionalized military man, one who followed the 'rules'.

According to Berkenhout, Byng's behaviour at Minorca can best be understood as a response to the controversy that had surrounded Mathews and Lestock: 'the only plausible argument that can be urged in extenuation of this admiral's conduct is, that he might be too strongly imprest by the recollection of Mathews and Lestock; the first of whom was punished for fighting, not according to rule, and the latter not punished, though he did not fight at all.'[17] A witness at the trial confirms that Mathews had indeed been uppermost in Byng's mind during the battle for Minorca. In answer to the question, 'Did you advise the Admiral to bear down [to engage the enemy]?', Arthur Gardiner, captain of Byng's flagship, stated that, 'the Admiral objected to it, lest an Accident of a similar Nature with that of Admiral *Matthews* on the same Seas, should be the Consequence.'[18] However, to note that Byng bore Mathews in mind is not to suggest that he sought to act as Mathews claimed to have acted; rather, it indicates that Byng sought to present himself as Lestock had presented himself. Certainly, Byng rested his defence on having behaved with 'Propriety and Naval Military Skill', that is, on having attempted 'a proper Execution of my Duty, conformable to the Rules of Prudence, the Art of War, and the established Discipline of the Navy.'[19] Like Lestock, Byng defined discipline as obedience to articles and instructions, the documents that made manifest the authority to which all officers were subject.

---

[16] *The Speech of the Honble Admiral Byng, Intended to have been Spoken on Board the Monarque at the Time of his Execution* (London: T. Lindsey, 1757), p. 4.
[17] Berkenhout, *Lives of the British Admirals*, IV, p. 81.
[18] *The Trial of Vice-Admiral Byng, at a Court-Martial, held on Board his Majesty's Ship the St. George, in Portsmouth Harbour* (London: J. Reason, 1757), p. 27.
[19] *Admiral Byng's Defence, as Presented by Him to the Court, on Board his Majesty's Ship St. George, January 18th, 1757* (London[?], 1757[?]), pp. 11, 34.

'No Commander … has a right to deviate from the established Discipline and Rules of the Navy, contained in the fighting Instructions', Byng argues, 'because if inferior Officers may judge for themselves, there is an End of all Discipline.'[20]

In Jeremy Black's view, Byng's behaviour at Minorca 'demonstrated the pernicious lack of initiative that had spread among the officers of the Royal Navy as a result of the Permanent Fighting Instructions.'[21] Certainly, Byng follows Lestock in emphasizing that he had obeyed where he was required to obey, thus laying claim to the specialist knowledge that allowed the modern military man to present himself as a professional. In fact, Byng expands this Lestockian line of argument by appealing to, not just the navy's articles and instructions, but also 'Men who have studied the Nature of Military Atchievements, [and] the Rules and Observations of ancient and modern Writers on this Head.'[22] Byng would have been by no means unusual in reading works on military matters. Azar Gat has traced the significant growth, particularly from the 1740s, in the publication of military literature that digested ancient and modern authors and extracted generalized maxims for warfare.[23] But given that Lestock had suffered from the accusation that he had held a suspicious correspondence with a French admiral, it is noticeable that Byng mentions 'ancient and modern' writers but actually refers to two foreign soldiers, both veterans of the War of the Spanish Succession: the French soldier turned theorist Antoine de Pas de Feuquières (1648–1711), whose memoirs had been published in London in 1736, and the Spanish soldier and diplomat Marquess Santa Cruz de Marcenado (1684–1732), author of *Reflections Military and Political*, published in London the following year.[24] With this, Byng openly aligns himself with the international officer class and, more broadly, the civil(ian) world, for in parading his

---

[20] *Admiral Byng's Defence*, p. 12.
[21] Jeremy Black, 'The Execution of Admiral Byng', *Military History Quarterly*, 11 (1999), 98–103 (at p. 103).
[22] *The Trial of Vice-Admiral Byng*, pp. 41–2.
[23] Azar Gat, *The Origins of Military Thought: From the Enlightenment to Clausewitz* (Oxford: Oxford University Press, 1989), pp. 25–31.
[24] *The Trial of Vice-Admiral Byng*, p. 42; *An Appeal to the People: Containing the Genuine and Entire Letter of Admiral Byng to the Secr. of the Ad—y: Observations on those Parts of it which were Omitted by the Writers of the Gazette: and what might be the Reasons for such Omissions. Part the First* (London: J. Morgan, 1756), pp. 46–8. For Feuquières and Marcenado see Mark H. Danley, 'The British Political Press and Military Thought During the Seven Years' War', in *The Seven Years' War: Global Views*, ed. by Mark H. Danley and Patrick J. Speelman (Leiden: Brill, 2012), pp. 359–97; Beatrice Heuser, *The Strategy Makers: Thoughts on War and Society from Machiavelli to Clausewitz* (Santa Barbara, CA: Praeger, 2010), pp. 124–9.

reading, Byng suggests that his military identity might be compatible with other identities, including the man of letters.[25]

If Byng followed Lestock's defence, it is also the case that he was prepared to make explicit that which Lestock had left implicit. Lestock had presented himself as one who, above all else, submitted to naval discipline and the pro-Mathews author of *A Just Genuine and Impartial History* had questioned Lestock's account of himself by pointing out that a commander needed more than rules and laws in order to cope with the elements: 'I should be glad to know, whether [Lestock] thought the Admiral's Order and Discipline, or that of the Sailors, could overcome the Western Winds, or Swelling of the Seas, which drove them confusedly together?'[26] At his trial, Byng inverts this argument in order to claim that even the most able of commanders would find his powers limited by circumstances that he could at best manage, rather than control. Given the unpredictable 'Nature of Sea Service', 'for a commander, even of the greatest Capacity, to provide against all contingencies, is impossible.' Since no-one has the capacity to succeed in all circumstances, Byng argues, the ideal commander must pick his battles according to his ability to assess and evaluate risk and reward. He explicitly ties professionalism to this kind of calculation, noting that 'the most approved Writers on Military Affairs' agree: 'it has been a settled Rule of all Generals, That no Commander should ever risque an Engagement, but when there is greater Expectations to gain by a Victory, than to lose by a Defeat.'[27] To do otherwise, he argues, would be ridiculous. 'Is a Commander expected to fight in all Situations, and under all Disadvantages?' Byng asks his judges, as 'surely all Extremes are culpable; and where nothing is to be gained, and all may be lost, Fighting becomes Presumptuousness, Rashness or Phrenzy.'[28]

Whereas Lestock had defined discipline in such a way as to align both militarism and masculinity with performance, Byng's defence goes beyond this by presenting a sustained critique of courage, and with it a candid attack on the notion that militarism ought to be understood to be bodily. Lestock had defended his devotion to discipline by arguing that the indecisive battle of Toulon had been the result of Mathews' rashness, his over-heatedness, in beginning the attack before the rear division had joined the line. In stating

---

[25] According to Stephen Moore, Byng deliberately inhabits the role of the gentleman officer. "A Nation of Harlequins'? Politics and Masculinity in Mid-Eighteenth-Century England', *Journal of British Studies*, 49.3 (2010), 514–39.
[26] *A Just, Genuine and Impartial History*, p. 239.
[27] *The Trial of Vice-Admiral Byng*, pp. 34, 41.
[28] *Admiral Byng's Defence*, p. 9.

that the commander must calculate risk and reward, Byng also argues that the ideal commander should offer more than hot-headed courage:

> Are Commanders then at all Events to show no other Token of Generalship, but what is to be learned from Brutes? An Excess of Courage only? And are all who use the superior Attributes of the human Understanding, to be considered as Delinquents in their Duty to their King and Country? What Commander of common Sense will serve his Country under such discouraging Conditions; where, unless he fights against all Kinds of Disadvantage, he is to be stigmatised with the eternal Infamy of Cowardice: and if he does not engage his Enemy, and does not succeed against this great Superiority of Force, he is to be deemed a Coward also, and given up to the rage of the Multitude?[29]

Rather than centralize courage as the military man's most essential quality, or even sideline hot-bloodedness for 'cool courage', as Lestock had done, Byng reduces courage to a merely animalistic attribute. In arguing that a commander must have more than an 'excess of courage', Byng argues that what is fundamentally bodily is inescapably brutish. The commander who aims to practise 'Generalship' – a deliberately generic term which encompasses all military officers, whether soldier or sailor – must rely on something other than that which can be reduced to the level of bodily capacity. An attack on the idea that the ideal military man should tender his body to military service, this has important implications for understanding eighteenth-century conceptualizations of masculinity. The notion that militarism must be more than an 'excess of courage' can be read as a rejection of the body as the point of origin for militarism, and with it, the point of origin for masculinity. While it is possible that Byng's Lestockian defence could have been rewarded with a similar verdict, with such a comment Byng made plain that to which Lestock's defence had only alluded and as this chapter goes on to explain, what had passed in the late 1740s was not to pass in the mid-1750s.

A Public Body

As with the aftermath of the battle of Toulon, the aftermath of the battle of Minorca can be explained with reference to party politics. The loss of Minorca was an embarrassment for the Newcastle administration, which sought to distance itself from the failure, and an opportunity for those out of office, notably Henry Fox and the popular 'patriot' William Pitt.[30]

---

[29] *The Trial of Vice-Admiral Byng*, p. 42; repeated in *An Appeal to the People*, p. 52.
[30] Richard Middleton, *The Bells of Victory: The Pitt-Newcastle Ministry and the Conduct of the Seven Years War, 1752–1762* (Cambridge: Cambridge University Press, 1985).

Byng's dispatch from the battle had reached London in June 1756 and the ministry published the letter in the *London Gazette* in an edited form which strengthened the impression of Byng's unwillingness to do his utmost. Byng's letter openly admitted that the ships of the rear of the British line had been adversely affected by a damaged ship in the middle of the line, the *Intrepid*, and that this had prevented them from fighting alongside the front section of the line, commanded by Rear-Admiral Temple West: '[the *Intrepid* being disabled] obliged that, and the ships ahead of me, to throw all a-back: This obliged me to do so also for some Minutes, to avoid their falling all on board me, ... this not only caused the Enemy's Centre to be unattacked, but left the Rear-Admiral's Division rather uncover'd for some very little Time.'[31] The suggestion that the confusion only lasted a 'very little Time' did little to avoid giving the impression that Byng had been more preoccupied with avoiding the enemy's ships rather than his own 'falling all on board me'. It is, however, problematic to subordinate the Byng affair to a narrative of mid-century party politics.[32] As N. A. M. Rodger points out, though it might seem that Byng's sentence was the result of 'political persecution' orchestrated by Newcastle, the execution occurred under the brief Devonshire–Pitt coalition and despite Pitt's appeal for clemency on Byng's behalf, an appeal which jeopardized his own political career.[33]

Like the trials of Mathews and Lestock, the Byng affair was political in a broader sense. As John Cardwell has documented, the Byng affair is particularly important for charting the growth of extra-parliamentary politics, for the controversy produced such an 'explosion of the more popular forms of political commentary – ballads, ephemeral verse, prose satire and prints' that it can be considered 'one of the few great crises in the eighteenth century when popular agitation and political opinion profoundly influenced the course of national politics.'[34] In an attempt to influence public opinion the pro-Byng *An Appeal to the People*, penned anonymously but likely at least paid for by Byng, was distributed to London's coffee houses. The *Appeal* attempted to shift responsibility for the indecisive battle to the government by restoring the excised sections of Byng's dispatch and arguing

---

[31] *London Gazette*, Tuesday 22nd June 1756.
[32] Marie Peters, *Pitt and Popularity: The Patriot Minister and London Opinion during the Seven Years' War* (Oxford: Clarendon, 1980), pp. 46–57.
[33] N. A. M. Rodger, *The Command of the Ocean: A Naval History of Britain, 1649–1815* (London: Penguin 2004; repr. 2006), p. 267. See also Peters, *Pitt and Popularity*, pp. 69–70.
[34] John Cardwell, *Arts and Arms: Literature, Politics and Patriotism during the Seven Years War* (Manchester: Manchester University Press, 2004), p. 51. See also Conway, *War, State and Society*, pp. 130–1.

that the ministry had tried to direct the blame for the loss of Minorca towards the most 'visible Object' and thereby 'fascinate the Understandings of the Multitude by delusive and partial Representations.'[35] When the manipulation of Byng's letter came to light it exposed ministerial misbehaviour and this prompted some sympathy for him: on the 8th of March the *London Evening Post* printed two letters side-by-side, one arguing that 'Minorca was rather sold than lost; rather given up by Treachery of some Persons at Home, than taken by us from Force', the other pleading for Byng's life on the basis that the court had been compelled to award a death sentence by the letter of naval law and not its conscience.[36] However, the *Appeal* sought to further secure sympathy for Byng by asking readers to put themselves in his shoes: 'Let me suppose that any one indifferent Man amongst you had been employed in a military Action of Consequence … What then must be the State of that Man's Bosom, who may have seen his own letter stripped?' Of course, by arguing that Byng had done that 'which every prudent Commander must have done, and was therefore highly reasonable to be concluded, would be done, by the Admiral, Council of War, and by all those who understand the Profession of Arms', the *Appeal* did little to establish a rapport with the people and much to deprive men, and women, of the right to pass judgement on military matters.[37] This dismissal of the public's capacity and right to judge is evident in other contributions to the broader 'pro-Byng' campaign. Seeking to strengthen the admiral's claim that he had made all possible haste to Minorca, the pamphlet states, 'for the benefit of Landsmen, … that no Man breathing on shore, can tell how long a Fleet might be going from Plymouth to Gibraltar', and then ridicules a 'naked head' overheard in a public place for presuming to judge Byng's conduct: 'it immediately began to roar, instead of a Ribbon, he shall have a String, &c. I walk'd off, and could not help reflecting how ridiculous it was, for Men bred Mechanics, to pretend to determine on the Propriety of an Admiral's Motions in naval Affairs.'[38]

Although Byng's *Appeal* was written for the people, it is clear that it was not written to appeal to the public that had condemned Lestock's definition of discipline and celebrated Mathews' rejection of it. The verse accompanying a satirical print published in September 1756 presented

[35] *An Appeal to the People*, p. 2.
[36] *London Evening Post*, Tuesday 8th March 1757.
[37] *An Appeal to the People*, pp. 10, 54.
[38] *A Modest Apology for the Conduct of a Certain Admiral in the Mediterranean. Being an Essay towards Silencing the Clamorous Tongue of Slander, til Facts can be Ascertained by Substantial and Circumstantial Evidence* (London: M. Cooper; B. Dodd, 1756), pp. 12–3.

the Byng affair as a chance to correct the earlier vindication of the admiral who had failed to fight: 'you're left to your Choice, / with L-st-k to Side or give M-th-ws your Voice.'[39] However, the second volume of the *Appeal*, printed after the trial and so at the point at which Byng's situation was quite desperate, repeated the Lestockian argument that all military men are limited by circumstances such that the ideal military man should learn to calculate rather than rely on innate courageousness: 'Does it not plainly appear, that the Resolutions seem to be founded on a Presumption, that a Commander in Chief ought to be *infallible*, rather than considered as *Man*; the most consummately excellent of which must be subject to Mistakes.'[40] Echoing the criticism of Lestock as an admiral too-easily-turned author, one anti-Byng author responded to what he assumed to be Byng's authorial efforts: 'Grammarians censure [certain] Passage[s] [of the *Appeal*]. But they should consider that an Admiral's Business is not to Write, but to Fight, and that our greatest Naval Heroes have been no Scholars – consequently B-g might have fought well.'[41]

Like the failure at Toulon, the loss of Minorca thrust attention on to the nation's military forces and its military men, but whereas the acquittal of Lestock had clashed with public opinion, the verdict at Byng's trial seems to have concurred with public anger. Some of the earliest prints issued in the aftermath of the loss of Minorca confirm that Byng was seen to exemplify modern militarism. In one of the earliest of the many prints to appear in the aftermath of the loss of Minorca, *The New Art of War at Sea*, the ships at the rear of the British line, labelled as Byng's, are identified as the practitioners of the 'new' way of fighting by a written key which contrasts the 'finely judged' distance between Byng and the enemy's line with the other British ships, directed by West, 'fighting in the old way.'[42] An even simpler and smaller, card-sized print produced in the same month, *Late Action, Bi-g, and Glassesoniere*, makes much the same point by highlighting 'the new way [Byng's] six fought.'[43] Also produced early in 1756, a print

---

[39] *Harry the Ninth to Goody Mahon*, September 1756, 3511. Reference numbers for prints are taken from Frederic George Stephens, *Catalogue of Prints and Drawings in the British Museum. Division I: Personal and Political Satires. Vol. III, Part II, March 28th 1751– c.1760* (London: 1877).

[40] *An Appeal to the People: Part the Second. On the Different Deserts and Fate of Admiral Byng and his Enemies: The Changes in the Last Administration: The Year of Liberty or Thraldom* (London: J. Morgan, 1757), p. 34.

[41] *A Real Defence of A – l B –'s Conduct: Wherein is Clearly Exploded the Common Error so Prevalent of Censuring this Gentleman's Behaviour, by a Series of Indisputable Facts, Hitherto Concealed* (London, 1756), p. 14.

[42] *The New Art of War at Sea*, May 1756, 3354.

[43] *Late Action, Bi-g, and Glassesoniere*, May 1756, 3355.

titled *Work for the Bellman* mocks Byng's 'Singular prudence in ye New arts of Policy & War.'[44] In each print the meaning of the word 'new' is clarified by the association between newness and cowardice. In the third print this is extended to suggest that Byng had concealed his cowardice behind 'prudence' and 'policy', terms which evoke Lestock's 'screen' of discipline.

As these examples indicate, by the mid-1750s the concept of newness in military matters was already old. However, of the many images produced in the aftermath of the loss of Minorca, the print *Cabin Council: A late Epistle to Mr. C – d* best makes clear the extent to which the criticism of Byng within the popular public sphere was criticism of the modernity of both his militarism and his masculinity.[45] The print depicts the second of two councils of war that had contributed to the loss of Minorca. On arriving at Gibraltar, Byng found that a council of war had been convened to decide whether or not to surrender troops from the garrison for landing on the island. Byng's first mistake was to abide by the council's decision rather than enforce the will of the Admiralty by requisitioning soldiers. The second council of war, called by Byng after the battle, decided that the fleet would return to cover Gibraltar rather than push for a second engagement. *Cabin Council* clearly concurs with Berkenhout's later assessment that 'councils of war seldom forebode much heroism. When a commander in chief, whose power is absolute, condescends to ask advice of his inferiors, it is a tacit acknowledgement, that his abilities are inadequate to his power.'[46] The image depicts Byng with four other officers, likely the key military officers in the Mediterranean at the time – General Stuart, Lord Effingham, Lord Bertie and Colonel Cornwallis – and suggests that they concocted excuses for cowardice collectively: 'we had the wind and weather: but run away together.' Here, the image suggests, are military, army and navy, officers – all equally smartly dressed and coiffured – for whom militarism is a performance, not unlike politeness. In this image the council of war is imagined as a social occasion, a form of conversation between polite participants; the captain's cabin, its walls lined with shelves of china, could be a room in an elegant house: even the canons have become toy-sized miniatures. Byng was well known to be a collector of fine china, and the same means are employed to make the same point in another print, *At Home: Abroad*.[47] In this print, Byng's ship is labelled

[44] *Work for the Bellman*, May 1756, 3352.
[45] *Cabin Council: A Late Epistle to Mr. C[levelan]d*, May 1756, 3358.
[46] Berkenhout, *Lives of the British Admirals*, IV, p. 82.
[47] *At Home: Abroad. Oh! Tempora.—Oh! Mores. Who could have thought it?*, 1756, 3526.

a 'China Ware House' and the satire is carried by a comment summarizing each of the two cartouches: 'China insur'd' and 'Canon secur'd'. Both prints imply that the military space has become a place for display, not action, and so the men merely ornaments. However, to make it clear that the pieces of china are not the only inappropriately fragile objects in what should be a military environment, *Cabin Council* includes an arrow hand that connects a perilously positioned porcelain bust to the centrally seated figure, Byng.

For Wilson, the public anxiety that emerged in the aftermath of Byng's failure at Minorca reveals 'widespread fears of the emasculation and degeneracy of the British body politic.'[48] Certainly, *Cabin Council* treats the modern military men as representatives of both the military and the ruling class, for as Cardwell has observed, the pieces of china displayed on the walls of the cabin indicate that these men have become cowardly due to the enervating effects of wealth and luxury.[49] This line of criticism is equally apparent in the pamphlet entitled *The Portsmouth Grand Humbug*, in which a boatswain, his mate and a midshipman discuss Byng's case. The petty-officer and his mate, Jack, turn on the midshipman, Tom Wholebones, whose surname indicates that not only is the would-be-commissioned officer unwilling to fight, but also that the whole 'family of *Wholebones* are great lovers of sleeping in *whole skins*'. The mention of Tom's familial inheritance highlights the importance of class conflict in this pamphlet: the hale and hearty mate, who asserts his right to comment on public matters – 'I say I have a right to speak, and so has every honest English tar' – and who possesses a 'noble British spirit', is contrasted with the cowardly family of Wholebones and shown to be the superior sailor.[50] That said, the pamphlet also suggests that courage should be understood to be part of the basic matter of the male body, for Tom's desire to keep his bones whole suggests that his inadequacy runs in his family's blood.

Like *The Portsmouth Grand Humbug*, *Cabin Council*, intervenes in the Byng affair by drawing attention to the problem of corporeality. To connect the modern military man to a badly balanced porcelain bust is to represent the *corpus rasa*, the blank body, or as Foucault has it, the 'fragment of mobile space', as a dangerous negation of the materiality of body. While

[48] Wilson, *The Sense of the People*, p. 185.
[49] Cardwell, *Arts and Arms*, pp. 62–3.
[50] *The Portsmouth Grand Humbug: Or, a Merry Dialogue Between the Boatswain and his Mate, on Board the Monarch Man of War, Relating to Admiral Byng, who is to be Shot one Time or Another* (London, 1757), p. 1.

Byng was confined at Greenwich under armed guard, during which it was widely rumoured that he had attempted to escape dressed in women's apparel, effigies were burnt in towns across England, from Southampton to Sunderland.[51] One anti-Byng author claimed that he had seen persons using a log dressed in a laced coat as a way to 'pelt him and piss upon him and then burn him'. The author does not join in, but he does not censure such behaviour on the basis that 'no body led them, no body drove them; but it was the cowardice, as you shall hear anon, that stuck in their stomachs.'[52] Here, the author contrasts Byng's cowardice with the protestors' stomachs, his lack of bodiliness with their bodily response. By dressing a log, the protestors were able to symbolically reconnect the modern military man with his materiality. The execution, which took place on board the *Monarque* on the morning of the 14th of March 1757, was to do something similar. In Voltaire's novella *Candide* (1759) the execution is described as a depressing spectacle of corporeality.[53] On arrival by boat to England, Voltaire's eponymous hero witnesses the execution: 'A multitude of people covered the shore, all gazing intently at a rather stout man who was kneeling blindfold on the deck of one of the naval ships. Four soldiers, posted opposite this man, each fired three shots into his skull, as calmly as you please, and the assembled multitude then dispersed thoroughly satisfied.'[54] Contemporaneous newspaper reports confirm that the event was well attended, for although few were allowed on board the *Monarque*, 'those ships that lay any ways near her, were greatly crowded with spectators, all their shrouds and tops being full, altho' it was difficult to see any thing on board the Monarque.'[55] In other words, the execution forced the Lestockian performer to confront his corporeality before a crowd that functioned, not as an audience for a theatrical performance, but as witnesses to the reality of mortality. Despite (but also because of) his attempt to align himself with Lestock during his trial, Byng's performance of modern professionalized militarism was halted by a sentence that reminded him of the importance of flesh and blood by depriving him of his life. In the contrast between Lestock's acquittal and Byng's death, then, it is possible to see the declining fortunes

---

[51] Cardwell, *Arts and Arms*, pp. 62, 65.
[52] [Issac Barclay], *Some Friendly and Seasonable Advice to Mr. Admiral Byng on his Approaching Court Martial* (London, 1756), p. 1.
[53] For the *philosophes* and anti-militarism see Armstrong Starkey, ' "To Encourage the Others": The Philosophes and the War', in *The Seven Years' War: Global Views*, pp. 23–46.
[54] Voltaire, *Candide and Other Stories*, ed. and trans. by Roger Pearson (Oxford: Oxford University Press, 1990), pp. 72–3.
[55] *Evening Advertiser*, Tuesday 15th March 1757. See also *London Evening Post*, Tuesday 15th March 1757; *London Chronicle*, Tuesday 15–17th March 1757.

of the modern military man, and, as I will go on to explain, the rising status of a powerful alternative model of militarism and masculinity: the old hero.

The New Old Hero

It is possible to say that Byng was simply unlucky to have been condemned to death, that it was merely an accident of timing. Once the court had unanimously agreed that the admiral had not done his utmost the sentence was determined by the revised *Articles of War* (1749). Had he been judged according to the previous *Articles*, the court would have had the licence to award a lesser punishment. As it was, the court could attempt to lessen the severity of the sentence only by recommending Byng to the king as an object of mercy. George II, who had led British forces to victory at Dettingen (1743), listened to the court's concerns but was not inclined to be clement, and despite last-minute efforts to raise the subject for discussion in the Lords, the course of naval justice could not be halted.[56] It is, however, equally possible to read further into the relationship between the revised *Articles* and the sentence, for if the revised *Articles* had been intended to punished those who failed to 'become' what was required by naval authority, Byng's sentence punished one who had failed to 'be' what he ought to have been. Much as the revision of the articles might have sought to legitimize the modern military man in the 1740s, in strengthening the power of naval authority it also produced a penal code that would, just a decade later, require a corporeal punishment and in so doing champion an alternative model of militarism that, while recognizably akin to the civic ideal of the citizen-soldier, was coming to be centred on heroism. This is not to suggest that the hero had not been important before; rather, by this mid-century moment, the cultural power once held by the civic citizen-soldier had passed to a particular iteration of the hero, one that could be presented as an equally 'old' model for militarism, but also a more obviously and robustly bodily counter to the modern military man's performance of professionalism.

There is some indication of this expansion of civic ideology in John Brown's *An Estimate of the Manners and Principles of the Times*, a text published shortly after Byng's death. As John Sekora and Emma Clery have recognized, Brown's strident critique of modernity draws from and revives civic discourse, but this is civic discourse shaped to suit the

---

[56] *London Chronicle*, Tuesday 26 February–1 March 1757; *London Evening Post*, Tuesday 26 February–1 March 1757.

mid-century.[57] Brown's central complaint is that modern men, brought up in the warmth of the nursery and educated at the universities, on the grand tour, or in London society, are wholly inadequate as men. The '*modern* man of Fashion' is dedicated to the conspicuous consumption of luxury, principally dress, equipage, champagne, poultry, entertainments, gaming, cards, and clubs: in short, '*despicable* and *effeminate Vanity*.'[58] Admittedly, Brown makes no explicit comment on the Byng affair, but he dismisses 'Superficial, though zealous, Observers, [who] think they see the Source of all our public Miscarriages in the particular and accidental Misconduct of Individuals' and the second volume of the *Estimate* (1758), notes that if individuals are delinquent in their offices, this is 'not merely personal or accidental; but founded in the established Manners and Principles of the Times.'[59] For Brown, whose personal experience of military service was limited to having been witness to the siege of Carlisle (1745–6), the modern man would do well to look to the classical soldier: 'The *Roman* killed himself, because he had been unfortunate in *War*; the *Englishman*, because he hath been unfortunate at *Whist*. The *old* Hero, because he had *disgraced* his *Country*; the *modern* because he dares not shew his head at *Arthur's*.'[60] With this, Brown exults an alternative model for masculinity, one derived from the classical past and identifiable by his militarism: the old hero. It is in the second volume that Brown indicates that although his notion of old heroism is derived from the classical past, it need not always appear to be so, for he hypothesizes that resolving the problem of the 'times' must inevitably result in restoring the relationship between the sexes that had also existed in the implicitly medieval and chivalric past, 'when [England's] *Daughters* were *chaste*, and her *Sons* valiant!'[61]

It should be noted that the old hero – a figure who functions as a vehicle for 'natural', essential masculinity – remains in the background of a text more concerned with diagnosis than cure. Brown's critique of modern masculinity includes a lament for the masculinization of modern

---

[57] Sekora, *Luxury*, pp. 63–109; Clery, *The Feminization Debate*, pp. 171–2. See also Gerald Newman, *The Rise of English Nationalism: A Cultural History, 1740–1830* (London: Weidenfeld and Nicolson, 1987), pp. 80–4.

[58] [John Brown], *An Estimate of the Manners and Principles of the Times*, 2nd ed. (London: L. Davis and C. Reymers, 1757), pp. 95–6.

[59] [Brown], *Estimate*, p. 11; [John Brown], *An Estimate of the Manners and Principles of the Times, Vol. II*, (London: L. Davis and C. Reymers, 1758), p. 15.

[60] [Brown], *Estimate*, p. 95.

[61] [Brown], *Estimate, Vol. II*, p. 82.

femininity. On the subject of female manners he writes, 'they are essentially the same with those of the Men, and are therefore included in this Estimate'. Brown's point is that there is little to tell men and women apart, 'the one Sex having advanced into *Boldness*, as the other have sunk into *Effeminacy*.'[62] In the second volume Brown likewise laments that 'the Sexes have changed Characters: The Men capering about, on *Hobbys* of thirteen Hands; while the Women are galloping full speed, on sized and *firey Hunters*.'[63] This sentiment is echoed by the pseudonymously (and in fact chronically) penniless poet 'Lancelot Poverty-Struck', Joseph Lewis, an artisan, author and briefly editor of the *Westminster Magazine*. Lewis imagines that a great reform of modern manners, particularly the twin evils of 'luxury and gaming', would realign modern feminized men and masculinized women with their male and female bodies:

> Then we shall have– pray; what shall we have then?
> Why– a new Set of Women, and of Men.
> Men, who'll wear Petticoats– and Women breeches;
> Players will thrive– and poets Roll in Riches.
> …
>
> Each Red-coat then shall act a noble Part
> For ev'ry one shall wear a Blakeney's Heart.
> No Cowardice shall taint the *British* Navy,
> *Britons* shall make the *Frenchmen* cry *Pecavi*.
> The Bards no more shall with derision sing,
> Of Admirals– like *Mathews– Lestock– Byng*.[64]

Here, Lewis predicts that a 'new' set of men and women will be formed once those who currently behave like men return to their petticoats and those who currently behave like women return to their breeches. The confirmation of this great return will be the end of military failures – such as those led by Mathews, Lestock and Byng – and the beginning of a new phase of military success, led by men who resemble one who became an exemplary new old hero in the aftermath of the loss of Minorca: General William Blakeney (1671/2–1761).

As Conway observes, the bellicose mid-century was a period in which public opinion managed to become an 'influence on elite political action rather than merely a tool to be shaped and then used by elite politicians'

---

[62] [Brown], *Estimate*, p. 51.
[63] [Brown], *Estimate, Vol. II*, p. 79.
[64] [Joseph Lewis], 'Lancelot Poverty-Struck', 'The Prophet', in *The Miscellaneous and Whimsical Lucubrations of Lancelot Poverty-Struck, an Unfortunate Son of Apollo; and Author of the Westminster Magazine. Adapted to the Present Times* (London, 1758), pp. 81–2.

but also a period which created 'long-lasting heroes'.[65] Admiral Edward Hawke, the admiral sent to relieve Byng at Minorca, is one example of this. Hawke had been one of the few captains to distinguish himself at the battle of Toulon and he went on to secure an important naval victory at Cape Finisterre (1747) during the War of the Austrian Succession by employing an aggressive, responsive style of fighting that would later be adopted by Horatio Nelson.[66] That said, during the Byng affair, Hawke's next triumph at Quiberon Bay, like General James Wolfe's victory at the Battle for Quebec, was still two years away. Given this, the hostility that greeted Byng is better compared with the enthusiasm that was directed towards another participant in the Minorca debacle, General Blakeney. Having served in Flanders during the War of the Spanish Succession, in the West Indies during the War of the Austrian Succession and as Lieutenant-Governor of Stirling Castle while it was besieged during the Jacobite Rebellion of 1745–6, the Irish octogenarian came to public attention for defending the besieged fort of St Philip on Minorca until the French invasion forced him to surrender.[67] The anonymous author of *Memoirs of the Life and Actions of General W. Blakeney* (1756) sings his praises in decidedly civic tones. According to *Memoirs*, Blakeney had begun his military life in support the Revolution of 1688 and on the basis that even 'Men of Fortune and influence' should give dutiful and patriotic military service. Motivated by this decidedly civic principle, Blakeney gathered together his family's tenants to form an armed band who, equipped with 'a kind of discipline' of his own creation, had all they needed in the way of the 'Art of War'.[68] This early outburst of civic feeling is presented as the foundation for a life spent 'in the peaceful exercises of War' and in opposing those whose 'principal aim is to debase the Spirits of the people … the better to fit them for the Yoke.'[69] The author is keen to refute the idea that such a man as Blakeney must necessarily be both incapable of mastering military discipline and unable to pass among the polite world, but while Blakeney is said to be socially competent and, notably, fond of dancing, it is significant that his interest in military discipline is directed towards making his own rules, and that his preferred dances are the humble jig and the lively rigadoon.

---

[65] Conway, *War, State and Society*, pp. 167, 213.
[66] Ruddock Mackay and Michael Duffy, *Hawke, Nelson and British Naval Leadership, 1747–1805* (Woodbridge: Boydell, 2009), pp. 30–6, 217–8.
[67] H. M. Stephens, 'Blakeney, William, Baron Blakeney (1671/2–1761)', rev. Richard Harding, *Oxford Dictionary of National Biography* (Oxford: Oxford University Press, 2004); online ed., January 2008.
[68] *Memoirs of the Life and Actions of General W. Blakeney* (London: 1756), pp. 5–6.
[69] *Memoirs of … General W. Blakeney*, pp. 9–10.

Blakeney can pass muster in the polite world, but the man 'Considered by all the Officers under him as a Kind of Father or Guardian, especially by the young men, whose Morals as well as Expenses he had a constant Eye on', stands apart from it, preferring to be a patrician figure to those who might otherwise be seduced by politeness and luxury.[70]

As the *Memoir* indicates, it is possible to find a broadly civic understanding of militarism in the mid-century. And yet, Lancelot Poverty-Struck's celebration of 'Blakeney's heart' indicates that this military man offers a more viscerally physical model for militarism. Whereas the anti-standing army authors had turned to the untrained, amateur citizen-soldier, whose courageous bearing of arms made manifest an inner military spirit and, by extension, an essential masculine nature, mid-century civic ideology looked to those, amateur or not, who willingly hazarded their life and limbs, without calculation of risk or peril, in the pursuit of victory. The official record of Byng's trial, taken from the judge advocate's minutes and published at the behest of the Admiralty, indicates that Blakeney presented himself as just such a man. As already noted, Byng had not attempted to land on the island of Minorca and this had led to the criticism that he had been too cautious. When Blakeney was asked for his opinion on the possibility of landing troops on an occupied island, he replied: 'I have served sixth-three Years, and I never knew yet any Enterprize undertaken without some Danger, and this might have been effected with as little Danger as ever I knew.'[71] In another published account of the trial, the veteran's opinion is exaggerated to heighten both the danger and his disregard for it: 'Danger! most certainly. It could not be so easy as stepping into this Ship. I have been upwards of fifty Years in the Service, and I never knew any Expedition of Consequence carried into Execution, but what was attended with some Danger: but of all the Expeditions I ever knew, this was certainly the worst.'[72] At a trial in which Byng re-fangled Lestock's definition of discipline in order to challenge what he considered to be the unrealistic expectation that a commander should fight, and win, against all odds, Blakeney's robust disregard for danger offered a dramatically different account of militarism, and one that replaced the performance of

---

[70] Ibid., p. 8.
[71] *The Trial of the Honourable Admiral John Byng*, p. 23. See also *The Trial of the Honble. Admiral Byng, at a Court-Martial held on Board his Majesty's Ship the St George, in Portsmouth Harbour, Tuesday, Dec 28, 1756* (London: J. Lacy, 1757), p. 53.
[72] *The Trial of Vice-Admiral Byng* (London: J. Reason, 1757), p. 6. See also *Minutes of the Proceedings of the Court Martial, on the Trial of Admiral Byng, held on Board his Majesty's ship St George, in Portsmouth Harbour; begun December 27, 1756, and continued till January 27, 1757* (London: H. Owen, 1757), pp. 11–2.

professionalism with an unambiguously physical kind of heroism that could challenge the modern military man's negation of the body.

When Carol Watts argues that Voltaire's barbed account of Byng's death 'punctures the notion of heroic sacrifice central to eighteenth-century patriotic accounts of war', she indicates how important this kind of heroism was becoming to the construction of the ideal military man during this period.[73] This can be seen in *The Contrast*, a woodcut print issued in July 1756, which depicts Britannia receiving the 'Illustrious, Brave and Magnanimous General Blakeney…and the Inglorious Cowardly Admirable A – B – g'. Blakeney, labelled 'The Christian Hero', is praised for acting 'as both a Man and a Christian' whereas a devil hovers behind Byng, who is depicted with an obviously phallic broken sword.[74] The same contrast between physical robustness and inadequacy can be found in *The British Hero and the Ignoble Poltron Contrasted*, an ambitious ode that, with classical pretensions and lengthy footnotes, sets out 'To sing the Man, / Who with undaunted Courage stood, / In Floods of Fire, and Seas of Blood.' According to the poem, age had been no impediment to the hero of Minorca, since 'Youth rekindles at the Trumpet's sound.' Faced with overwhelming odds, the elderly hero's body has incredible reserves of courage and fortitude. The poet, who inflates the size of the French force in the footnotes, concludes by asserting that, 'Blakeney fatigu'd almost to Death, / Would still the Fort have held, / And there resign'd his latest Breath', had his concern for his men not persuaded him to admit defeat.[75] Here, Blakeney reaches his body's limits – he is 'fatigu'd almost to Death' – but he is able to summon reserves of fortitude that exceed the physical limits of that fatigued body. Of course, Blakeney's old but also youthful, exhausted but also resilient, body reveals the central problem with the old hero. Though these lines can be read as flourishes of poetic licence they also expose the paradox of gender essentialism. The modern military man may be vulnerable to the criticism that his military identity is mere show, but the old hero offers his physical body as the guarantee for his inner qualities, the corporeal as the visible proof of that which is within, and thus the old hero must be fully bodily, but also exceed the basic materiality of his body to be more-than-bodily at the same time.

---

[73] Carol Watts, *The Cultural Work of Empire: The Seven Years' War and the Imagining of the Shandean State* (Edinburgh: Edinburgh University Press, 2007), p. 31.

[74] *The Contrast*, 10th July 1756, 3365. See also *The Admirable Admiral B—g Leading the Honourable and Brave General Blakeney through London in Triumph*, 23rd November 1756, 3422.

[75] *The British Hero and the Ignoble Poltron Contrasted; or, the Principle Actors in the Siege and Defence of Fort St. Philip, and the Mediterranean Expedition, Characteriz'd* (London: J. Robinson, 1756), pp. 1, 22.

Though the new old hero may appear to be more stable than the modern military man, whose performance is always vulnerable to the criticism that it lacks substance, he is no less problematic, for the old hero's authenticity is, reliant on an essential nature that is both material and immaterial, and thus inherently contradictory.

While the contradiction is largely hidden in the texts that responded to the loss of Minorca, in challenging the blankness of the body, the *corpus rasa*, the texts that champion new old heroes – be that Brown's *Estimate* or the memoir of Blakeney – do so in deeply coercive ways. On this basis, such texts can be set alongside those that sought explicitly to encourage men to join the services. During the early years of the war the government had great difficulty with military recruitment. Though the shortage of sailors was most acute in early 1756 and numbers gradually rose from 1757 to 1759, the navy was chronically strained by shortages and the ministry regularly had to resort to unpopular impressment or expensive bounties.[76] Likewise, the army, though always small in comparison to its European equivalents, was heavily criticized for resorting to employing foreign soldiers in order to be able to muster suitable numbers.[77] Echoing the anti-standing army argument that a nation needs only men with innate, inner military spirit, the author of *An Address to the British Army and Navy* (1756) questions the importance of needing to make, in his words 'moulding and framing', military men. The pamphlet stresses that without pre-existing courage 'bodily parts' will be 'motionless, defenceless, and like a dead and impotent Corpse.'[78] This choice of simile makes the point that the male body is innately capable of militarism and that failure to recognize and act on this is, in all senses, unnatural. Similar tactics are evident in *A Letter Adapted to the Present Critical Juncture* addressed to all the 'Military Gentlemen, by Sea or Land'(1758), which centres its argument on a biblical precept '*be of good courage*' in order to inspire its readers to a 'manly Greatness, a sedate Firmness and Resolution in the Midst of Danger.'[79] The author allows that some men do seem to be 'by Nature of such a weak and dastardly Spirit, that nothing can inspire them with Fortitude', but pushes the point that to

---

[76] Gradish, *The Manning of the British Navy*, pp. 41–53.
[77] Matthew McCormack, 'Citizenship, Nationhood, and Masculinity in the Affair of the Hanoverian Soldier, 1756', *The Historical Journal*, 49.4 (2006), 971–93.
[78] *An Address to the British Army and Navy. Intended to Remind our Brave Warriors of the Important Interests, in which they are now Engaged, and the Generous Motives and Incitements they have to act with Vigilance, Steadiness, and Resolution in Repelling Bold Insults, and Chastising the Insufferable Pride, Arrogance and Perfidy of France* (London: J. Buckland, 1756), pp. 1, 2.
[79] H. Worthington, *A Letter Adapted to the Present Critical Juncture. Addressed to all Military Gentlemen, by Sea and Land; Pointing out the True Soldier as Animated by Religion and Love of his Country*, 2nd ed. (London: R. Griffiths, 1758), pp. 5, 7.

be a man is to be naturally capable of and naturally disposed towards militarism. The author enforces this by invoking the gender binary: 'Imagine you see the Paleness and Horror of every Female Countenance; … your Virgin Daughters deflowered, your very Wives first prostituted, then cruelly murdered … Will it not call up all the Man within you?'[80]

The growing importance of the new old hero as a coercive model for militarism and masculinity is further illustrated by the rise and fall of the militia at this time. Sixty years earlier John Toland and Andrew Fletcher had put forward ambitious plans for militia reform, but the issue had been neglected throughout the first half of the eighteenth century. A serious campaign for militia reform, begun in 1756 and orchestrated by William Pitt, was completed soon after the execution of Byng with the passing of the Militia Act in June 1757.[81] As McCormack observes, at this point in the century 'nobody seriously talked of abolishing the army', but the enthusiasm for the militia was rooted in the belief that an amateur force would be 'the cure-all for the nation's political, military, moral and sexual ailments.' McCormack argues that the campaign for the revival of the militia relied on the idealization of 'natural' masculinity, constructed in opposition to femininity: 'the man's desire to protect his dependants was cited as a 'natural' masculine impulse: … the male political subject is attached to kin, country and abstract ideals (such as liberty) because they are cherished feminine objects.'[82] Unsurprisingly, John Brown's *On the Natural Duty of Personal Service, in Defence of Ourselves and Our Country* (1761) provides a further, vivid example of this. Brown attempted to impresses upon men that the obligation to serve in the militia was, in every sense, natural:

> The Magistrate hath a *Right* to the *personal Service of every Member* of the State, for the *Defence* and *Security* of the *Whole*. This Right arises in the clearest Manner, from the Nature and Condition of Man … And as no Man has a Right to destroy his own Life, so neither hath he a Right to submit it to Destruction by an Enemy, without exerting all possible resistance. What is thus a natural *Duty*, is no less the natural *Inclination* of all Men.[83]

---

[80] Worthington, *A Letter Adapted to the Present*, pp. 14–5.
[81] Western, *The English Militia*, pp. 127–69; Eliga H. Gould, 'To Strengthen the King's Hands: Dynastic Legitimacy, Militia Reform and Ideas of National Unity in England, 1745–1760, *The Historical Journal*, 32.2 (1991), 329–48. Peters, *Pitt and Popularity*, pp. 41–4, 67.
[82] Matthew McCormack, 'The New Militia: War, Politics and Gender in 1750s Britain', *Gender and History*, 19.3 (2007), 483–500 (at pp. 491, 494).
[83] John Brown, *On the Natural Duty of Personal Service, in Defence of Ourselves and Country. A Sermon Preached at St Nicholas Church in Newcastle, on Occasion of a Late Dangerous Insurrection at Hexham.* (London: L. Davies and C. Reymer, 1761), pp. 18–9.

The New Old Hero

But as much as Brown's pamphlet seems to attest to a continuing ideological investment in the militia as the ideal model for militarism, there is another narrative to be found in the fact that it was written in response to a militia riot. In principle the militia protected the liberty of all, but in practice it infringed the liberties of the few. Across the country, the gentry were unwilling to offer their services as officers, and the people, already discontented by rises in the cost of food and concerned that they might be drafted from the militia into overseas service, rioted.[84] Clearly, the militia was coming to be seen as something akin to the ever unpopular expediency of impressment, which, as a tool for increasing the size of the military establishment, was a manifestation of the growth of centralized authority. That said, public antipathy to forced service can be separated from public interest in the nation's military men.[85] The fact that support for the militia had declined even among politicians by 1761 suggests that, as the war turned in Britain's favour, the militiaman was only one version of an ideal that could equally be represented by daring heroism, like that which secured the victories of 1759, for the glamorous old hero was less overtly and so even more deeply coercive as a model (military) man.[86]

At his trial, Byng re-fangled a defence which had proved successful ten years earlier, and in so doing he offered himself as a modern military man, but the execution reunited the performer of professionalism with corporeality. The first volume of Byng's *Appeal* had tried to create a space for the modern military man by questioning the categories of villain and hero, arguing that 'between perfect Innocence and perfect Guilt there are innumerable Degrees in the Scale of Offence; and as no Man can say he is without Fault, so none can be pronounced all Guiltiness', but in the climate of the mid-century, tolerance for spaces 'in between' increasingly rigorously naturalized categories was increasingly limited.[87] In the aftermath of the loss of Minorca, critics like Brown called loudly for the reunion of gender and the sexed body. Just as the trials of Mathews and Lestock can be said to have reached their conclusion with the passing of the act for a naval uniform and the

---

[84] Tony Hayter, *The Army and the Crowd in Mid-Georgian England* (London: Macmillan, 1978), pp. 75–113; Harris, *Politics and the Nation*, pp. 142–4; Rogers, *Crowds, Cultures and Politics*, pp. 58–84.
[85] Conway, *War, State and Society*, pp. 140–2.
[86] Peters, *Pitt and Popularity*, p. 327.
[87] *An Appeal to the People*, p. 6. Trumbach, *Sex and the Gender Revolution*; Hitchcock, *English Sexualities, 1700–1800*.

revision of the *Articles of War*, so the trial and execution of Byng can be said to have reached a conclusion with the passing of the militia legislation. However, it is the celebration of the aged but youthful Blakeney which indicates that, by mid-century, the citizen-soldier ideal had found a new form, that of the more overtly 'natural' because physical military man, the new old hero.

CHAPTER 4

The Military Man and the Return to the Gothic Past
Hume, Hurd, Walpole

It seems apparent, that [Byng's] only wrong Step was leaving *Gibraltar* to give Battle to the *French*, and his Retreat to that Place the discreetest Act of Prudence and of a General, and in this Opinion the whole Council of War was unanimous: They did not imagine that a Commander in Chief with an inadequate Force was to engage at all Adventures, like *Moor* of *Moor-Hall*, who, with nothing at all, slew the Dragon of *Wantley*.[1]

An Appeal to the People (1756)

The concluding thought in this passage from the first volume of *An Appeal to the People*, an appeal written on behalf of Admiral Byng, contains three near-perfectly quoted lines from 'An excellent Ballad of a most dreadful Combat, fought between Moore of Moore-Hall, and the Dragon of Wantley' as printed in *A Collection of Old Ballads* (1723). 'The Dragon of Wantley' ought not to have been included in this collection of 'antique songs', for, as the editor's headnote to the poem admits, it was written in the mid-seventeenth century and 'is the same to Ballads of Chivalry, as *Don Quixot* is to Books of that kind.'[2] Rather than exemplify the style and themes of 'authentic' old balladry, the poem offers a farce on the gothic past: Moore, the knight of Moore-hall, agrees to hunt down a child-gobbling, village-terrorizing dragon in return for a pretty maid, but armed with wit and not strength, the 'cunning Champion' prevails by kicking the dragon's backside. Written in the tradition of satirical-political broadside balladry, 'The Dragon of Wantley' is a bawdy, scatological, pantomimic parody of tales of chivalry and romance.[3] As such, it is an obvious choice

---

[1] *An Appeal to the People*, p. 49.
[2] *A Collection of Old Ballads. Corrected from the Best and Most Ancient Copies Extant. With Introductions Historical, Critical, and Humorous*, 3 Vols (London: J. Roberts; J. Brotherton; A. Bettesworth; J. Pemberton; J. Woodman; J. Stag, 1723), I, p. 37.
[3] For distinctions between types of ballad see Albert B. Friedman, *The Ballad Revival: Studies in the Influence of Popular on Sophisticated Poetry* (Chicago: University of Chicago Press, 1961).

for the pro-Byng *Appeal*. Byng had been outmanoeuvred by French forces, but, so the allusion suggests, an admiral could hardly hope to prevail like Moore; naval battles can not be won by kicking backsides. To fight when rational calculation would dictate otherwise would be foolish and, so the intertextuality implies, ridiculous.[4] In quoting 'The Dragon of Wantley', then, the *Appeal* invokes a comedic, quixotic character – a parody of the chivalric knight of the gothic past – to counter the mid-century idealization of old heroism, against which Byng's modern military masculinity could only be found deficient.

As this chapter discusses, the eighteenth-century turn to the gothic past, and particularly its literature, can be mapped alongside the growing importance of the old hero in the popular public sphere. Dianne Dugaw has shown that the first substantial gathering of ballad texts, *A Collection of Old Ballads*, helped to popularize old songs, in large part because it was plundered by aggressively commercial publishers who discarded the editorial apparatus and recycled the ballads for cheaper chapbooks or single-sheet poems, giving 'ordinary people, who did not belong to … the "literary world", [access to] ballads marketed explicitly for their historical and antiquarian value.' As a result, Dugaw argues, the 'interest in "Old Ballads" at the popular level – conscious and purposeful in its own right – antedated and intersected with the literary "Ballad Revival".'[5] The close relationship between early interest in old songs and increasing enthusiasm for old heroism is further indicated by the more recent argument that the growth of interest in old English literature corresponds with the surge of popular patriotism and nationalism during the Seven Years' War.[6] With this in mind, this chapter suggests that the mid-century gothic revival opened up the possibility for a cultural (re)turn to a model military man, one that was alike and therefore an alternative to the civic citizen-soldier: the chivalric knight. However, having identified the intersection between nostalgia for the gothic past and nostalgia for gothic militarism, this chapter focuses on David Hume, Richard Hurd and Horace Walpole to show that each

---

[4] Here the *Appeal* reinforces what was a central pillar of Byng's defence. In correspondence with Horace Walpole, Horace Mann, who was otherwise critical of the loss of Minorca, conceded that Byng may have been right not to risk an engagement with insufficient 'strength'. Horace Mann to Horace Walpole, Saturday 3rd July 1756, *Horace Walpole's Correspondence*, ed. by W. Lewis and others (London: Oxford University Press, 1937–80), XX, pp. 565–9.
[5] Dianne Dugaw, 'The Popular Marketing of "Old Ballads": The Ballad Revival and Eighteenth-Century Antiquarianism Reconsidered', *Eighteenth Century Studies*, 21.1 (1987), 71–90 (at pp. 72, 84).
[6] See Angela Wright, *Britain, France and the Gothic, 1764–1820: The Import of Terror* (Cambridge: Cambridge University Press, 2013); Tony Wein, *British Identities, Heroic Nationalisms, and the Gothic Novel, 1746–1824* (Basingstoke: Palgrave Macmillan, 2002).

turned to the gothic past in order to write against the old hero dressed as a chivalrous knight.

Politicizing the Gothic Past

As J. G. A. Pocock has long since shown, the return to the gothic past – beginning in the late sixteenth century with the emergence of a new kind of historical interest – was pioneered by humanist legal scholars. Their 'constitutional antiquarianism' sought to establish, from written documents, that the law of England was, paradoxically, un-written, that is, customary, and that because it was un-made, it was therefore immemorial and unchangeable. This account of the ancient constitution, opposed as it resolutely was to the absolute sovereignty of a single ruler, was not originally a turn to a specific past; rather, establishing the un-beginning of English law helped in historicizing the slow formation of the English Parliament and thus the long history of English political representation.[7] However, the gothic past – a period which could be stretched from the fall of the Roman Empire to the arrival of the Stuarts – was also an age of feudalism. In the revolutionary 1650s, James Harrington's *The Commonwealth of Oceana* responded to the alliance and reliance of the commonwealth on the military might of the New Model Army by imagining a utopian republican future that could emerge only by consigning the feudal gothic past to the past.[8] It was not until after the Restoration and the Revolution of 1688 that a pessimistic attachment to the virtues of the gothic social order became widespread among those who opposed the new court Whigs.[9] For old Whigs, this entailed, in Pocock's words, 'a complete reversal of the historical order found in Harrington's own account of English government ... Harringtonian freedom was made to exist in the Gothic English past instead of being founded on its ruins.'[10] As anti-standing army author Samuel Johnson emphasized, the glory of the gothic past emanated from the signing of Magna Carta in 1215, by which the political power, and thus the liberty, of the Anglo-Saxon people was formally recognized by the Norman invaders. Samuel Johnson's first contribution to the standing

---

[7] J. G. A. Pocock, *The Ancient Constitution and the Feudal Law: A Study of English Historical Thought in the Seventeenth Century* (Cambridge: Cambridge University Press, 1957), pp. 18, 124–47.
[8] John Robertson, *The Scottish Enlightenment and the Militia Issue* (Edinburgh: John Donald Publishers, 1985), p. 14.
[9] R. J. Smith, *The Gothic Bequest: Medieval Institutions in British Thought, 1688–1863* (Cambridge: Cambridge University Press, 1987), pp. 11–3.
[10] Pocock, *The Machiavellian Moment*, p. 416.

army debate concludes with the assertion that 'there is no honest Englishman but if there was occasion would spend his blood for *Magna Charta*, that sacred Repository of all the English Liberties'. In his second tract, subtitled 'An occasional discourse in vindication of Magna Charta', Johnson urges his readers not to surrender political power that had been granted to them only after the pitched contest between the king and the barons over the signing of this document.[11] Thus, along with civic humanism, the neo-Harringtonians brought nostalgia for the gothic past into the centre of political debate, where it was to remain into the mid-eighteenth century as a hallmark of both old Whig and Tory opposition to Williamite and, later, Walpolian Whiggery.[12]

Like Harrington, the neo-Harringtonians opposed the creation of a standing army, but unlike Harrington, who planned for a new future, they planned to revive the militia as part of a return to the past, both classical and gothic.[13] Even John Trenchard, who held the classical citizen-soldier to be the ultimate embodiment of civic virtue, seems to have realized that the battle over the creation of a modern standing army could not be fought without reference to England's gothic past. In *A Short History of Standing Armies in England*, Trenchard argues that the first call for a standing army, and with it the beginning of the end for political liberty, came with the death of Elizabeth I, 'and with her all the Virtue of the *Plantagenets* and the *Tudors*.'[14] For Trenchard, Johnson, and the other anti-standing army authors, the gothic past was not so far in the past as to be beyond recovery, unless the nation should succumb to the king's request for a permanently embodied army and thereby surrender the blessings of a mixed constitution enshrined since the thirteenth century. Crucially, the anti-standing army argument found in feudal military service a model for the militia they hoped to restore, for as Thomas Orme opined, 'I think Knights Service was the composition of those Military Forces now commonly call'd Militia.'[15] The gothic constitution, so their argument went, had been forged alongside a feudal social order in which men had the right as well

---

[11] [Johnson], *A Confutation of a Late Pamphlet*, p. 35; [Johnson], *The Second Part of the Confutation of the Ballancing Letter*.
[12] Gerrard, *The Patriot Opposition to Walpole*; Isaac Kramnick, *Bolingbroke and his Circle: The Politics of Nostalgia in the Age of Walpole* (Cambridge, MA: Harvard University Press, 1968).
[13] Pocock, *The Machiavellian Moment*, pp. 409–16; Lawrence Cress, 'Radical Whiggery on the Role of the Military: Ideological Roots of the American Revolutionary Militia', *Journal of the History of Ideas*, 40 (1979), 43–60 (at p. 45).
[14] [John Trenchard], *A Short History of Standing Armies in England*, 3rd ed. (London: A. Baldwin, 1698), p. 8.
[15] [Orme], *The Late Prints for a Standing Army*, p. 12.

as the responsibility to take up arms. This close bond between the medieval baron and his vassals ensured that the sword stayed in the hands of the people, where, according to Andrew Fletcher, it would have remained had the pleasure-loving Renaissance Italians not abandoned the rigours of republicanism in favour of an 'expensive way of living' that,

> plunged [the barons] ... into so great Debts, that if they did not sell, or otherwise alienate their Lands, they found themselves at least obliged to turn the Military Service their Vassals owed them, into Money ... And by this means the Vassal having his Lands no longer at so easy a Rate as before, could no more be obliged to Military Service, and so became a Tenant. Thus the Armies, which in preceding times had been always composed of such Men as these, ceased of course, and the Sword fell out of the hands of the Barons. But there being always a necessity to provide for the Defence of every Country, Princes were afterwards allowed to raise Armies of Volunteers and Mercenaries.[16]

In Fletcher's narrative, the baron and vassal were as able to pick up the sword as their classical forebears, but the cost of luxury was such that 'easy' military service had to be replaced with onerous financial servitude.

At the end of the seventeenth century, then, the anti-standing army authors appealed to the classical citizen-soldier as a model for militarism, but they also returned to gothic feudalism in order to counter the call for a modernized military establishment. And yet, as Pocock observes, by the early eighteenth century the gothic past could just as readily be plundered to support that call for modernization:

> The humanists' stress on arms and land as the preconditions of individual civic and moral autonomy had heightened the dilemma [of how to preserve liberty within a modern commercial society] by presenting it in the form of an irreversible historical process. Virtue, in its paradigmatical social form, was now located in a past; but the era of freedom was also the era of barbarism and superstition, and the term 'Gothic' might, with excruciating ambivalence, be applied in both senses.[17]

In response to the anti-standing army authors, Defoe, who, during the standing army debate, preferred to stay away from matters historical as much as possible, pointed out that the anti-standing army argument was nostalgic for a gothic past of its own making. Defoe exposed the rampant

---

[16] [Fletcher], *A Discourse of Government*, pp. 13–4. For further discussion of Fletcher, see Robertson, *The Scottish Enlightenment*, pp. 22–30. For the standing army debate as a key phase in the attack on luxury, see Sekora, *Luxury*, pp. 78–9.
[17] Pocock, *The Machiavellian Moment*, p. 431.

romanticizing of 'the old *Gothick* Model of Government' that is, the feudal relationship between knight and vassal, arguing, 'in that [time] the Tyranny of the Barons was intolerable, the Misery and Slavery of the Common People insupportable, their Blood and Labour was at the absolute Will of the Lord, *and often sacrifice to their private Quarrels*: They were as much at his beck as his Pack of Hounds were at the Sound of his Horne.'[18] In Defoe's account, the vassal is not liberated by his right to take up arms since he is compelled to do so by his lowly status: his life is cheap enough to be thrown away by those who command. While the anti-standing army authors tended to elide the social difference between baron and vassal, in Defoe's summary the gothic knight is re-imagined as a petty and callous country squire.

Defoe was by no means alone in resisting the romanticizing of gothic militarism. The expansion of the reading public in England during the eighteenth century created demand from readers, including women, for the kind of narrative history already being written on the continent by Voltaire and others. British writers were slow to master the art of Enlightenment historical writing, but David Hume satisfied that demand with his six-volume *The History of England* (1754–62), a work spanning the centuries between the time of Julius Caesar and the Revolution of 1688.[19] Hume began writing his history of England, not from the beginning, that is, with the Romans, but with the reigns of the first Stuarts, James I and Charles I, the point at which, Trenchard had argued, the possibility of liberty and virtue had died. In choosing to begin with the seventeenth century, Hume had to engage with the turbulence and bloodiness of revolution and regicide, but this was a period, he argued, marked by the greatness of civil rather than military events.[20] Indeed, for Hume, this was the period in which an old and inadequate form of government had finally given way to the call for regular parliaments that anticipated the proper recognition of the political power of the people during the second of England's seventeenth-century revolutions: he writes,

---

[18] [Defoe], *An Argument Shewing*, p. 15.
[19] Karen O'Brien, *Narratives of Enlightenment: Cosmopolitan History from Voltaire to Gibbon* (Cambridge: Cambridge University Press, 1997), pp. 56–92; Laird Okie, *Augustan Historical Writing: Histories of England in the English Enlightenment* (Lanham, MD: University Press of America, 1991); David Wootton, 'David Hume: "The Historian"', in *The Cambridge Companion to Hume*, ed. by David Fate Norton and Jacqueline Taylor, 2nd ed. (Cambridge: Cambridge University Press, 1993; repr. 2009), pp. 447–79 (at pp. 447–51).
[20] Philip Hicks, *Neoclassical History and English Culture* (Basingstoke: Macmillan, 1996), pp. 179–80.

> In the ancient Gothic constitution, of which the English partook with other European nations, there was a mixture, not of authority and liberty, which we have since enjoyed in this island, and which now subsist uniformly together; but of authority and anarchy, which perpetually shocked with each other, and which took place alternately, according as circumstances were more or less favourable to either of them.[21]

Karen O'Brien argues that Hume's *History* presents the militaristic culture of the medieval age as 'an inversion of the outward-looking, commercially-minded and centralised states of his own era' and here Hume summarizes the gothic past, not as a golden age of political liberty, but as an inferior age of despotism and conflict.[22] By writing the history of England backwards, then, Hume wrote from a period in which the old heroes of the gothic past could have no place.

Hume's *History* swears allegiance to what David Spadafora has called the 'credo [of] canonizing change', that is, the organized optimism about the perfectibility of the present which countered all manner of 'historical pessimism'.[23] 'Progress' is one of the central ideas in eighteenth-century Enlightenment thought, and one that can easily be aligned with the ideology of politeness, for as Klein puts it, '"politeness" was not a form of nostalgia, but a program for modernity.'[24] To turn to Hume's mid-century essays – a form long since familiar to the polite readers of periodicals – the first of which were published in 1741 and the last new and revised essays in 1777, is to see Hume rejecting the gothic past, and its old heroes, in favour of the modern moment and its modern military men. This is not to deny that in 'Idea of a Perfect Commonwealth' Hume allows himself to essay in political utopianism, *pace* Harrington, and states that a perfect republican system of government should include a militia. Hume's republic is organized in line with a mathematical schema for ensuring fair political representation for all those who meet the minimum property requirements, and he includes a militia, composed of men marshalled by ballot, on the basis that this will protect the freedom of the government and ensure

---

[21] David Hume, *The History of Great Britain*, Vol. 1: *Containing the Reigns of James I and Charles I* (Edinburgh: Hamilton, Balfour and Neill, 1754), p. 79.
[22] O'Brien, *Narratives of Enlightenment*, p. 89. See also Smith, *The Gothic Bequest*, pp. 77–83. Wootton, 'David Hume: "The Historian"', pp. 468–71.
[23] David Spadafora, *The Idea of Progress in Eighteenth-Century Britain* (New Haven, CT: Yale University Press, 1990), pp. 2, 14.
[24] Klein, 'The Third Earl of Shaftesbury', p. 213. For progress see also Murray G. H. Pittock, 'Historiography', in *The Cambridge Companion to the Scottish Enlightenment* ed. by Alexander Broadie (Cambridge: Cambridge University Press, 2003), pp. 258–79; Sidney Pollard, *The Idea of Progress: History and Society* (London: Watts, 1968).

its 'stability [and] security'.[25] This civic affection for militia service is, however, checked by three caveats. First, Hume's system, which he explains briefly on the basis that such a topic is likely to become 'useless and chimerical', is not offered as a return to the past: it is explicitly forwarded as an alternative to any system of government rooted in the 'recommendation of antiquity'. Furthermore, the very perfection of this system renders it imperfect, since 'democracies are turbulent' and as likely to nurture individuals whose enthusiasm might incline them to 'conquest'. Though aristocracies are 'jealous and oppressive', they are 'better adapted for peace and order', concerns that have to be privileged above mathematical fairness.[26] Finally, he contemplates the militia as an adjunct to rather than replacement for a permanent army. As he writes elsewhere, though Britain may allow military campaigns to become ruinously expensive, the protection of the 'balance of power' in Europe is, on its own, a 'just cause' for war.[27] Crucially, Hume pragmatically accepts that trading nations need effective fighting forces to assist commercial ambition and so refutes the nostalgic idea that an amateur militia on its own could be in any way capable of meeting the nation's needs.[28]

Had Hume really wanted to champion the militia, he would have found allies for the cause. As during the standing army debate, so in the mid-eighteenth century civic-minded critics lamented the cost of maintaining standing soldiers and questioned the type of man that could be so purchased. Echoing Trenchard, John Brown deplored the fact that 'money … hath of late, more than ever, been among *us* regarded as the main *Engine of War*', and stridently opposed the idea that a nation need only concern itself with raising money to pay for military service: 'For will not *Cowardice*, at least as soon as *Courage*, part with a Shilling or a Pound, to avoid *Danger*? The capital Question therefore still remains, "Not who shall *Pay*, but who shall *Fight*."'[29] In 'Of Commerce', Hume makes the counter-argument. Hume defends the virtue of the modern soldier who goes to war for wages by contrasting modern military service with its equivalent in the 'ancient' past: 'A continual succession of wars makes every citizen a soldier: … This service is indeed equivalent to a heavy tax; yet it is less felt by a people who

---

[25] David Hume, 'Idea of a Perfect Commonwealth', in *Hume: Political Essays*, ed. by Knud Haakonssen (Cambridge: Cambridge University Press, 1994), pp. 221–33 (at p. 230).
[26] Hume, 'Idea of a Perfect Commonwealth', pp. 221–2, 232.
[27] David Hume, 'Of the Balance of Power', in *Hume: Political Essays*, pp. 154–60 (at p. 158).
[28] While Robertson argues that Hume is sympathetic to the idea of militia, he concedes that he does not advocate this. See *The Scottish Enlightenment*, pp. 60–74.
[29] [Brown], *Estimate*, p. 92. For Brown as a prophet of pessimism see Spadafora, *The Idea of Progress*, pp. 211–52.

are addicted to arms, who fight for honour and revenge more than pay, and who are unacquainted with gain and industry, as well as pleasure.'[30] Far from offering his service 'freely', this ancient soldier is part of a system that compels him to bear arms. Brutalized by bellicosity, this soldier cannot see his servitude as such. By likening ancient military service to a tax, Hume implies that a straightforward financial transaction of military service for payment is to be preferred.[31]

Just as 'Of Commerce' indicates that Hume inherited the pro-standing army position in opposition to the ancient military past, classical or gothic, so the essay 'Of Refinements in the Arts' reveals his support for specialized, professionalized military men, for here Hume observes that 'courage can neither have any duration, not be of any use, when not accompanied with discipline and martial skill.'[32] Furthermore, this essay and, perhaps more so, the essay 'Of National Characters' indicate that Hume also inherited the pro-standing army opposition to the notion of a timeless, innate connection between the male body and militarism. In the latter essay, Hume compares a soldier and a priest in order to make the case that their characters are created rather than innate. 'A *soldier* and a *priest* are different characters, in all nations, and all ages', Hume argues, not because their characters are fixed and unchanging but simply because of 'circumstances, whose operation is eternal and unalterable.' Thus, Hume suggests that military men do not come ready formed to their careers; rather, they are shaped by the conditions in which they serve. Thus Hume counters the notion that all men have the capacity to be military men. Hume draws to a conclusion that challenges the idealization of courage as an innately masculine quality, arguing that courage 'of all national qualities, is the most precarious; because it is exerted only at intervals, and by few in every nation; whereas industry, knowledge, civility, may be of constant and universal use, and for several ages may become habitual to the whole people.'[33] To claim that few men can show courage is to break the association between military service and the male body.

As a historian and essayist, then, Hume resisted the return to the gothic past. Despite flashes of fondness for republicanism and militia service, Hume's mid-century essays indicate that his allegiance lies with the modern moment and its modern military man. Hume measures the liberty of

---

[30] David Hume, 'Of Commerce', in *Hume: Political Essays*, pp. 93–104 (at p. 97).
[31] See also, 'Of Taxes', in *Hume: Political Essays*, pp. 161–5; 'Of Money', in *Hume: Political Essays*, pp. 115–25.
[32] David Hume, 'Of Refinement in the Arts', in *Hume: Political Essays*, pp. 105–14 (at p. 110).
[33] David Hume, 'Of National Characters', in *Hume: Political Essays*, pp. 78–92 (at pp. 79, 89).

the people, not by their access to the sword, but by the rise and progress of the arts and sciences in a polite and commercial nation.[34] Hume accepts that modern nations need fighting forces, but he defends luxury, construed as refinement in the arts, on the basis that it promotes 'mildness and moderation'. In a reworking of the civic idea that the citizen-soldier exchanges the sword for plough sheers on the basis that both are exercises of bodily labour, Hume indicates that the modern military man may assume the 'brute' in the field of battle, but he 'resume the man' after it.[35] In other words, this military man has no innate militarism; rather, he moves between identities, performing the role of the warrior when required, but divesting himself of it when able to do so in order to assume a contrary rather than compatible identity. That said, like his polite predecessors, Shaftesbury and Addison, Hume is wary of admitting the modern military man into polite society. The modern military man may perform variously, but for Hume, one of those performances remains brutish. In 'On the Middle Station of Life', Hume contrasts military men with men of letters to the detriment of the former: 'How many *Marlboroughs* were there in the confederate army, who never rose so much as to the command of a regiment? But I am persuaded there has been but one *Milton* in *England* within these hundred years, because everyone may exert the talents of poetry who is possessed of them.'[36] By imagining mute inglorious Marlboroughs, Hume suggests that although many ordinary soldiers might be capable of commanding men if given the chance, the fact that anyone might try their hand at literature shows that very few are capable of controlling metre. Whilst he hails the modern military man as a performer, then, Hume studiously avoids suggesting that the modern military man might be any more ideal than the historian, philosopher, poet or scholar.

On the Nature of Gothic Chivalry

In the mid-century, Humean confidence in the linearity of progress from barbarity and militarism to civility and peace was in danger of being undermined by the return to the gothic past and rediscovery of gothic chivalry. Chivalry is usually said to have reached its peak in the twelfth and thirteenth centuries and scholars have long been inclined to suggest that

---

[34] David Hume, 'Of the Rise and Progress of the Arts and Sciences', *Hume: Political Essays*, pp. 58–77.
[35] Hume, 'Of Refinement in the Arts', p. 109.
[36] David Hume, 'Of the Middle Station of Life', in *David Hume: Selected Essays*, ed. by Stephen Copley and Andrew Edgar (Oxford: Oxford University Press, 1996), pp. 5–9 (at pp. 8–9).

by the start of the eighteenth century there was very little serious interest in it.[37] Indeed, the decline of chivalry and the rise of modern militarism can be seen as stages in a simple narrative in which one simply replaced the other. However, as David Trim has argued, 'a widespread adherence to the chivalric ethos took a long time to be killed off by bourgeois, state-centred professionalism.'[38] The survival of a chivalric 'ethos' had much to do with the richness of chivalry as a guide for both military and civil behaviour. With his steadfast adherence to codes that governed all aspects of his conduct, the chivalric knight could be proffered by eighteenth-century commentators as a man who managed to be military and so manly, civilized but not polite. As Michèle Cohen notes, at the time when the modern refined man appeared to many to have degenerated into effeminacy, 'chivalry provided a vocabulary for refashioning the [polite] gentleman as masculine'.[39]

For those, like Hume, who subscribed to the idea of progress, the chivalric knight was problematic. The young Hume had wrestled with the merits of chivalry in an unpublished, unfinished essay, 'An Historical Essay on Chivalry and Modern Honour'. According to Ernest Mossner, Hume's essay can be dated to as early as 1725 on the basis that 'the youthfulness and precision of the handwriting, the widespread currency of the thesis ..., the brilliance and yet superficiality of the treatment, the tone of dogmatism, and the occasional awkwardness of the style' are sure signs of an undergraduate essay.[40] In the late 1720s, Hume took an interest in the early eighteenth-century union debate, for which Andrew Fletcher had revised his anti-standing army tract, *A Discourse of Government with Relation to Miltia's*.[41] It ought not to be surprising, then, that Hume's 'Essay on Chivalry' works against the idea of progress in the manner of a pessimistic civic-minded critic, not least when he suggests that medieval culture

---

[37] *Chivalry in the Renaissance*, ed. by Sydney Anglo (Woodbridge: Boydell Press, 1990). See also Mark Girouard, *The Return to Camelot: Chivalry and the English Gentleman* (New Haven, CT: Yale University Press, 1981).

[38] *The Chivalric Ethos and the Development of Military Professionalism*, ed. by D. J. B. Trim (Leiden: Brill, 2003), p. 31.

[39] Michèle Cohen, '"Manners" Make the Man: Politeness, Chivalry, and the Construction of Masculinity, 1750–1830', *Journal of British Studies*, 44 (2005), 312–29 (at p. 315). See also Catriona Kennedy, "A Gallant Nation': Chivalric Masculinity and Irish Nationalism in the 1790s', in *Public Men*, pp. 73–92.

[40] Ernest Campbell Mossner, 'David Hume's "An Historical Essay on Chivalry and Modern Honour"', *Modern Philology*, 45.1 (1947), 54–60 (at p. 54). Mossner's article includes a full transcript of the unfinished essay and all references to the text are to this article.

[41] John Robertson, 'The Scottish Enlightenment at the Limits of the Civic Tradition', in *Wealth and Virtue: The Shaping of the Political Economy of the Scottish Enlightenment*, ed. by Istvan Hont and Michael Ignatieff (Cambridge: Cambridge University Press, 1983), pp. 137–78 (at pp. 150–1).

emerged as a result of the barbarian passion for those 'polite and luxurious Arts' that had brought about the decline and fall of the classical world. However, in suggesting that gothic culture absorbed pre-existing 'polite' manners, Hume firstly historicizes politeness and secondly indicates that chivalry can be seen only as an early, and lesser because still partly barbarous, form of politeness.[42] Hume makes the point that chivalry was the product of a culture formed for violence, and war, he opines, is 'the chief Business and Source of Greatness, in all uncivilized Nations.' Far from truly civilized, gothic chivalry, he points out, offered, 'an affectation of civility' only, for 'a Knight-Errant … salutes you before he cuts your Throat, & a plain Man who understood nothing of the Mystery [of chivalry] wou'd take him for a treacherous Ruffian.'[43]

Though the young Hume was able to mark the distance between the rough civility of gothic chivalry and the polished manners of modern politeness, the issue was somewhat thornier for certain mid-century collectors of old English poetry, for whom the literature of the gothic past was intrinsically valuable. The publication of James Macpherson's tales of Ossian in the early 1760s (the authenticity of which Hume, ultimately, denied) contributed, albeit fraudulently, to the growth of interest in literature that offered 'aesthetic superiority to such "large scale cultural products" as the modern novel.'[44] In fact, a third of the 180 poems in Thomas Percy's important collection of old literature, *Reliques of Ancient English Poetry* (1765), were stock in trade for the publisher of the popular *A Collection of Old Ballads*, William Dicey.[45] However, to attend to Percy's collection is to see that he qualifies his investment in these texts by stressing that they are valuable for throwing light on the superiority of the polite present:

> In a polished age, like the present, I am sensible that many of the reliques of antiquity will require great allowances to be made for them. Yet they have, for the most part, a pleasing simplicity, and many artless graces, which in the opinion of no mean critics have been thought to compensate for the

---

[42] For Hume as sympathetic to chivalry see Ryu Susato, 'The Idea of Chivalry in the Scottish Enlightenment: The Case of David Hume', *Hume Studies*, 33.1 (2007), 155–78; Donald T. Siebert, 'Chivalry and Romance in the Age of Hume', *Eighteenth-Century Life*, 21.1 (1997), 62–79.

[43] Mossner, 'David Hume's "An Historical Essay"', pp. 58, 59, 60.

[44] Jonathan Brody Kramnick, 'The Cultural Logic of Late Feudalism: Placing Spenser in the Eighteenth Century', *ELH*, 63.4 (1996), 871–92 (at p. 873). See also Jonathan Brody Kramnick, *Making the English Canon: Print-Capitalism and the Cultural Past, 1700–1770* (Cambridge: Cambridge University Press, 1998). For Hume and Ossian, see Susato, 'The Idea of Chivalry', p. 168.

[45] Dugaw, 'The Popular Marketing of "Old Ballads"', p. 83.

want of higher beauties, and if they do not dazzle the imagination, are frequently found to interest the heart.[46]

In other words, rough diamonds shine, but not as dazzlingly as modern faceted jewels. For Percy, as for fellow literary antiquarian, Thomas Warton, the inevitable consequence of preserving the literature of the past is that it marks its own cultural inferiority as much as its achievement. The value in reading such literature lies in the way that it allows the reader to plot progress, from imperfect past to polite present. As Percy writes, 'no active or comprehensive mind can forbear some attention to the reliques of antiquity: It is prompted by natural curiosity to survey the progress of life and manners, and to inquire by what gradations barbarity was civilized, grossness refined and ignorance instructed.'[47] Warton makes a similar claim in his introduction to *The History of English Poetry* (1774), a work he dedicates to all those interested in 'tracing the transitions from barbarism to civility.' At a time 'advanced to the highest degree of refinement', following 'the progress of our national poetry, from a rude origin and obscure beginnings, to its perfection in a polished age, must prove an interesting and instructive investigation.' In Warton's view, 'we look back on the savage condition of our ancestors with the triumph of superiority.'[48]

If, in gathering ancient poetry, Percy and Warton necessarily value the cultural achievements of the past and ask their polite readers to do likewise, their prefatory matter also swear allegiance, albeit rather bluntly, to Enlightenment progress. Paradoxically, then, the poems included in *Reliques* are not, but also are, the 'rude songs of ancient minstrels', a phrase used by Percy in his dedication to Elizabeth Percy, Countess of Northumberland, a patron 'who adorns courts by her presence, and diffuses elegance by her example.'[49] Such is his commitment to marking progress that Percy draws a clear distinction between gothic literature and gothic culture: 'The reader is here presented with select remains

---

[46] Thomas Percy, *Reliques of Ancient English Poetry: Consisting of Old Heroic Ballads, Songs, and Other Pieces of our Earlier Poets (chiefly of the Lyric Kind). Together with Some Few of a Later Date*. Volume the First (London: J. Dodsley, 1765), p. x.
[47] Percy, *Reliques*, pp. vi–vii. For Percy as 'man of gothic letters' see Steve Newman, *Ballad Collection, Lyric and the Canon: The Call of the Popular from the Restoration to the New Criticism* (Philadelphia: University of Pennsylvania Press, 2007), pp. 118–28.
[48] Thomas Warton, *The History of English Poetry, From the Close of the Eleventh to the Commencement of the Eighteenth Century. To which are Prefixed Two Dissertations. I) On the Origin of Romantic Fiction in Europe, II) On the Introduction of Learning into England*. Volume the First, 4 vols. (London: J. Dosley; J. Walter; T. Beckett; J. Robson; G. Robinson; J. Bew, 1774), I, pp. i–ii.
[49] Percy, *Reliques*, p. vi.

of our ancient English Bards and Minstrels, an order of men who were once greatly respected by our ancestors, and who contributed to soften the roughness of a martial and unlettered people by their songs and their muse.'[50] In identifying medieval minstrels as the makers of gothic literature, Percy separates old poetry from a culture that is characterized as 'martial' rather than civilized. The minstrel may be 'rude' in comparison to the modern reader, but his mind and manners are more refined than those of the 'unlettered' warriors who are softened by his songs. With this the 'Old Heroic Ballads, Songs and Other Pieces' in the collection are positioned as middling mile markers on the road from the barbarous and militaristic past to the polished and peaceful present.

Percy is not alone in valuing gothic literature by separating that literature from gothic militarism. Richard Hurd's *Letters on Chivalry and Romance* (1762), as Kristine Haugen notes, has 'long been regarded as the primary exhibit in the story of how the eighteenth century rediscovered medieval literature' and, in Michèle Cohen's words, Hurd is 'usually credited with marking the shift in attitude to chivalry and the Middle Ages when he announced that Gothic manners were superior to classical as a subject for poetry.'[51] But whilst literary criticism has traditionally understood Hurd's enthusiasm for gothic romance as an important example of pre-Romanticism, Jonathan Kramnick has sought to move beyond the 'preromantic bind' by stressing the connection between Hurd and other mid-century antiquarians.[52] True, Hurd begins his examination of old literature by questioning the assumed inferiority of the barbarous ages: 'barbarians have their *own*, such as it is, if they are not enlightened by our reason.'[53] But though Hurd is charmed by the 'magic of the old romances', he, like Percy and Warton, places this within a narrative of progress, arguing that the 'bad writers' of the early gothic period failed to perfect the gothic style and that 'the Gothic system was … forced to wait for real genius to do it honour', in the form of Edmund Spencer's *Faerie Queene*.[54] Hurd also qualifies his enthusiasm by noting that the style of old

---

[50] Ibid., p. ix.
[51] Kristine Louise Haugen, 'Chivalry and Romance in the Eighteenth Century: Richard Hurd and the Disenchantment of *The Faerie Queene*', in *Medievalism and the Quest for the "Real" Middle Ages*, ed. by Clare A. Simons (London: Frank Cass, 2001), pp. 45–60 (at p. 45). Cohen, '"Manners" Make the Man', p. 316.
[52] Kramnick, 'The Cultural Logic of Late Feudalism', p. 872. For Hurd as pre-Romantic, see Audley L. Smith, 'Richard Hurd's Letters on Chivalry and Romance', *ELH*, 6.1 (1939), 58–81.
[53] Richard Hurd, *Letters on Chivalry and Romance* (London: A Millar; W. Thurlbourn; J. Woodyer, 1762), p. 3.
[54] Hurd, *Letters on Chivalry*, pp. 118, 105.

romance ought not to be attempted by modern writers: 'I would advise no modern poet to revive these faery tales in an epic poem.'[55]

Though Hurd praises the gothic imagination, his enthusiasm is couched by his effort to separate the culture of chivalry from the literature that was produced at the same time. He acknowledges that gothic romance emerged with 'that military institution, which we know by the name of CHIVALRY', but whilst 'the Spirit of Chivalry, was a fire which soon spent itself: ... that of Romance, which was kindled at it, burnt long, and continued its light and heat even to the politer ages.'[56] Hurd accepts that 'civility and politeness' were cultivated in the courtly environments controlled by feudal barons, where 'the free commerce of the ladies, in those knots and circles of the great, would operate so far on the sturdiest knight as to give birth to the attentions of gallantry.'[57] For proponents of modern politeness, conversation between men and women was to be celebrated, for by admitting women as participants, men became more civilized.[58] However, for one censorious mid-century commentator on 'gallantry', 'the modern Sense of that Word, is to be understood, as a constant Application to the good Works of Adultery and Fornication; or the prevailing Art of debauching, by any Methods.'[59] In praising the de-sexualized social spaces within gothic society, Hurd historicizes polite conversation and thus responds to the criticism that modern mixed-gender sociability provided a means to the ends of debauchery.[60]

However much gothic chivalry might resemble modern politeness, though, for Hurd, the connection between chivalry and militarism is such that it cannot and should not be read by mid-century Jeremiahs as superior to modern polite masculinity. Though Hurd approves of 'free commerce', he is equally keen to note that the chivalrous knight's gallantry took a 'refined turn' only because of the 'necessity there was of maintaining the strict forms of decorum, ... under the eye of the Prince and in his own family.'[61] Chivalry is not a form of civility that should be seen as superior

---

[55] Ibid., p. 101.
[56] Ibid., pp. 8, 3–4.
[57] Ibid., p. 17.
[58] For Enlightenment attitudes to women see Christopher J. Berry, *Social Theory of the Scottish Enlightenment* (Edinburgh: Edinburgh University Press, 1997), pp. 109–13. Laura L. Runge disputes this by suggesting that politeness valued female beauty, 'Beauty and Gallantry: A Model of Polite Conversation Revisited', *Eighteenth-Century Life*, 25.1 (2001), 43–63.
[59] *An Essay on Modern Gallantry. Address'd to Men of Honour, Men of Pleasure, and Men of Sense. With a Seasonable Admonition to the Young Ladies of Great Britain* (London: M. Cooper, 1750[?]), p. 5.
[60] For politeness and gallantry see Davidson, *Hypocrisy and the Politics of Politeness*, pp. 46–75.
[61] Hurd, *Letters on Chivalry*, p. 17.

to modern politeness, Hurd argues, for although it was 'the natural and even sober effect of the feudal policy', this meant that chivalry comprised 'nothing but war, and was fierce and military even in its amusements.'[62] Hurd observes that the chivalric knight's gallantry was simply an extension of his militarism: it was a product of 'those turbulent feudal times' and not the 'charms and graces … of the person addressed.' As a result, the gothic past was an age in which chivalric knights 'were extremely watchful over the chastity of their own women; but such as they could seize upon in the enemy's quarter, were lawful prize', hence ' "bastardy was in credit" '.[63] For those who subscribed to the idea of progress, an excessive regard for chastity is a sure sign of an unrefined society, one in which the sexes are unable to mix freely, as in polite society, because sexual appetites are not sufficiently restrained.[64] Hurd seems to concur, for he justifies his view of the inferiority of gothic chivalry with the argument that the fundamentally militaristic, feudal culture nurtured sexual as much, if not more, than social attachments between men and women, attachments which then provided justification for violence. For Hurd, the image of the knight as chivalrous protector aligns masculine behaviour with overly physical, in the sense of martial and sexual, prowess.

Like Hume, Hurd recognizes that the idealization of gothic chivalry has implications for conceptualizations of masculinity. The militaristic chivalric knight offers a robust because overtly bodily alternative to the modern performer. In response to this, both Hume and Hurd question whether the gothic knight is 'natural'. In *The History of England*, Hume suggests that chivalry arrived in England with the Norman Conquest and that 'no traces of these fantastical notions are to be found among the plain and rustic Saxons.'[65] It is significant that chivalry is said to be foreign, but more so that it is said to be 'fantastical', in the sense of excessive, illogical and irrational. In 'Essay on Chivalry', Hume identifies 'Courage or Warlike Bravery' as the chief quality of the chivalric knight, and second to this the 'extravagant Gallantry & Adoration of the whole Female Sex, & Romantic Notions of extraordinary Constancy, Fidelity & refin'd Passion for one Mistress.'[66] Here, Hume dismisses courage by likening it to the knight's 'extravagant' and 'extraordinary' attachment to women: both are unnatural in the sense

---

[62] Ibid., p. 10.
[63] Ibid., pp. 42, 35.
[64] Berry, *Social Theory of the Scottish Enlightenment*, p. 113.
[65] David Hume, *The History of England from the Invasion of Julius Caesar to the Accession of Henry VII*, 2 vols. (London: A. Millar, 1762), I, p. 423.
[66] Mossner, 'David Hume's "An Historical Essay', p. 60.

of illogical. Admittedly, the young Hume's proto-constructionism is limited by his views on women. Hume objects to gothic chivalry on the basis that the violent attachment to the 'fantastic Ornament' of female chastity empowered women in 'a curious Reversement of the Order of Nature.'[67] This seems to accord with his mid-century defence of modern gallantry in 'Of the Rise and Progress of the Arts and Sciences': 'As nature has given *man* the superiority above *woman*, by endowing him with greater strength both of mind and body, it is his part to alleviate that superiority, as much as possible, by the generosity of his behaviour, and by a studied defence and complaisance for all her inclinations and opinions.'[68] Though hardly a Butlerian rejection of sex/gender, Hume's argument bears scrutiny. As a philosopher, Hume resisted the explanatory power of a priori truths and this can be extended to the body, for as Sheriden Hough has argued, Hume asserts that gendered behaviours have physical beginnings, but that nature is pliable and can be bent by nurture to serve social ends.[69] Such scepticism about the meaning to be derived from the matter of the body can be traced in his mid-century essays that denounce as specious claims to authority based on birth on the basis that 'an anatomist finds no more in the greatest monarch than in the lowest peasant or day labourer.'[70] While bodies have literal matter, they cannot be more than matter, that is, special qualities and capacities do not run in the blood. Like the gothic knight, Hume's modern gentleman has a responsibility to 'protect', but rather than protect women from other men's sexual violence, the modern gentleman protects both her and himself from an illogical attachment to meaning derived from and enacted through the physical body.

In terming gothic chivalry 'fantastical', 'extravagant' and 'extraordinary', Hume's account of militaristic gothic chivalry defines what is 'natural' in terms of what is logical, not simply what is physical, and so challenges the cultural function of the chivalrous knight as a new old hero in the mid-century.[71] Hurd's *Letters* do the same. However, much Hurd champions

---

[67] Ibid., p. 60.
[68] Hume, 'Of the Rise and Progress of the Arts and Sciences', p. 74.
[69] Sheriden Hough, 'Humean Androgynes and the Nature of "Nature"', in *Feminist Interpretations of David Hume*, pp. 218–38. For Hume and feminism, see Lívia Guimarães, 'The Gallant and the Philosopher', *Hume Studies*, 30.1 (2004), 127–47; Lívia Guimarães, 'Hume and Feminism', in *The Continuum Companion to Hume*, ed. by Alan Bailey and Dan O'Brien (London: Continuum, 2012), pp. 319–31.
[70] David Hume, 'Of the Protestant Succession', in *Hume: Political Essays*, pp. 213–20 (at p. 214).
[71] According to Edgar Wind puts it, for Hume, all notions of military heroism are produced by an 'excess of imagination', and so are akin to fanaticism and superstition. Edgar Wind, *Hume and the Heroic Portrait*, ed. by Jaynie Anderson (Oxford: Clarendon Press, 1986), p. 9.

the literature of the past, he is clear that the old romances are not modern conduct manuals. For Hurd, as for Hume, the gothic knight is unnatural because he is a fantastical creation from a fantastical age. Rather than identify the knight as superior to the modern polite man, Hurd reduces chivalry to its fundamental excessiveness: 'the two most essential qualities of a Knight [were] COURAGE and FAITH', Hurd writes, and this explains why the Spanish 'were the furthest gone in every characteristic madness of true Chivalry.'[72] For Hurd, the knight's courage is, like faith, mental rather than physical, and, ultimately, the product of a diseased mind. True, Hurd is concerned with the effect the military culture of chivalry had in masculinizing women's behaviour, for he claims that romance tales of warrior-women, which, he notes, Samuel Butler dismissed as a 'most unnatural idea', are no 'mere extravagance of the imagination'.[73] However, Hurd's point seems to be that warrior-women are only as unnatural as warrior-knights. By resisting the allure of the chivalric knight, both Hume and Hurd indicate that to tie modern men to gothic chivalry is to render masculinity profoundly unnatural. Given this, it is fair to say that both champion 'natural' men, but this is not the nature of essentialism. However, limited both accounts are in conceptualizing the blankness of the female body, and thus the *corpus rasa*, both define what is natural in relation to what is logical rather than bodily. It would be the first gothic novelist of the mid-century, Horace Walpole, who would find the literary form in which to best represent the fantastical unnaturalness of the gothic knight.

On the Super(-)nature of Gothic Bodies

While scholars have, traditionally, turned to Richard Hurd's *Letters on Chivalry and Romance* to understand how the eighteenth century rediscovered gothic literature, they have turned to Horace Walpole's *The Castle of Otranto* (1764) to understand how that rediscovery prompted literary innovation. In fact, neither can be said to be overly representative of the period's return to the gothic past. For one thing, as Christine Gerrard notes, 'perhaps *the* distinctive hallmark of the [anti-Robert Walpole] Patriot literary programme [was] its imaginative engagement with British myth and legend.'[74] Such instrumentalizing of the gothic past during the 1730s in the service of (party) political ends is evident in Henry Carey's treatment of

---

[72] Hurd, *Letters on Chivalry*, pp. 21–2.
[73] Ibid., p. 12.
[74] Gerrard, *The Patriot Opposition to Walpole*, p. 99.

the tale of Moore of Moore-hall. Carey, credited with the first performance of the patriotic British anthem 'God Save the King', achieved renown with his dramatization of 'The Dragon of Wantley': the play, which premiered in 1737, proved to be more popular even than *The Beggar's Opera*.[75] The ballad of Moore of Moore-hall had originally burlesqued tales of the knights of old, only to be repackaged as an 'authentic' piece of old poetry. In Carey's hands, the tale of the chivalric knight became a rich resource with which to attack modern masculinity. As in the original ballad, Moore vanquishes the dragon without displaying courage or prowess with his sword, but this is not surprising given that to Carey's modern Moore dragon-slaying is decidedly less important than wheedling his lady and managing his mistress. With this, the tale of a dragon-kicking buffoon, a tale that once parodied the manners and principles of the gothic past, facilitates a critique of modern society.[76] While Carey's piece is distinctly party-political – it lampoons Walpole and his administration – its broader purpose as civic cultural criticism accords with a poem Carey had published eight years earlier, 'A Satyr on the Luxury and Effeminacy of the Age', the final lines of which condemn the manners of modern (military) men:

> Let's send our useless Dross beyond the Sea
> To fetch polite Imperial and Bohea:
> Let our Troupers to such a length extend,
> That vanquish'd *France* shall copy, but not mend;
> And Italy itself be forc'd to say,
> We fiddle and we sing as well as they.[77]

In restoring the ballad of 'The Dragon of Wantley' to its original satiric purpose, the pro-Byng author of the *Appeal* confronted those who, like Carey, sought to return to the gothic past in order to revive the old heroism that, as Walpole would have known, Byng was said to have so conspicuously failed to exhibit. In correspondence with a friend, George Montagu, Walpole records the public outcry over Byng's loss at Minorca: 'I have been but one night in town, and my head sung ballads about Admiral Byng, all

---

[75] Suzanne Aspden, 'Carey, Henry (1687–1743)', *Oxford Dictionary of National Biography*, online ed. (Oxford University Press, 2004).

[76] [Henry Carey], *The Dragon of Wantley: A Burlesque Opera, as Perform'd at the Theatres with Universal Applause. Set to Musick by Mr. John-Frederick Lampe. To which is Attached the Old Ballad, from whence this was taken* London: J. Shuckburgh, 1738.

[77] H[enry] Carey, 'A Satyr on the Luxury and Effeminacy of the Age', in *Poems on Several Occasions*, 3rd ed. (London: E. Say, 1729), p. 37. For Carey's satirical targets see Suzanne Aspden, 'Ballads and Britons: Imagined Community and the Continuity of English Opera', *Journal of the Royal Musical Association*, 122.1 (1997), 24–51.

night …: the streets swarm so with lampoons, that I begin to fancy myself a minister's son again.'[78] Walpole followed the preparations for the battle and the 'strange turn' of events at Minorca, and although initially predisposed to censure Byng, he came to sympathize with the admiral: 'the great doubtfulness of his crime, and the extraordinariness of the sentence, the persecution of his enemies who sacrifice him for their own guilt, and the rage of a blinded nation, have called forth all my pity for him – his enemies triumph, but who can envy the triumph of murder?'[79] At a time when the balance of opinion was firmly against Byng, Walpole 'used [his] utmost endeavours, but in vain, to save the unfortunate Admiral.'[80]

During this time, Walpole may have come into contact with anti-Byng pamphlets, poems and, crucially, prints, specifically *Byng in Horrors: Or, T---rr-ing-t-n's Ghost reproaching his cowardly Son* (1756) and *The Apparition* (1756), which cast the familial connection between Byng and his deceased father, the naval hero George Byng, Viscount Torrington, in gothic terms.[81] As Emma Clery has argued, the language of the supernatural had long been available for use in cultural communication, but the eighteenth century saw 'the growing commercialisation of spirits, … [and] a spiritualisation of commerce; a fundamental chiasmus.'[82] The number of anti-Byng prints to make use of the standard iconography of horned and cleft devils attest to this rampant commercialization of spirits, but the prints *Byng in Horrors* and *The Apparition* employ the supernatural in more complex ways. In both images, Byng is tormented by the shrouded figure of his late father, who lambasts his cowardly son: 'Could not my Honours fire thy Heart?' asks the hero in *Byng in Horrors*; 'Art thou, degenerate Wretch, my son?', cries the father in *The Apparition*. To say that Byng lacks his father's 'heart' is to indicate that his failings are moral but also physical: both prints make the point that Byng has his father's blood but that he has failed to follow

---

[78] Horace Walpole to George Montague, Monday 12th July 1756, *Horace Walpole's Correspondence*, IX, p. 192.
[79] Horace Walpole to Horace Mann, Thursday 3rd March 1757, *Horace Walpole's Correspondence*, XXI, p. 65.
[80] Horace Walpole, 'Short Notes', in *Horace Walpole's Correspondence*, XIII–XIV, p. 27. Walpole was still sympathetic toward Byng some twenty-five years later. See Horace Walpole to Horace Mann. Tuesday 20th August 1782, *Horace Walpole's Correspondence*, XXV, p. 307.
[81] *B-N-G in horrors; or T-rr-ing-t-on's Ghost reproaching his Cowardly Son*, August 1756, 3376; *The Apparition*, August 1756, 3374. For devils see *The Contrast*, 10th July 1756, 3365; *The Devil's Dance Set to French Music*, August 1756, 3373; *The Devil Turned Drover*, October 1756, 3416; *The Devil Turn'd Bird-Catcher*, 1756, 3499; *A Voyage to Hell or a Pickle for the Devil*, 1756, 3501.
[82] E. J. Clery, *The Rise of Supernatural Fiction, 1762–1800* (Cambridge: Cambridge University Press, 1995), p. 7. See also Kalter Barrett, 'DIY Gothic: Thomas Gray and the Medieval Revival', *ELH*, 70.4 (2003), 989–1019.

in his father's footsteps. These prints represent the old hero as a supernatural being on the basis that he was once superlatively 'natural', what I shall term 'super-natural'. In contrast, the modern military man is presented as 'unnatural', a failure as both a son and a man.

Though published seven years after Byng's trial, *The Castle of Otranto* responds to the celebration of old heroism in the mid-century by problematizing the super-natural old hero. Of course, the first 'gothic' novel can be read as an exercise in anti-modern nostalgia.[83] Walpole is well known for his fondness for the material culture of the gothic past: he gathered together an extensive collection of gothic artefacts, including a copy of Magna Carta, and remodelled his home at Strawberry Hill to create domestic splendour fit for a feudal baron. But as Sean R. Silver notes, Walpole's papier-mâché pastiche of gothic architecture was intended to create a giant cabinet in which to display his *objet*, more like a museum than a home.[84] Indeed, Walpole's house-sized cabinet of curios can be said to have much in common with Percy's collection of old poetry, that is, as a collection of artefacts at once valuable and inferior. Like Percy's *Reliques*, Walpole's *The Castle of Otranto* – a tale which was initially presented to the reading public as a 'found manuscript' authored by the fictitious Onuphrio Muralto and with a preface by the equally fictitious translator of Muralto's Italian, William Marshall – uses the gothic past to measure progress. Marshall's preface dates the tale to somewhere between the eleventh and thirteenth centuries, an age of learning when Italian letters were in their 'most flourishing state'. The preface identifies this as a period of schism between a thoroughly medieval culture, based on superstitious beliefs, and an emerging intellectual culture led by the 'innovators', one of whom wrote the text in a triumph of 'singular judgement'. Like Percy and Hurd, Walpole differentiates between the prevailing gothic culture and those who were ahead of their times; the luminous Latinate languages of the polite and polished world are juxtaposed with the obscure 'black letter [s]' belonging to the priest who, Walpole suggests, may have created, or at least rewritten, the text's 'preternatural events'.[85] Admittedly, the second edition and its second preface seem to question this narrative of progress, for in this preface Walpole

---

[83] See Maggie Kilgour, *The Rise of the Gothic Novel* (London: Routledge, 1995), pp. 16–23; Abby Coykendall, 'Chance Enlightenments, Choice Superstitions: Walpole's Historic Doubts and Enlightenment Historicism', *The Eighteenth Century*, 54.1 (2013), 53–70.

[84] Sean R. Silver, 'Visiting Strawberry Hill: Horace Walpole's Gothic Historiography', *Eighteenth-Century Fiction*, 21.4 (2009), 535–64 (at p. 537).

[85] Horace Walpole, *The Castle of Otranto: A Gothic Story*, ed. by E. J. Clery (Oxford: Oxford University Press, 1996), pp. 5–6.

confirms that this text is alive to the mid-century project to construct a history of English literature. Much of the second preface is dedicated to a dialogue with Voltaire on the use of low comedic characters in tragic scenes, which Walpole defends as commensurate with Shakespearean tragedy; he concludes the preface by stating that 'all I have said is to shelter my own daring under the cannon of the brightest genius this country, at least, has produced.'[86] For Angela Wright, Walpole's participation in establishing a canon of English literary excellence is evidence of his pragmatic genuflection to popular enthusiasm for old Englishness in the mid-century.[87] However, in praising Shakespeare, Walpole shows that the old bard might be a useful resource for modern innovators. In so doing, Walpole subtly reinforces the scale of value in which the past remains 'before'.

To understand the terms on which Walpole's text returns to the gothic past is to be able to uncover the novel's criticism of old heroism. In the second preface, Walpole asserts that the chivalrous knight and damsel-in-distress can hardly be said to be natural: 'the actions, sentiments, conversations, of the heroes and heroines of ancient days were as unnatural as the machines employed to put them in motion.' Walpole positions his text as a rejection of this, claiming 'my rule was nature':

> Desirous of leaving the powers of fancy at liberty to expatiate through the boundless realms of inventions, and thence of creating more interesting situations, [the author] wished to conduct the mortal agents in his drama according to the rules of probability; in short, to make them think speak and act, as it might be supposed mere men and women would do in extraordinary positions.[88]

For Walpole, what is natural is whatever is probable. Walpole's characters are, in his view, simply ordinary people managing the kinds of extraordinary situations found in gothic romance. The combination produces characters that are mere 'mortal agents': their decisions are clouded by ungovernable emotions; they are forced to piece together their understanding of events from limited and faulty knowledge; more most importantly, they are fallible, not in the dramatic sense of having a tragic flaw, but in the decidedly mundane sense of making clumsy mistakes. When Manfred attempts to exact revenge on Isabella, for example, he mistakenly kills his own daughter, Matilda. Similarly, when Theodore steps briefly into the role of chivalric knight in order to defend Isabella, he accidentally wounds

---

[86] Walpole, *The Castle of Otranto*, p. 14.
[87] Wright, *Britain, France and the Gothic*, pp. 16–30.
[88] Walpole, *The Castle of Otranto*, pp. 9–10.

her concerned father, Frederic. Walpole's 'natural' characters are carefully constructed so as not to be 'unnatural' paragons of perfection.

Like Hume and Hurd, for whom chivalry is a form of 'madness', Walpole aligns that which is natural to that which is reasonable, rational, logical. In his undergraduate essay, Hume had contrasted classical and gothic architecture, the one 'plain, simple and regular, withal majestic & beautyful' and the other 'a wild Profusion of Ornaments ... [and] rude Embellishments', and he goes on to state that, 'for the same Reason, when they wou'd rear up a new Scheme of Manners or Heroism, it must be strangely overcharged with ornaments, & no part exempt from their unskilled refinements.'[89] For Hume, gothic chivalry is inherently excessive or 'over-sized'. Walpole indicates that his novel will follow this line of argument with the death of Manfred's son and heir underneath the enormous helmet which belongs to the Knight of the Giant Sabre. The death can be read as an episode that asserts the power of the super-sized knight over the weak and feeble Conrad and thus promises that the text will call for a return to old, virile masculinity. For James Watt, Walpole's knight is over-sized in order to introduce a serious 'spectacle of legitimate nobility' in an otherwise frivolous text and Ellen Brinks has suggested that the later image of 'a hundred gentlemen bearing [the knight's] enormous sword, and seeming to faint under the weight of it' stages the anxiety of 'distressed masculinity'.[90] In contrast, I suggest that the over-sized gothic knight is to Walpole as the wild overcharged ornament is to Hume. As if to underscore the point that the knight is unnatural, he is only seen as dismembered bodily parts – a hand and leg – or represented synecdochally by his helmet or sword, as if the bulk of body and baggage can never be assembled into a stable whole.

Echoing Hume and Hurd, Walpole uses the gothic military man to define what is 'natural' in terms of that which is logical, rather than physical. According to Hume, the chivalric knight's courage is not a physical quality, something that inheres within the timelessly male body; rather, it is an overreaching of the matter of the body: as he puts it, '[the barbarians] ... exceed Nature, & overcharge their Courage with something excessive & monstrous.'[91] For Walpole, the quintessential gothic body, the body of the sword-weilding chivalric knight, is not super(latively)-natural,

[89] Mossner, 'David Hume's "An Historical Essay"', p. 58.
[90] James Watt, *Contesting the Gothic: Fiction, Genre and Cultural Conflict, 1764–1832* (Cambridge: Cambridge University Press, 1999), p. 38; Ellen Brinks, *Gothic Masculinity: Effeminacy and the Supernatural in English and German Romanticism* (Cranbury, NJ: Associated University Presses, 2003), p. 11.
[91] Mossner, 'David Hume's "An Historical Essay"', p. 59.

but irrational, excessive, and so supernatural. With this, Walpole's text responds to enthusiasm for the gothic military man, and also to essentialist conceptualizations of masculinity. Walpole certainly had reason to be preoccupied with the latter. As Clery notes, the novel was composed in the aftermath of a scandal that forced Walpole's cousin and close friend, the army officer Henry Seymour Conway, from civil office.[92] Walpole's anonymously published pamphlet in support of Conway was seized upon by William Guthrie, a civic-minded hack turned historian, who penned an extraordinarily bilious response:

> The complexion of the malice, the feeble tone of the expression, and the passionate fondness with which the *personal* qualities of the officer in question are continually dwelt on, would almost tempt one to imagine, that this arrow came forth from a female quiver; but as it wants both the true delicacy and lively imagination which characterize a lady's pen, the attack must probably have been made from a neutral quarter, from a being between both, neither totally male or female whom, if naturalists were to decide on, they would most likely class him by himself; by nature maleish, by disposition female, so halting between the two, that it would very much puzzle a common observer to assign to him his true sex. The description of the hermaphrodite horse which is just brought to town, may, perhaps, not unaptly represent him: "he possesseth all the characters of both sexes, but the odd situation and transposition of the parts, appear as it were the sport of nature, and render him the greatest curiosity ever seen."[93]

Guthrie's appeal to 'true sex' asserts that masculinity is a product of a timelessly sexed body and construes any gender identity that floats free of the physical body as a kind of monstrosity. In representing the chivalric knight as supernatural rather than super-natural, Walpole's novel inverts this so the supposedly natural body becomes monstrous.

In authoring the first gothic novel to reach the literary marketplace, Walpole participated subversively in the mid-century commercialization of old spirits. A literary exercise in the 'found text', the use of multiple false identities, and particularly the gradual divesting of those identities in the prefatory matter – from author to translator to Walpole himself – alerts readers to the import of the text's defence of modernity. After all, the acts of veiling and unveiling the 'real' author, played out in the first

---

[92] For a discussion of this relationship, see George E. Haggerty, *Men in Love: Masculinity and Sexuality in the Eighteenth Century* (New York: Columbia University Press, 1999).
[93] [William Guthrie], *A Reply to the Counter-Address; Being a Vindication of a Pamphlet Entitled, an Address to the Public, on the Late Dismission of a General Officer* (London: W. Nicoll, 1764), pp. 6–7. Guthrie's *A General History of England* (1744–51) condemned the pernicious effects of luxurious and corrupt manners. See Hicks, *Neoclassical History*, pp. 157–8.

and second prefaces, are integral to a text which, as Sue Chaplin observes, destabilizes the concept of origins.[94] In this chapter, I have argued that the novel's encounter with the gothic knight challenges the notion that masculinity, and gender more broadly, originates in and with the body. With this in mind, it becomes more significant that, according to the fictitious author, the text is concerned to show that '*the sins of fathers are visited on their children to the third and fourth generations*'.[95] In fact, the text disrupts the linearity of masculine inheritance: the past does not constrain the present, for the sins of the fathers are not passed on to their progeny. Admittedly Manfred's unfortunate children, Conrad and Matilda, suffer for their father's sins, but the fates of the grandchildren of Alphonso the Good complicate the central moral. Theodore is legitimately descended from Alphonso, but he does not inherit the castle and is tidied away into an unhappy marriage to a substitute bride. Like the use of supernatural knight, this marriage problematizes any attempt to define 'natural' in terms of the sexed body. Eve Kosofsky Sedgwick has argued that gothic literature emerged in concert with the increasing effort to categorize and demonize homosexuality and that gothic sexual 'decadence' seeks to either liberate or control sexuality.[96] *The Castle of Otranto* fits into either category rather awkwardly. The two patriarchs, Manfred and Frederick, are characterized by their libidinal desires for each other's daughters, but the text condemns the fathers' quasi-incestuous appetites without reasserting the primacy of the normatively heterosexual and reproductive body.[97] The marriage between Theodore and Isabella offers the chance to celebrate a heterosexual relationship, but this union leaves Theodore trapped with his cousin as a replacement for the dead Matilda, and the curious stasis of permanent mourning which surrounds the couple hardly suggests that theirs will be a marriage of fecund procreativity.

This chapter began with the anti-standing army authors' nostalgia for the gothic past, but it has concentrated on those authors who turned to that past, and even valued its literature, but without privileging its chivalric knight as an old hero and so model (military) man. As the young Hume

---

[94] Sue Chaplin, *The Gothic and the Rule of Law, 1764–1820* (Basingstoke: Palgrave Macmillan, 2007), pp. 48–51.
[95] Walpole, *The Castle of Otranto*, p. 7.
[96] Eve Kosofsky Sedgwick, *Between Men: English Literature and Male Homosocial Desire* (New York: Columbia University Press, 1985), pp. 83–96.
[97] On the queering of the father in early gothic see Dale Townshend, "Love in a Convent': or, Gothic and the Perverse Father of Queer Enjoyment', in *Queering the Gothic*, ed. by William Hughes and Andrew Smith (Manchester: Manchester University Press, 2009), pp. 11–35.

wrote in regard to gothic chivalry, 'there is nothing real in all this', for 'Heroism is formed only from Men's minds'; whereas the small societies of the ancient world curtailed individual ambitions to heroism, turning 'an empty Shadow ... [into] a solid Substance', the wide circulation of fantastical stories encouraged 'Moorish and Gothic Heroes' to reach for something beyond any human's grasp.[98] In the aftermath of the trial of Admiral Byng, amid the outpouring of hostility directed against one who was deemed to have failed both militarily and as a man, both Hurd and Walpole stressed the unnaturalness of the gothic knight. Whereas anti-Byng prints presented Byng's hero-father as super(latively)-natural, Walpole's text presents the chivalric knight as supernatural because illogical. In returning to the gothic past, then, Walpole rejects the naturalizing of gender, that is, the idea that the body has a 'true sex'. As a result, though *The Castle of Otranto* is usually referred to as the text which began a literary movement, it can also be read as a text that responded to its contemporary moment in radically proto-constructionist ways.

---

[98] Mossner, 'David Hume's "An Historical Essay"', pp. 59–60.

CHAPTER 5

The Military Man and the Culture of Sensibility
Smith, Ferguson, Mackenzie

> Mourn England, mourn in duller strain,
> Your chiefest hero Wolfe is slain.
> Adorn'd with every manly grace,
> In heart and body, mind and face.
> His virtue far and near was fam'd,
> A better man no age has nam'd.[1]

The British victory at the battle for Quebec in 1759 was a turning point in the Seven Years' War. The early years of the war had been marked by failures for Britain, not least the loss of Minorca that had resulted in the execution of an admiral. General James Wolfe's victory in Quebec was the mirror image of this, for the commander perished in his quest to secure victory. Unlike the death of the inglorious Byng, the death of England's 'chiefest hero' was a desirable subject for the eighteenth-century's culture of sensibility. The eighteenth-century's interest in sensibility is usually said to have emerged early in the century, clearly so by the 1740s, and to have reached the peak of its popularity by the 1780s even though it remained a significant term in the Romantic period.[2] In essence, the turn to sensibility was a turn to feeling and thus to the body. As Graham J. Barker-Benfield discusses, the ability to feel was understood to be a feature of the physical body: to feel was to possess a nervous system which produced bodily effects – blushes, tears and swoons – in response to external stimuli.[3] And yet, initially at least, the turn to sensibility was not a turn away from

---

[1] 'Britain in Tears for the Loss of Brave General Wolfe', *The Muse's Delight: or, the Songster's Jovial Companion* (London: Pridden et al., 1760), pp. 125–6, ll. 5–10.
[2] Janet Todd, *Sensibility: An Introduction* (London: Methuen, 1986); *Passionate Encounters in a Time of Sensibility*, ed. by Maximillian E. Novak and Anne Mellor (London: Associated University Presses, 2000); Christopher Nagle, *Sexuality and the Culture of Sensibility in the British Romantic Era* (New York: Palgrave Macmillan, 2007).
[3] G. J. Barker-Benfield, *The Culture of Sensibility: Sex and Society in Eighteenth-Century Britain* (Chicago: University of Chicago Press, 1992), pp. 1–36.

politeness. Such was the physicality of sensibility, Paul Goring argues, that this 'bodily rhetoric' of feeling could lend weight to the new 'performance of modern politeness'.[4] Indeed, for Philip Carter, sensibility is 'best viewed less as a complete replacement for than as a significant reworking of existing definitions of male refinement, whereby the potential for polite artifice was reduced through an accentuated attachment to the value of genuine emotion.'[5] That said, by the mid-century, sensibility could be pulled in quite the opposite direction. Jerome McGann has traced how the culture of sensibility changed during the mid to late century and argues that the sentimental writing which became so dominant promoted 'at least the appearance of traditional hierarchies of thought (religious vs. secular) and social relations (male vs. female).'[6] Emphasizing Edmund Burke's sentimentality for 'the age of chivalry' at the time of the French Revolution, Claudia Johnson likewise argues that by the end of the century sensibility had become integral to a masculine political identity that sought to centralize conservative and traditional ideologies.[7]

Like the return to the gothic past, then, there can be no single narrative for the eighteenth-century culture of sensibility. The very capaciousness of the key term meant that it could as easily reinforce the virtue of polite performance as corroborate essentialist argument, for that which was part internal and part external could anchor that which was suspiciously superficial or make manifest that which was invisibly innate. Such expansiveness also accommodates tensions, and these tensions are particularly acute with regard to the military man. An ancillary to politeness, the new cult of feeling emerged, as Barker-Benfield argues, alongside efforts to reform the 'old style of man', in particular his fondness for antisocial violence, such as duelling.[8] However, even Carter acknowledges that sensibility began to move to a very different direction, as he detects a 'pronounced equation of sensibility and militarism evident from the late 1750s.'[9] Drawing on texts by Adam Smith, Adam Ferguson and Henry Mackenzie, produced between the late 1750s and the early 1770s, this chapter argues that the culture of sensibility was able to accommodate both the modern military man and

---

[4] Paul Goring, *The Rhetoric of Sensibility in Eighteenth-Century Culture* (Cambridge: Cambridge University Press, 2005), p. ix.
[5] Carter, *Men and the Emergence of Polite Society*, p. 93.
[6] Jerome McGann, *The Poetics of Sensibility: A Revolution in Literary Style* (Oxford: Clarendon, 1996), p. 8.
[7] Claudia Johnson, *Equivocal Beings: Politics, Gender and Sentimentality in the 1790s, Wollstonecraft, Radcliffe, Burney, Austen* (Chicago: University of Chicago Press, 1995), pp. 34, 98.
[8] Barker-Benfield, *The Culture of Sensibility*, p. 86.
[9] Carter, *Men and the Emergence of Polite Society*, p. 108.

the 'natural' old hero. Whereas Smith's theorizing of moral sentiments employs the modern military man to help secure the virtue of modern performance, Ferguson and Mackenzie turn to the old hero, an honorific they extend to what the eighteenth century termed the 'savages' of North America and India, to highlight the social function of man's innate capacity for feeling. It is the appeal to the racialized 'other' that indicates how the military man was used within the culture of sensibility to centralize essentialist conceptualizations of gender.

Sympathy, Sentiment and the Military Man

The first edition of Adam Smith's *The Theory of Moral Sentiments* (1759) appeared in print just a few months before General Wolfe secured the victory that, with the successes at Minden, Lagos and Quiberon Bay turned the tide of the Seven Years' War. Given that, two years earlier, the public outcry over the loss of Minorca had led to the execution of an admiral, it is significant that, following the publication of Smith's *Theory*, David Hume wrote to 'commiserate' with his close friend: 'I proceed to tell you the very melancholy News, that your Book has been very unfortunate. For the Public seem disposed to applaud it extremely. It was looked for by a mob of foolish People with some Impatience; and the Mob of Literati are already beginning to be very loud in its Praises.' With this, Hume differentiates between their circle and the 'Public', a category that includes the 'mob of literati' and, implicitly, Smith's publisher, for as Hume goes on to write, 'you see what a Son of the Earth that is, to value Books only by the profit they bring him.' Hume further characterizes their circle when he reveals that he has circulated a copy of the book to carefully vetted individuals including Horace Walpole and the then unknown author of what Hume thought to be a 'very pretty' treatise on the sublime, Edmund Burke.[10] As participants in a closed community of intellectuals, to which Burke is only peripheral, Hume and Smith sought to occupy a space within the bourgeois public sphere, an insular space, insulated from the public and its views and opinions.

If, after decades of debate concerning the 'Adam Smith Problem', it is now thought to be too simplistic to say that the author of *The Theory of Moral Sentiments* later turned suddenly and unaccountably into the prophet of laissez-faire capitalism, it might also be admitted that Smith's

---

[10] David Hume to Adam Smith, 12th April 1759, in *On Moral Sentiments: Contemporary Responses to Adam Smith*, ed. by John Reeder (Bristol: Thoemmes Press, 1997), pp. 6, 7, 3.

theorizing of the concept of sympathy is broadly committed to furthering the culture of politeness.[11] According to Smith's *Theory*, the word sympathy 'denote[s] our fellow-feeling with any passion whatever': it is the human response to others' emotional states, whether those states are genuine or produced, like those conjured by actors in theatrical productions.[12] The virtue of sympathy lies in the fact that it does not attempt to discriminate on the basis of others' sincerity, for the involuntariness of the response to others' emotions countersigns the sincerity of the individual's responses to all those with whom she or he interacts. Tellingly, given the importance of conversation as the primary arena for polite performance, Smith reflects on the telling of a joke to illustrate the way sympathy operates. An individual ought to laugh when a joke is told in a social situation, Smith argues, for if no-one laughs the teller of the joke feels foolish. With this, Smith's *Theory* turns the affectation of amusement, which would otherwise be a polite but also duplicitous response, into an act of sympathy.[13] As this example illustrates, Smith's notion of sympathy lends moral weight to polite behaviour. That said, Smith's attempt to substantiate politeness with spontaneous sensibility ultimately subordinates emotional involuntariness to polite self-management, for the individual, Smith states, must submit to the 'measures and rules by which esteem and approbation are naturally bestowed.'[14] Thus, if the hearers of the joke are duty bound to laugh so as to alleviate another's distress, the teller of the joke is equally duty bound not to venture an unfunny remark. Following Smith's *Theory*, then, the capacity for feeling creates a double responsibility: individuals must sympathize with others' passions, but they must also regulate themselves so that others need not sympathize with them.

Though Smith defines sympathy as 'fellow-feeling' in ways that respond to the criticism that politeness operates as a mere screen for selfishness and duplicity, this remains 'self-centred sympathy', as Ildiko Csengei describes it, for his *Theory* turns what could be understood to be 'natural' feeling into the exercise of self-discipline.[15] Rather than seek to stabilize polite

---

[11] See Istvan Hont and Michael Ignatieff, 'Needs and Justice in *The Wealth of Nations*', in *Wealth and Virtue*, pp. 1–45; Nicholas Phillipson, 'Adam Smith as Civic Moralist', in *Wealth and Virtue*, pp. 179–202; Emma Rothschild, *Economic Sentiments: Adam Smith, Condorcet, and the Enlightenment* (Cambridge, MA: Harvard University Press, 2001). See also Janet Sorensen, *The Grammar of Empire in Eighteenth-Century British Writing* (Cambridge: Cambridge University Press, 2000), pp. 138–71.
[12] Adam Smith, *The Theory of Moral Sentiments* (London: A. Millar; A. Kincaid and J. Bell, 1759), p. 6.
[13] Smith, *Moral Sentiments*, pp. 15–18.
[14] Ibid., p. 245.
[15] Ildiko Csengei, *Sympathy, Sensibility and the Literature of Feeling in the Eighteenth-Century* (Basingstoke: Palgrave Macmillan, 2012), p. 53.

performance by centralizing the feeling body as the basis for politeness, Smith effectively reduces the capacity for spontaneous sympathy to one of the many 'duties of politeness, which are so easily observed, and which one can scarce have any serious motive to violate.'[16] After all, the individual must show sympathy to those who are in need of it, but the heavier duty is to manage him- or herself so as not to solicit or require that sympathy from others. The former is described as an exercise of the 'soft, the gentle and the amiable virtues', whereas the latter exhibits 'the great, the awful and respectable, the virtues of self-denial, of self-government, of that command of the passions which subjects all the movements of our nature to what our own dignity and honour, and the propriety of our own conduct require.'[17] In other words, Smith's enthusiasm for involuntary feeling only thinly disguises his greater investment in self-discipline. Of course, in asking individuals not to solicit others' sympathy, Smith allows the crowd of spectators the power to judge, if not to actually punish, and with this Smith seems to be aware that this discipline might be external in origin. Whereas Boswell was to find himself torn between self-discipline and discipline-from-an-external-source, Smith smooths over the tension by bringing the two together. The double-duty of sympathy requires the individual to anticipate the spectators' judgement and to internalize that judgement in the form of an impartial spectator who 'allows no word, no gesture, to escape' until it has been moderated.[18] By indicating that the individual must internalize a standard that originates outside of him- or herself, Smith's *Theory* moves further towards a Foucauldian understanding of performativity in which inscription from without creates the illusion of a soul within.

The argument that Smith's *Theory* reinforces the virtue of polite performance by turning the body's capacity for 'natural' emotional responses into the double-duty of self-discipline might seem to be far removed from any concern with militarism, but as Richard Sher claims, when it came to military matters 'Smith took his stand on the side of the moderns', that is, among those who supported the standing army.[19] Military men appear in Smith's *Theory* as exemplary modern performers of sympathy/discipline.

[16] Smith, *Moral Sentiments*, p. 277.
[17] Ibid., p. 41.
[18] Ibid., p. 43. This reading is supported by John Bender, *Imagining the Penitentiary: Fiction and the Architecture of the Mind in Eighteenth-Century England* (Chicago: University of Chicago Press, 1989), pp. 201–30.
[19] Richard B. Sher, 'Adam Ferguson, Adam Smith, and the Problem of National Defence', in *Adam Smith*, ed. by Knud Haakonssen (Aldershot: Ashgate, 1998), p. 258. See also Hont and Ignatieff, 'Needs and Justice in *The Wealth of Nations*'.

This is not immediately apparent in Smith's comments on what was a recent military event:

> There is many an honest Englishman, who in his private station would be more seriously disturbed by the loss of a guinea than by the national loss of Minorca, who yet, had it been in his power to defend that fortress, would have sacrificed his life a thousand times, rather than through his fault, have let it fall into the hands of the enemy.[20]

Here, Smith sounds rather like the civic social commentator John Brown. For Brown, the loss of Minorca had testified to the pernicious influence of fashionable manners on men's military spirit, particularly men in the higher ranks of society. Like Brown, Smith has little regard for 'the man of rank and distinction ... whose whole glory consists in the propriety of his ordinary behaviour ... To figure at a ball is his great triumph, and to succeed in an intrigue of gallantry, his highest exploit.'[21] The dissipated coxcomb 'may be willing to ... make a campaign when it happens to be the fashion', Smith observes, 'but he shudders with the horror at the thought of any situation that demands the continual and long exertion of patience, industry, fortitude, and application of thought.' Rather than censure all modern military men, though, Smith only takes against those men who reduce the performance of politeness – that which should be the 'virtue of the great' – to a hollow ritual, unsubstantiated by the discipline that produces sympathy.[22] Earlier on, Smith notes that the man who 'feels every defect in the highest ceremony of politeness, whether it be shewn to himself or any other person' deserves to be reprimanded.[23] Real politeness, Smith implies, is achieved only by submitting to the double-duty of sympathy, which is the same kind of submission that might lead a man to 'defend [a] fortress'. Rather than identify the military man as an alternative to the polite gentlemen, then, Smith indicates that the modern military man and the polite gentleman should share a similar disciplinary regime.

Although Smith's *Theory* does not explicitly address the standing or otherwise of the nation's military establishment, then, it is clear that Smith has little time for civic ideals. The modernity of Smith's position is apparent when, following in Steele's footsteps, he pauses to consider the nature of military courage:

---

[20] Smith, *Moral Sentiments*, p. 367.
[21] Ibid., p. 122.
[22] Ibid., pp. 123, 120.
[23] Ibid., p. 89.

The soldier who throws away his life in order to defend that of his officer, would perhaps be but little affected by the death of that officer, if it should happen without any fault of his own, and a very small disaster which had befallen himself might excite a much more lively sorrow. But when he endeavours to act so as to deserve applause, and to make the impartial spectator enter into the principles of his conduct, he feels that to everybody but himself his own life is a trifle compared with that of his officer, and that when he sacrifices the one to the other, he acts quite properly and agreeably to what would be the natural apprehensions of every impartial bystander.[24]

Although Smith commends the soldier who gives his life for his superior officer, he makes it clear that the soldier's courageous self-sacrifice is not entirely 'natural': it is not innate or essential. The soldier 'throws away' his own life only in order to comply with the impartial spectator. In other words, he performs courage in return for silent applause. Smith goes on to repeat his argument against natural courage by discussing men in the higher ranks. The officer who exposes his life in order to make a territorial gain for the nation does so not because he little values his life, but because he imagines the benefit of the gain to the people he serves. Rather than act from instinct, he disciplines his own feelings so as to act in accordance with the impartial spectator. It is the self-discipline required for the double-duty of sympathy, rather than natural courage, that enables the soldier and the officer alike to perform as military men.

Just as Smith concurs with Steele in his account of military courage, so his analysis of the military character shares much with Hume. When Hume contrasts the soldier and the priest he finds that 'the same principle of moral causes fixes the character of different professions, ... and this difference is founded on circumstances whose operation is eternal and unalterable.'[25] The 'circumstances' that shape the soldier are those that are 'eternally' different from those that shape the priest, not least the requirement that the soldier risk his life, and thus the character that seems to be essential to each is really a result of custom rather than nature. Echoing Hume's line of argument, Smith argues that the military character, in particular what seems to be uncountable cheerfulness, is forged by the rigours of professional military service: 'The ordinary situation ... of men of this profession, renders gaiety, and a degree of dissipation, so much

[24] Ibid., p. 366.
[25] Hume, 'Of National Characters', in *Hume: Political Essays*, p. 79.

their usual character; and custom has, in our imagination, so strongly connected this character with this state of life[,] that we are very apt to despise any man[,] whose peculiar humour or situation, renders him incapable of acquiring it.' There are subtle differences between Hume and Smith's approaches: whereas Hume argues that, because the soldier's business is the business of soldiering, the military character is 'eternally' different from that of the priest, Smith stresses the contingency of militarism by arguing that, 'a long peace […] is apt to diminish the difference between the civil and the military character.'[26] And yet, with this Smith's *Theory* equally emphasizes that the military character is merely circumstantial rather than corporeal.

When military men appear in Smith's *Theory*, then, they are championed only as thoroughly modern figures who have nothing of the old hero in them. According to Smith, it is the hero, rather than the polite gentleman, who is obviously and dangerously invested in promoting his own interests. For Smith, 'ambition' is,

> a passion, which when it keeps within the bounds of prudence and justice, is always admired in the world, and has even sometimes a certain irregular greatness, which dazzles the imagination, [but] when it passes the limits of both these virtues, [it] is not only unjust but extravagant. Hence the general admiration for Heroes and Conquerors, and even Statesmen, whose projects have been very daring and extensive, tho' altogether devoid of justice.[27]

In Smith's view of things, 'Heroes and Conquerors', unrestrained by 'limits', are, like the gigantic knight of Walpole's imagination, 'unjust and extravagant'. When Smith asserts that 'perils and misfortunes are not only the proper school of heroism, they are the only proper theatre which can exhibit its virtue to advantage, and draw upon it the full applause of the world', he defines virtue as a kind heroism, not heroism as a kind of virtue. After all, the officer who, like the soldier, is able to put the nation's interests above his own deserves praise, not for his military skills, but for mustering such self-discipline that he is able to counteract his 'natural' instinct for self-preservation: 'in thus thwarting from a sense of duty and propriety, the strongest of all natural propensities, consists the heroism of his conduct.'[28] Smith repeats this point when he notes that 'a brave man exults in those dangers, in which, from no rashness of his own, his fortune has involved him', because 'one who is master of all his passions, does not

---

[26] Smith, *Moral Sentiments*, pp. 395–6.
[27] Ibid., pp. 304–5.
[28] Ibid., pp. 129, 367.

dread any circumstance in which the superintendent of the universe may think proper to place him.'[29]

Taken together, Smith's observations on military courage, on the military character and on heroism suggest, not that a man is and ought to be capable of militarism, but that those who enter military life are shaped into military men by it. The inevitable conclusion is that the modern man might go to war, but he need not do so, for military service offers simply one arena in which a man might be able to display his mastery of himself. Given this, it is not surprising that Smith defends the view that politeness should bring about the feminization of masculinity. Smith encourages men to feminize their behaviour in mixed company: 'to talk to a woman as we should to a man is improper: ... their company should inspire us with more gaiety, more pleasantry, and more attention; and an intire insensibility to the fair sex, renders a man contemptible in some measure even to the men.'[30] As with Hume's essays, Smith's proto-constructionism reaches its limits when asked to account for the 'fair sex', but Smith's notion of gallantry makes the point that feminized behaviour in social spaces demonstrates self-control, and so although military service is one theatre in which self-discipline may be performed, it is by no means the most suitable for those with access to the polite world. It is the ordinary, 'private man', one who cannot achieve distinction through politeness, who 'looks forward with satisfaction to the prospect of foreign war, or civil dissension ... [and] sees through all the confusion and bloodshed which attend them ... [for] he may draw upon himself he attention and admiration of mankind.'[31] Ultimately, the military man may be capable of sympathy, as Smith understands it, but those capable of sympathy need not become military men. With this in mind, I want to compare the discussion of the modern military man in Smith's *Theory* with Adam Ferguson's appeal to old heroism in *An Essay on the History of Civil Society* (1767).

In comparison to Smith's *Theory*, Ferguson's *Essay* is not so obviously a significant contribution to the eighteenth-century culture of sensibility, but as an essay on the history of social organization, it was suited to its times. Whereas Smith published his *Theory* just a few months before a turning point in the war, Ferguson published his *Essay* four years after the end of the war, a period in which Britain was coming to terms with immense territorial gains that had

---

[29] Ibid., p. 133.
[30] Ibid., pp. 52–3.
[31] Ibid., pp. 121, 122.

considerably expanded Britain's horizons. Like many of his mid-century contemporaries, including Thomas Percy, Thomas Warton and Richard Hurd, Ferguson is concerned with the progress of human society from rudeness to civility, but whereas Percy, Warton and Hurd ultimately conclude that progress is synonymous with improvement, Ferguson takes issue with those who 'impute every advantage of our nature to those arts which we ourselves possess; and ... imagine, that a mere negation of all our virtues is a sufficient description of man in his original state.'[32] Ferguson's teleological account of the development of civil society is far from entirely hostile to modernity, particularly modern legal systems, but he does not consider progress to be a process which systematically replaces all that is imperfect because rude and old with all that is perfect because civilized and modern. As even-handed as the essay initially is about the advantages and disadvantages of both early and recent forms of human society, Ferguson ultimately forwards a thoroughly civic argument, one that looks back to the past in order to substantiate concerns about the present. Crucially, Ferguson strengthens his argument against unilinear progress by appealing to the timelessness of human nature. At the start of the essay, Ferguson considers the argument that mankind 'is in some measure the artificer of his own frame, as well as his fortune, and is destined, from the first age of his being, to invent and contrive.' Ferguson rejects this proto-constructionism on the basis that the capacity for 'invention' is innate and so the man who activates that capacity remains, fundamentally, the same.[33] And just as the capacity to invent is essential to human nature, so is the ability to feel. In the opening pages of the essay, Ferguson takes issue with the idea that in the 'state of nature' mankind exhibited a 'mere animal sensibility, without any exercise of the faculties that render them superior to brutes.' On the contrary, Ferguson argues, the ability 'to receive the informations of sense, is perhaps the earliest function of an animal combined with an intellectual nature.'[34]

To contrast Smith and Ferguson's essays is to see that Ferguson understands sensibility very differently. For Smith, to have feelings is to know that others have feelings, but this imposes the responsibility on individuals, the double-duty, to discipline their feelings in order to accept those who are unable to do likewise and, more importantly, to be acceptable to others. In Smith's account, the impartial spectator is a kind of mirror into

---

[32] Adam Ferguson, *An Essay on the History of Civil Society* (Dublin: Boulter Grierson, 1767), p. III.
[33] Ferguson, *Civil Society*, pp. 9, 12.
[34] Ibid., pp. 2, 38.

which the individual can peer and with which make adjustments to his or her behaviour so as to only appear in public in his or her best form. In Smith's hands, sympathy does not create intimate bonds between individuals, for although Smith claims that feeling has a social function – to facilitate the 'harmony of society' – the idea that the individual must replace his or her feelings with those of the impartial spectator hardens the formality of polite interpersonal relationships and so isolates individuals.[35] For Ferguson, in contrast, to understand that others have feelings is to be naturally disposed to feel for and then to form affectionate bonds with them: 'man, in the perfection of his natural faculties is quick and delicate in his sensibility; extensive and various in his imaginations and reflections; attentive, penetrating, and subtile, in what relates to his fellow-creatures; firm and ardent in his purposes; devoted to friendship or to enmity; jealous of his independence and his honour.'[36] Although Ferguson uses the term 'sensibility' here, it is significant that he generally prefers the term 'sentiment' to describe the 'emotions that pertain to society' and which, as he puts it, the heart should feel as naturally as the eye sees light and the ear hears sound.[37] Unlike Smith, Ferguson worries about the decline of real fellowship in civilized societies where 'private interest, and animal pleasure, [have] become the sovereign objects of care', and where 'men ... bestow their attention on trifles ... [and what they] are pleased to call *sensibility* and *delicacy*'. In societies that 'make no trial of the virtues or talents of men', Ferguson warns:

> We rate our fellow-citizens by the *figure* they are able to make; by their buildings, their dress, their equipage, and the train of their followers ... If the master himself is known to be a pageant in the midst of his fortune, we nevertheless pay our court to his station, and look up with an envious, servile, or dejected mind, to what is, in itself, scarcely fit to amuse children.[38]

Whereas Smith's double-duty of sympathy attempts to secure the virtue of polite sociability, Ferguson mounts an undisguised attack on what he calls the 'imbecility' of 'politeness', the pageantry of surfaces. Nothing, he reminds his readers, 'can turn the grimace of politeness into real sentiments of humanity and candour.'[39]

Ferguson's commitment to 'real sentiments' is reinforced by his comments on military matters. Some eight years previously, Ferguson had

[35] Smith, *Moral Sentiments*, p. 38.
[36] Ferguson, *Civil Society*, p. 167.
[37] Ibid., p. 5.
[38] Ibid., pp. 385, 377.
[39] Ibid., pp. 383, 58.

written a pamphlet that urged the nation's men to join the national militia, and the same civic impulses reappear in his *Essay*.[40] Like Trenchard and Brown, Ferguson is concerned with the growth of capitalism.[41] The first symptom of capitalism is the separation of work into professions which 'withdraw individuals from the common scene of occupation, on which the sentiments of the heart, and the mind, are most happily employed.'[42] The result of this is the decline of 'public spirit': 'we would have nations, like a company of merchants, think of nothing but the increase of their stock; assemble to deliberate on profit and loss; and, like them too, intrust their protection to a force which they do not possess in themselves.'[43] Echoing the anti-standing army argument, Ferguson reflects on the state of modern professionalized armies, peopled by men who serve for payment: 'A discipline is invented to inure the soldier to perform, from habit, and from the fear of punishment, those hazardous duties, which the love of the public, or national spirit, no longer inspire.'[44] Whereas Smith indicates that discipline creates, in every sense, the military man, Ferguson suggests that discipline is an inferior substitute for the emotions that first bonded people together and then motivated them to defend each other.

Ferguson's investment in 'real sentiments' is also an investment in real bodies. If love and compassion exist 'in the human breast', so the willingness to protect and preserve inheres within the body, and since military action is a consequence of the innate capacity to feel, both are necessarily 'natural'.[45] Indeed, Ferguson's argument that the feeling body precedes and prompts man's military actions leads him to argue that 'the frame of his nature requires him to be occupied'.[46] 'How many are there to whom war itself is a pastime, who chuse the life of a soldier, exposed to dangers and continued fatigues; of a mariner, in conflict with every hardship, and bereft of every conveniency', Ferguson muses. They do this, he asserts, because

> MAN, it must be confessed, notwithstanding all th[e] activity of his mind, is an animal in the full extent of that designation. When the body sickens,

---

[40] Adam Ferguson, *Reflections Previous to the Establishment of a Militia* (London: R and J Dodsley, 1759). For Ferguson and the militia, see Robertson, *The Scottish Enlightenment*, pp. 200–9.
[41] Iain McDaniel, *Adam Ferguson in the Scottish Enlightenment: The Roman Past and Europe's Future* (Cambridge, MA: Harvard University Press, 2013).
[42] Ferguson, *Civil Society*, p. 326. For Ferguson's opposition to commercial society, see Berry, *Social Theory of the Scottish Enlightenment*, pp. 132–49.
[43] Ferguson, *Civil Society*, p. 217.
[44] Ibid., p. 226.
[45] Ibid., p. 53.
[46] Ibid., p. 315.

the mind droops; and when the blood ceases to flow, the soul takes its departure. Charged with the care of his preservation, admonished by a sense of pleasure or pain, and guarded by an instinctive fear of death, nature has not intrusted his safety to the mere vigilance of his understanding, nor to the government of his uncertain reflections.[47]

Here, Ferguson seems to agree with Smith that men feel fear, but he then counters this by suggesting that the instinct for self-preservation, which is rooted in mere understanding and uncertain reflection, gives way to what is implicitly an equally natural capacity for action. For Ferguson, inactivity goes against men's innate, bodily nature such that 'in the absence of every manly occupation, [men] feel a dissatisfaction and languor which they cannot explain … like the disquiet of sickness'.[48]

Like the anti-standing army authors, Ferguson's hostility to standing forces is motivated by his civic fear for the people's liberty. Just as sentiment for others precedes military action, so military action should be directed towards communal action: 'liberty is a right which every individual must be ready to vindicate for himself', he argues, but on the basis that, 'when a people is accustomed to arms, it is difficult for a part to subdue the whole.'[49] For Ferguson, militarism should be used against those who wish to govern in ways that 'deprive the citizen of occasions to act as the member of a public; that crush his spirit; that debase his sentiments, and disqualify his mind for affairs', that is, for the benefit of the public-at-large.[50] However, to argue that the male citizen should be motivated by his love for others to defend his and their liberties is merely to soften the civic instruction to men to exercise their military capacity. Ferguson's ideal man of feeling is, in effect, required to be a man of action and Ferguson holds up as exemplary the 'old men, among the courtiers of Attila, [who] wept, when they heard of heroic deeds, which they themselves could no longer perform'.[51] While Smith's *Theory* promotes self-discipline, which the modern man might perform in any number of arenas, Ferguson's *Essay* takes on a coercive function in promoting old heroism. It is the connection between sentiment and old heroism that I want to explore in more detail.

---

[47] Ibid., pp. 65, 67.
[48] Ibid., pp. 388–9.
[49] Ibid., pp. 397, 404.
[50] Ibid., p. 320.
[51] Ibid., p. 157.

Fellow-Feeling and the 'Warrior-Savage'

Shortly after the publication of Smith's *Theory of Moral Sentiments*, the news of the death of Wolfe at the conquest of Quebec arrived in England. The cost of the much-needed victory was to test the culture of sensibility, as the *Annual Register* records:

> When the news of this decisive action arrived in England, we all remember, though it is very difficult to describe, the various and mixed emotions with which every one was affected ... the mixture of grief and pity, which attended the public congratulations and applauses, was very singular and affecting. The sort of mourning triumph, that manifest itself on that occasion, did equal honour to the memory of the general, and to the humanity of the nation.

The combination of a grand military success and a symbolically significant fatality produced an awkward confluence of emotions. For the editors of the *Register*, a 'mourning triumph' is still primarily a triumph, but they commend the neighbours of Wolfe's mother who forebore not to have any illuminations so as not to exacerbate her motherly grief: 'it shews a finesses of sentiment, and a justness of thinking, in the lower kind of people, that is rarely met with even amongst persons of education ... whoever knows the people, knows they made no small sacrifice on this occasion.'[52] With this, the *Register* recommends that the public manage its emotion in ways that accord with Smith's theory of the double-duty of sympathy. The *Register* permits the public to feel the loss of the general, but praises the respect shown towards one who was less able to manage her emotions. A similarly Smithean approach can also be seen in John Pringle's *The Life of General James Wolfe* (1760), the subtitle of which promises a biography written 'according to the rules of eloquence'. The author allows himself to be tossed from elation to despair: 'the Eye is seen to mourn; the Countenance in vain recalls its Sprightliness; nay, the whole Body, to shew its sympathies with the sincere Regret the Mind, would willingly clothe itself with a Garb of expressive sorrow!' However, this apex of sensibility is followed by a sudden narrowing of emotion: 'But cease ye unavailing Tears! ... Ye flow without reason.'[53] As he goes on to reason, there need only be so much

---

[52] *The Annual Register; or, A View of the History, Politicks and Literature of the Year 1759* (London: R. and J. Dodsley, 1762), p. 43.
[53] J[ohn] P[ringle], *The Life of General James Wolfe, the Conqueror of Canada: or the Elogium of that Renowned Hero* (London: G. Kearsley, 1760), pp. 3–4.

lamentation for one who has been rewarded for his sacrifice with recognition for his merits and a place in heaven.

Pringle's flight into sensibility and abrupt return to reason and restraint can be contrasted with the poem 'Britain in Tears', as the latter's lachrymose refrain, 'Mourn England, mourn in duller strain,/ Your chiefest hero Wolfe is slain', works to steadily increase the pitch of emotion. This strategy can also be seen in one important artistic response to the battle: Benjamin West's *The Death of General Wolfe* (1770). As Alan McNairn argues, Wolfe was 'granted eternal fame as the embodiment of distinct British values' in no small part because his death proved to be a popular subject with painters.[54] George Romney and Edward Penny produced pictures of Wolfe in the early 1760s, but none were as successful as Benjamin West's *The Death of General Wolfe*, exhibited at the Royal Academy in 1771. West's painting was heavily reproduced in the 1770s and established a vocabulary for military scenes which West himself reused for *The Death of Nelson* (1806). According to David Solkin, West's *Wolfe* was successful because it modernized history painting, traditionally the highest genre of painting, to better suit polite tastes: 'in Benjamin West's hands', Solkin writes, 'the most public form of art became an instrument for the cultivation of those refined and sympathetic virtues which Hume and other mid-century Whiggish philosophers identified as the crowning glory of a prosperous commercial state.'[55] Myrone has argued that history painting fared badly in the eighteenth century, certainly in comparison to portraiture, but by presenting military men in modern clothing and by capturing specific individuals' likenesses, a key to which was published with a print of the painting in 1776, West's *Wolfe* showed that an 'exemplary her[o] could be made meaningful for the modern public' as an 'icon of modernized masculinity.'[56] Following Solkin and Myrone, then, it would be possible to suggest that West's *Wolfe* promotes Smithean sensibility. In fact, Penny's intimate painting, which imagines Wolfe accompanied with just two attendants and in a secluded clearing some way from the battle, is a better candidate for this. West's painting makes use of a grander scale and the epic scene that stretches away behind Wolfe is suited to one whose death commands attention. The crescent of

---

[54] Alain McNairn, *Behold the Hero: General Wolfe and the Arts in the Eighteenth Century* (Liverpool: Liverpool University Press, 1997), p. 6.
[55] David Solkin, *Painting for Money: The Visual Arts and the Public Sphere in Eighteenth-Century England* (New Haven, CT: Yale University Press, 1992), p. 188.
[56] Myrone, *Bodybuilding*, p. 120.

witnesses, including a grenadier on Wolfe's right, an American ranger in green, a tartan-clad Scots highlander and an American Indian ally, are not restrained Smithean spectators. Wolfe's brothers-in-arms surround him – the ranger and the Scotsman appear to have just rushed to Wolfe's side and the grenadier's hands are clasped as though in prayer – and the cordon of representative figures includes a space for the viewer of the painting, who is invited to complete the circle as a fellow mourner. In accepting that invitation, the viewer is positioned to experience his or her emotional response to the death of the hero, and also his or her fellowship with those who are experiencing the same feelings. With this, the painting creates a virtuous circle of mourning, within which emotion circulates, steadily increasing rather than diminishing. As a result, the painting of a dying hero both depicts and promotes the kind of socially orientated fellow-feeling that the civic-minded Ferguson identifies as essential to the ideal society.

With its use of modern clothing and contemporary figures, West's *Wolfe* testifies to the tendency, increasingly apparent from the mid-century, for the arguments that were earlier easily distinguishable, no more so than during the standing army debate, to strategically cannibalize each other's claims and thereby come to resemble each other. However, my reading of West's *Wolfe* as a civic attack on modernization and a celebration of old heroism takes particular note of the powerful presence of the American Indian ally. The dying Wolfe is closely flanked by three kneeling figures, but he gestures away from them and towards the American Indian, who stares intently at him. The pair is placed on the same horizontal plane and the positions of their bodies address each other, establishing a physical as well as emotional bond between them. The relationship depicted here reprises one created in West's earlier work, *General Johnson Saving a Wounded French Officer from the Tomahawk of a North American Indian* (1764–8). For Jonathan Conlin, West's *General Johnson* indicates that, by the mid-century, 'the hero had for the most part given way to the 'prudent man' of Smith's *Theory of Moral Sentiments*'.[57] True, the painting depicts a British officer rescuing his imperial enemy from 'savagery', but West undercuts this celebration of European hegemony by harmonizing the British officer and the America warrior; West has used a limited palate for both figures, including their skin tones: their healthy, earthy hues are set against the French officer's plaid skin and stark white clothing. While *General Johnson* ostensibly celebrates the commonality among

[57] Jonathan Conlin, 'Benjamin West's *General Johnson* and Representations of British Imperial Identity, 1759–1770', *British Journal for Eighteenth-Century Studies*, 27.1 (2004), 37–59 (at p. 54).

civilized nations, the composition and colouring create a counter-narrative which, as in *Wolfe*, connects the British officer to what was, certainly after the Seven Years' War, a culturally pervasive figure of 'otherness', and with this both paintings complicate any easy association between the racialized 'other' and savagery.[58] In *Wolfe*, the American Indian is equipped with his traditional weapons of war to mark him as a warrior, but the bond between him and Wolfe ensures that the general, and by extension all those who are dressed in modern military uniforms, are anchored to a figure who functions, like the civic citizen-soldier or gothic chivalric knight, as an icon of old heroism, and one who exceeds the citizen-soldier and knight in terms of overt physicality. The American Indian's muscular body evokes the classical bodies that, as Myrone has shown, were critical to the survival of heroic manliness in eighteenth-century art.[59] In fact, the American Indian's physical presence is so powerful in West's *Wolfe* as almost to displace its new old hero. Rather than mark the American Indian as lesser because 'other', his semi-naked body is physically superior to Wolfe's slender, limp form, and thus the dying soldier, who looks almost more like the ghostly French officer, is in danger of being 'othered' by his inferiority. West may be using the American Indian to secure Wolfe's old heroism, but by highlighting the former's super(latively)-natural body, West permits the viewer to breathe a quiet civic sigh for the eighteenth-century's version of the old hero.

The American Indian warrior has as significant a role in Smith's *Theory* and Ferguson's *Essay*, for both Smith and Ferguson ruminate upon 'warrior-savagery' in ways that reinforce their accounts of sensibility. For Smith, the warrior-savage is far from barbarous: though savage societies are violent societies, the conduct of the warrior-savage is proof of his capacity for rationality and self-control. Every 'savage', he argues, prepares 'from his earliest youth for the dreadful end' by preparing a song to sing should he be taken as a prisoner of war, and if condemned to torture he 'submits to the most dreadful torments, without ever bemoaning himself, or discovering any other passion but contempt of his enemies.'[60] Smith's account of the inhabitants of the uncivilized world, particularly

---

[58] For the eighteenth-century's public interest in the American Indian as a warrior, see Troy O. Bickham, *Savages Within the Empire: Representations of American Indians in the Eighteenth-Century* (Oxford: Clarendon, 2005).

[59] Myrone, *Bodybuilding*. Vivien Green Fryd notes that West's used classical models in order to construct the American Indian as an ideal masculine figure, but for Fryd the 'Native American symbolizes the masculinity of an alien culture' and so remains in a 'secondary position' to Wolfe. See 'Rereading the Indian in Benjamin West's 'Death of General Wolfe'', *American Art* 9.1 (1995), 72–85 (at p. 84).

[60] Smith, *Moral Sentiments*, p. 401.

those of North America, goes so far as to state that 'their magnanimity and self-command … are almost beyond the conception of Europeans.'[61] For Maureen Harkin, Smith's willingness to praise the warrior-savage is indicative of a broader ambivalence about enlightened modernity: 'in Smith's version of history … the primitive and the modern compete for dominance, and the celebration of progress clashes with an intensely felt sense of decline and nostalgia.'[62] But though Smith praises the warrior-savage for his stoicism, that 'best school of heroes and patriots', this reflects the way his main thesis draws on Stoic philosophy to argue, as John Mullan puts it, 'that feeling be regulated and chastened', 'order[ed]' rather than 'celebrated'.[63] After all, in commending the warrior-savage's self-discipline, Smith pointedly does not praise his martial skills. Smith notes, for example, that the 'savage' is so self-disciplined as to be able to control pleasure as well as pain: he shows no preference in choice of a wife, as 'the weakness of love, which is so much indulged in ages of humanity and politeness, is regarded among savages as the most unpardonable effeminacy'. It is significant that Smith admires a society in which unrestrained sexual desire is considered a 'most indecent and unmanly sensuality', for with this Smith praises the warrior-savage for practising the kind of self-discipline that serves as the moral basis for modern politeness.[64]

As enthusiastic as Smith is about the warrior-savage's self-restraint, though, he is not offered as a model for modern man. Smith's *Theory* is not concerned principally with establishing a narrative of progress, but its encounter with the warrior-savage contributes to the text's underlying commitment to both proto-constructionism and the modern moment. Smith's 'savage' is not essentially and innately inclined to violence; rather, he is shaped by living in 'continual danger' which 'habituate[s] him to every sort of distress, and teach[es] him to give way to none of the passions which that distress is apt to excite.' As a result, the warrior-savage illustrates that people are formed by their circumstances – that 'the stile of manners which takes place in any nation … [is] that which is most suitable to its situation' – but as these circumstances change, so societies advance.[65] In praising the warrior-savage for his self-discipline, then, Smith

---

[61] Ibid., p. 399.
[62] Maureen Harkin, 'Adam Smith's Missing History: Primitives, Progress, and Problems of Genre', *ELH*, 72.2 (2005), 429–51 (at p. 443).
[63] Smith, *Moral Sentiments*, p. 136; John Mullan, *Sentiment and Sociability: The Language of Feeling in the Eighteenth Century* (Oxford: Clarendon Press, 1988), p. 56.
[64] Smith, *Moral Sentiments*, p. 400.
[65] Ibid., pp. 398, 409.

moves beyond what Sankar Muthu identifies as the earliest default narrative of savagery as the 'state of nature', but Smith's advance is limited, for his willingness to see the warrior-savage as complex, as a product of circumstances rather than nature, permits him to positions the warrior-savage within a unilinear narrative of progress that ends with polite civility.[66] Smith acknowledges that 'the delicate sensibility required in civilized nations sometimes destroys the masculine firmness of the character', and that as a result the modern man might not be as much a master of himself as the stoic warrior-savage: 'among civilized nations, the virtues which are founded upon humanity, are more cultivated than those which are founded upon self-denial and the command of the passions. Among rude and barbarous nations, it is quite otherwise.'[67] However, he seems not to conceive of this, as a civic critic might, as a loss, for this feminized man is also shaped by circumstances and so is more suited to the modern world. Ultimately, Smith concludes, the 'heroic and unconquerable firmness which the custom and education of [the warrior-savage's] country demand of every savage, is not required of those who are brought up to live in civil and civilized societies.'[68]

When Ferguson turns to the relationship between the warrior-savage and civilized society, he produces quite the opposite conclusion.[69] In the early pages of his *Essay*, Ferguson lays down a challenge to the Enlightenment narrative of progress by questioning whether 'the proper state of his nature … is not a condition from which mankind are for ever removed, but one to which they may now attain.'[70] Characteristically, Ferguson initially balances his argument by acknowledging there are some who have characterized early societies as lesser because more violent: '[they] have made the state of nature to consist in perpetual wars, … where the presence of a fellow-creature was the signal of a battle.'[71] He subsequently identifies the propensity for violence as one of the failings of rude nations: 'though they are patient of hardship and fatigue, though they are addicted to war … yet, in the course of a continued struggle, always yield to the superior arts, and the discipline of more civilized nations.[72] However, Ferguson is unwilling

---

[66] Sankar Muthu, *Enlightenment Against Empire* (Princeton, NJ: Princeton University Press), pp. 11–71.
[67] Smith, *Moral Sentiments*, pp. 408–9, 397.
[68] Ibid., p. 403.
[69] Here, I disagree with Tim Fulford's account of the similarity between Smith and Ferguson. See *Romantic Indians: Native Americans, British Literature, and Transatlantic Culture 1756–1830* (Oxford: Oxford University Press, 2006), pp. 41–6.
[70] Ferguson, *Civil Society*, p. 14.
[71] Ibid., p. 3.
[72] Ibid., p. 139.

to condemn the sentiments that prompt defensive violence: 'they are sentiments of generosity and self-denial that animate the warrior in defence of his country; and they are dispositions most favourable to mankind, that become the principles of apparent hostility to men.'[73]

Early man, Ferguson argues, loved and hated with equal vehemence, and it was this natural inclination to form friendships that also caused him to make enemies:

> Every tribe of warlike barbarians ... entertain among themselves the strongest sentiments of affection and honour, while they carry to the rest of mankind the aspect of banditti and robbers ...[O]ur sense of humanity, our regard to the rights of nations, our admiration of civil wisdom and justice, even our effeminacy itself, make us turn away with contempt, or with horror, from a scene which exhibits so few of our good qualities, and which serve so much to reproach our weakness.[74]

Here, Ferguson makes plain that those who seem to be merely 'barbarians' remind civilized societies that sentiment precedes violence, and thus so-called savage violence demonstrates the strength of fellow-feeling between fellow creatures. As a result, Ferguson's warrior-savage is fundamentally the same as the anti-standing army argument's civic citizen-soldier, since both take up arms for the love of their nation, and the 'humanity' that turns away is really that of a modernity that has degenerated into 'effeminacy' and 'weakness', for in the later stages of his argument, Ferguson firmly juxtaposes 'old' savage and modern civilized society, to the detriment of the latter:

> If the savage has not received our instructions, he is likewise unacquainted with our vices. He knows no superior, and cannot be servile; he knows no distinctions of fortune, and cannot be envious; he acts from his talents in the highest station which human society can offer, that of the counsellor, and the soldier of his country. Toward forming his sentiments, he knows all that the heart requires to be known; he can distinguish the friend whom he loves, and the public interest which awakens his zeal.[75]

So invested is Ferguson in the warrior-savage as a model man of feeling, he asks the modern man to recognize his past savage self as the superior man. Ferguson concedes that modern man has managed to 'obviate the casual abuses of passion' which once resulted from the closeness of feeling and violence, and he maintains that modern man should only be spurred

---

[73] Ibid., p. 34.
[74] Ibid., p. 232.
[75] Ibid., p. 278.

into action by love for his fellows rather than hatred of his enemy, that is, defence not attack. However, for Ferguson, the savage's martial spirit reminds the polite and commercial man that 'if the individual, not called to unite with his country, be left to pursue his private advantage; we may find him become effeminate, mercenary, and sensual.'[76] Whereas Smith indicates that savagery is one in a sequence of stages, Ferguson disrupts the linear narrative of progress by emphasizing the synchronicity of so-called savagery and modern civility in the contemporary moment: 'it is in their present condition, that we are to behold, as in a mirrour, the features of our own progenitors.' If Smith argues that modern man need only internalize the impartial spectator in order to appear at his best, Ferguson asserts that modern man would be improved by a (re)turn to the virtues of savagery. Ferguson turns to the 'wild American' to substantiate his point that modern man has sacrificed his essential nature for polite performance, for 'men who live in the simplest condition … have not learned to affect what they do not actually feel.[77] Like West's American Indian, Ferguson's warrior-savage is a model for the kind of militarism, and masculinity, in which the modern polite man is no longer interested, but to which he can and ought to return. For 'what should distinguish a German or a Briton, in the habits of his mind or his body, in his manners or apprehensions, from an American, who, like him, with his bow and his dart, is left to traverse the forest; and in a like severe or variable climate, is obliged to subsist by the chace?'[78]

Though the culture of sensibility could, as Smith's *Theory* shows, accommodate the celebration of progress and with it the feminization of masculinity, it was also the case that advocates for sensibility could seize on the apparently timeless 'nature' of feeling to denounce proto-constructionist understandings of masculinity. For Ferguson and, slightly later, West, the warrior-savage's capacity for feeling confirms that he is someone for whom civil society ought to have more regard, for in recognizing (dis)similarity, the modern man will see how far he has declined rather than progressed. The same argument is made in a novel published in the year West exhibited *The Death of Wolfe*: Henry Mackenzie's *The Man of Feeling* (1771). Like Walpole's *The Castle of Otranto*, the novel purports to be a 'found' text, though in this case the novel comprises a series of fragments contained by a frame

---

[76] Ibid., pp. 138, 374.
[77] Ibid., pp. 118, 25, 26.
[78] Ibid., p. 118.

narrative which explains how the original manuscript came to be so damaged. As episodic as it is, though, it is possible to discern a distinctly civic narrative: the protagonist, Harley, travels to London, the centre of the corrupt, duplicitous metropolitan world, in order to improve his fortunes, but he succeeds in failing and then returns to a place in which virtue is, or rather ought to be, possible. In other words, the text seems concerned primarily with the notion of recovering that which is old and original, that which, like the fictional original manuscript, is almost, but not quite lost.

As a young man in the 1760s, Mackenzie had travelled to London to finish his studies, but after returning to Edinburgh – a move he described as a retreat from the pursuit of 'rank and wealth' – he settled into the town as a freemason and member of various clubs including the Mirror Club, which supported his exercises in periodical publication: *The Mirror* (1779) and *The Lounger* (1785–7).[79] For Julie Ellison, the clubbable Mackenzie can easily be aligned with other Scottish Enlightenment intellectuals including Hume and Smith, who, she believes, 'produce[d] the fictional paradigm of tenderhearted manhood.'[80] However, Maureen Harkin has forwarded the argument that *The Man of Feeling* contains numerous 'indictments of contemporary society' and she places Mackenzie in 'an older conservative-reactionary tradition', nearer to Tobias Smollett than to Hume and his contemporaries.[81] One such indictment of modernity is evident in the text's suspicion of the modern, professionalized military man. The modern military man first appears in absentia: early in the text Mackenzie insinuates that the nation's standing soldiers might be less than virtuous when he notes that the beggar's dog had been stolen 'from the serjeant of a marching regiment (and by the way he can steal too upon occasion.)'[82] This implication is made into an accusation as the text builds to the emotional climax of Harley's visit to London: the rescue of the fallen woman, Emily Atkins. Emily's downfall began with the death of her mother, but Atkins' inadequacies as a father are intimately connected to his attachment to the army, as his pride in 'the honour of a solider', leads to his failure to instil within his daughter conventional moral and

---

[79] Mackenzie quoted in Richard B. Sher, *The Enlightenment and the Book: Scottish Authors and their Publishers in Eighteenth-Century Britain, Ireland and America* (Chicago: University of Chicago Press, 2006), p. 120.
[80] Julie Ellison, *Cato's Tears and the Making of Anglo-American Emotion* (Chicago: University of Chicago Press, 1999), p. 12.
[81] Maureen Harkin, 'Mackenzie's Man of Feeling: Embalming Sensibility', *ELH*, 61.2 (1994), 317–40 (at pp. 332, 325).
[82] Henry Mackenzie, *The Man of Feeling*, ed. by Stephen Bending and Stephen Bygrave (Oxford: Oxford University Press, 2001), p. 18.

religious principles.[83] And yet, the fact that Atkins has not progressed through the ranks means that he has not been entirely corrupted by his professional service. Thus, when Atkins, who has searched for Emily since her disastrous elopement, arrives at her shabby lodgings, the father and daughter are redeemed together. Atkins' intention to avenge his daughter evaporates at the sight of her: 'his lip quivered, his cheek grew pale! his eyes lost the lightening of their fury! … He laid his left hand on his heart – the sword dropped from his right – he burst into tears.'[84] Here, Atkins is overtaken by his innate capacity for feeling, made manifest in quivering, blanching, and, finally, weeping, such that he exchanges the modern professional soldier for the 'natural' because emotional father.

Of course, Atkins' transition from a proud soldier to a feeling father should not be read as a criticism of all militarism. When Atkins drops the sword with which he intends to avenge his daughter's destroyer and instead weeps, the text moves from criticizing the modern military man to sentimentalizing the old hero. Harley's final disappointment in London comes when he hears that the piece of land that he tried but failed to secure has not been presented to a worthy recipient, such as 'some war-worn officer, who like poor Atkins had been neglected from reasons which merited the highest advancement; whose honour could not stoop to solicit the preferment he deserved; perhaps with a family…'[85] The virtue of that which is 'old' is reaffirmed at the pivotal point in the novel. A passenger in the stagecoach that is carrying Harley back to the country, a young military officer, manipulates the seating arrangements, securing a seat next to one of the ladies by accusing an older man of trying to do likewise: '"So, my old boy", said he, "I find you have still some youthful blood about you."' The young officer maintains a conversation with the lady, 'by a variety of oaths, a sort of phraseology in which he seemed extremely versant', and her husband, a grocer, then joins them in making fun of the older gentleman passenger, leading Harley to reprove them: 'Harley looked sternly on the grocer: "You are come, Sir", said he, "to those years when you might have learned some reverence for age: as for this young man, who has so lately escaped from the nursery, he may be allowed to divert himself." "Dam'-me, Sir", said the officer, "do you call me young?"'[86] Here, the once bashful and easily duped Harley shames the 'young' officer,

---

[83] Ibid., p. 42.
[84] Ibid., p. 50.
[85] Ibid., p. 56.
[86] Ibid., pp. 58–9.

and the officer's attempt to assert his maturity only further enhances the value of that which is authentically old.

While Atkins represents the modern military man, albeit one who, unlike the young officer in the stagecoach, has not been irredeemably sullied by the machinery of modern war, the text introduces 'old Edwards', upon whom Harley happens because they are returning to the same village, as the old hero. Edwards is not a professional soldier: he had been forced to volunteer for service in order to spare his son, who, having angered the local Justice of the Peace, had been targeted by an army press-gang. Whereas Atkins must drop his military pride so as to reconnect with his child, Edwards had turned soldier for sentimental reasons and so his militarism is proof of his sensibility. Harley encounters Edwards asleep on the ground, like 'one of those figures which Salvator [Rosa] would have drawn; nor was the surrounding scenery unlike the wildness of that painter's backgrounds … A rock, with some dangling wild flowers, jutted out above where the soldier lay.'[87] Mackenzie's choice of artist is significant here. In *Discourses*, Joshua Reynolds rather cautiously praises Rosa's 'peculiar cast of nature, which though void of all grace, elegance, and simplicity, though it has nothing of that elevation and dignity which belongs to the grand style, yet, has that sort of dignity which belongs to savage and uncultivated nature.'[88] With his reference to Rosa, Mackenzie presents Edwards as one at ease with that which is 'savage and uncultivated': he is absorbed by the landscape, the rock and wild flowers guard and decorate the soldier's body and a 'twisted branch' shades the face which bears 'marks of manly comeliness'. Harley is drawn to this 'natural' figure by instinct: he hails the old man in a fit of 'romantic enthusiasm' and offers to carry his heavy knapsack, deducing that, '"you seem to have served your country, Sir, to have served it hardly too; 'tis a character I have the highest esteem for."'[89] Edwards responds with tears of gratitude, a language both men understand.

If Mackenzie's old Edwards' recumbent pose seems similar to that of West's dying Wolfe, it is because he serves the novel as a model of old heroism, and like West's *Wolfe*, Mackenzie secures the new old hero by establishing a bond between him and a 'savage' other. In conversation with Harley, Edwards reveals that the army had taken him to India, where an 'old Indian' who had been taken prisoner engages his sympathy:

> "Oh! Mr. Harley, had you seen him, as I did, with his hands bound behind him, suffering in silence, while the big drops trickled down his shrivelled

---

[87] Ibid., p. 64.
[88] Joshua Reynolds, *Discourses*, ed. by Pat Rodgers (London: Penguin, 1992), pp. 144–5.
[89] Mackenzie, *The Man of Feeling*, pp. 64, 65.

cheeks, and wet his grey beard, which some of the inhuman soldiers plucked in scorn. I could not bear it, I could not for my soul."[90]

Unlike Smith's warrior-savage, whose ability to suffer in silence is evidence of his proto-polite self-discipline, Mackenzie's tearful old Indian displays what Ferguson claims is the essential human capacity for sentiment. Edwards' fellow-feeling for his fellow human forces him to act, and he incurs military punishment for freeing the captive. The text does not condemn Edwards for this; on the contrary, the treatment of the old Indian and old Edwards indicates that the modern army – a tyrannical institution, dedicated to the commercial nation's imperial ambition – little deserves Edwards' loyalty. Though the figure of the American Indian was closely associated in the mid- to-late eighteenth century with topical stories of 'savage' violence, this figure could also, as Ian Haywood argues, be forwarded as a victim of British imperialism.[91] Whereas Ferguson recommends that modern man look at the so-called savage as though looking in a mirror, Mackenzie's novel stages such an encounter between Edwards and the old Indian and both men immediately recognize that they are fellows in 'natural' feeling and in their powerlessness against Britain's modern military machine. For Ferguson, the expansion of the British Empire is a matter of decline and fall: he frequently refers to the collapse of the Roman Empire to illustrate that 'the admiration of boundless dominion is a ruinous error'.[92] The legacy of seventeenth-century civic-republicanism is evident in his argument that empires erode the liberty of the people because boundlessness discourages peoples from marshalling their military capacity for their collective interests. When Mackenzie's 'Man of Feeling' speaks of 'what he does not understand', that is, of Britain's imperial expansion in India, he likewise condemns the desire for conquest and domination. For Harley, the desire for empire forces an army of old Edwardses abroad to be officered by men for whom ' "the fame of conquest, barbarous as that motive is, is but a secondary consideration: [for] there are certain stations in wealth to which the warriors of the East aspire." ' It falls to Edwards to remind Harley that he ought to castigate only militarism motivated by greed:

"For you know, Sir, that it is not the fashion now, as it was in former times, that I have read of in books, when your great generals died so poor, that

[90] Ibid., p.70.
[91] Ian Haywood, *Bloody Romanticism: Spectacular Violence and the Politics of Representation, 1776–1832* (Basingstoke: Palgrave Macmillan, 2006), pp. 141–7.
[92] Ferguson, *Civil Society*, p. 88.

they did not leave wherewithal to buy them a coffin; and people thought the better of their memories for it: for if they did so now-a-days, I question if any body, except yourself, and some few like you, would thank them."[93]

Here, the text's civic ideology is fully apparent, for Mackenzie separates the modern military men who serve only for their own personal gain, men like Robert Clive and Warren Hastings, from the virtuous old soldiers who, like the great generals of former times, serve as better models for modern men.

Though Mackenzie offers the encounter between old Edwards and the old Indian as an episode that reveals the connection between them, the text only takes this point of connection so far. Julie Ellison has examined the tendency for American war veterans and slaves to be coupled as 'others' in Anglo-American sentimental fiction; in Mackenzie's text the veteran and the prisoner become the virtuous 'others' to the corrupt modern British 'self'.[94] Having liberated the old Indian, Edwards is dismissed from the army and left to make his own way home. This allows for an awkwardly coincidental reunion in which their roles are reversed, as the old Indian assists Edwards in recognition of his debt to him, but also of their common humanity: '"You are an Englishman", said [the old Indian], "but the Great Spirit has given you an Indian heart."'[95] However, the shift from North America to India, from warrior-savage to military prisoner, reveals something of the conceptual knottiness of the ties that bind the politics of old heroism to the culture of sensibility. According to Muthu, representations of the 'noble savage' were crucial in facilitating the humanitarianism of the antislavery movement, but they struggled to fully break away from 'dehumanizing exoticism'.[96] Markman Ellis has charted the role of the sentimental novel in the development of a 'new humanitarian sensibility' and he concludes that, as in the case of Mackenzie's treatment of slavery in his novel *Julia de Roubigné* (1777), such writing stopped short of any 'radical' agenda.[97] This point stands for *The Man of Feeling* also, for when Mackenzie sentimentalizes the fellow-feeling between Edwards and the old Indian he rejects new commercial/imperial identities and relationships, but not traditional hierarchies. Having replaced the American Indian of Ferguson and West's imaginations with a 'safer' figure – a prisoner of war,

---

[93] Mackenzie, *The Man of Feeling*, p. 77.
[94] Ellison, *Cato's Tears*, pp. 151–2.
[95] Mackenzie, *The Man of Feeling*, p. 70.
[96] Muthu, *Enlightenment Against Empire*, p. 12.
[97] Markman Ellis, *The Politics of Sensibility: Race, Gender and Commerce in the Sentimental Novel* (Cambridge: Cambridge University Press, 1996), pp. 49, 117.

not a warrior with weapons – Mackenzie ensures that Edwards remains the principal model for old heroism. After all, the chapter merely pauses for Edwards to recall his encounter with the old Indian and then moves on to focus on Edwards' relationship with Harley. Soon after introducing himself to Edwards, Harley, whose early life has been marred by an absent father, embraces the old man with familial tenderness: ' "Edwards", said he, "let me hold thee to my bosom; let me imprint the virtue of thy sufferings on my soul. Come, my honoured veteran! let me endeavour to soften the last days of a life worn out in the service of humanity: call me also thy son, and let me cherish thee as a father." '[98] Old Edwards is as much in need of a son as Harley is in need of a father. Having been left to work the land on his own, Edwards' son had been unable to produce enough to pay the rent, leading to his death and the abandonment of his children. Once Harley has hailed Edwards as a father, then, the text begins to piece together a traditional family structure, for as Edwards' new son Harley bridges the gap between Edwards and his grandchildren. Of course, the sentimental bond between Harley and the old veteran sweetens the narrative, but does not disguise how strongly, as Barbara Benedict states, it 'advocates a reform of manners that yet reinscribes the necessity of social control.'[99] The urgency of the text's underlying patriarchal agenda is fully disclosed when Harley provides the Edwardses with a home on his land, for this muddles Harley's place in the family order so as to install Harley as an exemplarily benevolent land-owner.[100]

As Lyn Festa observes, though sentimental literature 'upholds a common identity' for humanity, the 'vagrant affect' which wanders in this borderless space threatens a 'menacing usurpation of the self.'[101] In its concluding stages, Mackenzie's novel works to reimpose traditional borders. As important as the warmth of natural feeling is between old Edwards and the old Indian, the text concludes with fragments which ensure that male emotion is channelled towards normatively masculine ends. As Janet Todd has shown, the culture of sensibility 'stressed those qualities considered

---

[98] Mackenzie, *The Man of Feeling*, p. 71.
[99] Barbara M. Benedict, *Framing Feeling: Sentiment and Style in English Prose Fiction, 1745–1800* (New York: AMS Press, 1994), p. 117.
[100] Here, I concur with Robert Markley's argument that Mackenzie's novel construes sensibility as a form of aristocratic noblesse oblige which maintains the social hierarchy. See Robert Markley, 'Sentimentality as Performance: Shaftesbury, Sterne, and the Theatrics of Virtue' in *The New Eighteenth Century*, ed. by Felicity Nussbaum and Laura Brown (New York: Methuen, 1987), pp. 210–30.
[101] Lynn Festa, *Sentimental Figures of Empire in Eighteenth-Century Britain and France* (Baltimore: Johns Hopkins University Press, 2006), pp. 4, 6.

feminine in the sexual psychology of the time', and so by the second half of the century 'excessive emotion', to borrow Adele Pinch's key term, was increasingly held to be an index of effeminacy.[102] Although Harley has undergone a civic journey and, as 'son' and landowner, become suitably patriarchal and patrician, his sensitivity is such that he is unable to reveal his affection for the local paragon of female modesty, Miss Walton, and so dies without becoming a husband and father. Harley's impotence does not render the novel likewise, of course. Just as the old Indian does not replace old Edwards as the model for old heroism, so Harley's romantic failure ensures that the younger man does not replace the old hero as the ideal 'man of feeling'. Though Edwards plays little part in the final stages of the narrative, he remains the model father, a conclusion that encapsulates the text's call for a return to the 'natural' feelings that underpin the 'natural' social order.

If the capaciousness of the culture of sensibility was such that both the modern professional military man and the old hero could be forwarded as model men of feeling, the presence of the 'warrior-savage' in the mid-century culture of sensibility reveals much about the limitations of both arguments. Though Smith's argument that sympathy is a form of self-discipline contains within it the proto-constructionist argument that character – whether that of the warrior-savage or the modern military man – is cultural rather than essential, any progressive energy generated by these ideas is restricted by his adherence to a narrative of progress from rude savagery to modern polite civility. In contrast, Ferguson's *Essay* and Mackenzie's novel understand sentiment to be an essential human attribute that knows no difference between an old Indian and an old Edwards, but these texts also contain deeply essentialist commitments. As pointed as Mackenzie's criticism of the modern British soldier and modern British imperialism is, the celebration of fellow-feeling does little to disrupt conservative race, class, and, crucially, gender hierarchies.

---

[102] Todd, *Sensibility*, p. 110; Adele Pinch, *Strange Fits of Passion: Epistemologies of Emotion, Hume to Austen* (Stanford, CA: Stanford University Press, 1996).

CHAPTER 6

The Making of Military Celebrity
The Trials of Admirals Augustus Keppel and Hugh Palliser, 1778–1779

> All Men would live somewhere eternally if they could, and they affect to become Immortal even here on Earth. To have their Names perpetuated, was the true Spring of several great Mens Actions; and for that only end, have they patiently undergon all manner of Toil and Danger.[1]
>
> John Toland (1699)

The trials of the Hon. Augustus Keppel and Sir Hugh Palliser occurred during a period of heightened anxiety in Britain. For four years, Britain and American had been at war over the relationship between local political representation and centralized political authority.[2] The American patriots had proved to be hardier opponents than their paper strength promised and the British response had been slower and less decisive than its standing after the Seven Years' War merited.[3] In the spring of 1778, France entered into the war as America's ally and this brought with it the threat of French invasion, which, coupled with Britain's domestic socio-economic problems, fuelled, in Wilson's assessment of it, the fear that 'the existence of the nation was at stake.'[4] In response, the government embodied the militia using legislation brought in shortly after the trial of Admiral Byng, the period in which John Brown had attacked modern manners and called for a return to old heroism. Rooted in the anti-standing army account of the classical citizen-soldier, augmented by the turn to the chivalric gothic knight and reinforced by mid-century sensibility, the new

---

[1] [Toland], *The Militia Reform'd*, p. 83.
[2] H. T. Dickinson, 'Britain's Imperial Sovereignty: The Ideological Case against the American Colonists', *Britain and the American Revolution*, ed. by H. T. Dickinson (Harlow, Essex: Longman, 1998), pp. 64–96.
[3] Richard Middleton, *The War of American Independence, 1775–1783* (Harlow: Pearson, 2012); Stephen Conway, *The British Isles and the War of American Independence* (Oxford: Oxford University Press, 2000).
[4] Wilson, *The Sense of the People*, p. 253. See also Middleton, *The War of American Independence*, p. 109.

old hero remained a powerful model of military masculinity in the 1770s, but this was also a period that was also coming to understand its heroes as 'celebrities'.

Although fame was hardly a new idea in the eighteenth century, its dominant meaning underwent a profound shift in this period. When Toland argues that men should act with a view to their name being perpetuated after their deaths, he indicates that men ought to see fame as compensation for services rendered and not a state that should be desired for its own sake. The same understanding of fame emerges in responses to Byng's loss of Minorca. In *An Ode of Consolation Upon the Loss of Minorca* (1756), Blakeney, 'mark'd with Age and Scars' and wrapped in 'deep Thought' on his 'hopeless State', is assured by an 'antique Figure' that should he die at St Philip, he would become as famous as Hannibal.[5] This can be read alongside the anti-Byng poem *A Poetical Epistle from Admiral Byng* (1757), which characterizes the modern military man as one who cannot see the value in posthumous compensation: 'Byng' exclaims, '"when once my Glass of Life is broke, / the Shouts of Fame are all a Joke!"'[6] And yet, even at the end of the seventeenth century there are signs of change. In response to the argument that men (should) desire the kind of 'Toil and Danger' that leads to immortality, one anonymous pro-standing army author asserts, '*the Itch of Popularity is an Epidemical Disease, and Men often are tickled with Fame of any Kind, though purchac'd like that of* Erostratus, *viz. by throwing the* firebrand.'[7] Erostratus was executed for having committed the dreadful act of setting fire to the temple of Diana in Ephesus, but although the Ephesians decreed death to anyone who mentioned the arsonist's name, the decree served to publicize his actions. The author might be dismissing such 'fame' as the mere 'itch of popularity', a phrase that resonates with class snobbery, but the example points to what was going to become a new kind of fame in the eighteenth century: 'celebrity'.

As Leo Braudy and others have recognized, increasingly so in recent years, during the eighteenth century the idea that fame ought to be a posthumous reward was put under pressure by the idea that fame could be achieved in one's own lifetime.[8] The study of early celebrity has tended

---

[5] John Free, *An Ode of Consolation Upon the Loss of Minorca. Humbly Address'd to his Royal Highness, the Duke of Cumberland, &c* (London: R. Baldwin, 1756), pp. 5–6.
[6] *A Poetical Epistle from Admiral Byng, in the Infernal Shades, to his Friend L – A –, an Inhabitant on Earth* (London: J. Fuller, 1757), p. 3.
[7] *Remarks Upon a Scurrilous Libel*, unnumbered pages.
[8] Leo Braudy, *The Frenzy of Renown: Fame and its History* (Oxford: Oxford University Press, 1986); Fred Inglis, *A Short History of Celebrity* (Princeton, NJ: Princeton University Press, 2010).

to focus on artists, particularly actors, for as Cheryl Wanko states, studying the celebration of 'activities traditionally considered not very useful or important (such as singing or acting, in comparison to military prowess)' reveals the dynamics of early celebrity culture.[9] However, Claire Brock goes further and suggests that the new fame of the eighteenth century displaced the military hero: 'inaccessible and irrelevant, the hero of old was out of place in a society eager to embrace those who offer[ed] more quotidian, intimate forms of heroism', such as authors.[10] In contrast, this chapter suggests that the emergence of the new understanding of fame is more complex than a shift from dead military heroes to living literary or theatrical lions. Chris Rojek and others have observed that a celebrity is, rather than just has, a visual/textual presence in public.[11] At a time when the bourgeois public sphere was being challenged by the emergence of a popular public sphere, a military man could cultivate just such a presence. By tracking an affair that began with the publication of a defamatory letter in a newspaper, I argue that the eighteenth-century debate about the relationship between masculinity and militarism was profoundly affected by the very suitability of old heroism to the culture of celebrity. This study of the Keppel–Palliser affair reveals that Keppel projected a performance of old heroism into that culture and thereby undermined the status of the old hero as a model of 'natural' masculinity. In mapping the trials of Keppel and Palliser, then, this chapter argues that, by the second half of the eighteenth century the once clear division between the modern military man and the new old hero was becoming unsustainable.

Keppel's Victory

The trials of Keppel and Palliser followed a British naval engagement with the French in July 1778 at which Palliser had been Keppel's third in command. Keppel had been given control of the Channel Fleet and tasked to patrol off Ushant in order to protect British naval and merchant ships and to attack passing French vessels. After several weeks at sea, Keppel met

---

[9] Cheryl Wanko, 'Celebrity Studies in the Long Eighteenth Century: An Interdisciplinary Overview', *Literature Compass*, 8.6 (2011), 351–62 (at p. 352). See also Frank Donoghue, *The Fame Machine: Book Reviewing and Eighteenth-Century Literary Careers* (Stanford, CA: Stanford University Press, 1996); *Romanticism and Celebrity Culture, 1750–1850*, ed. by Tom Mole (Basingstoke: Palgrave Macmillan, 2007); *Theatre and Celebrity in Britain, 1600–2000*, ed. by Mary Luckhurst and Jane Moody (Basingstoke: Palgrave Macmillan, 2005).
[10] Claire Brock, *The Feminization of Fame, 1750–1830* (Basingstoke: Palgrave MacMillan, 2006), p. 6.
[11] Chris Rojek, *Celebrity* (London: Reaktion, 2001); Graeme Turner, *Understanding Celebrity* (London: Sage, 2004).

and engaged Admiral d'Orvilliers' Brest Fleet. This was not the tidiest of naval battles and neither nation could claim to have advanced its superiority: the French sustained higher casualties, but damage to British masts and sails prevented Keppel pushing for a victory.[12] The action had shown that the British fleet could defend the nation's coastline, however, and Keppel received the customary thanks from the king and the Admiralty.[13] The history of the inglorious battle off Ushant might have rested there, had an anonymous letter not appeared in the *General Advertiser, and Morning Intelligencer*, the key newspaper for the Whig Opposition, some three months later. The letter denounced Palliser in the boldest of terms: its author claimed that 'the principal cause of Mr Keppel's not reattacking the French at half past three in the afternoon (being at that time totally refitted from the damages sustained in the morning) was Sir H- P-'s not joining him, agreeable to the signal to form the line.'[14] Affronted by the accusation that he had disobeyed orders and thereby prevented the fleet from claiming victory, Palliser visited Keppel and demanded that he sign a pre-written statement to the contrary. Keppel refused to do so. Thus began the Keppel–Palliser affair, which deepened in early December during a debate in the Commons, where Keppel sat for Windsor and Palliser for Scarborough.

Like all military matters in the eighteenth century, the Keppel–Palliser affair was enmeshed in party politics; in fact, in J. H. Broomfield's opinion the disagreement led to 'a political feud unparalleled in British history.'[15] True, the admirals were closely associated with the rival parties. Having begun his military career in the 1730s, Palliser saw decades of active service before accepting an administrative role as comptroller of the navy in Lord North's Tory administration (1770–1782). It was through working closely with Lord Sandwich, the first Lord of the Admiralty that Palliser, the son of an army captain of no particular note, received a baronetcy and the position of Lieutenant-General of the Marines, a position Keppel had coveted. Keppel, the second son of the second Earl of Albemarle, was born into a militantly 'new' Whig family: the first earl had accompanied William to England in the Revolution of 1688. Having achieved the rank of rear-admiral in 1762 following the successful

[12] Middleton, *The War of American Independence*, pp. 115–6.
[13] Philip Stevens to Augustus Keppel, 2nd August 1778, National Maritime Museum, KEP/9.
[14] *The General Advertiser, and Morning Intelligencer*, Thursday 15th October 1778.
[15] J. H. Broomfield, 'The Keppel–Palliser Affair, 1778–9', *The Mariner's Mirror*, 47 (1961), 195–207 (at p. 203). See also David Franklin Wells, *The Keppel–Palliser Dispute, 1778–9: A Case Study in Eighteenth-Century English Politics*, unpublished manuscript, British Library, DSC qX22/9349.

Havana campaign, Keppel served as First Lord of the Admiralty in Lord Rockingham's short-lived Whig administration (1765–6). His naval and political identities remained closely linked throughout his career, and at the start of war with America, Keppel followed his party's line by refusing to serve directly against the colonists.[16] Keppel was so well known to be closely allied to the party that opposed the war that some commentators hypothesized that Palliser's charges had been created in concert with his allies in the ministry to blacken Keppel and by extension the Opposition. And yet, when the dispute about the battle off Ushant spilled over into the Commons, Sandwich – Palliser's patron, but also the man responsible for Keppel's appointment as commander-in-chief of the Channel Fleet – expressed his high regard for both admirals and countered calls for a more formal investigation by recalling the parliamentary inquiry that had preceded the trials of Mathews and Lestock some thirty years earlier:

> [That] enquiry raised a kind of commotion in the nation, every person almost taking one side or the other; and at the conclusion no one good purpose was answered, but the whole terminated to the dissatisfaction of the nation, and established no rule whatever, which might serve to lead or direct the conduct of naval commanders, or those serving under them, in future.[17]

Rather than seize on the Keppel–Palliser dispute as an opportunity for political point scoring, Sandwich seems to have been keen to put the matter to rest.

Though the Keppel–Palliser affair could not but involve party politics – John Crossland suggests that 'the political parties were determined to exploit the quarrel between these two aging and sick naval officers for their own advantage' – Sandwich's reference to the trials of Mathews and Lestock is an indication that there were broader issues at stake.[18] The earlier trials had contributed significantly to the Admiralty's attempts to secure modern militarism in the late 1740s, but such was the 'dissatisfaction of the nation' that the verdicts had also contributed to popularizing the old hero as a model military man. Unlike Palliser, Keppel had reason to remember this. In late 1747, just a year after the trials of Mathews and Lestock, Keppel,

---

[16] Piers Mackesy, *The War for America, 1775–1783* (Lincoln: University of Nebraska, 1964; repr. 1993), p. 202.
[17] *The Parliamentary Register, or, History of the Proceedings and Debates of the House of Commons* (London: J. Almon, 1779), XIV, p. 29.
[18] John Crossland, 'The Keppel Affair', *History Today*, 46.1 (1996), 42–8 (at p. 46).

then aged twenty-two, had faced a court martial for the loss of the ship *Maidstone*. The *Maidstone* had run aground in very poor weather while in pursuit of a much larger vessel, likely with a view to securing a handsome financial reward. It was a reckless act, and Keppel was called to account for the loss of a ship and many of the lives aboard it. The punishment for the loss of a ship was affected by the revision of the *Articles of War* in 1749, after which capital punishment was available at the court's discretion, but given that the older set of *Articles* allowed the court to award a fine or imprisonment, Keppel had reason to be worried. However, in the closing lines of a letter to his father written shortly before the trial, he makes only brief mention of the impending proceeding: 'I am at Portsmouth waiting to be tried for the loss of the Maidstone and then shall be in London til the Anson is ready for sea before which time I flatter myself with hopes of seeing you.'[19] In a letter to an unidentified correspondent he likewise eagerly anticipates commanding the sixty-gun *Anson*, a larger and more prestigious ship than the *Maidstone*, 'if I can come well off at my trial, which I don't apprehend can be otherwise.'[20] Given that Lestock had only recently been acquitted on the grounds that he had prioritized discipline over pursing the enemy, such optimism is surprising, but Keppel's confidence was rewarded. Keppel's judges restricted their enquiry to showing that the likelihood of striking rocks could not have been foreseen and that Keppel had done all he could to save lives.[21] In other words, they read the quest for a prize as an exercise in Lestockian professionalism.

The Lestockian Keppel of the 1740s re-emerges in documents concerned with the months prior to the battle off Ushant. In the spring of 1778, while the Channel Fleet was being readied for operation, Keppel had corresponded tersely with Sandwich in order to establish whether he, with limited numbers, would be expected to fight a combined French and Spanish fleet, should the Bourbon allies unite and attempt to invade Britain. Shortly after setting sail, Keppel captured intelligence that disclosed to him the superiority of the French fleet at Brest and this prompted him to turn back for reinforcements.[22] However, when making his defence to the court, he disavowed explicitly such Lestockian calculation, arguing that he had been thinking, not of discipline and risk, but of doing his duty: 'I have done my best and utmost, not merely to comply with an article of war

[19] Augustus Keppel to George Keppel, 4th and 6th October 1747, National Maritime Museum, KEP/X/7.
[20] Augustus Keppel, National Maritime Museum, MS 88/057.
[21] Court Martial Records, 4th April to 31st October 1747, National Archives, ADM 1/5290.
[22] Mackesy, *The War for America*, pp. 205–7.

(I should be ashamed that such a thing, at such a time could have engaged my thoughts) but to defend the kingdom.'[23] During the Commons debate Lord Mulgrave, captain of a ship in Keppel's division at the battle but also a member of Sandwich's Admiralty, asserted that the tightening of the *Articles of War* in the aftermath of the Toulon trials had been intended to ensure that admirals would be punished, rather than rewarded, for failing to do their utmost.[24] When standing before his judges, the fate of the Lestockian Admiral Byng might well have been uppermost in Keppel's mind. As a judge at Byng's trial, Keppel had been party to the court's verdict and then its ultimately unsuccessful recommendation that Byng be treated as an object of mercy. As the defendant at his own trial, Keppel must have realized that he was facing a charge that used the wording of the twelfth article of war, by which Byng had been executed. Certainly, Keppel was aware that an early publication had called for the leaders of the battle off Ushant to suffer Byng's fate.[25] Critics of both Lestock and Byng had attacked those admirals for penning excuses for failure and at his trial Keppel distanced himself from any such behaviour: 'I shall not be very uneasy, if I have been thought to have wrote a bad letter [by way of an official report after the battle], if I shall be found, as I trust I shall be found, to have done my duty in fighting the enemy.'[26]

Rather than follow Lestock's definition of discipline, as Byng had done, Keppel defended himself by claiming that he had shown simple and unwavering commitment to defending the kingdom. To strengthen his case, Keppel harnessed the explanatory power generated by a direct opposition or contrast, like that of Lestock and Mathews, Byng and Blakeney. Keppel declared:

> I am not to be considered in the light in which Sir Hugh Palliser seems to consider me, merely as an officer with a limited commission, confined to a special military operation, to be conducted upon certain military rules, with an eye toward a Court Martial, for my acquittal or condemnation, as I adhered to those rules, or departed from them. My commission was of a very different sort: I was entrusted with ample discretionary powers for the immediate defence of the kingdom ... Every thing which I did as an officer was solely subservient and subordinate to the great end of national defence. I manoeuvred; I fought; I returned to port; I put to sea; just as it seemed the best to me for the purpose of my destination. I acted on these principles

---

[23] *The Defence of Admiral Keppel* (London: J. Almon, 1779), p. 8.
[24] *The Parliamentary Register*, XI, p. 140.
[25] *The Defence of Admiral Keppel*, p. 12.
[26] Ibid., p. 17.

of large discretion, and on those principles I must be tried. If I am not, it is another sort of officer, and not one with my trust, and my powers, that is on trial.[27]

Here, Keppel frames his disagreement with Palliser as a contest between two types of military men: the one who is subordinate to external authority, and so preoccupied by the possibility of being called to a court martial, and the one who acts under his own discretion and so purely in the interest of the nation. It is Palliser, he argues, who believes that the role of the military officer is limited to a specific operation and executed in line with a given set of rules, that is, performed only as and when required. The officer who is truly dedicated to 'the great end of national defence' leads on his own and not by rule or council. This officer relies on his instincts and capacities, that which he carries with him because they inhere within him.

The Parliamentary Register records that in the early stages of the affair Keppel had been less willing to attack a fellow officer: '[Keppel] impeached no man of a neglect of duty, because he was satisfied that [Palliser] … had manifested no *want* of what was most essential in a British seaman – courage.'[28] Like Sandwich, Keppel seems to have initially wanted to close down further discussion of the disagreement with Palliser, but his language also shows an awareness of the potency of a certain key term: courage. Lestock had been accused of hiding cowardice behind a screen of discipline; Keppel was not to be so caught out: when asked by the court to account for whether or not he had given chase to some stray French ships the day after the battle, Keppel argued, 'I was resolved, as I have already before observed, in the introduction to my defence, not to sacrifice [my duty] to an empty show and appearance, which is beneath the dignity of an officer.'[29] With the words 'empty show', Keppel positions robustness and substance in opposition to the mere performance of militarism and masculinity, old heroism against the modern military man. In distancing the Lestockian modern military man, then, Keppel offered himself, not just as a particular 'sort of officer', but as a particular sort of 'man'. At his trial, Keppel asked his witnesses to specify who had engaged with the enemy, clarifying this at one point, 'what I mean by engaging, is like Men, not at a Distance.'[30] In forging a link between close combat and manliness, the admiral who had privately

[27] Ibid., pp. 7–8.
[28] *The Parliamentary Register*, XI, p. 90.
[29] *The Defence of Admiral Keppel*, p. 32.
[30] *Minutes of the Proceedings at a Court-Martial, assembled for the Trial of the Honourable Admiral Augustus Keppel, on a Charge Exhibited Against him by Vice-Admiral Sir Hugh Palliser, Baronet* (London: W. Strahan and T. Cadell, 1779), p. 24.

questioned whether or not he would be expected to fight against a superior enemy publically connects the willingness to fight, to risk life and limb, to masculinity. Keppel was to make the same point when giving evidence at Palliser's trial by describing their brother-in-arms Vice-Admiral Robert Harland's willingness to fight in terms of courage and manliness: 'as soon as the smoke cleared away, the first Thing that presented itself was the Vice-Admiral of the Red trying to weather me, coming along in a Manner that made my heart warm, for he was doing it like a Man.'[31] Harland then reinforced Keppel's argument that those who fought closely did so 'like Men' by recalling Palliser's movements as follows:

> I saw [Palliser's ship] when she came out of the cannonade, – my observation was, I think there was merit, and in firing [Palliser's ship] was equally entitled to that credit with other ships; ... but the Court must have observed, that in pursuing the enemy that day, a bold, a necessary, and a noble stroke of war was required, – where nothing but risque, as it appeared, could stop the French fleet from getting off; the great and decisive strokes of the day were to follow by closing the enemy, and fighting it out.[32]

Harland credits Palliser's ship for firing, but by suggesting that Palliser was incapable of producing a 'bold' and 'noble stroke' and thereby 'fighting it out', Harland indirectly accuses the admiral of lacking the kind of courage that becomes a man. Like Keppel, Harland seems to have been alert to the extent to which courts martial called officers to account for their understanding of the nature of militarism, and with it masculinity. Whereas Lestock and Byng had offered accounts of themselves as military men that had challenged essentialist conceptualizations of masculinity, both Keppel and Harland reinforced their versions of militarism by not questioning what it meant to be a 'man'. Given this, the fact that Keppel triumphed at his trial suggests that the Keppel–Palliser affair provided a clear victory for old heroism. This is less straightforward than it seems, however, for the change in Keppel's self-presentation over the course of the affair – from Lestockian calculation to innate courage – indicates that, by the 1770s, the debate had moved beyond the earlier bifurcation of modern militarism and old heroism.

---

[31] *Minutes of the Proceedings at a Court-Martial, assembled for the Trial of Vice-Admiral Sir Hugh Palliser, Bart* (London: W. Strahan and T. Cadell, 1779), p. 4.

[32] *An Authentic and Impartial Copy of the Trial of the Sir Hugh Palliser, Vice-Admiral of the Blue, held on Board his Majesty's Ship the Sandwich, in Portsmouth Harbour on Monday, April 12, 1779, and Continued by Several Adjournments to Wednesday the 5th of May, 1779* (Portsmouth: Messrs Wheldon and Co; Jos. White; H. Payne; R. Faulder; J. Fisk; M. Davenhill, 1779), p. 88.

Private Vices, Public Benefits

Although the basic outline of the courts martial of Keppel and Palliser is not unlike that of the trials of Mathews and Lestock – both sets of trials concerned a disagreement between a commander-in-chief and a subordinate officer following a lacklustre battle – the Keppel–Palliser affair ended rather differently, as Lieutenant-General William Keppel observed in a letter sent to his older brother on his acquittal:

> Thank God my brother has gained a complete victory over his enemys, and has come from Portsmouth in a more Triumphant manner than his most sanguine friends could have expected, for let you very properly observe the Court faction meant at his life and his honour, and had found a [...] Fool, who had served under Admiral Lestock in the Mediterranean, to perpetuate their black design– but the event turned out differently from Matthews' court martial. He was made a victim to party, my Brother [rose above] it for the honour of the whole Sea Profession, who, one and all, stood up for innocence, and shewed their Persecutors, though high in Power, that honour bound them in defiance of all Power and future favours.[33]

Here, William congratulates his brother for not falling victim to a ministerial plot fronted by a 'fool' who had served under and, so the letter implies, modelled himself on, Lestock. With this, William likens his brother to Mathews, the admiral who had been censured by his judges but celebrated by the public. He goes on to observe that Keppel's fellow 'sea profession[als]' were very aware of the importance of public opinion. Prior to Keppel's trial, twelve admirals, including the hero of the Seven Years' War, Edward Hawke, had written to the king to complain that the Admiralty had called a court martial on the basis of one man's grievance against another, but their letter also asserted that 'the honour of an officer is his most precious possession and best qualification; the public have an interest in it; and ... it is often impossible perfectly to restore military fame by the mere acquittal of a court martial.'[34] With this, the twelve officers define 'fame' not as posthumous reward for military service, but as a state determined by and within the popular public sphere.

As William Keppel's letter indicates, the trials of Keppel and Palliser offer an insight into the relationship between power and the people in

---

[33] William Keppel to Augustus Keppel, 19th March 1779, National Maritime Museum, MS 88/057.
[34] *The Trial of the Honourable Augustus Keppel, Admiral of the Blue Squadron, for a Charge of Misconduct and Neglect of Duty, Exhibited Against him by Vice-Admiral Sir Hugh Palliser* (Bath: R. Cruttwell, 1779[?]), p. xx.

the later eighteenth century. Just as Cardwell has argued that 'the Minorca demonstrations of late 1756 illustrate the existence of a vocally and visually rich tradition of extra-parliamentary political protest', so Wilson has identified a surge in public protest during the trials of Keppel and Palliser.[35] Nicholas Rogers agrees that the Keppel–Palliser affair reveals the increasing power of the popular public sphere: 'by the [1770s] there was a greater insistence upon the 'people' as the source of political authority … This change in the legitimacy of public opinion, something crucial to the full operation of the public sphere in the Habermasian sense of the term, was registered in the newspapers.'[36] According to Habermas, the growth of the newspaper press contributed significantly to changing the bourgeois public sphere – that small, closed world of rational-critical debate – into a larger, looser space dominated by a broader populace and its opinions. Habermas qualifies his argument by suggesting that the newspapers democratized 'information' only insofar as the sale of information would allow, but Hannah Barker contends that, by generating income from sales and advertising, the newspaper press freed itself from reliance on political patronage and was able to serve its own agenda.[37] The newspaper press, Barker argues, 'appealed to the English people en masse, presuming to speak both to them and for them, and in facilitating the exchange of information and ideas and providing a new institutional context for political action, it was instrumental in the development of public opinion and, with it, the political public sphere.'[38]

The Keppel–Palliser affair, beginning as it did with the publication of the anonymous letter in the Whiggish *General Advertiser, and Morning Intelligencer*, reflects the shift from a bourgeois public sphere to an increasingly powerful popular public sphere. The unsigned letter is prefaced by

[35] Cardwell, *Arts and Arms*, p. 67. Wilson's argues that the swelling 'of anti-administration sentiment out-of-doors marked one of the first convergences of extra-parliamentary political action with that of the [Whig] opposition.' *The Sense of the People*, p. 259. For the Opposition and public opinion see also James E. Bradley, 'The British Public and the American Revolution: Ideology, Interest and Opinion', *Britain and the American Revolution*, pp. 124–54 and *Popular Politics and the American Revolution in England: Petitions, the Crown and Public Opinion* (Macon, GA: Mercer University Press, 1986).
[36] Nicholas Rogers, 'The Dynamic of News in Britain During the American War: The Case of Admiral Keppel', *Parliamentary History*, 25.1 (2006), 49–67 (at p. 65). See also Rogers, *Crowds, Culture, and Politics*, p. 129.
[37] Habermas, *Structural Transformation*, p. 169; Hannah Barker, *Newspapers, Politics, and Public Opinion in Late Eighteenth-Century England* (Oxford: Clarendon Press, 1998).
[38] Hannah Barker, 'England, 1760–1815' in *Press, Politics and the Public Sphere in Europe and North America, 1760–1820*, ed. by Hannah Barker and Simon Burrows (Cambridge: Cambridge University Press, 2002), pp. 108–9. See also, *Newspapers, Politics, and Public Opinion*.

another letter, signed only by an 'E' who claims that the inflammatory document had been given to him or her at a coffee-house and that she or he had offered it to the newspaper in order to counter Sandwich's attempts, via hired scandalmongers, to 'cry down the *Whig Admiral* [Keppel], that he might raise his minion the V. Admiral [Palliser] upon the other's ashes.' This might be thought to confirm that the Keppel–Palliser affair was little more than a piece of party-political infighting, but the framing of the accusatory letter with another letter allows the newspaper to claim that it has put information that might have remained private into public circulation, and thus to position itself in opposition to official power. As John Brewer has pointed out, the rise of a bureaucratically sophisticated fiscal-military state in the eighteenth century generated an increasing amount of 'information' that was not designed for public consumption.[39] In the 1770s, for example, Sandwich managed an intelligence network of agents and ambassadors that fed back information regarding the French and Spanish navies.[40] With the use of the framing device, the *General Advertiser* responds to such control of information by indicating that it too has a network of informants.

If the publication of the accusatory letter is an indication of the growth of the popular public sphere, the way that Keppel and Palliser responded to it reveals how they wanted to position themselves in relation to that public. Crucially, in the early stages of the affair neither admiral was overly keen to contribute to the public circulation of information. It was Keppel's refusal to sign Palliser's pre-prepared statement that pushed Palliser to publish a lengthy account of his conduct at the battle, which began as follows:

> Having seen since my late arrival at Portsmouth, a very scandalous paragraph in the [General Advertiser, and] Morning Intelligencer of the 15th of last month … containing many gross falsehoods, calculated expressly for the purpose of wounding my reputation, and to represent me in a culpable light to the whole nation; and being well informed that injurious reports of the like nature have been industriously propagated for the same purpose by some malignant, wicked people, it becomes necessary for me, in order to vindicate my own conduct, to publish such particulars relating to the battle on that day, as may enable the public, who have a right to be fully informed of the truth in a matter of so much importance to them, to judge whether *I* was the cause of the French fleet not being re-attacked on that afternoon: I therefore request that you will publish the inclosed paper,

---

[39] Brewer, *The Sinews of Power*, pp. 181–204.
[40] Nicholas Tracy, *Navies, Deterrence and American Independence: Britain and Seapower in the 1760s and 1770s* (Vancouver: University of British Columbia, 1988), pp. 12–22.

containing the facts necessary to be known, for justifying me from the said foul aspersions. After the nation is in full possession thereof[,] if any individual, or if Parliament, or the nation at large, call for a public enquiry, I am ready to stand the issue of such enquiry; but I shall not answer any questions, or queries in newspapers, or otherwise.[41]

Although Palliser supports the public's right to be 'fully informed' about the battle, he states that he has written to the newspapers in order to correct falsehoods that are already in circulation and to offer only the 'facts' necessary to clear his reputation. In other words, Palliser makes it plain that he has submitted his account to the public unwillingly, and although he promises to respond to any enquiry, even from the 'nation at large', he refuses to conduct further dialogue through newspapers. Paradoxically, then, Palliser's explanatory letter in the *Morning Post*, like Byng's unsuccessful *Appeal to the People*, addresses the public while at the same time questioning the public's right to information.

Keppel's contributions to the Commons debate suggest that he instinctively felt very similarly. Keppel may have been behind the accusatory letter, but he made much of Palliser's decision to reply to it in print, noting peevishly that 'he had himself been frequently the subject of news-paper abuse; but he had not appealed to the public, nor refused to serve his country, when his services were demanded'. Rather than demonstrate any warmth towards the newspapers, Keppel's comment censures Palliser for allowing what had been written in the public press to rile him. *The Parliamentary Register* records that, Keppel objected most particularly to the fact that Palliser's agitation had put private matters into public hands:

> Admiral Keppel seemed to disapprove much of relating the private conversation [at which Palliser had asked Keppel to sign the statement], which had now been reported to the vice admiral, to have passed between them at his own house. He said, nothing of a nature merely private was a matter of public discussion … As to any insinuations or indirect charges, he knew not whence they came; for his part he had made none; nor did he know any part of the vice admiral's conduct deserving of censure; but his seeing the name of "Hugh Palliser", signed to a letter in the Morning Post.[42]

Keppel might have taken Palliser's decision to sign his name in the newspaper can be taken as a rebuke to the network of anonymous

---

[41] Palliser's letter was printed on Tuesday 3rd November 1778 in the *General Evening Post*, the *London Chronicle* and the *St James Chronicle or the British Evening Post*, and reprinted on Thursday 5th November in the *Morning Post and Daily Advertiser* and on Friday 6th November in the *Morning Chronicle and London Advertiser*.

[42] *The Parliamentary Register*, XI, p. 93.

and pseudonymous newspaper correspondents, but by objecting to the publication of a 'private conversation' and to the signing of the letter with a 'real' name, Keppel attempts to draw a firm line between public and private. The minutes of parliamentary sessions were published in the newspapers before appearing in *The Parliamentary Register*, and although the Opposition-leaning *General Advertiser* made no mention of Keppel's hostility to public information, the *Morning Post* noted his annoyance at seeing 'the name of "Hugh Palliser"' in print.[43] But if Palliser decisively turned his back on the popular public sphere in the early stages of the affair, the records of Keppel's trial indicate that he, ultimately, did not want to be seen to do likewise.

The position Keppel adopted during his trial is made clear in the following extract from the proceedings. Here, Palliser responds to Keppel's request to the court for permission to read his printed letter and to question him about it:

> SIR HUGH PALLISER. "If you have any questions to ask me, I will answer them in a proper place."
> ADMIRAL KEPPEL. "I do assure the Court I never will call on Sir Hugh Palliser as a private gentleman."
> SIR HUGH PALLISER. "I will answer no questions here, but in any other place, I will answer any question."
> COURT. "We must put an end to this sparring at each other."
> ADMIRAL KEPPEL. "Mine cannot be termed sparring for I declare I will not call on him as a private gentleman, but as he has called for my letters, and published his story to all the ladies and gentlemen present in a newspaper, I think he could not have received so good an answer as this trial has produced."
> SIR HUGH PALLISER. "I do object to my letters being read."[44]

Palliser's hostility to the request comes as no surprise: having in his letter refused to answer questions or queries by way of the newspapers, he refuses to provide answers that he must have known would be recorded by the short-hand writers and then published in newspapers and pamphlets. Keppel clearly understands what Palliser means by a 'proper place', as he refuses to call on Palliser as a 'private gentleman'. Indeed, the sarcasm in Keppel's comment that, having 'published his story', Palliser can

---

[43] *General Advertiser, and Morning Intelligencer*, Thursday 3rd December 1778; *Morning Post and Daily Advertiser*, Thursday 3rd December 1778.

[44] *An Authentic and Impartial Copy of the Trial of the Hon. Augustus Keppel, Admiral of the Blue, Held as Portsmouth on the 7th of January, 1779, and Continued by Several Adjournments to the 11th day of February, 1779* (Portsmouth: Messrs. Wheldon and Co; Messrs. Richardson and Urquhart; R. Faulder; J Fisk, 1779), pp. 351–2.

hardly refuse to provide an answer to the court, suggests that Keppel is less than enthusiastic about becoming a public person. And yet, by refusing to countenance conducting his dispute with Palliser in private, Keppel opposes privacy.

Although Keppel had initially refused to participate in the public sphere by providing a signed statement for the newspapers, the records of his trial show that he changed his position with regard to the public circulation of private information, and in so doing ensured that he could be seen as a 'public' person. When Palliser, acting as prosecutor, called for Keppel's private letters to Sandwich, Keppel seconded Palliser's request, claiming that, 'so far from having any Objection to what is proposed by the Vice-Admiral, there is not one Act in my Life that I do not wish may come before you – whether it is private or public.'[45] In another published record of the trial, the word 'private' is removed and this strengthens Keppel's claim that he is open to public scrutiny: 'there is not, I will assure you, a single transaction of my life that I do not wish to have made public.'[46] Palliser might have hoped to force Keppel to object to his private letters becoming matters of public record, but he succeeded only in damaging his own position, as his request pushed Sandwich, rather than Keppel, to refuse: 'I only beg Leave to mention, it certainly does seem to me, as I perceive it has to the Court, that private Letters are a very unusual Kind of Evidence to be given.'[47] The court interrupted this tense stand-off between Keppel, Palliser and Sandwich by ruling that private letters were inadmissible, but by this time the hostility shown by Palliser's patron to admitting private letters had served to enhance the impression that Keppel was a fully 'public' person. Keppel's cause received a further boost when the court asked Lord Mulgrave to state whether or not Keppel had tarnished the honour of the British flag. Mulgrave declined to provide an answer for the following reasons:

> I hope the Court will not press upon me to give my Opinions; I have always thought that the Opinions and Thoughts of Individuals were sacred: I have declined to my most intimate Friends giving any Opinion upon this Case ... Whether I am of Opinion that the Admiral was guilty of negligently performing his Duty, or no? does not become me as a Witness ... I am an injured Man, if I must answer that Question.

---

[45] *Minutes of the Proceedings ... Keppel*, p. 92.
[46] *An Authentic and Impartial Copy of the Trial of the Hon. Augustus Keppel*, p. 246.
[47] *Minutes of the Proceedings ... Keppel*, p. 93.

In response, a member of the court warned Mulgrave that his refusal would be judged harshly by the public: 'My Lord, the Language you have made use of to this Court, will appear without Doors in a very strange Light.'[48]

Just as Keppel had transformed into an old hero during his trial, so he metamorphosed into a 'public' person, someone prepared, in fact eager, to provide those 'without Doors' with information about his private self. The two identities supported each other: his claim to old heroism reinforced and was reinforced by his apparent willingness to be open to public scrutiny, since both were claims to be more than mere surface or 'empty show'. To be a natural old hero and an open, public person was to be doubly undisguised, genuine, authentic and so with these twin performances Keppel courted both his judges and public opinion. That said, the details of the affair that expose his performances undermine those performances. For example, during the trial, the apparently publicly-orientated Keppel expressed his annoyance at the court taking evidence from those he deemed to be inferior in rank and status. Keppel's witnesses included two admirals and twenty captains, but only six lieutenants and four masters. He seems to have found the latter particularly irksome, as he refused to cross-examine a warrant officer, Robert Christian, master of the *Ramillies*, stating: 'as I shall not condescend to measure my Conduct as Commander in Chief of the Fleet, by the Opinion of a Master of a Ship, I shall put no Questions to the Witness at all.'[49] Keppel returned to this grievance when putting his defence to the court by noting that 'masters have been called to give their opinions on the higher departments of command. Higher authorities should have been taken.'[50]

According to one account of the trial, Keppel 'went to his trial with the *vox populi* in his favour almost to a man'.[51] It was customary for naval courts martial to take place on ships, but a last-minute bill had been passed to allow Keppel's trial to take place on land and when Keppel left the court, accompanied by eminent military and political figures, including admirals Harland and Campbell, the Duke of Cumberland and Lord Effingham, Rockingham and Richmond, he was met by an immense cheering crowd. According to another account of this, Keppel, emerged from the court to 'receiv[e] the heart-felt gratulations of the multitude. He … walked home in procession, preceded by a band of music, and attended by the Admirals

---

[48] Ibid., p. 91.
[49] Ibid., p. 95.
[50] *An Authentic and Impartial Copy of the Trial of the Hon. Augustus Keppel*, p. 272.
[51] *The Trial of the Honourable Augustus Keppel* (Cruttwell), p. xviii.

and Captains of the fleet.' However, the details, perhaps inadvertently, reveal a rather more segregated celebration:

> The noblemen and gentlemen had light blue ribbons in their hats, which they carried in their hands, with the word 'KEPPEL' inserted in gold letters, presented to them for the occasion by the Duchess of Cumberland, the Duchess of Richmond, the Marchioness of Rockingham, the Countess of Effingham, and other ladies of fashion. The band played "He comes, he comes, the hero comes", while the whole concourse, noblemen, gentlemen in the procession, and ladies from the windows, supplied the vocal part, and the crowd closed each period of the harmony with a choral cheer.[52]

The 'whole concourse' are said to have been signing what was a very popular tune, but the scene is one of social hierarchy rather than harmony. The elite men and women – who have exchanged blue ribbons with gold letters between themselves – sing the 'vocal part'. This differentiates them from the general crowd, whose cheers create a simple accompaniment, more like the musicians' instrumental parts than the singers' vocal embellishments.

The views of the blue-ribboned ladies and gentlemen can be imagined from comments made in private letters by one Frederick Robinson to his brother Thomas Robinson, then British ambassador to Madrid. There can be no doubt where Robinson's sympathies lie: 'I am a Keppelist in thinking that Sir Hugh Palliser's accusations were scandalous and ill-founded, [and] that previous to it and immediately after the trial Keppel's conduct was that of a great[,] an able and honest man'.[53] However, his first letter to include mention of Keppel does so as part of a short summary of recent happenings in town:

> I think the Queen cannot come out again[.] [T]he Lady's heads are something lower than they were last winter[.] There are not many people in town; not a few are at Portsmouth[.] [A]ll reasonable people are agreed in disapproving of those who are gone there as supporters of Admiral Keppel, prejudging his cause, and giving the appearance of a popular contested election to a most solemn trial.[54]

It is significant that Robinson is led to the subject of the 'solemn trial' by reflections on the queen's pregnancy and changing fashions in ladies' hairstyles. Elsewhere Robinson identifies himself as a member of the polite

---
[52] *An Authentic and Impartial Copy of the Trial of the Hon. Augustus Keppel*, pp. 414, 415.
[53] Frederick Robinson to Thomas Robinson, 16th March 1779, Bedfordshire and Luton Archives and Records Service, L 30/14/333/188.
[54] Frederick Robinson to Thomas Robinson, 15th January 1779, L 30/14/333/170.

world: his letters make reference to artists – including a friend of Keppel's, Joshua Reynolds, to whom Robinson was distantly related by marriage – and society events. While Keppel's court martial is of interest to the man who is interested in ladies' hairstyles, Robinson seems to regard Keppel as one in whom he can be interested because he really belongs to his sphere. Robinson records that, when news of the acquittal reached London, '[the illumination] was universal. The mob broke the windows of Lord North's, Lord Germaine's, Lord Mulgrave's and Lord Bute's houses, most of those in the Admiralty were destroyed as was Capt Hood's Harley Street and the inside of a house in Pall Mall where Sir Hugh Palliser did live was entirely pulled to pieces.'[55] Some eleven days later, such apparently disorderly goings-on were still going on: Robinson records that, on leaving a dinner, 'we heard a great noise and … perceived that Admiral Keppel was returning from his dinner in the city attended by a mob who insisted on an illumination in all the streets through which they passed and broke the windows before the light could be got ready.' Robinson terms this an 'instance of the tyranny of the people', and a few days later he writes approvingly that Keppel had declined a dinner invitation on the basis that the mob had grown uncontrollable.[56]

Keppel may have courted the popular public sphere with his performances of old heroism and public person, but to Robinson at least the admiral belongs to the polite social world, in which 'true' character was not required. Fittingly, Robinson's final letter to mention Keppel ends by quoting a sermon on 'character' in private and public life: '"it is quite astonishing and unaccountable that the very same persons who in private life are considerate, reasonable, impartial, good natured and humane will in publick affairs be impetuous, [vehement], acrimonious, ungenerous and unjust."' The author of the sermon writes against the Mandevillian argument that public and private characters need not be harmonized, but Robinson breezily dismisses the sermon's moralizing: 'you will say that that when I begin to quote sermons it is high time that I should conclude to adieu[.] [M]y Dearest Brother believe me to be with unfeigned and constant affection, publickly and privately, ever and ever, Geo F R.'[57] In assuring his brother of both his public and private affection, Robinson indicates that, for him, his brother and those in their circle, public and private characters should never be assumed to be the same.

---

[55] Frederick Robinson to Thomas Robinson, 12th February 1779, L 30/14/333/178.
[56] Frederick Robinson to Thomas Robinson, 23rd February 1779, L 30/14/333/181.
[57] Frederick Robinson to Thomas Robinson, 26th February 1779, L 30/14/333/182.

The Real Deal

Keppel's transformation into an old hero and public person might not have been so successful, had it not been for the scandal that emerged during his trial with regard to Alexander Hood, a captain in Palliser's division, and his altered log-book. As the primary record of signals and movements, ship log-books contained what should have been a complete and reliable record of fact. At the start of Keppel's trial, the master of each ship had been required to submit his log to the court and to swear to its veracity. The master of Hood's ship, the *Robuste*, had refused to take the oath, and when Hood appeared as a witness for the prosecution the state of his log-book became a major issue. Hood admitted that he had ordered alterations to be made to the log, but he sought to justify this on the basis that, '[they were] not done, Sir, in private but known to every Officer in the Ship. It was done to set forth a fair and faithful Representation of the Transaction on the 27th July.' In arguing that the log had not been altered in 'private', meaning without the master's knowledge, Hood defines 'public' in a way that jars with the idea of a public 'without Doors'. Hood went on to openly challenge the legitimacy of this public when giving his evidence:

> Sir, I stand here an attacked Man; from the 11th *August* last, to the present Hour, my Honour has been wounded. In Papers of that Date, I was put under Arrest for Disobedience of Orders. In other Papers, I was broke: since which, Letters have been circulated to the greatest Characters in the Kingdom, charging the Rear Division with the Loss of that Day. The Words are from the Information I have received from one of the First Men in the Kingdom, that had the Rear Division done their Duty Half as well as the Van and Centre, a complete Victory would have been obtained; since which, there have been many anonymous Publications which I very much despise. But, Sir, I became alarmed greatly when in a public Assembly the whole of that Division seemed to be aimed at.[58]

Hood's statement echoes Palliser's printed letter, but Hood goes beyond Palliser's refusal to conduct his affairs in the newspapers as he harangues the press for issuing false reports, with the implication that, in 'arresting' and breaking him, they were reaching so far beyond themselves as to usurp the disciplinary power held by the Admiralty.

In his examination of Hood, Keppel attempted to prove that the witness had conspired with Palliser to conceal the facts of the battle by altering his log-book. Hood freely admitted that his friendship with Palliser had included an

---

[58] *Minutes of the Proceedings ... Keppel*, p. 27.

exchange of letters in the months leading up to the trial, but he claimed that they had not discussed the trial. In order to confirm that they had, in fact, colluded, Keppel pushed Hood on when exactly the changes had been made to the log:

> Q. When you ordered the Alterations and Corrections to be inserted, had you not heard of Admiral *Keppel's* Court-Martial?
>
> A. I had not heard of Admiral *Keppel's* Court-Martial, but it was rumoured here.
>
> Q. What do you mean by a Rumour of a Court-Martial which you had never heard of?
>
> A. What I mean by a Rumour is, that a great many People were talked of to be tried, as common Conversation.[59]

Hood's attitude to rumour is significant. According to Ann Dean, spoken information was integral to print media in the eighteenth century: '[newspapers] allowed readers to "overhear" the whispers and reports that constituted political information …, and they provided those readers with ample material for speculation and conjecture.'[60] Having already criticized the newspapers, Hood differentiates between official, authorized information and the public circulation of unofficial information. However, Hood's distinction between reliable because official information and mere rumour was undermined by the president of the court, Sir Thomas Pye: 'I believe, if you recollect, it was very well known at that Time, though not officially, that Mr. *Keppel* was to be tried.'[61] The division between those prepared to credit rumour and those opposed to its currency deepened when a further log-book scandal came to light: the removal of the pages concerned with the battle from Palliser's ship's log. Convinced that the master of the *Formidable*, William Forfar, had been coached by Palliser in advance of his appearance in court, Keppel asked Forfar when he came to know that the court had discovered a problem with the *Formidable*'s log. Forfar replied: 'I heard it in a Shop Yesterday- a Woman in a Shop telling another Person, that there had been some Leaves torn out of the *Formidable*'s Log-Book, which was the first I heard of it.'[62] Forfar's explanation relies on the legitimacy of rumour in order to deflect the accusation of a conspiracy. Whether or not he had first heard about the log in a shop, he appealed to the public

---

[59] Ibid., p. 34.
[60] Ann C. Dean, 'Court Culture and Political News in London's Eighteenth-Century Newspapers', *ELH*, 73.3 (2006), 631–49 (at p. 647).
[61] *Minutes of the Proceedings … Keppel*, p. 35.
[62] Ibid., p. 68.

circulation of unofficial information and no member of the court openly questioned this. As a repository for official information, a ship's log-book was supposed to contain a record of the 'truth', but the log-book scandals revealed that rumour might be more truthful than official information, or at least, that the popular public sphere could determine, rather than simply receive, 'truths'.

On closer inspection, then, the records of Keppel's trial say less about the solidity of old heroism – as a model for a particular military man and a vehicle for a particular conception of the 'real', essential 'nature' of masculinity – than they do about the quiet collapse of earlier polarization of model military men at a time when the public was coming to know its strength, and to make that strength manifest, through the culture of celebrity. According to Leo Braudy, the rise of a new kind of fame in the eighteenth century can be understood as the rise of a new kind of status, one that did not need to be underpinned by traditional sources of power: 'once the validation of a class distinction', Braudy writes, fame became 'not only distinguishable from class but perhaps even opposed to it.'[63] However, if celebrities break, as well as break away from, old class distinctions, the public makes demands upon those whom it ennobles. As Richard Dyer argues, a celebrity must offer an 'irreducible core of inner individual reality', that is, this core must be exteriorized so as to be available for public inspection. In other words, she or he must become a 'private sel[f] in public'.[64] As already indicated, Keppel seems to have done just this. Despite initially refusing to participate in the public exchange of private letters, Keppel began his defence to the court by proclaiming, 'I now stand before you, not merely to save my life, but for a purpose of infinitely greater moment – to clear my fame.'[65] Here he acknowledges that the court will examine his behaviour as a military officer, even noting that the charges could lead to a capital punishment, but he also refers to this as a trial of his reputation, using 'fame' where he might have said 'name'.

Of course, a culture that rewards authenticity in order to establish its own legitimacy is inherently liable to mistake crafted performance for 'real' substance. According to P. David Marshall, 'the celebrity is one form of resolution of the role and position of the individual and his or her potential

---

[63] Braudy, *The Frenzy of Renown*, p. 371.
[64] Richard Dyer, *Heavenly Bodies: Film Stars and Society*, 2nd ed. (London: Routledge, 1986; repr. 2004), pp. 10, 12.
[65] *An Authentic and Impartial Copy of the Trial of the Hon. Augustus Keppel*, p. 272. See also, 'I stand here for my fame, as well as for my life, and for my station in the Navy', *The Defence of Admiral Keppel*, p. 5.

in modern society. The power of the celebrity, then, is to represent the active construction of identity in the social world.'[66] Put differently, the individual who opens his or her private self to public scrutiny cannot but 'perform' that self in exchange for celebrity status. Furthermore, the mechanisms that facilitate the exchange also complicate any easy connection between celebrity and authenticity. As Tom Mole explains, celebrity became possible when three components came together: a 'confessional author', a 'curious reader' and, most importantly, 'an industry' created by those seeking to profit from print.[67] The industry – Rojek prefers the term 'cultural intermediaries' – forges a relationship between the confessional individual and the curious readers, creating and sustaining, Mole argues, 'an impression of unmediated contact'.[68] For Eric Eisner, this was actually 'impossible intimacy', not just because the individual could exercise some control over his or her confessions, but also because of the commercialization of access to those confessions.[69] If, as Marshall puts it, 'celebrities are manifestations of the organization of culture in terms of democracy and capitalism', they function in the absence of rigid categories for social identity as standard bearers for social groups united primarily by limited consumer choices. The culture of celebrity may be a manifestation of the power of the non-bourgeois public sphere, but in a capitalist system '[the] celebrity as public individual who participates openly as a marketable commodity serves as a powerful type of legitimation of the political economic model of exchange and value', within which the 'celebrity sign is pure exchange value cleaved from use value', and so, Marshall argues, the 'centre of false value'.[70]

As much as Keppel's performances of old heroism and public person benefitted from others' efforts to protect their private selves and their altered log-books, his claim to be the 'real' deal was reinforced by 'cultural intermediaries', specifically the publishers of commercially produced

---

[66] P. David Marshall, *Celebrity and Power: Fame in Contemporary Culture* (Minneapolis: University of Minnesota Press, 1997), p. xi. See also David Gritten, *Fame: Stripping Celebrity Bare* (London: Allen Lane, 2002).

[67] Tom Mole, *Byron's Romantic Celebrity: Industrial Culture and the Hermeneutic of Intimacy* (Basingstoke: Palgrave Macmillan, 2007), p. 2.

[68] Rojek, *Celebrity*, p. 10; Mole, *Byron's Romantic Celebrity*, p. 22.

[69] Eric Eisner, *Nineteenth-Century Poetry and Literary Celebrity* (Basingstoke: Palgrave Macmillan, 2009), p. 13. See also Mole, *Byron's Romantic Celebrity*; Shearer West, 'Siddons, Celebrity and Regality: Portraiture and the Body of the Ageing Actress', in *Theatre and Celebrity in Britain*, pp. 191–213; Claire Knowles, 'Hazarding the Press: Charlotte Smith, the *Morning Post* and the Perils of Literary Celebrity', *Romanticism*, 20.1 (2014), 30–42.

[70] Marshall, *Celebrity and Power*, pp. 246, x–ix. See for example, Felicity Nussbaum, 'Actresses and the Economics of Celebrity, 1700–1800', in *Theatre and Celebrity in Britain*, pp. 148–68.

reports of the trial proceedings. As Forfar's evidence to the court indicates, pieces of information about Keppel's trial circulated in various ways before and during the trial. Several newspapers followed the proceedings in detail: the *General Advertiser, and Morning Intelligencer*, perhaps unsurprisingly, but also the *Public Advertiser*, the *London Evening Post* and *Lloyd's Evening Post*. There were numerous short-hand writers in the courtroom, a fact that troubled Captain Digby of the *Ramillies* who complained that they were writing down his words in their own way and for their own ends. The court could only reassure him that their clerks were 'to receive no information from the short hand writers; the court has no connection with them.'[71] By publishing information about the trial, newspapers provided access to the closed proceedings in advance of the publication of the official account in the standard authorized form, the version taken from the judge advocate's notes and published by the 'lord Commissioners of the Admiralty'. However, after the trial alternatives to the official text, *Minutes of the Proceedings*, could compete in the marketplace for print. Four other versions of Keppel's trial have survived the passage of time, assuming the numerous editions published by R. Cruttwell, publisher and shareholder in the *Bath Chronicle*, are counted as one text. Cruttwell sold his version of the trial through numerous booksellers, including two based in London: five shillings if bought from W. Goldsmith in Paternoster Row, but only two shillings and six pence if bought from C. Etherington at St. Paul's Churchyard. It is possible that Cruttwell had been motivated to publish an account of the trial by party-politics: his brother, William, clearly had strong political sympathies given that he started a provincial newspaper in Sherborne as a rival to a local publication with strong Whig sympathies. However, Cruttwell's pricing structure and distribution strategies give cause to suggest that he responded to the affair first and foremost as a businessman.

The fierceness of the competition for a share of the Keppel market can be gauged from the quantity of small mistakes, such as errors with names and dates, in the four unauthorized versions of the trial, but also from their use of prefaces and appendices. Cruttwell's version, for example, offers a narrative of the events preceding the trial, created by pulling together pieces from newspapers in the manner of a provincial paper borrowing from the London gazettes. But though each competitor in the market tried to offer something different, when seen as a group it is apparent that they all make

---

[71] *The Trial of the Honourable Augustus Keppel*, (Cruttwell), p. 22.

a virtue of their status as unofficial publications.[72] By offering records of the whole trial, but with extra details, particularly details that lifted the veil of formality, the unofficial versions could claim to be the more truthful. For example, whereas the officially sanctioned *Minutes of the Proceedings* concealed the judges' identities by declining to specify which member of the court was speaking at any point, Cruttwell's version went so far as to record individuals' off-the-cuff comments: 'Admirals Montague and Arbutnot said, they did not care sixpence in this case for law: we come here to do justice, and hope, in God's name it will be done.'[73] Cruttwell also shows that tempers started to fray towards the end of the month-long trial, noting that Captain Duncan complained to the court about the tediousness of the proceedings:

> Mr. President, I must beg that we have no more examination of masters as to log-books; we have been upwards of an hour trying the master of the Queen, and not one point to the purpose of the trial we sit here for. The log-books were delivered in for our inspection, and if the prosecutor examines more witnesses the same as the last, I must beg the court to withdraw.[74]

Similarly, *An Authentic and Impartial Copy of the Trial of the Hon. Augusts Keppel*, records that 'Admiral Arbutnot was suddenly overcome with the heat of the Court, and obliged to retire for some time' and that Sir John Lindsay had to be carried out of the court by two men on account of his gout.[75] Such candid additions add little to the record of the legal substance of the case, but they appeal to an audience that values newspaper correspondence and rumour.

The close relationship between the unofficial accounts of the trial and the wider print industry is amply demonstrated in the interplay between one of the versions of the trial and a 'pro-Keppel' pamphlet. *An Authentic and Impartial Copy of the Trial* is the only version to record a brief exchange between the two admirals on the seemingly trivial subject of smiling: Palliser asked the court to 'take notice that the prisoner smiles' and Keppel responded, 'does the court preclude me that? It is my natural countenance.'[76] This detail forms the basis for a pamphlet entitled *The Indictment, Trial, and Condemnation, of Admiral Keppel, for Knowingly Bringing into the Court-Martial his Own Natural Countenance, to the Great*

---

[72] Ibid.
[73] Ibid., p. 18.
[74] Ibid., p. 130.
[75] *An Authentic and Impartial Copy of the Trial of the Hon. Augustus Keppel*, pp. 242, 349.
[76] Ibid., p. 149.

Confusion of Sir Hugh Palliser (1779). The pamphlet imagines Keppel on trial for maintaining a 'natural countenance' during the court martial. Keppel is called by Palliser to answer five charges relating to his natural countenance, but a lawyer defends Keppel's 'steadiness of countenance, which could not be wrought *into confusion* ..., as it is the native result of conscious innocence', and commends 'the Admiral's amiable qualities as a man'.[77] In other words, the author defines 'natural' as open, genuine, authentic, and with this, the pamphlet parades its, as much as Keppel's, calculated investment in 'truth'.

While the versions of Keppel's trial participated in the circulation of unauthorized and unofficial information which sustained and legitimized the popular public sphere, these texts also participated in the culture of celebrity by marketing the possibility of genuine intimacy between an authentic individual and the curious public, and in so doing undermined that possibility. This doubleness is apparent in the spat between the publishers of two accounts of the trial that both claimed a personal relationship with Keppel. *The Proceedings at Large of the Court-Martial*, published by John Almon, claimed to have been 'taken in short hand, by W. Blanchard, for the Admiral and published by his permission.'[78] *The Trial of the Honourable Augustus Keppel*, as taken down by Thomas Blandemor, claimed to have been produced at the request of 'many Gentlemen of the Navy, and several other very respectable characters, the friends of the Honourable Admiral Augustus Keppel'.[79] The tension between the two camps is evident in an edition of the *London Chronicle* which printed advertisements side-by-side in which they attacked the other. The Blanchard/Almon advert alerts the public to an imposter publication – one that replaces 'Blanchard' with 'Blandemor' – and desires the public to know that the Blanchard text is 'the only Trial published with the Admiral's knowledge and permission, and that the Admiral's Defence, Letters and Papers, have all been examined by George Rogers, Esq., the Admiral's Secretary. No other Edition will, or

---

[77] The Indictment, Trial, and Condemnation, of Admiral Keppel, for Knowingly Bringing into the Court-Martial his Own Natural Countenance, to the Great Confusion of Sir Hugh Palliser (London: J. Johnson, 1779), pp. 38, 62.

[78] *The Proceedings at Large of the Court-Martial, on the Trial of the Honourable Augustus Keppel, Admiral of the Blue. Held on Board his Majesty's Ship Britannia, on Thursday, January 7th, 1779* (London: J. Almon, 1779).

[79] *The Trial of the Honourable Augustus Keppel, Admiral of the Blue Squadron, at a Court Martial held on his Majesty's ship Britannia, in Portsmouth Harbour, on Thursday 8th January 1779, on Charges Exhibited by Sir Hugh Palliser, for Misconduct and Neglect of Duty* (Portsmouth: Messrs J. Wilkes, Breadhower and Peadle, 1779).

can, contain authentic copies of these Papers.' In reply, the advert for the version produced by the 'friends of Admiral Keppel' includes an affidavit from Blandemor and a statement to expose 'the bare-faced and matchless effrontery of W. Blanchard, in publicly asserting [Blandemor] to be an Impostor, [who is] endeavouring to impose on the public, by personating [Blanchard], and pretending the copy [Blandemor] has taken of this Trial, to be the same as published by Almon – A most ingenious mode of profiting at the expense of other people's credit.' Though, on the surface, these advertisements are concerned to establish the reality of their editors' identities and relationships with Keppel, as Blandemour's final point reveals, the underlying issue is one of credit. By raising the issue of 'credit', the advert claims to be offering something reliable, that is, something the public can believe to be true, but also something they can purchase. The advert states that Blandemor's text was printed at a Portsmouth press, 'erected for the purpose' by Messrs. J Wilkes, Breadhower and Peadle, and that, 'it may be proper to inform the Public, that this Edition [is] published by the above gentlemen at their own proper expense, in order to preserve an unbiased and impartial state of the evidence on this extraordinary affair.' This cannot but suggest that the backers for Blandemor are largely concerned with recouping printing costs.[80]

The tussle between these two publications indicates how far such texts reinforced the importance of the 'real' while simultaneously undermining any such thing. Given that both claim to be the only text to have a close association with the admiral himself, neither can be trusted. As such, these texts are not unlike a range of other mid-century products that marketed Keppel as a celebrity. Alan McNairn suggests that '[General] Wolfe was blessed in departing this world just at the moment when it became possible to reach a huge audience through print, music, theatre, pictures, and other affordable consumer goods.'[81] This is true enough, though it would be more accurate to note that the manufacturers of such items were somewhat luckier than the dead soldier.[82] Like Wolfe, Keppel became a commodity within the popular public sphere and others benefitted from this. Various ceramic goods were produced at the time of the trial, many featuring the pro-Keppel slogan 'Keppel forever'. Temporarily unable to access this market for lack of a suitable picture to copy, Josiah Wedgwood

---

[80] *The London Chronicle*, Thursday, 4–6th March, 1779.
[81] McNairn, *Behold the Hero*, p. xii.
[82] Benjamin West was one such beneficiary of this system, for as Solkin notes, West's *Wolfe* was fundamentally 'consumer-orientated'. Solkin, *Painting for Money*, p. 211.

lamented being unable to 'sell *thousands* of Keppels at any price': '"Oh Keppel Keppel – Why will you not send me a Keppel. I am perswaded if we had our wits about us ... we might have sold £1000 worth of this gentleman's head."'[83] Like pieces of printed china, the multiple printed versions of Keppel's trial were part of the sale of intimacy, but rather than provide access to the 'real' person, all such products contributed to opening up the space between the apparently confessional individual and the curious public. In such a climate, old heroism could all too easily be performed by one whose sympathies seem to side with Lestock's discipline and Robinson's polite society at least as much as with the popular public sphere.

The End to Opposition?

The triumph of the 'natural' Keppel in the Keppel–Palliser affair attests to the continued allure of old heroism at a time when, Conway concludes, the demands that the American war placed on British society 'bolstered traditional attitudes' to gendered behaviour.[84] Though still firmly rooted in civic humanism, the old heroism of the mid-century had been reinforced by the return to the gothic past and turn to sensibility, both of which emphasized the 'nature' of masculinity by construing the ability to take up arms for the nation as an essentially masculine capacity. And yet, it is equally fair to say that Keppel's claim to old heroism contributed to undermining the once clear division between the modern military man and the old hero, for at a time when Britain was fighting for and against its own self, the business of opposition was becoming more complex. Robert Jones has argued that during the 1770s and early 1780s once neatly opposed conceptions of masculine political identity came under pressure as 'all sides, Whig and Tory, Ministry and Opposition, adverted to masculinity as a way of condensing claims for probity, honour and independence into a single figure.' In particular, Jones notes, the Whig Opposition, with whom Keppel was associated, borrowed the old Whig language of civic humanism, augmented by sensibility, to stabilize its claim to authority.[85]

---

[83] Josiah Wedgwood quoted in N. McKendrick, 'Josiah Wedgwood: An Eighteenth-Century Entrepreneur in Salesmanship and Marketing Techniques', *The Economic History Review*, New Series 12.3 (1960), 408–33 (at p. 422). See also Conway, *The British Isles and the War of American Independence*, p. 127.
[84] Conway, *The British Isles and the War of American Independence*, p. 89.
[85] Robert Jones, *Literature, Gender and Politics in Britain during the War for America, 1770–1785* (Cambridge: Cambridge University Press, 2011), p. 31, 119–58. For the argument that the Opposition's

In response to the Opposition's cannibalizing of Tory ideological positions, at least one contemporary commentator sought to reinstate clear lines between opposing views. According to James Macpherson, in his post-Ossian phase as a political writer under the Tory patronage of Lord Bute, the behaviour of the Opposition in opposing the war for America had sunk the manners of the times to a new low. Macpherson highlights 'the conduct of Opposition, during the trial, and after the acquittal of A-l K-l' as a case in point:

> Their abrogating the old forms of the Admiralty, by removing a trial for a naval offence to the land, to accommodate their own purposes, their appearance at Portsmouth, upon the occasion, their biasing witnesses, their carrying all the indecencies of a play house audience into a Court of Justice, their soliciting the officers of the navy, their sowing discontents among the common seamen, their parading the streets, for the purpose of inflaming the populace, were such mean, scandalous, and unjustifiable tricks of faction, as can scarcely be paralleled by any example in history.[86]

If the Opposition are the 'play house audience', Keppel is their star actor; together they are equally responsible for dismantling 'old forms'. It becomes clear that, for Macpherson, one such 'form' is the necessary because 'natural' relationship between masculinity and militarism. Macpherson criticizes the Opposition for stirring 'the general depression [over the war], by their unmanly oratory' and urging reconciliation where they should have, 'exhibited a spirited and disinterested love for their country, ... a manly boldness to meet, to break, to disconcert ... enemies.'[87] With this, Macpherson's pamphlet harks back to the comparative conceptual clarity of the anti-standing army argument, during which Andrew Fletcher had envisioned new militia training camps to which 'none but Military Men' would be admitted. In the summer of 1778 the militia had been mustered to join strategic encampments that had been established in case the French should mount an invasion, but these camps became social spaces in which genders and classes mixed freely and to civic-minded critics they fermented what Jones terms the 'unsettling mutability of identity ... in

---

ideology made strategic use of recognizably seventeenth-century defences of virtue and liberty, see also John Derry, *English Politics and the American Revolution* (London: Dent, 1976), pp. 1–38

[86] [James Macpherson], *A Short History of the Opposition during the Last Session of Parliament*, 2nd ed. (London: T. Cadell, 1779), pp. 17, 18.

[87] [Macpherson], *A Short History of the Opposition*, pp. 42, 50.

contemporary culture.'[88] Writing just a year later, Macpherson calls for a proper revival of martial spirit among the male population:

> The present situation of Public Affairs calls forcibly upon every good Subject to exert himself in the Public Service. Every individual possesses a power, which can aid and support his country. He can draw his sword in her defence, contribute to her resources, or combat with argument, and expose to the just indignation, those, who have proved themselves her internal, and consequently, her unnatural enemies.[89]

Here, he genders 'every individual' male and imagines that individual in the militaristic role of the chivalrous protector of the feminized nation. It has to be noted that Macpherson tempers his criticism by indicating that a man might contribute to the great remasculinization by wielding the pen rather than the sword, or even contributing financial resources to the nation's military services. It seems that even Macpherson is not immune to the temptation of cannibalizing others' arguments. However, in arguing that every man can recognize an 'unnatural' enemy, he invests in the coercive ideal of masculine 'nature' as the opposite to modern performance.

When Macpherson warns Keppel and his allies in the Opposition that 'the applause of a mob is the coarsest commodity either a gentleman or his friends can purchase', he both resists the power of the popular public sphere and highlights how far the culture of celebrity had contributed to creating conditions within which once old and solid 'forms' could be so hollowed out.[90] During the parliamentary debate which preceded the trials, Earl Nugent, then aligned with North's ministry but more generally a man of fluctuating political affiliations, had spoken against both admirals in ways that anticipated Macpherson's argument for a turn away from popular applause and towards 'real' masculinity. Nugent cautions Keppel and Palliser against allowing what had been a disagreement between them to become more than this:

> As to the professional reputation of the two officers, in what instance had either of them suffered? In the public prints: and were those anonymous imputations a sufficient ground for an enquiry? Suppose every fine woman who sees herself calumniated in the same manner, by one of her own sex, who is envious of her charms, was in like manner to demand an enquiry, where would it end? The idea was too absurd to reason upon it.[91]

---

[88] Robert W. Jones, 'Notes on *The Camp*: Women, Effeminacy and the Military in Late Eighteenth-Century Literature', *Textual Practice*, 11.3 (1997), 463–76 (at p. 464). See also *Literature, Gender and Politics*, pp. 124–7.
[89] [Macpherson], *A Short History of the Opposition*, p. v.
[90] Ibid., p. 20.
[91] *The Parliamentary Register*, XI, p. 135.

Here, Nugent warns both admirals that in reacting to the letter in the newspaper they were chasing the wrong kind of reputation, implicitly a modern kind of fame which he dismisses as the concern of 'fine women'. Though Brock asserts that 'fame as a concept underwent a process of feminization [in the eighteenth century] [that] enabled women to embrace celebrity', Nugent's comment indicates that the new idea of fame could equally be characterized as feminine in order to trivialize and so neutralize its threat to old, traditional forms.[92] A similar argument is made by a contributor to the 'pro-Palliser' *Morning Post* who challenges Keppel's claim to old heroism by wilfully conflating fame with femininity. In a seven-stanza poem 'The Ladies hero' is welcomed to 'his *Tea-table* throne', not as a chivalric protector, but as a man more interested in women's gossip than naval battles. The fourth stanza makes the point that all Keppel has achieved by his acquittal is 'but a kindred sound to fame / Honour and Wealth so near the same', and although the poet argues that the Opposition are deeply implicated in this – for 'false Oratory' creates '*unreal* fame', 'So Fame was crown'd, but Int'rest won the cause' – the insistence that this aligns Keppel with the 'lovely ladies' reveals the broader concern with the public's insensitivity to what is 'false' as opposed to what is 'real', for the former 'raised a mortal [Keppel] to the skies, / That threw a Hero [Palliser] down.'[93]

Though there were efforts made during the Keppel–Palliser affair to destabilize Keppel's performances as public person and old hero and thereby draw attention to the danger of the commodified celebrity becoming a 'false' hero, Keppel and his supporters had a vested interest in maintaining the illusion of a structured opposition. From the beginning, Palliser had made little effort to conceal his distaste for the curious readers of the popular public sphere and the newspapers had responded to this slight, with one correspondent, writing as 'Nauticus', reminding him that, 'a person in your exalted Station … appealing to the Publick for the Vindication of your *supposed* injured Reputation, gives every individual of that Publick the Liberty of criticising upon your Appeal, whether under real or anonymous Signatures.'[94] With this, the correspondent warns the recently titled Sir Hugh Palliser of the power of the papers, and the point is repeated by a contributor to the *General Advertiser*, who urged the editor to,

---

[92] Brock, *The Feminization of Fame*, p. 1. Linda Zionkowski argues that men could inhabit the culture of celebrity by rejecting politeness and displaying aggression. 'Celebrity Violence in the Careers of Savage, Pope and Johnson' in *Romanticism and Celebrity Culture*, pp. 168–85.
[93] *The Morning Post and Daily Advertiser*, Wednesday 22nd September 1779.
[94] *St James Chronicle, or the British Evening Post*, Tuesday 17th November 1778.

write immediately to your correspondents at Portsmouth for a list of ALL the officers without distinction who associate with Sir Hugh Palliser, that their names may be published at full length in large capitals, that they may be transmitted to posterity, and they receive a portion of that ignominy which belongs to the man whom they are indiscreet or abandoned enough to favour with their company.[95]

In reminding Palliser that a newspaper can publicize the names of his friends, the contributor defends the power of the newspapers to make and break reputations. That said, a poem printed in the *General Advertiser* on the third day of Keppel's trial accused Palliser of being the author of his own undoing: 'For once Sir Hugh, your cards you've manag'd ill, ...Foully you plotted Keppel's fame to kill; [But] you have quickene'd and destroy'd your own.[96] This menacing of the man who had refused to become a public person is comparable to another piece of newspaper commentary, written a fortnight before the end of Keppel's trial, in which 'Byng's ghost' also admonishes Palliser, again characterized as a card-shaper as civic shorthand for modern degeneracy, for following in his footsteps:

> Sir, You are playing a confounded losing game; for although you have, by shuffling and cutting, and packing and altering, got a very odd trick or two, you have not the least chance of winning the game, as all the *honours* are constantly against you ... for depend upon it, Sir Hugh, should you obstinately persist in playing a losing game, as your masters do in America, you will in the end meet with *my fate*.[97]

To turn to Palliser's account of himself, forwarded during the parliamentary inquiry and at his trial, is to see that he inadvertently presented himself as just such a modern military man. During the Commons debate, Palliser stated that although 'the hon. Admiral had been kind enough to do him justice on the essential point of courage; he should be nevertheless exceedingly uneasy if he was thought deficient in other respects as an officer', and that 'he despised all the means resorted to, both within and without doors, to vilify and traduce him, as a professional man.' Though alert to the currency of 'courage', Palliser positioned himself as a professional man, and though this was not disastrous in itself, Palliser further weakened his case by ruminating upon his response to the accusations that had been levied at him in the anonymous letter that Keppel had refused to counter:

---

[95] *General Advertiser, and Morning Intelligencer*, Saturday 30th January 1779.
[96] Ibid., 9th January 1779.
[97] *London Evening Post*, Tuesday 26th January 1779.

> To say anything against a friend, was, to a man of sensibility, the most disagreeable thing in nature; but where an officer's reputation was at stake, the removing of an unjust stigma was certainly the first object; [Palliser] had therefore appealed to the public, he had stated facts to them, and by those facts he would stand or fall.[98]

Here, Palliser identifies himself as a 'man of sensibility' only to then state that he was forced to sacrifice his sensibility in order to defend his 'officer's reputation'. In the one statement, then, Palliser seems to claim that he can and cannot be a 'man of sensibility' and a military man simultaneously. This paradox can be explained by the fact that Palliser seems to align himself with Smithean sensibility, for Palliser's claim that friendship follows what is '[a]greeable in nature' invokes the physicality of feeling only in order to reinforce the greater importance of rules for social interactions. This sense of sensibility is very far from the kind of innate fellow-feeling that better became the old hero because it was, so Ferguson had argued, of a piece with his essential 'nature'.

Palliser's failure to capitalize on the currency of 'natural' courage and sentiment meant that he became Keppel's opposite, the modern military man to his old hero. The published accounts of Keppel's trial made much of the senior admiral's capacity for unrestrained, natural feeling: several make reference to his 'sincere Heart' and one records how, 'with the most feeling sensibility, and the tear bursting from his eye, he exclaimed that his astonishment could not be expressed, when he first heard that his conduct on the 27th and 28th days of last July was accused.'[99] 'Nauticus', the newspaper commentator, had addressed Palliser on the subject of Keppel's irreproachable sensibility: 'Mr Keppel is a Man of approved true Courage! A Man of a most benevolent, humane, affectionate, and sincere Heart! whose chief Delight is "in serving of others". *Many, many*, Sir Hugh, can vouch for the Truth of this short, but just, Character, of as worthy a little Man as ever existed.'[100] At Palliser's trial, Keppel drew attention to his depth of feeling for others' distress. When asked to explain a letter he had written to the Admiralty after the battle in which he had praised his officers in general, thus giving no indication of any unhappiness with Palliser's conduct, Keppel said:

> I wrote that letter to the Admiralty, that they might, if they pleased, give it to the World, that I thought well of those Captains ... There is one of

---

[98] *The Parliamentary Register*, XI, p. 92–3. Previously printed in the *Morning Chronicle and London Advertiser*, Thursday 3rd December 1778.
[99] *The Trial of the Honourable Augustus Keppel* (Cruttwell), pp. 37–38. See also *The Trial of the Honourable Augustus Keppel* (Wilkes, Breadhower and Peadle), p. 82.
[100] *St James Chronicle, or the British Evening Post*, Tuesday 17th November 1778.

them a Member of this Court, whose Bravery and good Conduct I have no Reason to doubt of; but he had delicate Feelings. There was another Officer, who was abused in the Newspapers, and his feelings about Newspapers differed very much from mine; he felt it much, and came to me very uneasy. ... and therefore I wrote that Letter in general Terms, that the First Lord of the Admiralty might either put it in Print, or shew it to any Gentleman he pleased.[101]

Here, Keppel presents the commendatory letter as a response to others' inappropriately delicate feelings with regard to newspapers, feelings so different to his vital, robust and, implicitly, manly feelings.

Palliser began his defence by announcing that 'there is some consolation in lamenting my misfortunes in the presence of persons with generous minds', but in seeking 'the tribute of commiseration' he did not manage to create the impression of openness and authenticity that the sensitive Keppel had so carefully cultivated.[102] When making his defence, Palliser attempted to draw attention to Keppel's performances of authenticity. He implied that Keppel had been responsible for the anonymous letter in the newspaper, arguing that despite 'his having at first *publicly approved* of my conduct in his dispatch from the battle, I had too good grounds to suspect, that *privately he did not discourage* a very opposite representation of me.'[103] For Palliser, the difference between Keppel's dispatch and Keppel's evidence pointed to '*the greatest duplicity*', but Palliser extended this accusation by implicating Keppel in a conspiracy of 'powerful enemies', noting that 'all accuse *secretly*; but *not one* of the whole list chooses to come forth in a manly way to *avow his accusations*.'[104] Had Palliser concentrated on arguing that he had shown courage and that he had been solely dedicated to the defence of the nation, that is, had he claimed old heroism, he would have better alerted his audience to Keppel's manipulation of the structure of opposition. After all, Keppel may have become the celebrity, but Palliser seems to have more regard for 'ordinary' people. Whereas Keppel had relied primarily on admirals and captains as witnesses, Palliser called fifteen captains, five lieutenants and fourteen masters. The impression that Palliser had a warmer relationship with lower ranking sailors is also suggested by one published account of his trial that records how his acquittal was celebrated by the crews of his ships: 'the

---

[101] *Minutes of the Proceedings ... Palliser*, p. 11.
[102] *The Defence of Vice-Admiral Sir Hugh Palliser, Bart. At the Court-Martial lately held upon him, with the court's sentence* (London: T. Cadell, 1779), p. 1.
[103] *The Defence of Vice-Admiral Sir Hugh Palliser*, pp. 3–4.
[104] Ibid., pp. 55, 4.

whole audience joined in three shouts of acclamation, which were instantly returned by three cheers from the Formidable's and other barges along side the Sandwich, the crews of which immediately put blue ribbons in their caps, bearing the inscription, PALLISER *and* INNOCENCE *protected*.'[105]

This reading of the Keppel–Palliser affair has sought to show that, by the 1770s, the structure of the debate about militarism and masculinity was changing within a culture that was inherently liable to mistake performance for authenticity. At his trial, Keppel carefully differentiated himself from the Lestockian modern military man and transformed himself into an old hero, but his claim to old heroism was supported by his turn towards the popular public sphere. Whereas Palliser maintained his resistance to the public circulation of information throughout the period of the affair, Keppel underwent a dramatic transformation during it, metamorphosing from one initially unwilling to sign a statement which Palliser would then have published in a newspaper to one who participated openly with the press and its curious readers. As a result, Keppel's popularity is less a sign of the strength of old heroism than of the increasing complexity of the debate about militarism and masculinity, complexity exacerbated by the commercialism at the centre of the culture of celebrity. Palliser did attempt to expose Keppel's twin performances of old heroism and public person, but his refusal to lay claim to either for himself meant that he appeared to be the modern military man. As a result, the Keppel–Palliser affair can be said to have both hastened and concealed the collapse of the kind of rigid opposition that had emerged with the standing army debate some eighty years earlier.

---

[105] *The Trial of Sir Hugh Palliser, Vice-Admiral of the Blue Squadron, at a Court-Martial, held on Board his Majesty's Ship the Sandwich, in Portsmouth Harbour on Monday, April 19th, 1779*, 3rd ed. (London: J. Murray; C Etherington, 1779), pp. 231–2.

CHAPTER 7

(De)Romanticizing Military Heroism
Clarke, Southey, Austen

> We saw a countless number of Postchaises full of Boys pass by yesterday morn[ing] – full of future Heroes, Legislators, Fools, & Vilains. … You will not pay us a visit yet of course, we must not think of it. Your Mother must get well first, & you must go to Oxford & <u>not</u> be elected; after that, a little change of scene may be good for you, & Your Physicians I hope will order you to the Sea, or to a house by the side of a very considerable pond.[1]
>
> Jane Austen to James-Edward Austen (1816)

Although this 'letter' written by Jane Austen just over a year after the end of the French Revolutionary and Napoleonic Wars, and less than two weeks before she finished the first draft of the novel *Persuasion* (1817), assembles fragments of conversation in a seemingly haphazard fashion, her comment on the carriages of boys is more than just a passing observation. At the end of the seventeenth century, the anti-standing army authors had defended the citizen-soldier as the virtuous guardian of the people's liberty, but by the end of the eighteenth century the language of republicanism and citizenship had been commandeered by the newly independent American patriots and the *sans-culottes* of Revolutionary France. The threat posed by the possibility of a French invasion of Britain, and perhaps more so by the circulation of French ideas, allowed the government to counter political activism by disrupting Jacobin societies and prosecuting controversial writers.[2] This was matched, certainly

---

[1] Jane Austen to James-Edward Austen, 9th July 1816, *Jane Austen's Letters*, ed. by Deirdre Le Faye, 4th ed. (Oxford: Oxford University Press, 2011), p. 330.

[2] Clive Emsley, *British Society and the French Wars, 1793–1815* (Basingstoke: Macmillan, 1979); Emma Vincent Macleod, *A War of Ideas: British Attitudes to the Wars Against Revolutionary France 1792–1802* (Aldershot: Ashgate, 1998); Edward Royle, *Revolutionary Britannia? Reflections on the Threat of Revolution in Britain, 1789–1848* (Manchester: Manchester University Press, 2000); Mark Philp, *Reforming Ideas in Britain: Politics and Language in the Shadow of the French Revolution 1789–1815* (Cambridge: Cambridge University Press, 2014).

after the resumption of war in 1803, by a significant growth in what H. T. Dickinson terms 'popular conservatism.'[3] The latter is reflected in *The Life of Admiral Nelson* (1813), in which poet laureate Robert Southey celebrates one 'whose presence in every village through which he might have passed would have wakened the church bells, have given school-boys a holyday, have drawn children from their sports to gaze upon him, and "old men from the chimney corner" to look upon Nelson ere they died.'[4] Here, Southey borrows from Philip Sidney's defence of poetry: '[the poet] commeth to you ... with a tale which holdeth children from play, and old men from the chimney corner.' In replacing the poet with Nelson, Southey becomes one with the children at play and the old men at rest, both of whom idolize the naval hero, but he also creates a palimpsestic connection between himself, as a poet, and the celebrated military man. Austen's letter to her nephew James-Edward, recently of Winchester College, stands in marked contrast to this. Her swift mockery of the occupants of the post-chaises, who, she implies, both desire and are destined to inhabit the masculine public sphere, prefigures her advice to James-Edward not to seek election at Oxford University, for both the mockery and the advice puncture young men's aspirations with regard to masculine roles and male patriarchal privilege. Indeed, her advice to James-Edward is interwoven with her concern for his and his mother's health and this reminder of their shared physicality warns against putting too much distance between male and female, masculine and feminine.

According to Linda Colley, the general enthusiasm for the wars with Revolutionary and Napoleonic France created the conditions in which 'a cult of heroism', a cult that ultimately bolstered the patrician and propertied classes and protected the prevailing social order, could thrive.[5] Colley may be too quick to suggest that the popular public sphere was easily led; after all, the vogue for battlefield visiting which began after the climatic final engagement of the war at Waterloo (1815) enabled military tourists, even of the 'shopkeeping class', to walk in their heroes' footsteps.[6] As Catriona Kennedy argues, the many and varied opportunities for the 'pleasurable consumption of war' as 'exciting and romantic spectacle' – including theatrical afterpieces and panorama displays – allowed a greater number of

---

[3] H. T. Dickinson, 'Popular Conservatism and Militant Loyalism', in *Britain and the French Revolution, 1789–1815*, ed. by H. T. Dickinson (Basingstoke: Macmillan, 1989), pp. 103–25.
[4] Robert Southey, *The Life of Nelson*, 2 vols. (London: John Murray, 1813), II, p. 273.
[5] Colley, *Britons*, p. 178 See also Timothy Jenks, *Naval Engagements: Patriotism, Cultural Politics and the Royal Navy, 1793–1815* (Oxford: Oxford University Press, 2006).
[6] Philip Shaw, *Waterloo and the Romantic Imagination* (Basingstoke: Palgrave Macmillan, 2002), p. 67.

people than ever before to participate in a collective 'fantasy of military power, glamour and heroism.'[7] This chapter explores that fantasy by positioning works by James Stanier Clarke and Robert Southey, principally the latter's *The Life of Nelson*, as texts that attest to the interdependence of civic argument and popular conservatism at the beginning of the nineteenth century. That said, this chapter also explores resistance to the idealization of new old heroism by reading Jane Austen's *Persuasion* as a proto-feminist novel.[8] Austen's awareness of war has long been a subject for scholarly discussion and Toby Tanner, Claudia Johnson and others have argued that her last completed novel celebrates the self-made men of the navy as figures who can challenge the social dominance of the old elite.[9] However, in arguing that *Persuasion* questions military heroism, I follow Gillian Russell's opinion that, while British society celebrated the victory at the battle of Waterloo, Austen seems to have developed a 'profoundly ambivalent view' of the military.[10] My reading suggests that Austen's modernity lies not with her willingness to allow new middle-class men to assume the positions once held by the elite; rather, it lies with her capacity to question the nature of masculinity, and more specifically, the use of military heroism as a vehicle for a privileged ideal of 'natural', essential masculinity. Just as Austen advises James-Edward not to be seduced, like the boys in the post-chaises, so in *Persuasion* she resists romanticizing military heroism and in so doing highlights the cultural function of even the newest of old heroes in glamorizing and justifying gender inequality.

Sailors of Fortune

In the winter of 1815, while she was completing *Persuasion*, Austen became embroiled in an exchange of letters with James Stanier Clarke. The three

---

[7] Kennedy, *Narratives of the Revolutionary and Napoleonic Wars*, pp. 172, 175.
[8] This argument is indebted to work on Austen and feminism by Margaret Kirkham, *Jane Austen, Feminism and Fiction* (Sussex: Harvester Press, 1983); Margaret Poovey, *The Proper Lady and the Woman Writer: Ideology as Style in the Works of Mary Wollstonecraft, Mary Shelley and Jane Austen* (Chicago: University of Chicago Press, 1984); Johnson, *Equivocal Beings*.
[9] Tony Tanner, *Jane Austen* (London: Macmillan, 1986); Claudia L. Johnson, *Jane Austen: Women, Politics and the Novel* (Chicago: University of Chicago Press, 1988); Rogers Sales, *Jane Austen and Representations of Regency England* (New York: Routledge, 1994); Jocelyn Harris, *A Revolution Almost Beyond Expression: Jane Austen's* Persuasion (Newark: University of Delaware Press, 2007).
[10] Gillian Russell, 'The Army, the Navy, and the Napoleonic Wars', in *A Companion to Jane Austen*, ed. by Claudia L. Johnson and Clara Tuite (Oxford: Blackwell, 2009), pp. 266–7.

letters sent by Clarke, a clergyman and the Prince Regent's librarian at Carlton House, written between November 1815 and March 1816, ostensibly with respect to a copy of *Emma* requested by the prince, are rare examples of surviving correspondence between Austen and a man other than one of her family members or publishers.[11] In his opening letter (November), Clarke urges Austen to 'delineate in some future Work the Habits of Life and Character and enthusiasm of a Clergyman.'[12] He presses the point in his second (December), a letter which stretches his acknowledgement of the receipt of Austen's novel to some eight paragraphs:

> Do let us have an English Clergyman after your fancy – much novelty may be introduced – shew dear Madam what good would be done if Tythes were taken away entirely, and describe him burying his own mother – as I did – because the High Priest of the Parish in which she died – did not pay her remains the respect he ought to do. I have never recovered the shock. Carry your Clergyman to Sea as the Friend of some distinguished Naval Character about a Court – you can then bring foreward like Le Sage many interesting Scenes of Character & Interest.

With this, Clarke again urges Austen to make a close study of just such a clergyman as himself, one who would challenge the parish priest 'as I did'. But having taken the opportunity to stress his own exemplary qualities, Clarke suddenly changes tack and suggests that this not-so-hypothetical clergyman would be a suitable companion for a 'distinguished Naval Character'. Lest Austen should miss the point that a clergyman might be every bit as 'distinguished', Clarke goes on to promise to send his *Naval Sermons* (1798), a volume of ten sermons which he 'wrote & preached on the Ocean'.[13]

If Clarke's letters attempt to draw Austen into further correspondence, they also seem designed to seduce with that which he found to be seductive. By the time Austen met Clarke at the Prince Regent's library, to which she had been offered a tour, he had long since established himself as one of the period's preeminent authors on naval matters.[14] Clarke was the founding editor of *The Naval Chronicle*, a successful monthly miscellany of naval news, parliamentary debates, discussion of tactical and engineering matters and light literary entertainment, issued from 1798 until 1818

---

[11] Clarke escorted Austen around Carlton House library and may have painted her portrait from memory. See Joan Klingel and Richard James Wheeler, 'James Stanier Clarke's Portrait of Jane Austen', *Persuasions*, 27 (2005), 112–8.
[12] James Stanier Clarke to Jane Austen, 16th November 1815, *Letters*, p. 309.
[13] Ibid., 21st December 1815, *Letters*, p. 320.
[14] Brian Southam, *Jane Austen and the Navy* (London: Hambledon and London, 2000), p. 221.

and read widely within and beyond the wooden walls of the navy. Austen may also have been aware of his three-volume *Naufragia, or, Historical Memoirs of Shipwrecks* (1803); his edition of William Falconer's epic poem *The Shipwreck* (1806), which he also promised to send to her; or his co-authored *The Life of Admiral Lord Nelson* (1809). Of course, by offering his *Naval Sermons*, Clarke drew attention to his own, first-hand experience of naval life. Clarke had spent three years during the war with Revolutionary France as the naval chaplain onboard the *Impétueux* under the command of Captain John Willet Payne. Clarke and Payne had first met socially through their mutual friend the Prince Regent but the clergyman's *Naval Sermons* are dedicated to Payne as one whose 'brave, zealous and sincere … character and abilities adorn the naval profession.'[15] Payne had been commended for gallantry during the War of American Independence and had received a gold medal for his contribution to the battle of the Glorious First of June (1794). In dedicating a volume of sermons to a man who had so distinguished himself, Clarke discloses his susceptibility to military heroism.

As Clarke's dedication suggests, his views on militarism and masculinity are recognizably civic. Granted, this is not exactly the same as the civic republican thinking that had been deployed by the anti-standing army authors. Given that Clarke had gone to sea as a naval chaplain in 1796, his sermons must have been written at the time of the naval mutinies at the Spithead and Nore anchorages (1797). Notably, then, he addresses the sailors as men who have it in their power to protect Britain from 'republican pestilence' rather than ferment it: 'you, my Brethren, are of a profession, whose predominant features are loyalty, courage, and active patriotism: and, in which, a willingness to shed your blood, and a noble exposure of your lives; must ever become a duty.'[16] Here, as elsewhere, Clarke uses the term 'profession' without reservation. However, Clarke's 'profession' is a cannibalized term; no longer the preserve of Lestockian discipline and calculation, Clarke uses professionalism to describe the product of the 'native courage of [the sailors'] hearts'.[17] When Clarke acknowledges that the professional sailors on the *Impétueux* might not have enlisted voluntarily, he reminds any one of them who might 'repine … to *get his bread*

---

[15] James Stanier Clarke, *Naval Sermons, Preached on Board his Majesty's Ship The Impetueux, The Western Squadron During Its Services off Brest: To Which Is Added a Thanksgiving Sermon for Naval Victories* (London: T. Payne, B. White, 1798).
[16] Clarke, *Naval Sermons*, pp. 165, 81. For religion and responses to the Revolution see Macleod, *A War of Ideas*, pp. 135–57.
[17] Clarke, *Naval Sermons*, p. 60.

with the peril of his life' that they have courage within: 'Have you not, when encountering the fury of battle, found your minds elevated and ennobled by its dangers? – ... You must remember what superior sensations animated your souls, when, preparing for action, you first beheld the line extending to oppose the arrogance of an approaching enemy.'[18] As might be expected from a clergyman, Clarke identifies Christianity as the only 'pure source' of courage, but he invokes a civic binary when he cautions against relying on 'false and uncertain courage, [derived] merely from the force of habit or constitution', as this juxtaposes 'true' innate courage with 'false' courage that is merely acquired. Clarke's civic appeal to innate capacity also bends a little to accept that there are some who 'eagerly pursue what is perfectly opposite to the nature of their calling', but his point is not that they are the exceptions that disprove the rule; rather, that such men have misconceived notions of what military service entails and so think that militarism is compatible with what an earlier critic might have termed politeness: selfishness, affection for trifling forms and parade and aversion to 'manly exertion'.

As a chaplain on a naval ship, Clarke had initially addressed his civic moralizing to a captive audience; as a writer on naval topics, he, like the novelist to whom he recommended the naval character, addressed a broader audience, and nowhere more so than in his *The Life of Admiral Lord Nelson*. Though Clarke's civic sermons advise the sailors to model themselves on their ancestors – 'consider the earth as sacred, where these Heroes have long slept in death' – the 'distinguished naval character' mentioned in the letter to Austen almost twenty years later seems more likely to have been intended to evoke the contemporary naval figure whose career Clarke and his co-author James McArthur had recorded in an impressive two-volume quarto designed as a 'history of a Life, which is to be held out as an example of Heroism and professional Talent to future Generations': Admiral Nelson.[19] The career of the exemplary hero had begun inauspiciously during the war with America. According to Southey's *The Life of Nelson*, Nelson looked back on this as a period in which he had abandoned himself to ' "a feeling that I should never rise in my profession" ' until overcome by a surge of patriotic feeling: ' "Well then", I exclaimed, "I will be a hero! and, confiding in Providence, I will brave every danger!" '[20] Nelson

---

[18] Ibid., pp. 6–7.
[19] Ibid., p. 157; James Stanier Clarke and John McArthur, *The Life of Admiral Lord Nelson, K. B. From His Lordship's Manuscripts*, 2 vols. (London: Cadell and Davies, 1809), I, p. iv.
[20] Southey, *Life of Nelson*, II, p. 24.

became a hero by distinguishing himself for his courage and daring, first at the battle of St Vincent (1797), at which he led a boarding party onto an enemy ship, hazarding pistol and musket shot, and then in the attack on Santa Cruz (1797). Nelson's dogged pursuit of victory, his 'naked thirst for glory', led to further, spectacular, successes at the battles of the Nile (1798), Copenhagen (1801) and finally, fatally, Trafalgar (1805).[21] Southey enthused about the significance of these victories, crediting him with creating 'a new [e]ra in our naval history.'[22] Certainly, his death helped to stimulate the public's interest in, and willingness to pay subscriptions for, grand public monuments to the nation's military heroes.[23]

Southey approached the subject of the life of Nelson after digesting Clarke and McArthur's *Life* for the Tory *Quarterly Review*, and by the time his biography of the hero had been published he had become Poet Laureate, but as David M. Craig has argued, the young radical Southey who planned to establish a pantisocratic community in America and the older, more conservative Southey who supported the war against Revolutionary France are equally indebted to seventeenth-century republicanism. As the war dragged into the 1810s, Southey sided with those who questioned the decline in the nation's martial spirit and argued that the army could be reformed to be more like a militia, not least in the softening of military discipline and corporeal punishments.[24] This civic-mindedness can be found in *The Life of Nelson* when Southey describes the French revolution as a case of 'good principles ... perilously abused by ignorant and profligate men', and when he indulges in a digressive account of the history of Corsican republicanism that concludes, 'if France had not interfered, upon its wicked and detestable principle of usurpation, Corsica might, at this day, have been as free, and flourishing, and happy a commonwealth, as any of the Grecian States in the days of their prosperity.'[25]

---

[21] N. A. M. Rodger, 'Nelson and the British Navy: Seamanship, Leadership, Originality', in *Trafalgar in History: A Battle and Its Afterlife*, ed. by David Cannadine (Basingstoke: Macmillan, 2006), pp. 7–29 (at p. 28). For Nelson and popularity see Jordan and Rogers, 'Admirals as Heroes', 201–24; Kate Williams, "Nelson and Women: Marketing, Representations and the Female Consumer", in *Admiral Lord Nelson: Contexts and Legacy*, ed. by David Cannadine (Basingstoke: Macmillan, 2005), pp. 67–89; Mark Philp, *Reforming Ideas in Britain*, pp. 232–59.

[22] Southey, *Life of Nelson*, I, p. 225.

[23] Marianne Czisnik, 'Representations of the Hero: Monuments to Admiral Nelson', in *Reactions to Revolution: The 1790s and Their Aftermath*, ed. by Ulrich Broich, H. T. Dickinson and Martin Schmidt (Berlin: Lit Verlag, 2007), pp. 263–88.

[24] David M. Craig, *Robert Southey and Romantic Apostasy: Political Argument in Britain, 1780–1840* (Woodbridge, Suffolk: Boydell, 2007), pp. 50–3. See also David Eastwood, 'Robert Southey and the Meanings of Patriotism', *Journal of British Studies*, 31.3 (1992), 265–87.

[25] Southey, *Life of Nelson*, I, pp. 87, 100–101.

Southey's account of Nelson's character is just as infused with civic thinking. As a child, Southey records, Nelson 'had already given proofs of that resolute heart and nobleness of mind, which, during his whole career of labour and of glory, so eminently distinguished him.' Just as the young Nelson is innately disposed to be courageous – ' "Fear! Grandmamma", replied the future hero, ' "I never saw fear:—What is it?" ' – so the older Nelson counsels others against giving into timorousness: ' "these are not times for nervous systems." '[26] True, Southey's courageous Nelson is a 'professional' sailor: the Duke of Clarence's first impression of the sailor who would become his 'firm friend' was of a man 'dressed in a full laced uniform, an old fashioned waistcoat with long flaps, and his lank unpowdered hair tied in a stiff Hessian tail', but the duke concludes that ' "[Nelson's] address and conversation were irresistibly pleasing; and when he spoke on professional subjects, it was with an enthusiasm that showed he was no common being." '[27] Had this meeting occurred some forty years earlier, a pleasing conversationalist in a full uniform might have been a Lestockian professional and member of the international officer class. However, the Nelson in an old-fashioned waistcoat, with lank hair and an enthusiasm for military subjects, is also the Nelson who, when faced with a superior number of French ships, joked that he might soon have to learn something he had presumably never wanted or needed to know: how to speak French.[28]

Like Clarke's sermons, Southey's biography cannibalizes the term 'professional', but just as there is no contradiction between innate courage and professionalism, so there is no contest. The difference between the modern professional military man of the 1740s and Southey's civic Nelson is confirmed by Southey's emphasis on Nelson's disregard for 'rules'. When Lestock had been charged with the failure to fight, he argued that he had followed the 'discipline' of the navy. Nelson, who was often critical of naval administrators, asserts that rules can only ever be a distraction from the crucial business of fighting: ' "to obey orders, is all perfection. To serve my king, and to destroy the French, I consider as the great order of all, from which little ones spring." '[29] Southey indicates that this was particularly the case at the battle of Copenhagen. The civic-leaning Southey claims that Nelson considered this battle to be his greatest achievement because of the strength of Danish men's innate military

---

[26] Ibid., I, pp. 5, 6; II, p. 94.
[27] Ibid., I, p. 46.
[28] Ibid., I, p. 30.
[29] Ibid., II, p. 74.

spirit: 'All ranks offered themselves to the service of their country...: – it was one of those emergencies in which little drilling or discipline is necessary to render courage available.'[30] This was also a battle in which Nelson deliberately ignored the signal to leave off the action: ' "I have fought contrary to orders, and I shall, perhaps, be hanged. Never mind: let them!" '[31] In Southey's view, Nelson is exemplary because he always followed his own, inner convictions. 'A higher compliment could not have been paid to any commander-in-chief', Southey writes, 'than to say of him, that he understood the merits of Nelson, and left him, as far as possible, to act upon his own judgement.'[32]

But while it is possible to see Southey's civic leanings in his characterization of Nelson as innately courageous and dedicated to duty rather than discipline, his civic intent is clearest in his close attention to the subject of military service and money. The anti-standing army authors had argued that virtuous militiamen should not be replaced with avaricious standing soldiers who serve only for pay and upon whom no Briton could depend. Writing in the mid-century, Adam Ferguson agrees that men must not think of national defence as something that they can pay others to do on their behalf:

> Men frequently, while they study to improve their fortunes, neglect themselves; and while they reason for their country, forget the considerations that most deserve their attention. Numbers, riches, and the other resources of war, are highly important but nations consist of men and a nation consisting of degenerate and cowardly men, is weak; a nation consisting of vigorous, public-spirited, and resolute men, is strong.[33]

Southey's *Life of Nelson* offers a similarly robust account of the problems caused by mixing military service and financial motivation. Just four years earlier, the probity of the nation's monarchy had been exposed by the revelation that the Duke of York's mistress had undertaken to secure army officers' promotions in return for payments that supplemented her already generous allowance.[34] Southey seems to respond to this scandal in the moments where Nelson opines on the quality of Britain's partners in the fight against Napoleon. Nelson's admiration for the leaders of the Corsican revolution is coupled with his criticism of England's hired allies: ' "I begin

---

[30] Ibid., II, p. 113.
[31] Ibid., II, p. 138.
[32] Ibid., I, p. 152
[33] Ferguson, *Civil Society*, p. 337.
[34] Colley, *Britons*, pp. 217–8.

to think that the [Austrian] Emperor is anxious to touch another four millions of English money. As for the German generals, war is their trade, and peace is ruin to them; therefore we cannot expect that they should have any wish to finish the war."'[35] So stridently civic is this criticism of hired soldiers' moral bankruptcy that it is hardly surprising that Southey then reverts to his own voice to condemn soldiers and sailors of fortune for their inability to be 'vigorous or manly.'[36]

Southey secures his account of Nelson's heroism with an unremitting attention to the hero's virtuous poverty. Southey begins this by noting that the young Nelson spent some time learning seamanship on board a merchant vessel, from which he acquired a 'hatred of the King's service', but the lure of a life on a merchant ship was soon replaced by the allure of naval service.[37] Once he had begun his career as a naval officer, he devoted himself to duty rather than personal gain. For Southey, 'it is characteristic of Nelson, that the chance by which he missed a share in [what would have been his first] prize [money earned by capturing an enemy ship], is never mentioned in any of his letters; nor is it likely that it ever excited even a momentary feeling of vexation.'[38] On being sent to North America during the War of American Independence, Nelson responds to a senior officer who states that it is a 'fine station for making prize money': ' "Yes, sir, ... but the West Indies is the station for honour." ' In Southey's hands, Nelson is proud to have ended his service in that war ' "without a fortune" ': ' "True honour, I hope, predominates in my mind far above riches." '[39] Southey repeats the point in his account of the engagement at Aboukir Bay, the battle of the Nile. He notes that Nelson burnt three of the captured ships rather than weaken his battle fleet by allowing it to tow all the ships as prizes, and that those he kept were intended to reward the sailors. In response to the Admiralty's decision to distribute the resulting prize money 'unfairly', in his eyes, Nelson refuses to take any money at all: ' "I desire that no such claim may be made: – no, not it if were sixty times the sum, and, – poor as I am, I were never to see prize money." '[40] In simultaneously recognizing the importance of money to the junior officers and denying its importance to him, Southey's Nelson presents prize money as a reward for those who cannot be heroes; after all, ' "an Admiral may be amply

---

[35] Southey, *Life of Nelson*, I, p. 140.
[36] Ibid., II, p. 21.
[37] Ibid., I, p. 10.
[38] Ibid., I, p. 29.
[39] Ibid., I, pp. 45, 50.
[40] Ibid., II, p. 87.

rewarded by his own feelings ... but what reward have the inferior officers and men, but the value of the prizes?"'[41]

To see that, for Southey, heroes have no need of financial reward is to be able to appreciate why, in what is a hagiographic account of Nelson's heroic military career, Southey highlights his efforts to police others' financial misbehaviour, first by preventing illegal trade between American and British colonies and then in exposing the fraudulent activities of West Indies naval contractors and agents. The former involved enforcing the Navigation Act at the cost of countermanding his senior officers and angering American traders, who attempted to sue him personally, firstly for £40,000 and later £20,000. Nelson's efforts to restrain others financial activities brought him little in the way of reward and he comes to reflect, somewhat uncharacteristically ruefully, that '"my fortune, God knows, has grown worse for the service: so much for serving my country."'[42] Of course, it might have been problematic for Southey that Nelson's victories were rewarded in ways that could be accounted. Southey records that Nelson was presented with lavish gifts including jewelled boxes from the mother of the Sultan of the Ottoman Empire, Czar Paul of Russia and the King of Sardinia, and a 'simple offering' from the Greeks of Zante, 'a golden-headed sword, and a truncheon, set round with all the diamonds that the island could furnish, in a single row.' Southey negotiates this by suggesting that such rewards were, like the numerous titles he received, 'the outward and visible signs of honour, which he had so fairly won.'[43] As such, Southey considers Nelson to have been justifiably peeved at the English baronetage he received after the battle of the Nile and pardonably proud of the Italian dukedom granted to him the following year. Southey makes plain that pursuing the nation's interest and the public good remained Nelson's first concern by adding that 'it was some days before he could be persuaded to accept' the Dukedom of Bronte, worth £3,000 a year, and that he later quickly pledged to sell the title in order to finance efforts to break the French siege at Malta.[44]

According to Linda Colley, Nelson's public persona has to be understood as a product of 'self-interested' 'showmanship': 'Nelson did what the majority of the men who dominated Great Britain sought to do more elegantly and discreetly: use patriotic display to impress the public and cement their own

[41] Ibid., I, p. 252.
[42] Ibid., I, p. 79.
[43] Ibid., II, p. 67.
[44] Ibid., II, p. 65.

authority.'⁴⁵ Southey is somewhat less critical, for although he is clear that Nelson had no interest in financial reward, in allowing him to be flattered by gifts and titles, Southey permits him to be interested in his status both within the navy and beyond. Southey admits that Nelson had an 'unspeakable pride in the prospect of the fame to which he aspired', but he does not condemn him for this, indicating instead that Nelson desired only recognition for his virtues: '"an uniform course of honour and integrity"', Nelson reasons, '"seldom fails of bringing a man to the goal of fame at last."'⁴⁶ Thus, when Nelson's activities in Corsica are overlooked by the British naval authorities, Southey records that he 'felt himself neglected' and consoled himself with the idea that his naval exploits would have to be recognized eventually: '"never mind, I'll have [an official naval] gazette of my own."'⁴⁷ Southey does seem to be sceptical about the proximity of Nelson's fame to celebrity. 'Now that the fame of Nelson has given interest to everything connected with his name', Southey observes, even pieces of naval paperwork have acquired the status of a 'relic'.⁴⁸ The fame to which Southey's Nelson aspires is the modern fame that emerged in opposition to older markers of status. This kind of fame could not be acquired without the assistance of commercial intermediaries, particularly those industries dedicated to forging an apparently intimate relationship between a confessional individual and an interested audience. Publications like Clarke's *Naval Chronicle*, which drew on private, or pseudo-private, letters and diaries, Clarke and McArthur's *The Life of Admiral Lord Nelson*, which included facsimile copies of Nelson's letters, and Southey's *The Life of Nelson*, which uses the first person and imagined speech rather than simple commentary, fulfil this role. But as complicit as Southey's *Life* might be with the commercial culture of celebrity, it is clear that Southey's civic intent is to present Nelson to the reader as a new old hero, and, crucially, one who deserves fame for not seeking private fortune.

Jane Austen's novels are all, in some way, alert to the necessity of money to those who have little and the damage that money can cause to those who have plenty, and in the novel she was writing at the time that she was corresponding with Clarke her awareness of this is combined with a study of military, specifically naval, men. Austen began working on *Persuasion* just a few months after the battle of Waterloo (1815), a circumstance that

---

[45] Colley, *Britons*, p. 183.
[46] Southey, *Life of Nelson*, I, pp. 102, 79.
[47] Ibid., I, pp. 119–20.
[48] Ibid., I, p. 43.

might be taken to suggest that the text was inspired by the celebrations for the victory that brought the lengthy wars to a close. In fact, Austen's more complex relationship with contemporary military matters is apparent in her decision to set the novel in the false peace following the defeat of Napoleon and his abdication (April 1814) and lasting until his return from exile on Elba (March 1815). The false peace was a result of the containment of a French hero, Napoleon, and the end of the peace, anticipated in the novel's final lines, was the result of a 'heroic' return. By obliquely alluding to this, military heroism is tarnished by association with one who was at once hero and villain. That said, the fact that the novel focuses on men in sea-service rather than land-service is a greater indication that this text critiques the heroism of Clarke and Southey's imaginations. Had Austen set the text ten years earlier, that is, in the period that ended with the battle of Trafalgar, her focus on the navy would have been more overtly celebratory, for it was this battle that won Britain 'an unchallenged command over the sea.'[49] As a result, in the years after Trafalgar, British sea power was concentrated in the less obviously glamorous duties of blockading French ports, protecting British convoys and supporting Wellington's campaigns. Naval action could still be found in the West Indies, in the ancillary war with North America and in skirmishes with neutrals and France's allies, but in the aftermath of Trafalgar, as Christopher D. Hall notes, 'Napoleon's sailors always tried to avoid battle if possible.'[50] While the navy and its most celebrated figure, Nelson, had been central to British success in the first ten years of the war, the remaining years and particularly the final battle at Waterloo allowed the army to secure 'pride of place' in the nation's hearts.[51] After Waterloo it was, as Clive Emsley observes, 'something special to be a "Waterloo man"' and the battle created a new national hero, Arthur Wellesley, Duke of Wellington.[52] With this in mind, Austen's decision to write about naval officers seems less a move in concord with the national mood than a deliberate counter to it.

It would be fair to suggest that Austen's decision to foreground naval characters in *Persuasion* may have been prompted by her family connections. Austen had three military-minded brothers. The eldest, Henry-Thomas

---

[49] Rodger, *The Command of the Ocean*, pp. 528–74 (at p. 543). See also David Gates, *The Napoleonic Wars, 1803–1815* (London: Pimlico, 2003), pp. 38–48.
[50] Christopher D. Hall, *Wellington's Navy: Sea Power and the Peninsular War, 1807–1814* (London: Chatham, 2004), p. 123. On the war with America as a 'side-show' see Emsley, *British Society and the French Wars*, p. 167.
[51] Lincoln, *Representing the Royal Navy*, pp. 185–90. See also Southam, *Jane Austen and the Navy*, pp. 257–64; Czisnik, 'Commemorating Trafalgar'.
[52] Emsley, *British Society and the French Wars*, p. 171.

(Henry) Austen, had joined the Oxfordshire militia in his early twenties and for some years earnestly, though unsuccessfully, sought a commission to a regular regiment, a failure Austen eagerly anticipated: 'I heartily hope', she wrote 'that he will, as usual, be disappointed in this scheme.'[53] Henry's younger brothers Francis-William (Frank) and Charles-John (Charles) were more successful in their naval careers and at the time that Austen was writing *Persuasion* both were junior captains. It would be overly generous to suggest that her brothers' careers led her to romanticize naval heroism, however. Austen's brothers' naval experiences must have been useful, but largely for the quotidian details and tarnished realities of naval life. Despite the fact that naval rank could not be purchased, as in the army, a naval career was extremely hard to forge on merit alone: a young officer needed friends among the upper echelons of the navy, and ideally on the board of the Admiralty. Austen's father made every effort to exploit the family's slim connections with senior admirals and in a letter to her sister, Cassandra, Austen reflects on the unofficial system of naval patronage with dry comedy: 'I have sent the … sweets of [Admiral Gambier's letter promising help] to Charles, who poor fellow! Tho' he sinks into nothing but an humble attendant on the Hero of the peice, will I hope be contented with the prospect held out to him.'[54] Here Austen hails Gambier, not Charles, as the hero, and his 'heroism' consists of little more than potentially useful seniority. Charles did make progress in his career in the end, but neither brother was to become anything like a Nelsonian hero. As a captain in Nelson's fleet during 1805, Frank might have been at the battle of Trafalgar had it not occurred so late in the season that Nelson had already sent a number of ships to be refitted. As a result, Frank missed out on the honour of having participated in the most celebrated naval battle of the war – a battle described by Admiral Collingwood as one at which 'every individual appeared a Hero on whom the Glory of his country depended' – a loss Frank lamented bitterly in letters to his wife.[55]

While Austen's sailor brothers' careers were rich sources of information, neither provided her with examples of heroism. In fact, during the period in which Austen composed *Persuasion*, both naval brothers were at low points in their careers. This was, in part, because of factors beyond their control, for as N. A. M. Rodger has outlined, the French Revolutionary

---

[53] Jane Austen to Cassandra Austen, 9–10th January 1796, *Letters*, p. 2.
[54] Ibid., 24–26th December 1798, *Letters*, p. 30.
[55] Clarke and McArthur, *The Life of Admiral Lord Nelson*, II, p. 457. Southam, *Jane Austen and the Navy*, p. 95.

and Napoleonic Wars brought forth a 'crisis in the naval career structure.'[56] Throughout the war there were far more men qualified to command than there were ships in need of captains. The result was a high degree of unemployment among officers at the lower captaincy ranks of commander and post-captain. Given this, Frank was lucky to have been constantly employed almost throughout the war, but with the peace of 1814 he was set ashore and reduced to half-pay. No-one could have known that he would not sail for another thirty years, but in the summer of 1815, when Austen began *Persuasion*, the fact that the war had ended must have made his situation seem rather more than temporary. Frank was promoted in 1815, but as Austen would have known, promotions for all ranks above captain were based on length of time enrolled on the active service list rather than actual, continuous service at sea.[57] In comparison, Charles fared slightly better. In late 1814, he had been dispatched to help with the hunt for Napoleon's collaborators and so was still in active service when the war recommenced. However, in the spring of 1816, his ship was wrecked off Turkey, and although he was exonerated by a court martial, he seems to have fallen under a cloud which was to keep him on shore for the next ten years. By the end of the period in which Austen composed *Persuasion*, then, both brothers were restricted to shore-based roles. They remained in the service, and in this sense both were naval men, but, like the naval characters of Austen's novel, they were not actually engaged in seafaring endeavours.

For Brian Southam, Austen's decision to write about the navy within which her brothers served at a time when, in the aftermath of Waterloo, it was held in comparatively low esteem, is evidence of her desire to 'show the navy in its best light.'[58] Jocelyn Harris seems to agree, as she argues that Wentworth's career is modelled closely on Southey's Nelson's, so much so that he becomes a 'distinctly Nelsonian war hero'.[59] In fact, Wentworth's narrative of his career, as delivered principally to Henrietta and Louisa Musgrove, is decidedly lacking in heroic exploits. Wentworth tells Henrietta and Louisa that he first went to sea in 1806, but he means by this that he first achieved a command at this time. In practice, a young man born in 1783/4, as Wentworth must have been, would have first gone to sea at the age of fourteen or fifteen, if not earlier. As his sister had

---

[56] Rodger, *The Command of the Ocean*, p. 518.
[57] David Hopskinson, 'The Naval Career of Jane Austen's Brother', *History Today*, 26.9 (1976), 576–83.
[58] Southam, *Jane Austen and the Navy*, p. 265
[59] Jocelyn Harris, '"Domestic Virtues and National Importance": Lord Nelson, Captain Wentworth, and the English Napoleonic Hero', *Eighteenth-Century Fiction*, 19.1&2 (2006), 181–205 (at p. 189).

married an admiral, Wentworth would have had better family connections than either Frank or Charles Austen, but he seems to have missed out on Nelson's battles at Aboukir Bay, Copenhagen and Trafalgar. True enough, Wentworth was promoted from lieutenant to commander (a captain of a small vessel) 'in consequence of the action off St. Domingo [1806].'[60] This battle, at which Frank was present, was one of the navy's highpoints after Trafalgar, but it was on a comparatively small scale. The action was an undoubted success, and Clarke's *Naval Chronicle* listed the names of officers who deserved recognition – Frank Austen was not among them, though he did receive public recognition from the Lloyd's Patriotic Fund in the standard form of a congratulatory vase – but it had not furnished the nation with any examples of Nelsonian heroism. According to the *Chronicle*, 'to compare the contest off Domingo with the noble triumphs of Nelson, would be invidious and absurd'. The *Chronicle* concludes that nothing more could have been asked from the fleet, but that the outcome was due more to 'the superior skill and adroitness displayed by the British officers and seamen, than of the ensanguined fury with which [the French fleet] was fought, completely captured, or annihilated.'[61]

To compare Southey's courageous and celebrated Nelson and Austen's competent but undistinguished Wentworth is to see that Austen's Wentworth is defined by that which Southey's Nelson dismisses: financial reward. In a letter to Cassandra, Austen notes of 'Southey's life of Nelson; – I am tired of Lives of Nelson, being that I never read any. I will read this however, if Frank is mentioned in it.'[62] Here, she replaces Southey's hero with her unheroic brother, Frank, whose career, like Wentworth's, is best measured in terms of money accrued rather than laurels won. Having missed out on Trafalgar, Frank made enough to live comfortably from the strategically important job of escorting fleets of merchant shipping, for protecting trading ships during war was as necessary as destroying enemy ones. If the vessels arrived in their destined port safely the captain of the convoy was entitled to a percentage of the value on board, known as freight-money. Wentworth's fortune of £25,000 is acquired from the rather more glamorous-sounding activity of capturing prize ships, but for a naval officer in Austen's era making prize money was not straightforwardly the result of winning battles and in many respects these two activities, the heroic

---

[60] Jane Austen, *Persuasion*, ed. by Patricia Meyer Spacks (New York: W. W. Norton, 1995), p. 18.
[61] James Stanier Clarke and John McArthur, *The Naval Chronicle*, ed. by Nicholas Tracy, 5 vols. (London: Chatham, 1998) III, p. 262.
[62] Jane Austen to Cassandra Austen, 11–12th October 1813, *Letters*, p. 245.

and the economic, were best pursued independently. After all, battles created opportunities for capturing enemy ships, but in practice, any ship in sight of the prize could be deemed to be involved in its capture, and thus the numbers of ships involved in any sizeable battle reduced the amount of prize money available. Furthermore, the captured ship had to be taken to port, judged to determine the legality of the capture and, if approved, valued and 'bought' by the Admiralty. In other words, a captured ship was not a prize unless it could be towed to port, and even then a ship in a very poor state might be deemed to be only salvage. The difference between heroic and economic success is well illustrated by the battle of Trafalgar, a battle in which so many potential prizes were lost rather than captured that the government created a fund with which to augment the meagre amounts available to the sailors.

While it might be thought that the size of Wentworth's fortune is indication enough of courage and daring, his good fortune points away from and not towards heroism in battle. As J. R. Hill observes, given that battle reduced the likelihood of profit, it is remarkable that naval ships did not spend most of their time 'picking up merchant prizes and enriching themselves, with no serious fighting', though this is explained by, among other things, the navy's stiff punishments for those deemed to have shirked their patriotic duty.[63] As this suggests, rather than hope to captain a heavily gunned and prestigious battleship like Nelson's *Victory*, a naval officer with a mind to prize money would have aspired to the command of a smaller, lightly gunned and relatively nimble frigate, the type of ship that could break away from a fleet and cruise independently in search of stray naval ships or isolated merchant vessels. As a young officer, Frank Austen spent his early sailing career hoping to be appointed to a frigate, only to move from a sloop to the ill-fated warship which missed Trafalgar and then to convoy duty. Wentworth, in contrast, succeeds in captaining small ships and thereby picking up easy prizes. In his attempt to impress the uninformed Henrietta and Louisa Musgrove, Wentworth lists the ships from which he has earned prize money. His earliest prizes came to him in the West Indies: numerous privateers (privately owned ships licensed to capture enemy ships for private profit and therefore likely to have been sailing independently of a naval fleet) and one French frigate, a larger ship than his own sloop but not as formidable an opponent as a ship of the line. The encounters with these ships must have involved some element of unequal

---

[63] J. R. Hill, *The Prizes of War: The Naval Prize System in the Napoleonic Wars, 1793–1815* (Stroud: Sutton, 1998), p. 60.

combat, but Wentworth twice allows that his prizes were the result of '"luck"', and while he may be playing down any struggles for the benefit of his impressionable female audience, his willingness to assist Henrietta and Louisa at one point by swiftly opening a volume of naval lists suggests that he is not concealing any heroic endeavour out of modesty. His latter captures are explained geographically, rather than by the class of the ships involved: first a '"lovely cruise … off the Western Islands"', implicitly of Scotland, and then service in the Mediterranean.[64] The latter certainly suggests that he was engaged in convoy or blockade duties, but neither description locates him in the most volatile naval theatres further into the Baltic or over to North America.[65]

Wentworth's substantial fortune does mark him as especially fortunate, both in terms of opportunity and outcome. Prize money was divided among the crews of all ships involved in a capture using a set scale of payments, but few officers other than flag officers acquired enormous wealth through prize money, a state of affairs exacerbated after 1808 when the scale of payments was altered to reduce the amount given to admirals and captains. Though Charles Austen was luckier with prizes than his brother, he earned slightly less than 5 percent of Wentworth's £25,000.[66] But if Wentworth is a sailor of good fortune, extremely good fortune, his luck does not equate to Nelsonian heroism. Wentworth's fortune is the result of learning how to save rather than destroy, for the young officer who proposed to Anne prior to becoming a captain had already 'been lucky in his profession, but spending freely, what had come freely, had realized nothing.'[67] Much as he might want to play the hero for the female audience, he does not produce any tales of daring and courage, and the absence of both is further underlined by his comparative obscurity, for as competent a sailor as Wentworth undoubtedly is, none of his actions seem to have brought his name to prominence among the Elliots and Musgroves. As Hill concludes, 'to become known, to gain kudos and probable promotion, was to succeed in action against enemy fighting forces', whereas capturing even the most financially rewarding prizes 'would scarcely bring the ship's name to notice, let alone the names of individuals.'[68] Wentworth's

---

[64] Austen, *Persuasion*, pp. 44–45.
[65] See Black, *Britain as a Military Power*, pp. 221–40.
[66] Sheila Johnson Kindred, 'Captain Charles Austen's Influence on *Persuasion* and *Mansfield Park*', *Persuasions*, 31 (2009), 115–29 (at p. 117).
[67] Austen, *Persuasion*, p. 19.
[68] Hill, *The Prizes of War*, p. 64.

arrival at the Musgrove's residence is anticipated by Mrs Musgrove's anxious desire to make acquaintance with one who was once her son, Dick Musgrove's, captain, but when Mrs Musgrove cuts short Wentworth's narrative of his career in order to claim that '"*we* shall never forget what you did"', she is referring only to his role in relation to her dead son rather than to any particularly noteworthy contribution to the nation's war effort.[69]

The limits of Wentworth's account of himself are marked during the conversation with Henrietta and Louisa by the spectral presence of their late sailor brother. Mary Favret has argued that *Persuasion* reduces the spectacle of war to the level of the everyday by meditating on loss and absence.[70] The death of the unremarkable Dick Musgrove is one such loss. The time and place of Dick's death is unexplained, but Austen provides enough information to allude to a well-known naval failure. That Dick served with Wentworth on the *Laconia*, which Wentworth must have commanded from some point in 1808, indicates that he died after 1809, a date that cannot but invoke the ill-fated Walcheron expedition (1809). This attack on the French naval base at Antwerp exposed the deeply unheroic reality of military service for most of its participants, as more sailors died from sickness than from enemy fire, a situation made worse by the poor provision of medical aid. The failure of the expedition led to high profile recriminations and it was a significant factor in the very public disagreement between the Foreign Secretary, George Canning, and the Secretary of State for War, Lord Castleregh, which was settled by means of a duel.[71] Dick is said to have served six months under Wentworth '"a great while before he died"', or so Louisa guesses, and it is indicated that the news of his death had reached his family in or around 1812. However, by not pinpointing the date of Dick's death, Austen invokes the Walcheren disaster, not as a specific event, but as an example of the most likely narrative for ordinary men at war.[72] Even Wentworth seems to acknowledge that he might, but for chance, have exchanged places with the unheroic sailor whose death is unrecorded and marked only by a mother's grief; Wentworth admits that, due to a gale, he had once been twenty-four hours from becoming just

---

[69] Austen, *Persuasion*, p. 45.
[70] Mary Favret, *War at a Distance: Romanticism and the Making of Modern Wartime* (Princeton, NJ: Princeton University Press, 2010), pp. 145–51.
[71] Emsley, *British Society and the French Wars*, p. 130.
[72] Austen, *Persuasion*, p. 34. As Roger Sales notes, Austen deals severely with Mrs Musgrove's desire to remember Dick warmly, *Jane Austen and Representations of Regency England*, pp. 185–7.

'"a gallant Captain Wentworth, in a small paragraph at one corner of the newspapers: and being lost in only a sloop, nobody would have thought about me."'[73] In comparison to the 'thick-headed, unfeeling, unprofitable' Dick, whose unexplained death points to the ubiquity of undistinguished mediocrity, the skilful Wentworth is a far more fortunate, in every sense, but the sense that fortune might just have easily changed their places indicates that they are more double than opposites.[74]

By drawing Wentworth as a financially successful but undistinguished sailor, more like her brothers than the celebrated Nelson, Austen writes against Southey's civic connection between heroism and virtuous poverty, or rather, between soldiers and sailors of fortune and vicious avarice. Austen's account of Wentworth's career, haunted as it is by the 'unprofitable' Dick Musgrove, distances Southey's romanticized ideal of the hero, the ideal that Mrs Musgrove 'remembers' in place of Dick. Of course, the end of the novel leaves Wentworth 'as [one] high in his profession as merit and activity could place him, … no longer nobody', but his move from 'nobody' to the husband of a baronet's daughter has been facilitated by his fortune and he remains undistinguished in the way that Nelson is distinguished, as one loved by all for the heroism that, ultimately, killed him.[75] Louisa Musgrove's haziness regarding the reason for Wentworth's sudden reappearance – '"[he] is just returned to England, or paid off, or something"' – hints at the possibility that he might not be on leave, but might have been retired on half-pay. Although officially at peace in 1814, the navy still had commitments and Wentworth's presence throughout the period of time covered by the narrative, justified only as his not being 'immediately employed', strongly hints at a more than temporary cessation.[76] Indeed, Mrs Musgrove's sudden allusion to Dick brings an abrupt end to Wentworth's account of himself and metonymically raises the possibility that he has suffered a similarly abrupt interruption to his sea service, like those suffered by Austen's brothers. The text does leave open the possibility that Wentworth will go to sea again, and perhaps to a battle, but the idea that Anne must pay the 'tax' of 'quick alarm' for her marriage subtly ties any future performance of militarism to the accrual of further financial reward.[77]

---

[73] Austen, *Persuasion*, p. 44.
[74] Ibid., p. 34.
[75] Ibid., p. 165.
[76] Ibid., pp. 34, 18.
[77] Ibid., p. 168.

Domestic Happiness

When Clarke suggested to Austen that she should write a clergyman, one who might be a suitable friend for an alluringly 'distinguished Naval Character', he did so in a letter that he begins by noting that he was himself 'getting Spirits for a Winter Campaign'.[78] Both the advice and the flirtation met with little in the way of enthusiasm. In response to his initial suggestion that she should commit her pen to the life of a clergyman, Austen asserted that, a 'Woman, who ... knows only her own Mother-tongue' and has read as little of the moderns as the ancients could never attempt 'Man's Conversation'.[79] In highlighting the difference between boys' and girls' education, Austen formulates a proto-feminist response. There is no record of Austen's reply to Clarke's second recommendation, made in his second letter, that she write a naval character, but his last letter (March) is shorter and less personal than his previous letters and continues to attempt to establish a rapport only by way of the suggestion that Austen write a historical romance, a genre favoured by women writers of the period. This was another proposition she rebuffed:

> I am fully sensible that an Historical Romance ... might be much more to the purpose of Profit or Popularity, than such pictures of domestic Life in Country Villages as I deal in – but I could no more write a Romance than an Epic Poem. – I could not sit seriously down to write a serious Romance under any other motive than to save my Life & if it were indispensible for me to keep it up & never relax into laughing at myself or other people, I am sure I should be hung before I had finished the first Chapter. – No – I must keep to my own style & go on in my own Way.[80]

As before, the profession of incapability actually questions the 'nature' of gendered behaviours. Austen's lack of interest in either 'feminine' romance or 'masculine' epic can be read as a refusal to write the chivalric or classical past and thus to perpetuate old mythologies in which men are heroes and women the reward for heroism. Furthermore, in joining romance and epic, Austen brings together opposites – feminine and masculine, prose and poetry, low and high – only to state that she is no more likely to write one than the other. The threat of laughter sweeps aside binary opposition.

Austen makes no mention of reading Clarke's *Naval Sermons*: had she done so, she would surely have seen that he defends gender binaries by

---

[78] James Stanier Clarke to Jane Austen, 21st December 1815, *Letters*, p. 320.
[79] Jane Austen to James Stanier Clarke, 11th December 1815, *Letters*, p. 319.
[80] Jane Austen to James Stanier Clarke, 1st April 1816, *Letters*, p. 326.

appealing to the physicality of the body. Like Adam Ferguson, Clarke rests his account of militarism on the notion that the male body is naturally active. In his first sermon, Clarke dismisses the notion that happiness is achieved only when the 'wants of nature are provided or procured without labour.' Clarke stresses the importance of physical activity to men: 'we cannot but perceive, that man, both from the structure of his body, the powers of his mind, and the combined operations of both, is formed for active progress, and continual exertion.'[81] To say that the 'structure of the body' is 'formed' for activity is to indicate that the male body has an essential capacity for militarism. Admittedly, Clarke acknowledges that man's innate capacity for activity is both mental and physical, for 'as the body, from want of exercise, is disposed to generate those corrupt humours which destroy the health', so an idle and inactive mind will 'undermine virtue'.[82] However, the importance of the body to his binary thinking is nowhere clearer than in his assertion that the sailors' activity is akin to Adam's 'laborious occupation' after the fall, a move that fixes male in opposition to female, masculinity in opposition to femininity.[83] When he argues that 'they who have passed through the rigid school of discipline, which the naval profession continues to preserve, are often known to form the best of fathers, of husbands, and of friends', he cannibalizes 'discipline' to mean that which aids men in fulfilling their 'natural' roles as men.[84] As Geoff Quilley points out, in the aftermath of the great naval mutinies of 1797 conservative voices deliberately connected military and familial duty to counter the threat of rebellion from within.[85] Clarke reaches just such a climax in the conclusion to the eighth sermon, 'On the Love of Our Country':

> On that Altar, which our forefathers reared to Liberty, the flame of patriotism arises! Around it, let every age and rank assemble: the Nobles, and the Rulers, and the Elders of the People, and take that oath, which the Genius of Britain proffers;--WE SWEAR, THAT WE WILL REMEMBER THE LORD! WE WILL FIGHT FOR OUR BRETHREN, OUR SONS, OUR DAUGHTERS, OUR WIVES, AND OUR HOUSES! AND WILL FIRMLY UNITE IN THE PRESERVATION AND DEFENCE OF HER WHO DWELLETH, WITH SO MUCH TERRIBLENESS, IN

---

[81] Clarke, *Naval Sermons*, pp. 1, 5.
[82] Ibid., p. 8.
[83] Ibid., p. 9.
[84] Ibid., p. 74.
[85] Geoff Quilley, 'Duty and Mutiny: The Aesthetics of Loyalty and the Representation of the British Sailor c.1789–1800', in *Romantic Wars: Studies in Culture and Conflict, 1793–1822*, ed. by Philip Shaw (Aldershot: Ashgate, 2000), pp. 80–109.

THE CLEFTS OF THE ROCK; WHOSE RAMPART, AND WHOSE WALL, – IS FROM THE SEA![86]

Clarke's homily requires sailors to pledge their military capacity as husbands, fathers and sons. As defenders of their wives and children and of the feminized land, they provide military service in return for patriarchal privilege. Given this, Clarke's admonition to all sailors to attend to religious devotions and thereby 'withdraw the only shade' cast on the navy by 'the vices of a few individuals' may be referring to the mutineers, but also seems intended to police non-heterosexual behaviour and promote heterosexual domesticity.[87]

Whereas Clarke's civic understanding of militarism appeals to the essential 'nature' of the male body to reinforce the gender binary, Southey's equally civic account of the nation's hero has to work harder to do likewise. The biography begins with Nelson's early life, including Nelson's father's belief, 'that in whatever station he might be placed, [his son] would climb, if possible, to the very top of the tree.'[88] The now-hackneyed idiom uses the metaphor of climbing to introduce Nelson's essential disposition towards physical activity. As Southey later notes, Nelson sought to command because he became so frustrated by others' inactivity: '"to be an admiral, and in command of the English fleet; I should very soon either do much, or be ruined; my disposition cannot bear tame and slow measures."'[89] However, Southey's biography is relentlessly occupied with the hero's seemingly inadequate body. That the young Nelson should want to go to sea is something of a surprise to his naval uncle, for as a child, Nelson 'was never of a strong body; and the ague, which at that time was one of the most common diseases in England, had greatly reduced his strength.'[90] The early stages of Nelson's career are remarkable for the continuousness of his physical suffering: he is 'reduced almost to a skeleton' by service in India, poisoned by manchineel and weakened by dysentery in Nicaragua, and then sent to the harsh conditions of the Baltic before fully recovered.[91] Southey notes that 'the asperity with which he mentioned [the latter] so many years afterwards, evinces how deeply he resented a mode of conduct equally cruel to the individual and detrimental to the service.'[92] Such

---

[86] Clarke, *Naval Sermons*, pp. 171–2.
[87] Ibid., p. 37.
[88] Southey, *Life of Nelson*, I, pp. 4–5.
[89] Ibid., I, p. 128.
[90] Ibid., I, p. 5.
[91] Ibid., I, p. 23.
[92] Ibid., I, p. 40.

is Nelson's propensity to fall ill that he even manages to contract a sore throat and fever when stationed at the Nore during the, admittedly often inclement, British summer. More significantly, Southey connects Nelson's willingness to hazard danger to his sustaining more lasting bodily damage: the loss of sight in one eye and the loss of a lower arm. Southey expands on the latter by noting that the damage was made worse by a mistake with the amputation that left him in pain for many months.

But as much as Southey's cataloguing of Nelson's bodily fallibility might seem to work against any endeavour to present the hero with the laurels of old heroism, this is better thought of as a response to the necessary contradiction within essentialist argument. The old hero offers more than a mere performance of militarism, and masculinity, but although the authenticity of this is guaranteed by his bodiliness, that which is innate and inheres within is also, by necessity, more than tangible, fleshy matter. In Southey's account of it, illness and accidents confirm that the qualities which inhere within the body cannot be destroyed by damage to the body. Thus, when Southey writes that, after nearly five years fighting in the French Revolutionary War, Nelson's needed to repair his 'shattered frame', he draws attention to Nelson's 'real' body and to his super-natural fortitude in continuing to serve. That said, as well as suffering physically, Southey's Nelson is subject to frequent bouts of depression. Nelson returns from India with a 'body broken down by sickness, and spirits which had sunk with his strength'; the loss of his lower right arm convinces him that he is ' "a burthen to my friends, and useless to my country." '[93] However, Southey makes plain that Nelson's spirits are lowered only when his military activities are threatened or actually curtailed, either as a result of illness and injury. The fact that Southey's Nelson overcomes even the most physically debilitating of setbacks means that his body is presented as more super(latively)-natural as a result. Fittingly, Southey's final statement on Nelson's body concerns his corpse. Southey states that 'there was reason to suppose, from the appearances upon opening the body, that, in the course of nature, he might have attained, like his father, to a good old age.'[94] Having focused so much on the combination of Nelson's susceptibility to disease and injury and ability to overcome physical setbacks, this strange detail can be read as a move to ensure that the text's interest in super-natural resilience does not compromise the hero's status as a straight-forwardly 'natural' military man.

[93] Ibid., I, pp. 23, 195.
[94] Ibid., II, p. 274.

It is noticeable that Southey's narrative strikes another odd note when he asserts that 'he, who was familiar with wounds and death, suffered like a woman.'[95] But if the intended contrast between masculine resilience and feminine fragility goes somewhat awry, it reflects the fact that, just as Southey wrestles with Nelson's 'natural' body, so he wrestles with Nelson's attitude to domestic happiness. For all his patriotic dedication to the public good, Nelson had succumbed to an adulterous passion for Emma Hamilton, Southey writes, after which the celebrated hero 'had every earthly blessing, except domestic happiness: he had forfeited that forever.'[96] However, Southey's discussion of the extramarital relationship is more nuanced than this direct criticism suggests. Southey prepares for the arrival of Emma by presenting Nelson's inclinations towards women as positively as possible. Southey stresses that Nelson's feelings always tended towards matrimony rather than debauchery: his first romantic attachment is interrupted by friendly interventions which prevent an 'imprudent marriage' and he is able to give up his second attachment when he reflects on 'the evils of a straitened income to a married man.'[97] Nelson's third attachment, to a young widow, Frances Nisbert, leads to marriage, the circumstances of which are described by Southey so as to indicate that his romantic enthusiasm is quickly subordinated to duty. Too noble to benefit financially from a rift between Frances' father and brother that would have enriched Frances and so Nelson, the newly married Nelson facilitates their reunion. The honourable Nelson is unwilling to tear himself from his new wife's side, but he does so on the basis that ' "private convenience or happiness must ever give way to the public good." ' At this point in his narrative, Southey takes the opportunity to respond to an unnamed critic who asserts that a naval hero ought to be unmarried; Southey counters this by stressing that to read Nelson's letters to Frances is to 'understand the effect of domestic love and duty upon a mind of the true heroic stamp.'[98]

According to Clarke's homily to domesticity, a man ought to see himself as the counterpart to femininity. This seems to be the position Southey adopts in order to excuse Nelson's relationship with Emma, for the author who managed to enjoy close friendships with women other than his wife seems unable to entirely condemn Nelson's connection with Emma.[99]

[95] Ibid., II, p., 186.
[96] Ibid., II, p. 91.
[97] Ibid., I, pp. 44, 51.
[98] Ibid., I, pp. 69.
[99] For Southey and women, see Mark Storey, *Southey: A Life* (Oxford: Oxford University Press, 1997).

Southey details Emma's many virtues, including her success in continental diplomacy on behalf of the navy, in order to indicate that her personal qualities were sufficient to draw an honourable man's attention. Her 'manners and accomplishments', her 'uncommon intellectual endowments' and character 'which, both in its strength and in its weakness, resembled [Nelson's] own' were, according to Southey, sufficient to allay Nelson's father's concerns about their relationship.[100] As Southey asserts, 'there is no reason to believe that this most unfortunate attachment was criminal.'[101] To further sanitize their mutual affection, Southey presents Nelson's interest in Emma as just as domestic because just as dutiful as his relationship with his wife. Southey points out that Nelson fulfilled his domestic duty by providing for his wife financially: '"the little I have, I have given to you … I wish it was more; but I have never got a farthing dishonestly: – it descends from clean hands."'[102] In the second edition of the biography, published in 1814, Southey insists that Nelson continued to give away much of what he received in pay and pension to his estranged wife, so much so that even in the final years of his life he remained 'comparatively a poor man'.[103] This establishes a precedent which helps explain why, after the death of William Hamilton, Nelson supports Emma by furnishing her with funds equal to her husband's pension.

And yet, for all his effort to neutralize the 'unfortunate attachment' to the woman Nelson called '"Brave Emma! – Good Emma!"', Southey does condemn the woman he holds responsible for Nelson's shameful actions at Naples: 'it was obvious that he was influenced by an infatuated attachment, – a baneful passion, which destroyed his domestic happiness, and now … stained ineffaceably his public character.'[104] Southey can allow Nelson and Emma to 'resemble each other', as this explains their innocent attraction to each other, and he can even excuse Nelson's suspicious generosity to a widow, but Southey sympathizes only in so far as the relationship remains 'natural', that is, until it becomes clear that Emma holds sway over Nelson. Although Southey likens Emma to 'a heroine of modern romance', he comes to see her not as a chaste damsel and counterpart to the chivalric knight, but as a temptress, more like Matilda in Mathew Lewis' infamous gothic novel *The Monk* (1796).[105] The woman who 'totally

---

[100] Southey, *Life of Nelson*, II, p. 179.
[101] Ibid., II, p. 42.
[102] Ibid., I, p. 115.
[103] Robert Southey, *The Life of Nelson*, 2nd ed., 2 vols (London: John Murray, 1814), II, p. 183.
[104] Southey, *Life of Nelson* (1813), II, pp. 228, 52.
[105] Ibid., II, p. 28.

weaned [Nelson's] affections from his wife' is unduly venerated by the 'spell bound' admiral and 'the undisguised and romantic passion with which he regarded [her image], amounted almost to superstition.'[106] While Southey permits Nelson's desire for Emma, a desire which can be understood in terms of the hero's 'natural' masculinity, the masculinity that finds its necessary counterpart in femininity, Southey ultimately attacks Emma for wielding an 'unnatural' power over him, that is, for conquering the hero's super(lative)-nature with her supernatural womanly powers.

According to Tim Fulford, Southey's *The Life of Nelson* offers a narrative of redemption: Nelson succumbs to Emma's temptations but then becomes 'a paragon of a properly self-restrained manliness' and so much so that Southey, like Austen, identifies the navy's middle-class men as new 'models of British manliness on which a stable domestic society could be founded'. However, to say that Austen allows such men to be, in Fulford's words, 'chivalric, authoritative, paternalist' is to underestimate the depth of her engagement with others' use of the military man as a model of 'natural' masculinity.[107] For Clarke and Southey, there is a natural, in every sense, reciprocity between the new old hero and orthodox patriarchal domestic happiness: the vigorous body that fights is also a virile body that fathers. Austen's *Persuasion* satirizes this connection.[108] When Mrs Clay offers the opinion that a naval officer would be a very '"desirable tenant"' for Sir Walter Elliot's Kellynch Hall, she does so on the basis that she knows a '"good deal"' about the profession. Though the sexual innuendo is more apparent to the reader once it has been revealed that she hopes to trade her personal charms for Sir Walter's favour, Sir Walter is quick to catch her meaning. His reticence to let Kellynch to a naval officer is born of his refusal to associate with men who might have raised themselves from '"obscure birth"' to positions that command respect, but he also instinctively characterizes such men as troublingly potent. Sir Walter assumes that any such tenant would want to hunt and he worries about allowing a military man, '"sailor or soldier"',

---

[106] Ibid., II, pp. 42, 62, 245.
[107] Tim Fulford, 'Romanticizing the Empire: The Naval Heroes of Southey, Coleridge, Austen, and Marryat', *MLQ*, 60.2 (1999), 161–96 (pp. 177, 187, 171). See also Tim Fulford, 'Sighing for a Soldier: Jane Austen and Military Pride and Prejudice', *Nineteenth-Century Literature*, 57.2 (2002), 153–78; Anne Frey, 'Nation Without Nationalism: The Reorganization of Feeling in Austen's *Persuasion*', *Novel: A Forum on Fiction*, 38.2&3 (2005), 214–34; Alice Drum, 'Pride and Prestige: Jane Austen and the Professions', *College Literature*, 36.3 (2009), 92–115.
[108] For further discussion of sexual knowledge in *Persuasion*, see Jill Heydt-Stevenson, *Austen's Unbecoming Conjunctions: Subversive Laughter, Embodied History* (Basingstoke: Palgrave Macmillan, 2008), pp. 181–205.

the right to his '"pleasure-grounds"'. Despite Mrs Clay's assurances that the grounds will be respected, even Elizabeth Elliot's '"sweet"' borders, he fears for his eldest daughter and recommends that she '"be on her guard with respect to her flower-garden."'[109] A widowed baronet whose only son had been still-born, Sir Walter is anxious about the strength of what he believes to be the essential 'nature' of military men. In his state of anxiety, Sir Walter begins to argue against their potency: he asserts that active military service can only be detrimental to a military man's '"youth and vigour' and that naval service has a particularly deleterious effect on the body, for such is the damage caused by exposure to sunshine and sea air that 'a sailor grows old sooner than any other man"'. Somewhat strategically, Mrs Clay revises her position on the desirability of the military man in order to concur with Sir Walter: she opines that since all professions take a toll on men's bodies, only propertied men '"hold the blessings of health and a good appearance to the utmost."'[110]

The novel's early satire on the sexual appeal of 'naturally' potent military men opens out to a study of their romantic appeal. It has been some time since Randolph Trumbach suggested that the rising importance of sentimentalized romantic domesticity in the eighteenth century served to reinforce the naturalization of heterosexuality and thus as a 'strategy for reconstructing patriarchy.'[111] Though hardly engaged in queering heterosexuality, Austen's *Persuasion* resists romanticizing the 'natural' military man and instead offers naval officers who are characterized as much by their unheroic careers as they are by the unremarkable materiality of their bodies and their unconventional domestic felicity. The Elliots' tenant, Admiral Croft, is exemplary in this regard. Of all the naval men in the novel, Croft is the closest to a hero. Unlike Wentworth and his fellow officers Captains Harville and Benwick, Croft fought at the battle of Trafalgar. However, it is not clear what position he held at Trafalgar or what he contributed to that action, and his subsequent naval service is described by Mrs Croft in terms of locations: she mentions the East and possibly West Indies, various European ports and the North Seas. The latter places Croft in one of the more volatile naval theatres after the battle of Trafalgar, but as a rear-admiral of the white, Croft holds a relatively modest admiral's rank, one that suggests lengthy rather than exceptional service. Like Wentworth, Croft is introduced to the text as a wealthy but not a celebrated sailor: only

---

[109] Austen, *Persuasion*, pp. 13–14.
[110] Ibid., pp. 14–15.
[111] Trumbach, *Sex and the Gender Revolution*, p. 430.

Anne has heard of the admiral prior to his arrival at Kellynch, and her reasons for scanning the naval news with more than common assiduity can easily be fathomed.

Though the oldest sailor in the novel, Admiral Croft does not serve as a model old hero. For all Sir Walter's worrying about what a military tenant might do to his property, Croft shows little interest in the dogged pursuit of victory; Sir Walter is informed that though 'he sometimes took out a gun [to hunt], [he] never killed.'[112] The admiral who fails to fulfil the vacancy for a Nelsonian hero also possesses the most ordinary of bodies. The Elliots retreat to Bath to cure their finances; the Crofts retire there to cure his gout. There's little in the way of super-natural fortitude here, merely acceptance of a mundane ailment. Just as importantly, Croft has not fathered any children. Given that the text begins with the issue of generation, it is, as Eric C. Walker has noted, significant that the Crofts are childless.[113] It is not clear which of their bodies is infertile, and so the text casts doubt on Mr as much as Mrs Croft's reproductive capacity. Furthermore, with her portrait of Admiral Croft, Austen presents the character most likely to have been the superlatively bodily old hero as the character most obviously happy in his very un-patriarchal domesticity. Like Southey, the admiral is an advocate for the benefits of a naval life for an unmarried man, but whereas Southey asserts that love spurs a man to do his patriotic and patriarchal duty, Croft warns Wentworth that marriage exposes chivalric gender roles as idealistic, for a married military man will want to accommodate his wife on board his ship rather than leave her with the hearth and home. Mrs Croft can attest to this: she has seen a good deal of naval service and is able to say that '"the happiest part of my life has been spent on board a ship."' True, Austen makes no claim to military heroism on Mrs Croft's behalf: when Admiral Croft is in the North Seas, she waits at the port of Deal, fearing for his life at sea and hers on shore.[114] But as Claudia Johnson, Peter Knox-Shaw and others have argued, Austen is at her most proto-feminist in her presentation of Mrs Croft, the character who punctures what Michael Kramp identifies as Wentworth's 'performance' for Henrietta and Louisa by upbraiding him for talking '"as if women were all fine ladies, instead of rational

---

[112] Austen, *Persuasion*, p. 16.
[113] For the Croft's troublesome status as a childless, unsettled couple, see Eric C. Walker, *Marriage, Writing and Romanticism: Wordsworth and Austen After War* (Stanford: Stanford University Press, 2009), pp. 51–8.
[114] Austen, *Persuasion*, pp. 47.

creatures." '[115] With Admiral and Mrs Croft, Austen creates a relationship not unlike that of Southey's Nelson and Emma, one in which her strength and weakness 'resemble' his, but rather than conclude that this is a threat to masculine authority, Austen offers the Crofts' equality as the model for domestic happiness.[116] The couple who seem always to be together share the role of the sailor as much as they do the reins of their carriage, and it is in only nearly overturning their carriage that they successfully overturn the binary opposition within Clarke's sermons and Southey's *Life*.[117]

Whereas Admiral Croft serves the novel as an old military man who has no interest in old heroism, Captain Harville's place within the text is more complicated. Harville has profited less from his naval service than Wentworth – his accommodation in a lodging-house reveals his straitened circumstances – and rather than accrue prize money he has acquired a 'severe wound'. That said, the latter does little to introduce Nelsonian glamour into the text, for the unexplained wound is as underwhelming as Croft's gout: 'ha[ving] never been in good health' since being wounded, Harville is left a 'little lame' and so altered by his bodily complaints as to look older than his years. Unable to serve at sea, Harville is able to use his military skills to 'supply the deficiencies of lodging-house furniture, and defend the windows and doors against the winter storms.'[118] Karen Harvey has warned scholars to take care when assessing the men's activities in the domestic sphere during the eighteenth century: in the household 'male authority … [was] consolidated and embedded in the subtle but potent everyday material practices of the house'.[119] This would be the case for the Harvilles, were it not for the fact that Harville's lameness has also left him with a 'mind of usefulness and ingenuity' that he turns to small, domestic rather than defensive, tasks: 'he drew, he varnished, he carpentered, he glued; he made toys for the children, he fashioned new netting needles and pins with improvements.'[120] That said, it is Harville who, at the end of the text, asserts that masculinity inheres within the male body.

---

[115] Michael Kramp, *Disciplining Love: Austen and the Modern Man* (Columbus: Ohio State University Press, 2007), p. 130; Austen, *Persuasion*, p. 47. See also Johnson, *Jane Austen*, pp. 151; Peter Knox-Shaw, *Jane Austen and the Enlightenment* (Cambridge: Cambridge University Press, 2004), pp. 227–8.

[116] For the Crofts as a model of equality see, for example, Megan A. Woodworth, *Eighteenth-Century Women Writers and the Gentleman's Liberation Movement: Independence, War, Masculinity and the Novel 1778–1818* (Aldershot: Ashgate, 2011), pp. 205–78.

[117] Austen, *Persuasion*, p. 62.

[118] Ibid., pp. 63, 65, 66.

[119] Karen Harvey, *The Little Republic: Masculinity and Domestic Authority in Eighteenth-Century Britain* (Oxford: Oxford University Press, 2012), p. 22.

[120] Austen, *Persuasion*, p. 66.

In response, Anne claims that women love longer for social rather than biological reasons: '"we live at home, quiet confined, and our feelings prey on us. You are forced on exertion. You have always a profession, pursuits, business."' Harville agrees about the effects of the different opportunities given to each gender, but he retreats from Anne's proto-constructionism to a more essentialist view of masculinity: '"I believe in a true analogy between our bodily frames and our mental; and that as our bodies are the strongest, so are our feelings; capable of bearing most rough usage, and riding out the heaviest weather."'[121] Harville's opinions serve an important purpose: he helps Anne to see that Wentworth's apparent desire to marry 'as soon as he could be properly tempted' is bravado and so to realize that he is still attached to her.[122] However, once again the text undermines Harville, for in exposing Wentworth's performance of masculinity he punctures his own essentialist argument. Harville's standing in the text is further questioned by the introduction of his double, Mrs Smith. Confined to her sick chamber by rheumatism of the legs, Mrs Smith is relieved, not by a 'submissive spirit', but by 'that elasticity of mind, ... finding employment which carried her out of herself, which was from Nature alone.'[123] With this pairing, Austen indicates that, though thrust into different spheres, the minds, and indeed bodies, of men and women are not essentially different.

According to Knox-Shaw, the 'celebration of the strength of women' in *Persuasion* shows that, 'at a time when war had conferred a premium on the male virtues of courage and daring, Jane Austen reopened debate on sexual roles'.[124] Indeed, for Nina Auerbach, 'the revolutionary vision of *Persuasion* encompasses ... the polemics of a Mary Wollstonecraft'.[125] While it is all too tempting to view Wentworth through Henrietta and Louisa's eyes, just as Henrietta comes to see that a military man is no more desirable than a clergyman, so it is helpful to see that Austen does not allow the fortunate Wentworth's military activities to be connected to his romantic ones. Wentworth explains that he was willing to set sail in an old and unseaworthy ship in 1806 because he wanted '"to be doing something"', but the 'something' is really to recover from Anne's rejection of his proposal, and thus the text sets what Clarke and Southey might identify

---

[121] Ibid., p. 155
[122] Ibid., p. 41.
[123] Ibid., p. 102.
[124] Knox-Shaw, *Jane Austen and the Enlightenment*, pp. 222, 228.
[125] Nina Auerbach, 'O Brave New World: Evolution and Revolution in *Persuasion*', *ELH*, 39.1 (1972), 112–28 (p. 128).

as 'naturally' masculine military activity and domestic happiness at odds from the beginning.[126] True enough, Wentworth is provided with romantic rivals who he can treat as military enemies, one of whom, Charles Hayter, is made to 'quit the field' as a result of Wentworth's assault on Henrietta.[127] However, as Jill Heydt Stevenson has argued, the collision of military terms and domestic matters in this novel creates an 'unbecoming conjunction' of ideas, one of many comic and destabilizing combinations aimed at frustrating 'rigid expectations of gender roles.'[128] Wentworth's active, militaristic pursuit of a romantic conquest comes to nothing: Wentworth does not win Henrietta and his prize for securing Louisa is to be bound unhappily to her, restrained 'in a state of inaction' until she consents to release him. Once freed, Wentworth finds that ' "[he] could exert [him]self, [he] could do something" ' to bring about a reconciliation with Anne, but Austen's decision to rewrite the final chapters of the novel ensures that Wentworth does not control the final stages of the narrative.[129]

In the original ending to *Persuasion*, Anne and Wentworth meet at the Crofts' lodgings in Bath and the Crofts are instrumental in ensuring that the lovers renew their affections: 'during that time, the Husband and wife, either by the wife's contrivance, or simply by going on in their usual way, were frequently out of the room together.'[130] In the rewritten ending, Anne and Wentworth's reconciliation is completed by their chance meeting in the street. In this fortunate moment the wind is momentarily taken out of Wentworth's sails and he is set adrift; in response to Charles' question about his intended direction he can only muster, ' "I hardly know" '.[131] Wentworth is far from heroic in this encounter, and to underline this point Charles, a decidedly unmilitary man, strikes out to buy a gun, leaving Wentworth and Anne to secure each other's hearts. The revision works at the cost of losing the valuable role played by the Crofts and the implication that Anne and Wentworth will grow to be like them, but the rewritten ending makes it clearer that Anne and Wentworth will be as happy because as equal. This is achieved by the strengthening of Anne's refusal to accept that she had erred in rejecting Wentworth's first proposal. In the original final chapters, Anne concedes: ' "If I *was* wrong, in yielding to Persuasion

---

[126] Austen, *Persuasion*, p. 44.
[127] Ibid., p. 55.
[128] Heydt-Stevenson, *Austen's Unbecoming Conjunctions*, p. 198. See also Knox-Shaw, *Jane Austen and the Enlightenment*, pp. 226–9.
[129] Austen, *Persuasion*, p. 162.
[130] Ibid., p. 172.
[131] Ibid., p. 160.

once, remember that it was to Persuasion exerted on the side of Safety, not of Risk."' In the rewritten chapters the same conversation is drawn out into two parts and in the second Anne gives less ground: '"I must believe that I was right, much as I suffered from it, that I was perfectly right in being guided."'[132] Of course, Anne was right. To have accepted would have been to succumb, like Isabella Thorpe, Lydia Bennet and Louisa Musgrove, to 'scarlet fever'; that is, Anne would have conformed to a gender stereotype which buttressed the patriarchal gender order.[133] Unlike Louisa, Anne is able to resist the man in uniform and in refusing to apologize for having earlier rejected Wentworth she avoids taking the subordinate position of one asking for forgiveness from a superior.

Persuasion is unusually closely connected to its contemporary moment by its inclusion of dates and references, but for all its timeliness with regard to the end of the Napoleonic wars, the novel that avoids the post-Waterloo moment in which it was written contributes to a debate that can be traced back to the early eighteenth century. Clarke's *Naval Sermons* and Southey's *Life of Nelson* indicate that the civic ideal of citizen-soldiering retained some potency in the early nineteenth century; for both, the new old hero is now inescapably a professional military man, but he remains a courageous servant to the public good, rather than personal emolument, and is now even more obviously the patriarchal defender of hearth and home. Austen's final words on the navy, that it may be 'more distinguished in its domestic virtues than in its national importance', imply that the two need not be joined together as the 'natural' concerns of the essentially male body.[134] By resisting the allure of civic old heroism and instead drawing on her brothers' distinctly unheroic careers, Austen presents Wentworth as a one who is fortunate, but whose militarism and masculinity are neither innate nor essential. Rather than idealize Wentworth as a romantic because military hero, then, Austen de-romanticizes military men, offering men whose underwhelming bodies and harmonious domestic arrangements question the cultural function of old heroism, including middle-class heroism, in sustaining a binary gender order predicated on the essential 'nature' of the male – and female – body.

---

[132] Ibid., pp. 174, 164.
[133] For this stereotype see Louise Carter, 'Scarlet Fever: Female Enthusiasm for Men in Uniform, 1780–1815', in *Britain's Soldiers: Rethinking War and Society, 1715–1815*, ed. by Kevin Linch and Matthew McCormack (Liverpool: Liverpool University Press, 2014), pp. 155–79.
[134] Austen *Persuasion*, p. 168.

Conclusion
Rethinking Military Masculinity

> Liberty, Gentlemen, has during my long life been regularly progressive; and I am sorry to say, it is now getting too much into a *system* of licentiousness, calculated either to throw us back within the grasp of a standing army and an absolute Monarch, or into the most horrid extensive quagmire, from which it will be difficult to reach any solid foundation, even should we flee to the shores of a democratic republic.[1]
>
> *A Letter to the Reforming Gentlemen* (1817)

William Atkinson's *Letter*, ostensibly a response to a proposal made by one Godfrey Higgins, a Yorkshire magistrate and, in Atkinson's scathing words, a 'Gentleman of *consummate wisdom*, and great celebrity', for the building of a local asylum, is largely concerned with the clarion of reform in the early nineteenth century.[2] According to 'Mr Higgins' Address', as reproduced in Atkinson's *Letter*, the call for reform has been 'peaceably – manfully – honourably' made by the people, and should the gentlemen fail to heed that call, dire consequences may ensue. Higgins' faith in 'awful physical strength, in union with a general enlightened sentiment' seems to draw on seventeenth-century civic republican ideology; he echoes Trenchard, Brown and Ferguson in his attempt to stir the nation's gentlemen to join in the people's crusade: 'Oh! that I could rouse you from your fatal lethargy! If *I* cannot, ... when the blood of civil strife flows down your streets, ... what will be your reproaches should you be alive to make them?' But though Higgins is alert to the dangers of inequality, to the poverty of what he estimates to be a quarter of the population, he looks for a 'gap betwixt military despotism [the rule of the monarch with a standing

---

[1] [William Atkinson], *A Letter to the Reforming Gentlemen, by the Old Inquirer* (Bradford: T. Inkersley, 1817), p. 12.
[2] [Atkinson], *A Letter to the Reforming Gentlemen*, p. 3.

Conclusion: Rethinking Military Masculinity

army and popular anarchy', that is, for reform led by, rather than simply including, gentlemen.[3] It falls to Higgins' opponent, the 'Old Inquirer', to warn against allowing the call for reform to be co-opted by a 'snug little faction' that hopes to marshal the people for its own ends. Atkinson explicitly rehearses civic republican fears of falling into 'the grasp of a standing army and an absolute Monarch'. Following Trenchard, Brown and Ferguson, Atkinson argues that 'the Reform wanted is in [certain] *men*', in their weaknesses for personal advancement and addiction to the 'vices of paper currency'.[4] And yet, Atkinson is really no more kindly disposed towards the people than Higgins. To Atkinson, Jacobin ideas concerning electoral reform are like an empty breeches pocket, impressive only from the outside. Despite all his civic rhetoric, Atkinson rebuffs the notion that there is any nation, America included, so revolutionary as to allow the people, or even the majority of the people, to choose their representatives.

The disagreement between Atkinson and Higgins illuminates something of the complexity of attitudes to militarism in the long eighteenth century, for both employ civic language, but not in the ways or to the ends for which it had been used a century earlier. From one perspective, this seems to confirm Pocock's sense that, by the end of the eighteenth century, the force that had propelled the intellectual tradition of civic republicanism, and with it the model of the citizen-soldier, was all but exhausted. For Pocock, the American Revolution was, 'in some sense ... the last act of the civic Renaissance.'[5] The new states of America defined themselves in civic republican terms, as a community formed on the principles of liberty and democracy, but as the American states began to invest power in leaders, so, Pocock argues, Britons began to reaffirm the importance of the monarchy. Ultimately, Pocock concludes, civic republicanism was 'challenged by modernity: namely, by the perception that under the conditions imposed by the territorial and commercial state, it was no longer possible for the individual to be the autonomous proprietor, arms-bearer, and direct participant in self-government, as presupposed by antiquity.'[6]

The decline in civic thinking can be said to be matched by the rise of modern militarism, and with this the modern military man. For historians of the military revolution, the process of modernization that had started in

---

[3] Ibid., pp. 4, 5.
[4] Ibid., pp. 7, 16.
[5] Pocock, *The Machiavellian Moment*, p. 462.
[6] J. G. A. Pocock, 'States, Republics and Empires: The American Founding in Early Modern Perspective', in *Conceptual Change and the Constitution*, ed. by Terence Ball and J. G. A. Pocock (Lawrence: University of Kansas Press, 1988), pp. 55–77 (at p. 65).

the sixteenth century reached its conclusion by the end of the eighteenth century, even if further revolutions, particularly the advent of 'total war', had only just begun.[7] And yet, Atkinson and Higgins' use of civic language also suggests that civic thinking retained some of its former potency in the early nineteenth century. Indeed, Pocock offers an important postscript when he argues that centralized and centralizing modernity was not so successful as to prevent the persistence of older ideals. The citizen-soldier and, perhaps more so, his descents, the militiaman and the new old heroes of varied kinds, can be included in this, for in the modernized state, Pocock argues, 'the ancient image of virtue was never overthrown or abandoned, and in consequence it had to be recognized that the virtue of commercial and cultivated man was never complete, his freedom and independence never devoid of the elements of corruption.'[8] Rather than offer a simplified narrative of decline and fall, then, Pocock asks scholars to take seriously the survival of older ideals: 'to dismiss all discussion of [modernity by eighteenth-century thinkers] as "nostalgic" and "reactionary", on the one hand, or "progressive" and "bourgeois", on the other, is proof of an incessant desire to misunderstand … What was under discussion was not a simple choice between opposed ideals but a painful and complicated process.'[9]

This study has traced models of militarism – civic and modern – that functioned as vehicles for ideas about the 'nature', or lack thereof, of masculinity, and has mapped those models across the long eighteenth century. On the one hand, then, this has been a study of 'opposed ideals'. I have argued that defences of militiamen and of new old heroes, whether dressed in classical, chivalric or 'savage' garb, are defences of the essential, bodily nature of masculinity. These arguments are rooted in the past, as the appeal to past times confirms that their models are timeless, but they also prioritize courage and daring, particularly the willingness to risk life and limb, as markers of a nature that was innately and necessarily male. At the heart of this model is a concern with the 'reality' or 'truth' of masculinity. As I have argued, the alternative to this – the modern military man – serves as a vehicle for proto-constructionist ideas about masculinity. Though not yet conceptualizing the body as 'a reality fabricated by th[e] specific technology of power that [Foucault] called "discipline"', defences of the modern military

---

[7] Parker, *The Military Revolution*, p. 149; Henninger, 'Military Revolutions and Military History', pp. 18–19.
[8] Pocock, *Virtue, Commerce and History*, p. 147.
[9] Pocock, 'States, Republics and Empires', p. 65.

man are defences of the trained professional who is paid for acquiring a range of skills and deploying those skills as instructed. The notion that this modern military man was a model performer, in a Butlerian sense, indicates that this was a century that was able to see that there might be a space between gender and the sexed, and sexual, body. As such, these arguments are beginning to conceive of the modern body as a *corpus rasa*, a blank, empty space, waiting to project back that which is projected on to it. If this body is not yet an illusion, it is at least a present absence.[10]

The first chapter began with the late seventeenth-century standing army debate as an episode in which these opposing arguments were organized into a structured conflict. The king's proposal to introduce an army of permanently embodied soldiers prompted Trenchard, Toland, Fletcher and the other anti-standing army authors to look to the past for a model of militarism that could reshape the present. The principles that motivated those anti-standing army authors were forged long before there was a proposal for a standing army to oppose and in response to the argument that change was inevitable and the nation's military services must be willing to be changed or be left behind, Trenchard and his allies drew on the history of civic republicanism to argue that while a standing army would threaten the liberty of the people, the fact that any Englishman might become a militiaman meant that all Englishmen would be free men. This call for the militarization of the nation's men was predicated upon the idea that the male body was formed for militarism. The anti-standing army appeal to the traditions of the past corroborated this by confirming the timelessness of men's essential nature. With this, the anti-standing army authors responded to the fact that the king's proposal had created the opportunity for their opponents to discursively reconceptualize militarism and in so doing to forward a new understanding of masculinity. The modern military man emerged in pamphlets by Defoe, Somers, and others as one who must be set aside to acquire the skills needed for modern warfare and then maintained by payment so that he might be available whenever required. Whereas the anti-standing army authors argued that the militiaman had all that was needed within, principally courage, their opponents argued that the male body should be understood as raw material and not as matter imbued with innate, essential capacities. By breaking with civic thinkers' essentializing connection between militarism and the male body, the pro-standing army authors offered an account of masculinity that can be termed proto-constructionist.

[10] Foucault, *Discipline and Punish*, p. 194.

This study may have begun with 'opposed ideals' of militarism and masculinity, but it has sought to reveal the complexity of these ideals by locating them within eighteenth-century culture, both 'high' and 'low'. The pro-standing army authors imagined a new kind of professionalized military man and he is described in Steele, Hume and Smith's writings on military courage and military character. The pro-standing army position was inherited by proponents of politeness, for those already invested in the social construction of the self were predisposed to agree with the argument that modern men must be trained to make military men. But though modern militarism shared much with politeness, the connection was also problematic, for the coming together of professional militarism and politeness exposed that which made both vulnerable to criticism: the emptiness of the *corpus rasa*. Addison and Steele, and even Hume and Smith, wrestled with how to position politeness in relation to a similar performance, but the desire to keep some distance is clearest in Boswell's inability to reconcile his interest in polite self-discipline – the discipline that Smith termed 'sympathy' and argued could give substance to polite performance – and the Foucauldian discipline governing the modernized military man.

The modern professional military man can also be found in the clash between Admirals Mathews and Lestock. In claiming to have obeyed the 'discipline of the navy', Lestock submitted himself to the 'rules' that made manifest the power of centralized naval authority. In so doing, he presented himself as an individual whose militarism was acquired rather than essential, performed rather than expressed. Given that the Mathews and Lestock controversy recaptured the intensity of the standing army debate, it would seem fair to suggest that Lestock's acquittal, a ruling that prefigured the introduction of a naval uniform and the revision of the *Articles of War* in the final years of the 1740s, legitimized the professional military man, but at the time of the trials Lestock was widely said to have concealed cowardice and self-interest behind a 'skreen of discipline'. Much though the Admiralty's reforms might have wanted to formalize 'change', then, the standing of the modern military man remained uncertain after these trials, as Admiral Byng discovered. Like Lestock, Byng presented himself as a surface that reflected back what the Admiralty projected, but in the mid-1750s the open advertisement of such emptiness was not to be rewarded and the execution of Byng seems to have been intended to restore the modern military man to his body by depriving him of his life.

Though the anti-standing army authors had forwarded the militiaman as their ideal model for militarism, by the mid-century the 'natural' military man was as likely to be represented as one of many types of new old hero. In the late 1750s John Brown could still appeal to the 'Roman' old hero, but his contemporaries had other old heroes from which to choose, in particular the medieval knight. One advantage of the chivalric knight for those inclined to civic thought was that he could be proffered as a superior version of both modern militarism and modern politeness. As I have argued, those who opposed this did so without necessarily conceding the achievements of the past to their opponents. Just as Hume argued that the gothic culture of chivalry ought not to be idealized, so Hurd celebrated romance literature by separating gothic literary innovation from gothic militarism. It might seem odd to suggest that Walpole, the author of the first gothic novel, thought likewise, but he had found a form that could challenge the vaunted 'nature' of old heroism. Walpole questioned the model of the knight by turning the apparently super(lative)-nature of this old hero into something supernatural, something unnatural in its excessiveness and illogicality. Of course, the 'natural' body was also at the centre of the culture of sensibility. While Smith's theory of sensibility co-opted feeling to underpin the virtue of modern, polite manners, Ferguson identified the common sentiment of fellow-feeling as essential to man's nature and the basis of masculine military action. His argument that mankind is innately predisposed towards fellow-feeling for fellow creatures is extended to the inhabitants of 'barbarous' nations, past and present; for Ferguson, the warrior-savage is a model for the old heroism that could be revived, if the modern commercial man were to return to his bodily nature. In Mackenzie's hands, sentiment reinforces old heroism even more strongly. Mackenzie echoes Ferguson's concerns with regard to commercialism and colonialism, but having figured the 'savage' as a military prisoner rather than a warrior, Mackenzie's narrative privileges the old veteran as guardian of the patrician and patriarchal masculine 'self'.

As dynamic as the debate conducted by Trenchard and Defoe, Mathews and Lestock, Brown and Hume, Ferguson and Smith was, and not least due to the cannibalizing of each other's terms, the debate began to collapse during the Keppel–Palliser controversy, and in large part due to the growth in the power of the popular public sphere. During the Toulon trials, but also for decades after, Lestock proved to be remarkably unpopular. The equally unpopular Byng responded directly to the public criticism of his conduct with *An Appeal to the People*, but to no avail. Some twenty years later, Keppel managed not to make the same mistakes. In the early stages of the affair Keppel showed little inclination to explain his military conduct to the judging public, but once the trials were underway he took pains to distance himself from the Lestockian conception of correct conduct and to stress that he had dedicated himself to defending the nation. His apparent willingness to be open to public scrutiny reinforced his claim to old heroism, just as his claim to old heroism reinforced his apparent willingness to be open to public scrutiny. However, in performing that which was most desired within the embryonic culture of celebrity – authenticity – Keppel's triumph produced a hollow victory, for the cause of modern militarism had triumphed as much as old heroism. Of course, the French Revolutionary and Napoleonic Wars were to produce more celebrated heroes and both Clarke and Southey made this heroism available to men as their fair share of the patriarchal dividend. Such heroism made little impression upon Austen, however. Rather than allow modern middle-class military men to become new old heroes, she questioned the cultural function of military heroism in sustaining gender inequality. In presenting the modern military man as fortunate but not heroic – a sign of continuity with the standing army debate – Austen contrasts the old certainties of binary masculinity and femininity with new formulations for domestic happiness.

This study has followed parallel narratives of militarism and masculinity in order to understand the tensions and contradictions that are internal to each, but also how they were shaped by their relationships with each other and with public opinion. Just as those narratives are complex, so neither is necessarily more progressive. Civic argument for militarism borne from the essential nature of masculinity was always complicated by the need to articulate how that masculinity might be bodily and more than bodily at once. That said, the support for old heroism was rooted in revolutionary republican politics and hostile to empire-building, its radicalism as vital, in theory if not always in practice, as its patriarchalism. The modern military man was even more unstable, for performance lacked substance; to its critics, performance was unreliable, deceptive and dangerous. But while the supporters of modern militarism may have articulated proto-constructionist ideas about the nature of masculinity, these ideas were enmeshed in commitments to politeness and progress and wary of the emerging popular public sphere. As Mark Philp points out, 'perhaps the most lasting influence of the French Revolution and the reform movement of the 1790s was the recognition by governments that they needed to attend to the opinions of a much wider portion of society than those who cast votes in elections.'[11] Though Colley suggests that the French Revolutionary and Napoleonic Wars rescued the elite from redundancy, I hope to have indicated that

---

[11] *Resisting Napoleon, Resisting Napoleon: The British Response to the Threat of Invasion, 1797–1815*, ed. by Mark Philp (Aldershot: Ashgate, 2006), p. 11.

enthusiasm for celebrity heroes like Admiral Nelson is less an indication of the power of braid and buttons to mesmerize the masses and more an indication of the power of the popular public sphere to challenge old hierarchies and to create new standards for worth, albeit with the 'help' of commercial intermediaries.

As neatly opposed as the standing army debate initially was, then, this study has suggested that parallel lines do not necessarily run true. The situation at the end of the period covered by this book strengthens this point. When Defoe argued that change was inevitable France had already established a standing army; by the end of the eighteenth century, those committed to modernization could, once again, cite French innovation. Whereas the various efforts to revive the English militia in the eighteenth century had sought to effect a militarization of the nation's apparently innately militaristic men through balloted service, the French *levée en masse* (1793) actually militarized a nation in that it made men into soldiers by conscription.[12] The centralizing of military authority seems to have finally conquered the old ideal of the militiaman, but only by cannibalizing the civic assumption that all men are capable of militarism and turning this into an assertion that all men can be made to be military men. If the conscript seems to resemble the militiaman it is also because the balloted militiaman had always resembled a conscript. In Britain, the declaration of war with France, 1793, raised the perennial problem of manning the nation's military services and attempts to increase the militia in 1796–7 were met with widespread rioting, in part by those for whom service would disrupt family economies, but also because it was well known that the wealthy could buy their way out of the ballot and because the distinction between regulars and militia was no longer closely guarded.[13] As McCormack notes, many of the soldiers on the field of Waterloo fought and died in their militia uniforms and their deaths made it difficult to sustain the militia in the nineteenth century.[14] The scale of the hosililty to centralized military authority in this period can be further gauged from the unprecedented surge of 'volunteering' for military bands that were independent of even the balloted militia.[15]

---

[12] Hagemann, 'The Military and Masculinity', pp. 348–50; William J. Philpott, 'Total War', in *Palgrave Advances in Modern Military History*, pp. 131–52 (at pp. 133–4).

[13] John Bohstedt, *Riots and Community Politics in England and Wales, 1790–1810* (Cambridge, MA: Harvard University Press, 1983), pp. 14, 173–84.

[14] McCormack, *Embodying the Militia*, p. 195.

[15] See Colley, *Britons*, pp. 287–319; Kevin Linch, 'Creating the Amateur Soldier: The Theory and Training of Britain's Volunteers', in *Soldiering in Britain and Ireland*, pp. 200–18; J. E. Cookson, 'The English Volunteer Movement of the French War, 1793–1815: Some Contexts', *The Historical Journal*, 32.4 (1989), 867–91.

Although volunteering might be thought to reassert the civic anti-standing army argument that men can exchange the ploughshares for the sword because they are naturally formed for either, the volunteer elected to move in and out of militarism as and when he wanted, and in so doing revealed that he, like his citizen-soldier forebears, is not really naturally formed for either. The volunteer may seem to be a blood relative of the new old heroes, but he is as much a modern military man, for the nature of volunteering reveals that both militarism and masculinity are, essentially, performances.

Bibliography

Primary Sources

A Collection of Old Ballads. Corrected from the Best and Most Ancient Copies Extant. With Introductions Historical, Critical, and Humorous, 3 Vols. London: J. Roberts; J. Brotherton; A. Bettesworth; J. Pemberton; J. Woodman; J. Stag, 1723.

A Full and Particular Account of a Most Dreadful and Surprising Apparition which appeared to a Certain Great Man, at his Great House, on Monday Last, at Midnight. London[?], 1757[?].

A Just, Genuine, and Impartial History of the Memorable Sea-Fight, in the Mediterranean: Between the Combined Fleets of France and Spain, and the Royal Fleet of England, under the Command of the Two Admirals Mathews and Lestock. London: R. Walker, 1745.

A Key to the Trial of Admiral Byng: or A Brief State of Facts Relating to the Action on the Mediterranean on the 20th of May, 1756. London: J. Wilkie, [1756].

A Letter from a Friend in the Country to a Friend at Will's Coffee-House; in Relation to Three Additional Articles of War. London: J. Bromage, 1749.

A Letter Humbly Addrest to the Most Excellent Father of his Country, the Wise and Victorious Prince, King William III. London: J. Darby, 1698.

A Letter to a Foreigner, on the Present Debates about a Standing Army. London: Dan Brown, 1698.

A Letter to Robert Lord Bertie, Relating to his Conduct in the Mediterranean, and his Defence of Admiral Byng. London: R.Griffiths, 1757.

A Modest Apology for the Conduct of a Certain Admiral in the Mediterranean. Being an Essay towards Silencing the Clamorous Tongue of Slander, til Facts can be Ascertained by Substantial and Circumstantial Evidence. London: M. Cooper; B. Dodd, 1756.

A Narrative of the Proceedings of his Majesty's Fleet in the Mediterranean, and the Combined Fleets of France and Spain, from the Year 1741 to March 1744, 3rd ed. London: J[ohn] Millan, 1745.

A Particular Account of the Late Action in the Mediterranean. London: T. Tons, 1744.

A Poetical Epistle from Admiral Byng, in the Infernal Shades, to his Friend L – A –, an Inhabitant on Earth. London: J. Fuller, 1757.

A Real Defence of A – l B – 's Conduct: Wherein is Clearly Exploded the Common Error so Prevalent of Censuring this Gentleman's Behaviour, by a Series of Indisputable Facts, Hitherto Concealed. London, 1756.

Addison, Joseph, Richard Steele and others, *The Spectator*, 8 vols. London: S. Buckley; J. Tonson, 1712–1715.

Admiral B—g in Horrors, at the Appearance of the Unhappy Souls, who was kill'd in the Engagement crying for Revenge. London[?], 1756[?].

Admiral Byng's Defence, as Presented by Him to the Court, on Board his Majesty's Ship St. George, January 18th, 1757. London[?], 1757[?].

Admiral Matthews's Account of the Action in the Mediterranean, as Publish'd by Authority, which Mr. Lestock in Part only has Thought Proper to Quote in his Recapitulation, before the Honble House of Commons, April 9th 1745. London: M. Cooper, 1745.

Admiral Mathews's Charge Against Vice-Admiral Lestock Dissected. London: John Millan, 1745.

Admiral Mathews's Remarks on the Evidence Given, and the Proceedings Had, on his Trial, and Relative Thereto. London, 1746.

[Almon, John], *A Review of the Reign of George II*, 2nd ed. London: J. Wilkie; Mr. Smith, 1762.

An Address to the British Army and Navy. Intended to Remind out Brave Warriors of the Important Interests, in which they are now Engaged, and the Generous Motives and Incitements they have to act with Vigilance, Steadiness, and Resolution in Repelling Bold Insults, and Chastising the Insufferable Pride, Arrogance and Perfidy of France. London: J. Buckland, 1756.

An Address to the Lords of the Admiralty, on their Conduct towards Admiral Keppel. London: J. Almon, 1778.

An Appeal to the People: Containing the Genuine and Entire Letter of Admiral Byng to the Secr. of the Ad—y: Observations on those Parts of it which were Omitted by the Writers of the Gazette: and what might be the Reasons for such Omissions. Part the First. London: J. Morgan, 1756.

An Appeal to the People: Part the Second. On the Different Deserts and Fate of Admiral Byng and his Enemies: The Changes in the Last Administration: The Year of Liberty or Thraldom. London: J. Morgan, 1757.

An Authentic and Impartial Copy of the Trial of the Hon. Augustus Keppel, Admiral of the Blue, Held as Portsmouth on the 7th of January, 1779, and Continued by Several Adjournments to the 11th day of February, 1779. Portsmouth: Messrs. Wheldon and Co; Messrs. Richardson and Urquhart; R. Faulder; J Fisk, 1779.

An Authentic and Impartial Copy of the Trial of the Sir Hugh Palliser, Vice-Admiral of the Blue, held on Board his Majesty's Ship the Sandwich, in Portsmouth Harbour on Monday, April 12, 1779, and Continued by Several Adjournments to Wednesday the 5th of May, 1779. Portsmouth: Messrs Wheldon and Co; Jos. White; H. Payne; R. Faulder; J. Fisk; M. Davenhill, 1779.

An Essay on Modern Gallantry. Address'd to Men of Honour, Men of Pleasure, and Men of Sense. With a Seasonable Admonition to the Young Ladies of Great Britain. London: M. Cooper, 1750[?].

An Heroic Congratulation, Addressed to the Honourable Augustus Keppel, Admiral of the Blue; On his being unanimously, Honourable, and Fully acquitted of the Five Malicious *and* Ill-founded Charges *exhibited Against Him by* Sir Hugh Palliser, *Vice-Admiral of the Blue.* London: J Dodsley; J. Almon; Richardson and Urquhart; J Bew; P. Broke, 1779.

Another Estimate of the Manners and Principles of the Present Times. London: G. Kearsley, 1769.

[Atkinson, William]. *A Letter to the Reforming Gentlemen, by the Old Inquirer.* Bradford: T. Inkersley, 1817.

Austen, Jane. *Persuasion*, ed. by Patricia Meyer Spacks. New York: W. W. Norton, 1995.

Authentic Letters from Admiral Mathews to the Sec— t- - - - s of St- - te, the L- - - - ds of the Ad- - - - - - ty &c. London: W. Webb, 1744[?].

[Barclay, Issac]. *Some Friendly and Seasonable Advice to Mr. Admiral Byng on His Approaching Court Martial.* London, 1756.

Berkenhout, [John]. *Lives of the British Admirals: Containing a New and Accurate Naval History, from the Earliest Periods. Written by Dr. J Campbell. With a Continuation Down to the Year 1779*, 4 vols. London: Alexander Donaldson, 1779.

Bond, Donald F., ed. *The Spectator*, 5 vols. Oxford: Clarendon, 1965.

Boswell, James. *The Life of Samuel Johnson*, 2 vols. London: Charles Dilly, 1791.

— *Boswell's London Journal 1762–63*, ed. by Frederick Pottle. London: Heinemann, 1952.

'Britain in Tears for the Loss of Brave General Wolfe', *The Muse's Delight: or, the Songster's Jovial Companion.* London: Pridden et al., 1760.

[Brown, John]. *An Estimate of the Manners and Principles of the Times*, 2nd ed. London: L. Davis and C. Reymers, 1757.

— *An Estimate of the Manners and Principles of the Times, Vol. II.* London: L. Davis and C. Reymers, 1758.

— *On the Natural Duty of Personal Service, in Defence of Ourselves and Country. A Sermon Preached at St Nicholas Church in Newcastle, on Occasion of a Late Dangerous Insurrection at Hexham.* London: L. Davies and C. Reymer, 1761.

Captain Gascoigne's Answer, to a Pamphlet Entitled Admiral Mathews's Remarks on the Evidence Given, and the Proceedings Had, on His Trial. London: M. Cooper, 1746.

Captain Opie's Appeal Against the Illegal Proceedings of Vice-Admiral Mathews, to the Late Lords Commissioners for Executing the Office of Lord High Admiral of Great Britain. London: M. Cooper, 1745.

Carey, H[enry]. 'A Satyr on the Luxury and Effeminacy of the Age', *Poems on Several Occasions*, 3rd ed. London: E. Say, 1729.

— *The Dragon of Wantley: A Burlesque Opera, as Perform'd at the Theatres with Universal Applause. Set to Musick by Mr. John-Frederick Lampe. To which Is Attached the Old Ballad, from Whence This Was Taken.* London [?], 1737[?].

Clarke, James Stanier. *Naval Sermons, Preached on Board His Majesty's Ship The Impetueux, The Western Squadron During Its Services Off Brest: To Which *is Added a Thanksgiving Sermon for Naval Victories.* London: T. Payne, B. White, 1798.

Clarke, James Stanier, and John McArthur. *The Life of Admiral Lord Nelson, K. B. From His Lordship's Manuscripts*, 2 vols. London: Cadell and Davies, 1809.

The Naval Chronicle, ed. by Nicholas Tracy, 5 vols. London: Chatham, 1998.

Cooper, Anthony Ashley, third Earl of Shaftesbury. *Characteristics of Men, Manners, Opinions and Times*, ed. by Lawrence E. Klein. Cambridge: Cambridge University Press, 1999.

Copley, Stephen, and Andrew Edgar, eds. *David Hume: Selected Essays*. Oxford: Oxford University Press, 1996.

Corbett, Julian S., ed. *Fighting Instructions, 1530–1816*. Publications of the Navy Records Society, 29 (1905).

Cowley, Charlotte. *The Ladies History of England; From the Descent of Julius Cæsar, to the Summer of 1780*. London: S. Bladon, 1780.

[Defoe, Daniel]. *A Dialogue betwixt Whig and Tory, aliàs Williamite and Jacobite.* London, 1693.

Some Reflections on a Pamphlet Lately Publish'd, Entituled, An Argument Shewing That a Standing Army Is Inconsistent with a Free Government, and Absolutely Destructive to the Constitution of the English Monarchy. London: E. Whitlock, 1697.

An Argument Shewing, That a Standing Army with Consent of Parliament Is Not Inconsistent with a Free Government. London: E. Whitlock, 1698.

A Brief Reply to the History of Standing Armies in England with Some Account of the Authors. London, 1698.

Ferguson, Adam. *Reflections Previous to the Establishment of a Militia.* London: R. and J. Dodsley, 1759.

An Essay on the History of Civil Society. Dublin: Boulter Grierson, 1767.

[Fletcher, Andrew]. *A Discourse of Government with Relation to Militia's.* Edinburgh, 1698.

Free, John. *An Ode of Consolation Upon the Loss of Minorca. Humbly Address'd to His Royal Highness, the Duke of Cumberland, &c.* London: R. Baldwin, 1756.

General B---y's Account to his Majesty, Concerning the Loss of Minorca. A Political Satire. London[?], 1756[?].

Goldsmith, [Oliver]. *The History of England, From the Earliest Times to the Death of George II*, 4 vols. London: T. Davies, Beckett and De Hondt, T. Cadell, 1771.

[Gordon, John]. *A New Estimate of Manners and Principles: Being a Comparison between Ancient and Modern Times in the Three Great Articles of Knowledge, Happiness and Virtue.* Cambridge: J. Bentham; W. Thurlbourn and J. Woodyer; A. Millar; R. & J. Dodsley; J. Beercroft, 1760.

[Guthrie, William]. *A Reply to the Counter-Address; Being a Vindication of a Pamphlet Entitled, an Address to the Public, on the Late Dismission of a General Officer.* London: W. Nicoll, 1764.

Haakonssen, Knud, ed. *Hume: Political Essays.* Cambridge: Cambridge University Press, 1994.

[Hayley, William]. *Epistle to Admiral Keppel*. London: Fielding and Walker, 1779.
Hervey, Frederic. *The Naval History of Great Britain; Including the Lives of the Admirals, and the Other Illustrious Commanders and Navigators, Who Have Contributed to Spread the Fame, and Increase the Power of the British Empire; from the Earliest Times to the Rupture with Spain in 1779*, 2nd ed., 4 vols. London: William Alard; J. Bew, 1780–83.
Horsley, William. *The Fool: Being a Collection of Essays and Epistles, Moral, Political, Humourous, and Entertaining*, 2 vols. London: Nutt, Cooke and Kingman, et al, 1748.
Hull, Mr, ed. *Selected Letters Between the Late Duchess of Somerset, Lady Luxborough, Miss Dolman, Mr. Whistler, Mr. R. Dodsley, William Shenstone, Esq., and Others*, 2 vols. London: J. Dodsley, 1778.
Hume, David. *The History of Great Britain, Vol. 1: Containing the Reigns of James I and Charles I*. Edinburgh: Hamilton, Balfour and Neill, 1754.
The History of England from the Invasion of Julius Caesar to the Accession of Henry VII, 2 vols. London: A. Millar, 1762.
Hurd, Richard. *Letters on Chivalry and Romance*. London: A Millar; W. Thurlbourn; J. Woodyer, 1762.
[Johnson, Samuel]. *A Confutation of a Late Pamphlet Intituled, A Letter Ballancing the Necessity of Keeping a Land Force in Times of Peace with the Dangers That May Follow on It*. London: A. Baldwin, 1698.
The Second Part of the Confutation of the Ballancing Letter. Containing an Occasional Discourse in Vindication of Magna Charta. London: A. Baldwin, 1700.
Le Faye, Deirdre, ed. *Jane Austen's Letters*, 4th ed. Oxford: Oxford University Press, 2011.
Letter from an Officer of the Naval Army of France to the Hon. Admiral Keppel; Dated on Board a French Squadron off Ushant, 9th of August, 1778. London, 1778.
[Lewis, Joseph]. 'Lancelot Poverty-Struck', 'The Prophet', in *The Miscellaneous and Whimsical Lucubrations of Lancelot Poverty-Struck, an Unfortunate Son of Apollo; and Author of the Westminster Magazine. Adapted to the Present Times*. London, 1758.
Lewis, W. S. and Ralph S. Brown, eds. *Horace Walpole's Correspondence with George Montagu*, Volume IX. London: Oxford University Press, 1941.
Lewis, W. S., George L. Lam and Charles H. Bennet, eds. *Horace Walpole's Correspondence with Thomas Gray, Richard West and Thomas Ashton*, Volume XIII–XIV. London: Oxford University, 1948.
Lewis, W. S., Warren Hunting Smith and George L. Lam, eds. *Horace Walpole's Correspondence with Sir Horace Mann*, Volumes XX, XXI, XXV. London: Oxford University Press, 1955–1971.
Mackenzie, Henry. *The Man of Feeling*, ed. by Stephen Bending and Stephen Bygrave. Oxford: Oxford University Press, 2001.
[Macpherson, James]. *A Short History of the Opposition during the Last Session of Parliament*, 2nd ed. London: T. Cadell, 1779.

Mason, W[illiam] *Ode to the Naval Officers of Great Britain. Written Immediately after the Trial of Admiral Keppel, February the Eleventh, 1779*. London: T. Cadell, 1779.
Memoirs of the Life and Actions of General W. Blakeney. London, 1756.
Minutes of the Proceedings at a Court-Martial, Assembled for the Trial of the Honourable Admiral Augustus Keppel, on a Charge Exhibited Against Him by Vice-Admiral Sir Hugh Palliser, Baronet. London: W. Strahan and T. Cadell, 1779.
Minutes of the Proceedings at a Court-Martial, Assembled for the Trial of Vice-Admiral Sir Hugh Palliser, Bart. London: W. Strahan and T. Cadell, 1779.
Minutes of the Proceedings of the Court Martial, on the Trial of Admiral Byng, Held on Board His Majesty's Ship St George, in Portsmouth Harbour; begun December 27, 1756, and Continued till January 27, 1757. London: H. Owen, 1757.
[Moyle, Walter]. *The Second Part of an Argument Shewing that a Standing Army is Inconsistent with a Free Government, and Absolutely Destructive to the Constitution of the English Monarch*. London, 1697.
Original Letters and Papers, Between Adm---l M----ws, and V. Adm---l L-----k. London: M. Cooper, 1744.
[Orme, Thomas]. *The Late Prints for a Standing Army and in Vindication of the Militia Consider'd, Are in Some Parts Reconcil'd*. London, 1698.
[Osborn, Sarah]. *Letter to the Lords of the Admiralty*. London[?], 1757[?].
Past Twelve o'Clock, or Byng's Ghost, an Ode, Inscribed to the Triumvirate; More Particularly His Grace the Duke of N--------. London: J. Scott, 1757.
Percy, Thomas. *Reliques of Ancient English Poetry: Consisting of Old Heroic Ballads, Songs, and Other Pieces of our Earlier Poets, (Chiefly of the Lyric Kind). Together with Some Few of a Later Date. Volume the First*. London: J. Dodsley, 1765.
P[ringle], J[ohn], *The Life of General James Wolfe, the Conqueror of Canada: or the Elogium of that Renowned Hero*. London: G. Kearsley, 1760.
[Prior, Matthew]. *A New Answer to an Argument Against a Standing Army*. London[?], 1697[?].
Remarks Upon a Scurrilous Libel Called an Argument, Shewing That a Standing Army Is Inconsistent with a Free Government. London, 1697.
Resolutions of the Court-Martial, Upon the Several Articles of the Charge Against Thomas Mathews, Esq; Previous to the Pronouncing Sentence. London[?], 1746[?].
Reynolds, Joshua. *Discourses*, ed. by Pat Rodgers. London: Penguin, 1992.
Several Reasons for the Establishment of a Standing Army, and Dissolving the Militia. London[?], 1700[?].
Smith, Adam. *The Theory of Moral Sentiments*. London: A. Millar; A. Kincaid and J. Bell, 1759.
Smollett, T[obias]. *A Complete History of England, Deduced from the Descent of Julius Caesar, to the Treaty of Aix La Chapelle, 1748. Containing the Transactions of One Thousand Eight Hundred and Three Years*, 4 vols. London: James Rivington and James Fletcher, 1757–58.
Some Doubts Occasioned by the Second Volume of an Estimate of the Manners and Principle of the Times. Humbly Proposed to the Author or to the Public. London: W. Sandby, 1758.

Some Further Considerations about a Standing Army. London, 1699.

Some Remarks upon a Late Paper, Entituled, An Argument, Shewing, That a Standing Army Is Inconsistent with a Free Government, and Absolutely Destructive to the Constitution of the English Monarchy. London[?], 1697.

[Somers, John]. *A Letter Ballancing the Necessity of Keeping a Land-Force in Times of Peace: With the Dangers that May Follow on It*. London[?], 1697.

Southey, Robert. *The Life of Nelson*, 2 vols. London: John Murray, 1813.

——— *The Life of Nelson*, 2nd ed., 2 vols. London: John Murray, 1814.

Stephens, Frederic George. *Catalogue of Prints and Drawings in the British Museum. Division 1: Personal and Political Satires*. Vol. III, Part II, *March 28th 1751–c.1760*. London, 1877.

[Stevenson, John]. *An Address to the Honourable Augustus Keppel, Containing Candid Remarks on His Late Defence with some Impartial Observations on such Passages as Relate to the Conduct of Vice-Admiral Sir Hugh Palliser*. London: Richardson and Urquhart, 1779.

Swaby, [Edward Lamport]. *An Ode, Most Humbly Inscribed to the Right Hon. Lord Blakeney, on His Arrival to England from Minorca*. London, 1757.

[Tasker, William]. *A Congratulatory Ode to Augustus Keppel, Admiral of the Blue*, 2nd ed. London: Dodsley; Becket; Richardson and Urquhart; Johnson; Kearsley; Ridley; W. Davis, 1779.

The Argument Against a Standing Army Rectified, and the Reflections and Remarks Upon it in Several Pamphlets, Consider'd in a Letter to a Friend. London, 1697.

The Annual Register; or, A View of the History, Politicks and Literature of the Year 1759. London: R. and J. Dodsley, 1762.

The British Hero and the Ignoble Poltron Contrasted; or, the Principle Actors in the Siege and Defence of Fort St. Philip, and the Mediterranean Expedition, Characteriz'. London: J. Robinson, 1756.

The Case of a Standing Army Army [sic] Fairly and Impartially Stated. In Answer to the Late History of Standing Armies in England: and Other Pamphlets Writ on That Subject. London, 1698.

The Case of the Hon. Admiral Byng, Ingeniously Represented. London: H. Owen, 1757.

The Charge Against Thomas Mathews, Esq; Also the Answer and Defence of Admiral Mathews to the Said Charge, 2nd ed. London: E. Cooper, 1746[?].

The Charge Against Vice-Admiral Lestock, to Which Is Added the Sentence Pronounc'd by the Court-Martial. London: J. Millan, 1746.

The Defence of Admiral Keppel. London: J. Almon, 1779.

The Defence of Vice-Admiral Sir Hugh Palliser, Bart. At the Court-Martial Lately Held upon Him, with the Court's Sentence. London: T. Cadell, 1779.

The Field of Mars: Being an Alphabetical Digestion of the Principal Naval and Military Engagements, in Europe, Asia, Africa, and America, particularly of Great Britain and her Allies, from the Ninth Century to the Present Period, 2 vols. London: J. MacGowan, 1781.

The History of the Mediterranean Fleet from 1741 to 1744, with the Original Letters, &c. that Passed between the Admirals Matthews and Lestock, 2nd ed. London: J[ohn] Millan, 1745.

The Indictment, Trial, and Condemnation, of Admiral Keppel, for Knowingly Bringing into the Court-Martial His Own Natural Countenance, to the Great Confusion of Sir Hugh Palliser. London: J. Johnson, 1779.

The Parliamentary Register; or, History of the Proceedings and Debates of the House of Commons. London: J Almon, 1779.

The Portsmouth Grand Humbug: Or, a Merry Dialogue Between the Boatswain and His Mate, on Board the Monarch Man of War, Relating to Admiral Byng, Who Is to be Shot One Time or Another. London, 1757.

The Proceedings at Large of the Court-Martial, on the Trial of the Honourable Augustus Keppel, Admiral of the Blue. Held on Board His Majesty's Ship Britannia, on Thursday, January 7th, 1779. London: J. Almon, 1779.

The Prosperity of Britain, Proved from the Degeneracy of Its People. A Letter to the Rev. Dr. Brown, Occasioned by His Estimate of the Manners. London: R. Baldwin, 1757.

The Real Character of the Age, in a Letter to the Rev. Dr. Brown, Occasioned by His Estimate of the Manners and Principles of the Times, 2nd ed. London: M. Cooper, 1757.

The Seaman's Opinion of a Standing Army in England in Opposition to a Fleet at Sea, As the Best Security of This Kingdom. In a letter to a Merchant, Written by a Sailor. London: A. Baldwin, 1699.

The Sentence Pronounc'd by the Court-Martial, Sitting Aboard His Majesty's Ship, the Prince of Orange, *at* Deptford, *on* Tuesday, *the 3rd of* June, *1746, on Vice-Admiral* Lestock. London: M. Cooper, 1746.

The Speech of the Honble Admiral Byng, Intended to have been Spoken on Board the Monarque at the Time of his Execution. London: T. Lindsey, 1757.

The Trial of the Honble. Admiral Byng, at a Court-Martial held on Board his Majesty's Ship the St George, in Portsmouth Harbour, Tuesday, Dec 28, 1756. London: J. Lacy, 1757.

The Trial of the Honourable Admiral John Byng, at a Court Martial, as Taken by Mr. Charles Fearne, Judge Advocate of his Majesty's Fleet. Published by Order of the Right Honourable the Lords Commissioners of the Admiralty, at the Desire of the Court-Martial. London: R. Manby; J. Whiston and B. White; W. Sanby; J Newbery; W. Faden, 1757.

The Trial of the Honourable Augustus Keppel, Admiral of the Blue Squadron, at a Court Martial held on His Majesty's ship Britannia, in Portsmouth Harbour, on Thursday 8th January 1779, on Charges Exhibited by Sir Hugh Palliser, for Misconduct and Neglect of Duty. Portsmouth: Messrs J. Wilkes, Breadhower and Peadle, 1779.

The Trial of the Honourable Augustus Keppel, Admiral of the Blue Squadron, for a Charge of Misconduct and Neglect of Duty, Exhibited Against Him by Vice-Admiral Sir Hugh Palliser. Bath: R. Cruttwell, 1779[?].

The Trial of Sir Hugh Palliser, Vice-Admiral of the Blue Squadron, at a Court-Martial, Held on Board His Majesty's Ship the Sandwich, in Portsmouth Harbour on Monday, April 19th, 1779, 3rd ed. London: J. Murray; C. Etherington, 1779.

The Trial of Vice-Admiral Byng, at a Court-Martial, Held on Board His Majesty's Ship the St. George, in Portsmouth Harbour. London: J. Reason, 1757.

Thoughts on the Conduct of Admiral Keppel, Together with Reasons for Restoring Sir Hugh Palliser into the Full Confidence and Good Opinion of His Country. London: Richardson and Urquhart, 1779.

Tindal, N[icholas]. *The Continuation of Mr. Rapin's History of England; From the Revolution to the Present Times*, 9 vols. London: Mr. Knapton, 1759.

To the Annonimus Author of the Argument Against a Standing Army. London[?], 1697[?].

[Toland, John]. *The Danger of Mercenary Parliaments.* London[?], 1698[?].

The Militia Reform'd: Or, An Easy Scheme of Furnishing England with a Constant Land-Force Capable to Prevent or to Subdue any Forein Power, and to Maintain Perpetual Quiet at Home Without Endangering the Public Liberty, 2nd ed. London: Daniel Brown; Andrew Bell, 1699.

[Trenchard, John]. *An Argument Shewing that a Standing Army Is Inconsistent with a Free Government and Absolutely Destructive to the Constitution of English Monarchy.* London, 1697.

A Letter from the Author of the Argument Against a Standing Army, to the Author of the Balancing Letter. London, 1697.

A Short History of Standing Armies in England, 3rd ed. London: A. Baldwin, 1698.

Vice-Adm---l L-st--k's Account of the Late Engagement Near Toulon, Between His Majesty's Fleet, and the Fleets of France and Spain; as Presented by Him the 12th of March 1744–5. Also Letters to and from Adm---l L-st--k, Relating Thereto Since His Arrival in England. London: M. Cooper, 1745.

Vice-Admal Lestock's Recapitulation, as Spoke by Him at the Bar of the Honble House of Commons, on Tuesday the 9th of April, 1745. London: John Millan, 1745.

Vice Admiral Lestock's Defence to the Court-Martial, Giving a Short View of the Nature of His Evidence. London, 1746.

Vice-Admiral Lestock's Vindication, as Spoke by Him at the Bar of the Hon. House of Commons, on Tuesday the 9th of April, 1745. Portsmouth[?]: J. Jingle, 1745.

Voltaire. *Candide and Other Stories*, ed. and trans. by Roger Pearson. Oxford: Oxford University Press, 1990.

Walpole, Horace. *The Castle of Otranto: A Gothic Story*, ed. by E. J. Clery. Oxford: Oxford University Press, 1996.

Warton, Thomas. *The History of English Poetry, From the Close of the Eleventh to the Commencement of the Eighteenth Century. To Which are Prefixed Two Dissertations. I) On the Origin of Romantic Fiction in Europe, II) On the Introduction of Learning into England. Volume the First*, 4 vols. London: J. Dosley; J. Walter; T. Beckett; J. Robson; G. Robinson; J. Bew, 1774.

Worthington, H. *A Letter Adapted to the Present Critical Juncture. Addressed to All Military Gentlemen, by Sea and Land; Pointing Out the True Soldier as a Animated by Religion and Love of his Country*, 2nd ed. London: R. Griffiths, 1758.

Secondary Sources

Alryyes, Ala. 'War at a Distance: Court-Martial Narratives in the Eighteenth Century'. *Eighteenth Century Studies*, 41.4 (2008), 525–42.

Anderson, Fred. *Crucible of War: The Seven Years War and the Fate of Empire in British North America, 1754–1766*. London: Faber, 2000.
Anderson, M. S. *The War of the Austrian Succession, 1740–1748*. New York: Longman, 1995.
Anglo, Sydney, ed. *Chivalry in the Renaissance*. Woodbridge: Boydell Press, 1990.
Aspden, Suzanne. 'Ballads and Britons: Imagined Community and the Continuity of English Opera'. *Journal of the Royal Musical Association*, 122.1 (1997), 24–51.
'Carey, Henry (1687–1743)'. *Oxford Dictionary of National Biography*, online ed. Oxford: Oxford University Press, 2004.
Auerbach, Nina. 'O Brave New World: Evolution and Revolution in *Persuasion*'. *ELH*, 39.1 (1972), 112–28.
Averill, James H. 'The Death of Stephen Clay and Richard Steele's *Spectators* of August 1711'. *The Review of English Studies*, 28 (1977), 305–10.
Bailey, Alan, and Dan O'Brien, eds. *The Continuum Companion to Hume*. London: Continuum, 2012.
Ball, Terence, and J. G. A. Pocock, eds. *Conceptual Change and the Constitution*. Lawrence: University of Kansas Press, 1988.
Barker, Hannah. *Newspapers, Politics, and Public Opinion in Late Eighteenth-Century England*. Oxford: Clarendon Press, 1998.
Barker, Hannah, and Simon Burrows, eds. *Press, Politics and the Public Sphere in Europe and North America, 1760–1820*. Cambridge: Cambridge University Press, 2002.
Barker, Hannah, and Elaine Chalus, eds. *Gender in Eighteenth-Century England: Roles, Representations and Responsibilities*. Longman: London, 1997.
Barker-Benfield, G. J. *The Culture of Sensibility: Sex and Society in Eighteenth-Century Britain*. Chicago: University of Chicago Press, 1992.
Barrell, John. *The Political Theory of Painting from Reynolds to Hazlitt*. New Haven, CT: Yale University Press, 1986.
The Birth of Pandora and the Division of Knowledge. Basingstoke: Macmillan, 1992.
Barrett, Kalter. 'DIY Gothic: Thomas Gray and the Medieval Revival', *ELH*, 70.4 (2003), 989–1019.
Baugh, Daniel. *British Naval Administration in the Age of Walpole*. Princeton, NJ: Princeton University Press, 1965.
The Global Seven Years War, 1754–1763: Britain and France in a Great Power Contest. Harlow: Pearson, 2011.
Bender, John. *Imagining the Penitentiary: Fiction and the Architecture of the Mind in Eighteenth-Century England*. Chicago: University of Chicago Press, 1989.
Benedict, Barbara M. *Framing Feeling: Sentiment and Style in English Prose Fiction, 1745–1800*. New York: AMS Press, 1994.
Benyon, John. *Masculinities and Culture*. Buckingham: Open University Press, 2002.
Berry, Christopher J. *Social Theory of the Scottish Enlightenment*. Edinburgh: Edinburgh University Press, 1997.
Bickham, Troy O. *Savages Within the Empire: Representations of American Indians in the Eighteenth Century*. Oxford: Clarendon, 2005.

Black, Jeremy. *Robert Walpole and the Nature of Politics in Early Eighteenth-Century Britain*. Basingstoke: Macmillan, 1990.
  A Military Revolution? Military Change and European Society, 1550–1800. Basingstoke: Macmillan, 1991.
  Britain as a Military Power: 1688–1815. London: UCL Press, 1999.
  'The Execution of Admiral Byng'. *Military History Quarterly*, 11 (1999), 98–103.
Black, Jeremy, and Philip Woodfine, eds. *The British Navy and the Uses of Naval Power in the Eighteenth Century*. Atlantic Highlands, NJ: Humanities Press International, 1989.
Black, Scott. 'Social and Literary Form in the Spectator'. *Eighteenth-Century Studies*, 33.1 (1999), 21–42.
Bohstedt, John. *Riots and Community Politics in England and Wales, 1790–1810*. Cambridge, MA: Harvard University Press, 1983.
Bonehill, John. 'Reynolds' Portrait of Lieutenant-Colonel Banastre Tarleton and the Fashion for War'. *British Journal for Eighteenth-Century Studies*, 24.2 (2001), 123–44.
Bonehill, John and Geoff Quilley, eds. *Conflicting Visions: War and Visual Culture in Britain and France, c.1700–1830*. Aldershot: Ashgate, 2005.
Botting, Fred. *Gothic*. London: Routledge, 1996.
Bowen, Scarlet. '"The Real Soul of a Man in Her Breast": Popular Opposition and British Nationalism in the Memoirs of Female Soldiers, 1740–1750'. *Eighteenth-Century Life*, 28.3 (2004), 20–45.
Bradley, James E. *Popular Politics and the American Revolution in England: Petitions, the Crown and Public Opinion*. Macon, GA: Mercer University Press, 1986.
Braudy, Leo. *The Frenzy of Renown: Fame and Its History*. Oxford: Oxford University Press, 1986.
Brewer, John. *The Sinews of Power: War, Money and the English State, 1689–1783*. London: Unwin Hyman, 1989.
  The Pleasures of the Imagination: English Culture in the Eighteenth Century. Abingdon: Routledge, 1997; repr. 2013.
Brinks, Ellen. *Gothic Masculinity: Effeminacy and the Supernatural in English and German Romanticism*. Cranbury, NJ: Associated University Presses, 2003.
Broadie, Alexander, ed. *The Cambridge Companion to the Scottish Enlightenment*. Cambridge: Cambridge University Press, 2003.
Brock, Claire. *The Feminization of Fame, 1750–1830*. Basingstoke: Palgrave Macmillan, 2006.
Brod, Harry, and Michael Kauffman, eds. *Theorizing Masculinities*. Thousand Oaks, CA: SAGE, 1994.
Broich, Ulrich. *The Eighteenth-Century Mock-Heroic Poem*, trans. by David Henry Wilson, 2nd ed. Cambridge: Cambridge University Press, 1990, repr. 1968.
Broich, Ulrich, H. T. Dickinson and Martin Schmidt, eds. *Reactions to Revolution: The 1790s and their Aftermath*. Berlin: Lit Verlag, 2007.
Broomfield, J. H. 'The Keppel–Palliser Affair, 1778–9'. *The Mariner's Mirror*, 47 (1961), 195–207.

Butler, Judith. 'Foucault and the Paradox of Bodily Inscriptions'. *The Journal of Philosophy*, 86.11 (1989), 601–7.
    Gender Trouble: Feminism and the Subversion of Identity. New York: Routledge, 1990; repr. 2007.
    Bodies that Matter: On the Discursive Limits of "Sex". New York: Routledge, 1993.
Cannadine, David, ed. *Admiral Lord Nelson: Contexts and Legacy*. Basingstoke: Macmillan, 2005.
    ed. *Trafalgar in History: A Battle and Its Afterlife*. Basingstoke: Macmillan, 2006.
Cardwell, John. *Arts and Arms: Literature, Politics and Patriotism during the Seven Years War*. Manchester: Manchester University Press, 2004.
    'The Rake as Military Strategist: Clarissa and Eighteenth-Century Warfare'. *Eighteenth-Century Fiction*, 19.1&2 (2006), 153–80.
Carter, Philip. 'An 'Effeminate' or 'Efficient' Nation? Masculinity and Eighteenth-Century Social Documentary'. *Textual Practice*, 11.3 (1997), 429–43.
    Men and the Emergence of Polite Society: Britain, 1660–1800. Harlow, Essex: Pearson, 2001.
Chaplin, Sue. *The Gothic and the Rule of Law, 1764–1820*. Basingstoke: Palgrave Macmillan, 2007.
Chickering, Roger, and Stig Förster, eds. *War in an Age of Revolution, 1775–1815*. Cambridge: Cambridge University Press, 2010.
Childs, John. *Armies and Warfare in Europe, 1648–1789*. Manchester: Manchester University Press, 1982.
    The British Army of William III, 1689–1702. Manchester: Manchester University Press, 1987.
    'War, Crime Waves and the English Army in the Late Seventeenth Century'. *War and Society*, 15.2 (1997), 1–17.
Clark, Anna. 'The Chevalier d'Eon and Wilkes: Masculinity and Politics in the Eighteenth Century'. *Eighteenth-Century Studies*, 32.1 (1998), 19–48.
Clayton, Timothy, *The English Print 1688–1802*. New Haven, CT: Yale University Press, 1997.
Clery, E. J. *The Rise of Supernatural Fiction, 1762–1800*. Cambridge: Cambridge University Press, 1995.
    The Feminization Debate in Eighteenth-Century England: Literature, Commerce and Luxury. Basingstoke: Palgrave Macmillan, 2004.
Cohen, Michèle. *Fashioning Masculinity: National Identity and Language in the Eighteenth Century*. London: Routledge, 1996.
    '"Manners" Make the Man: Politeness, Chivalry, and the Construction of Masculinity, 1750–1830'. *Journal of British Studies*, 44 (2005), 312–29.
Colley, Linda. *Britons: Forging the Nation, 1707–1837*, 2nd ed. New Haven, CT: Yale University Press, 2005.
Conlin, Jonathan. 'Benjamin West's General Johnson and Representations of British Imperial Identity, 1759–1770'. *British Journal for Eighteenth-Century Studies*, 27.1 (2004), 37–59.
Connell, R. W. *Masculinities*. Cambridge: Polity Press, 1995.
Conniff, James. 'Hume on Political Parties: The Case for Hume as a Whig'. *Eighteenth-Century Studies*, 12.2 (1978–9), 150–73.

Conway, Stephen. *The British Isles and the War of American Independence.* Oxford: Oxford University Press, 2000.
—— "'A Joy Unknown for Years Past': The American War, Britishness and the Celebration of Rodney's Victory at the Saints'. *History*, 86.2 (2001), 180–200.
—— 'War and National Identity in the Mid-Eighteenth-Century British Isles'. *The English Historical Review*, 116 (2001), 863–93.
—— *War, State and Society in Mid-Eighteenth-Century Britain and Ireland.* Oxford: Oxford University Press, 2006.
Cookson, J. E. 'The English Volunteer Movement of the French War, 1793–1815: Some Contexts'. *The Historical Journal*, 32.4 (1989), 867–91.
Copley, Stephen. 'Commerce, Conversation, and Politeness in the Early Eighteenth-Century Periodical'. *British Journal for Eighteenth-Century Studies*, 18.1 (1995), 63–77.
Corfield, Penelope J. *Power and the Professions in Britain 1700–1850.* London: Routledge, 1995.
Cowan, Brian. 'Mr Spectator and the Coffeehouse Public Sphere'. *Eighteenth-Century Studies*, 37.3 (2004), 345–66.
—— 'What Was Masculine about the Public Sphere? Gender and the Coffeehouse Milieu in Post-Restoration England'. *History Workshop Journal*, 51(2001), 127–57.
Coykendall, Abby. 'Chance Enlightenments, Choice Superstitions: Walpole's Historic Doubts and Enlightenment Historicism'. *The Eighteenth Century*, 54.1 (2013), 53–70.
Craig, David M. *Robert Southey and Romantic Apostasy: Political Argument in Britain, 1780–1840.* Woodbridge, Suffolk: Boydell, 2007.
Creighton, Margaret S., and Lisa Norling, eds. *Iron Men, Wooden Women: Gender and Seafaring in the Atlantic World, 1700–1920.* Baltimore: Johns Hopkins University Press, 1996.
Cress, Lawrence. 'Radical Whiggery on the Role of the Military: Ideological Roots of the American Revolutionary Militia'. *Journal of the History of Ideas*, 40 (1979), 43–60.
Crossland, John. 'The Keppel Affair'. *History Today*, 46.1 (1996), 42–8.
Csengei, Ildiko. *Sympathy, Sensibility and the Literature of Feeling in the Eighteenth Century.* Basingstoke: Palgrave Macmillan, 2012.
Danley, Mark H., and Patrick J. Speelman, ed. *The Seven Years' War: Global Views.* Leiden: Brill, 2012.
Davidson, Jenny. *Hypocrisy and the Politics of Politeness: Manners and Morals from Locke to Austen.* Cambridge: Cambridge University Press, 2004.
Davies, J. D. *Gentlemen and Tarpaulins: The Officers and Men of the Restoration Navy.* Oxford: Clarendon Press, 1991.
Dean, Ann C. 'Court Culture and Political News in London's Eighteenth-Century Newspapers'. *ELH*, 73.3(2006), 631–49.
Derry, John. *English Politics and the American Revolution.* London: Dent, 1976.
Deslandes, Paul R. 'The Boundaries of Manhood in Eighteenth- and Nineteenth-Century Britain'. *Gender and History*, 19.2 (2007), 376–79.

Dickinson, H. T., ed., *Britain and the French Revolution, 1789–1815*. Basingstoke: Macmillan, 1989.
  ed. *Britain and the American Revolution*. Harlow, Essex: Longman, 1998.
Dickinson, H. W. *Educating the Royal Navy: Eighteenth- and Nineteenth-Century Education for Officers*. London: Routledge, 2007.
Donoghue, Frank. *The Fame Machine: Book Reviewing and Eighteenth-Century Literary Careers*. Stanford, CA: Stanford University Press, 1996.
Downie, J. A. 'Chronology and Authorship of the Standing Army Tracts: A Supplement'. *Notes and Queries*, 23.8 (1976), 342–6.
Dudink, Stefan, Karen Hagemann and John Tosh, eds. *Masculinities in Politics and War: Gendering Modern History*. Manchester: Manchester University Press, 2004.
Duffy, Christopher. *The Military Experience in the Age of Reason*. London: Routledge and Kegan Paul, 1987.
Duffy, Michael, ed. *The Military Revolution and the State, 1500–1800*. Exeter: University of Exeter Press, 1980.
Dugaw, Dianne. 'The Popular Marketing of "Old Ballads": The Ballad Revival and Eighteenth-Century Antiquarianism Reconsidered'. *Eighteenth-Century Studies*, 21.1 (1987), 71–90.
Dull, Jonathan R. *The French Navy and the Seven Years War*. Lincoln: University of Nebraska Press, 2005.
Duncan, Alison. 'The Sword and the Pen: The Role of Correspondence in the Advancement Tactics of Eighteenth-Century Military Officers'. *Journal of Scottish Historical Studies*, 29.2 (2009), 106–22.
Drum, Alice. 'Pride and Prestige: Jane Austen and the Professions'. *College Literature*, 36.3 (2009), 92–115.
Dyer, Richard. *Heavenly Bodies: Film Stars and Society*, 2nd ed. London: Routledge, 1986; repr. 2004.
Eastwood, David. 'Robert Southey and the Meanings of Patriotism'. *Journal of British Studies*, 31.3 (1992), 265–87.
Eder, Markus. *Crime and Punishment in the Royal Navy of the Seven Years War, 1755–1763*. Aldershot: Ashgate, 2004.
Eisner, Eric. *Nineteenth-Century Poetry and Literary Celebrity*. Basingstoke: Palgrave Macmillan, 2009.
Eley, Geoff. 'Politics, Culture and the Public Sphere'. *Positions*, 10.1 (2002), 219–36.
Elias, Norbert. 'Studies in the Genesis of the Naval Profession'. *The British Journal of Sociology*, 1.4 (1950), 291–309.
Ellis, Markman. *The Politics of Sensibility: Race, Gender and Commerce in the Sentimental Novel*. Cambridge: Cambridge University Press, 1996.
  The History of Gothic Fiction. Edinburgh: Edinburgh University Press, 2000.
Ellison, Julie. *Cato's Tears and the Making of Anglo-American Emotion*. Chicago: University of Chicago Press, 1999.
Emsley, Clive. *British Society and the French Wars, 1793–1815*. Basingstoke: Macmillan, 1979.

Ennis, Daniel James. *Enter the Press-Gang: Naval Impressment in Eighteenth-Century British Literature*. London: Associated University Presses, 2002.
Fairer, David. 'The Origins of Warton's *History of English Poetry*'. *Review of English Studies*, New Series 32 (1981), 37–63.
  'Historical Criticism and the English Canon: A Spenserian Dispute in the 1750s'. *Eighteenth-Century Life*, 24.2 (2000), 43–64.
Fate Norton, David, and Jacqueline Taylor, eds. *The Cambridge Companion to Hume*, 2nd ed. Cambridge: Cambridge University Press, 1993; repr. 2009.
Favret, Mary. *War at a Distance: Romanticism and the Making of Modern Wartime*. Princeton, NJ: Princeton University Press, 2010.
Felsenstein, Frank. 'Unravelling Ann Mills: Some Notes on Gender Construction and Naval Heroism'. *Eighteenth-Century Fiction*, 19.1&2 (2006), 206–16.
Festa, Lynn. *Sentimental Figures of Empire in Eighteenth-Century Britain and France*. Baltimore: Johns Hopkins University Press, 2006.
Fletcher, Anthony. *Gender, Sex and Subordination in England 1500–1800*. New Haven, CT: Yale University Press, 1995.
Folkenflik, Robert, ed. *The English Hero, 1660–1800*. London: Associated University Presses, 1982.
Foucault, Michel. *Discipline and Punish: The Birth of the Prison*, trans by Alan Sheridan. London: Penguin, 1975; repr. 1991.
Frey, Anne. 'Nation Without Nationalism: The Reorganization of Feeling in Austen's *Persuasion*'. *Novel: A Forum on Fiction*, 38.2&3 (2005), 214–34.
Frey, Sylvia. 'Courts and Cats: British Military Justice in the Eighteenth Century'. *Military Affairs*, 43.1 (1979), 5–11.
Friedman, Albert B. *The Ballad Revival: Studies in the Influence of Popular on Sophisticated Poetry*. Chicago: University of Chicago Press, 1961.
Fulford, Tim. 'Romanticizing the Empire: The Naval Heroes of Southey, Coleridge, Austen, and Marryat'. *MLQ*, 60.2 (1999), 161–96.
  'Sighing for a Soldier: Jane Austen and Military Pride and Prejudice'. *Nineteenth-Century Literature*, 57.2(2002), 153–78.
  Romantic Indians: Native Americans, British Literature, and Transatlantic Culture 1756–1830. Oxford: Oxford University Press, 2006.
Fryd, Vivien Green. 'Rereading the Indian in Benjamin West's 'Death of General Wolfe''. *American Art*, 9.1 (1995), 72–85.
Gardner, Kevin J. 'George Farquhar's *The Recruiting Officer*: Warfare, Conscription, and the Disarming of Anxiety'. *Eighteenth-Century Life*, 25.3 (2001), 43–61.
Gat, Azar. *The Origins of Military Thought: From the Enlightenment to Clausewitz*. Oxford: Oxford University Press, 1989.
Gates, David. *The Napoleonic Wars, 1803–1815*. London: Pimlico, 2003.
Gatrell, Vic. *City of Laughter: Sex and Satire in Eighteenth-Century London*. London: Atlantic, 2006.
Gerrard, Christine. *The Patriot Opposition to Walpole: Politics, Poetry and National Myth, 1725–1742*. Oxford: Clarendon, 1994.
Gilbert, Arthur N. 'Law and Honour Among Eighteenth-Century British Army Officers'. *The Historical Journal*, 19.1 (1976), 75–87.

'Military and Civilian Justice in Eighteenth-Century England: An Assessment'. *The Journal of British Studies*, 17.2 (1978), 41–65.

'The Changing Face of British Military Justice, 1757–1783'. *Military Affairs*, 49.2 (1985), 80–4.

Girouard, Mark. *The Return to Camelot: Chivalry and the English Gentleman*. New Haven, CT: Yale University Press, 1981.

Glover, David, and Cora Kaplan. *Genders*. London: Routledge, 2000.

Goring, Paul. *The Rhetoric of Sensibility in Eighteenth-Century Culture*. Cambridge: Cambridge University Press, 2005.

Gould, Eliga H. 'To Strengthen the King's Hands: Dynastic Legitimacy, Militia Reform and Ideas of National Unity in England, 1745–1760'. *The Historical Journal*, 32.2(1991), 329–48.

Gradish, Stephen F. *The Manning of the British Navy During the Seven Years War*. London: Royal Historical Society, 1980.

Gregg, Stephen. '"A Truly Christian Hero": Religion, Effeminacy, and the Nation in the Writings of the Societies for Reformation of Manners'. *Eighteenth-Century Life*, 25.3 (2001), 17–28.

Gritten, David. *Fame: Stripping Celebrity Bare*. London: Allen Lane, 2002.

Grosz, Elizabeth. *Volatile Bodies: Towards a Corporeal Feminism*. Crows Nest, NSW: Allen and Unwin, 1994.

Guimarães, Lívia. 'The Gallant and the Philosopher'. *Hume Studies*, 30.1 (2004), 127–47.

Haakonssen, Knud, ed. *Adam Smith*. Aldershot: Ashgate, 1998.

Habermas, Jürgen. *The Structural Transformation of the Public Sphere*, trans. by Thomas Burger. Cambridge: Polity Press, 2006; repr. 1989.

Haggerty, George E. *Men in Love: Masculinity and Sexuality in the Eighteenth Century*. New York: Columbia University Press, 1999.

Hall, Christopher D. *Wellington's Navy: Sea Power and the Peninsular War, 1807–1814*. London: Chatham, 2004.

Hallett, Mark. *The Spectacle of Difference: Graphic Satire in the Age of Hogarth*. New Haven, CT: Yale University Press, 1999.

Harding, Richard. *Amphibious Warfare in the Eighteenth Century: The British Expedition to the West Indies, 1740–1742*. Woodbridge: Boydell, 1991.

The Emergence of Britain's Global Naval Supremacy: The War of 1739–1748. Woodbridge: Boydell, 2010.

Harkin, Maureen. 'Mackenzie's Man of Feeling: Embalming Sensibility'. *ELH*, 61.2 (1994), 317–40.

'Adam Smith's Missing History: Primitives, Progress, and Problems of Genre'. *ELH*, 72.2 (2005), 429–51.

Harrington, Peter, ed. *The Martial Face: The Military Portrait in Britain, 1760–1900*. Providence, RI: Brown University Press, 1991.

Harris, Jocelyn. '"Domestic Virtues and National Importance": Lord Nelson, Captain Wentworth, and the English Napoleonic Hero'. *Eighteenth-Century Fiction*, 19.1&2 (2006), 181–205.

A Revolution Almost Beyond Expression: Jane Austen's Persuasion. Newark: University of Delaware Press, 2007.
Harris, Robert. *A Patriot Press: National Politics and the London Press in the 1740s*. Oxford: Clarendon, 1993.
Politics and the Nation: Britain in the Mid-Eighteenth Century. Oxford: Oxford University Press, 2002.
Harvey, Karen. *Reading Sex in the Eighteenth Century: Bodies and Gender in English Erotic Culture*. Cambridge: Cambridge University Press, 2004.
'The History of Masculinity, circa 1650–1800'. *Journal of British Studies*, 44 (2005), 296–311.
The Little Republic: Masculinity and Domestic Authority in Eighteenth-Century Britain. Oxford: Oxford University Press, 2012.
Harvey, Karen, and Alexandra Shepard. 'What Have Historians done with Masculinity? Reflections on Five Centuries of British History, circa 1500–1950'. *Journal of British Studies*, 44 (2005), 274–80.
Hayter, Tony. *The Army and the Crowd in Mid-Georgian England*. London: Macmillan, 1978.
Haywood, Ian. *Bloody Romanticism: Spectacular Violence and the Politics of Representation, 1776–1832*. Basingstoke: Palgrave Macmillan, 2006.
Heuser, Beatrice. *The Strategy Makers: Thoughts on War and Society from Machiavelli to Clausewitz*. Santa Barbara, CA: Praeger, 2010.
Heydt-Stevenson, Jill. *Austen's Unbecoming Conjunctions: Subversive Laughter, Embodied History*. Basingstoke: Palgrave Macmillan, 2008.
Hicks, Philip. *Neoclassical History and English Culture*. Basingstoke: Macmillan, 1996.
Higate, Paul R., ed. *Military Masculinities: Identity and the State*. Westport, CT: Praeger, 2003.
Hill, J. R. *The Prizes of War: The Naval Prize System in the Napoleonic Wars, 1793–1815*. Stroud: Sutton, 1998.
Hill, Mike. 'The Crowded Text: E. P. Thompson, Adam Smith, and the Object of Eighteenth-Century Writing'. *ELH*, 69.3 (2002), 749–73.
Hitchcock, Tim. *English Sexualities, 1700–1800*. Basingstoke: Macmillan, 1997.
Hitchcock, Tim, and Michèle Cohen, eds. *English Masculinities 1660–1800*. Harlow, Essex: Addison Wesley Longman, 1999.
Hogle, Jerrold E., ed. *The Cambridge Companion to Gothic Fiction*. Cambridge: Cambridge University Press, 2002.
Holmes, Geoffrey. *Augustan England: Professions, State and Society, 1680–1730*. Hemel Hempstead, George Allen & Unwin, 1982.
Hont, Istvan, and Michael Ignatieff, eds. *Wealth and Virtue: The Shaping of the Political Economy of the Scottish Enlightenment*. Cambridge: Cambridge University Press, 1983.
Hoppit, Julian. *A Land of Liberty? England 1689–1727*. Oxford: Clarendon, 2000.
Hopskinson, David. 'The Naval Career of Jane Austen's Brother'. *History Today*, 26.9 (1976), 576–83.

Hughes, Matthew, and William J. Philpott, eds. *Palgrave Advances in Modern Military History*. Basingstoke: Palgrave Macmillan, 2006.
Hughes, William, and Andrew Smith, eds. *Queering the Gothic*. Manchester: Manchester University Press, 2009.
Inglis, Fred. *A Short History of Celebrity*. Princeton, NJ: Princeton University Press, 2010.
Jacobson, Anne Japp, ed. *Feminist Interpretations of David Hume*. Philadelphia: Pennsylvania State University Press, 2000.
Jarrett, Dudley. *British Naval Dress*. London: J. M. Dent, 1960.
Jenks, Timothy. *Naval Engagements: Patriotism, Cultural Politics and the Royal Navy, 1793–1815*. Oxford: Oxford University Press, 2006.
Johnson, Claudia. *Equivocal Beings: Politics, Gender and Sentimentality in the 1790s, Wollstonecraft, Radcliffe, Burney, Austen*. Chicago: University of Chicago Press, 1995.
  Jane Austen: Women, Politics and the Novel. Chicago: University of Chicago Press, 1988.
Johnson, Claudia L., and Clara Tuite, eds. *A Companion to Jane Austen*. Oxford: Blackwell, 2009.
Jones, Robert W. 'Notes on *The Camp*: Women, Effeminacy and the Military in Late Eighteenth-Century Literature'. *Textual Practice*, 11.3 (1997), 463–76.
  Literature, Gender and Politics in Britain during the War for America, 1770–1785 (Cambridge: Cambridge University Press, 2011).
Jordan, Gerald, and Nicholas Rogers. 'Admirals as Heroes: Patriotism and Liberty in Hanoverian England'. *Journal of British Studies*, 28.3 (1989), 201–24.
Keen, Maurice. *Chivalry*. New Haven, CT: Yale University Press, 1984
Kennedy, Catriona. *Narratives of the Revolutionary and Napoleonic Wars: Military and Civilian Experience in Britain and Ireland*. Basingstoke: Palgrave Macmillan, 2013.
Kennedy, Laurence. 'Standing Armies Revisited. 1697–1700: Authorship, Chronology and Public Perception'. *Notes and Queries*, 43.3 (1996), 287–92.
Kilbourne, H. R. 'Dr Johnson and War'. *English Literary History*, 12.2 (1945), 130–43.
Kilgour, Maggie. *The Rise of the Gothic Novel*. London: Routledge, 1995.
Kimmel, Michael S., and Michael A. Messner, eds. *Men's Lives*, 2nd ed. New York: Macmillan, 1989; repr. 1992.
Kindred, Sheila Johnson. 'Captain Charles Austen's Influence on *Persuasion* and *Mansfield Park*'. *Persuasions*, 31 (2009), 115–29.
Kirkham, Margaret. *Jane Austen, Feminism and Fiction*. Sussex: Harvester Press, 1983.
Klein, Lawrence. 'The Third Earl of Shaftesbury and the Progress of Politeness', *Eighteenth-Century Studies*, 18.2 (1984–5), 186–214.
  'Liberty, Manners and Politeness in Early Eighteenth-Century England'. *The Historical Journal*, 32.3 (1989), 583–605.
  'Gender, Conversation and the Public Sphere in Early Eighteenth-Century England'. In *Textuality and Sexuality: Reading Theories and Practices*, ed. by

Judith Still and Michael Worton. Manchester: Manchester University Press, 1993, pp. 100–15.
Shaftesbury and the Culture of Politeness: Moral Discourse and Cultural Politics in Early Eighteenth-Century England. Cambridge: Cambridge University Press, 1994.
'Politeness and the Interpretation of the British Eighteenth Century', *The Historical Journal*, 45.4 (2002), 869–98.
Klingel, Joan, and Richard James Wheeler. 'James Stanier Clarke's Portrait of Jane Austen'. *Persuasions*, 27 (2005), 112–8.
Knowles, Claire. 'Hazarding the Press: Charlotte Smith, the *Morning Post* and the Perils of Literary Celebrity'. *Romanticism*, 20.1 (2014), 30–42.
Knox-Shaw, Peter. *Jane Austen and the Enlightenment.* Cambridge: Cambridge University Press, 2004.
Kramnick, Isaac. *Bolingbroke and His Circle: The Politics of Nostalgia in the Age of Walpole.* Cambridge, MA: Harvard University Press, 1968.
Kramnick, Jonathan Brody. 'The Cultural Logic of Late Feudalism: Placing Spenser in the Eighteenth Century'. *ELH*, 63.4(1996), 871–92.
Making the English Canon: Print-Capitalism and the Cultural Past, 1700–1770. Cambridge: Cambridge University Press, 1998.
Kramp, Michael. *Disciplining Love: Austen and the Modern Man.* Columbus: Ohio State University Press, 2007.
Kuchta, David. *The Three-Piece Suit and Modern Masculinity-England, 1550–1850.* Berkeley: University of California Press, 2002.
Lacqueur, Thomas. *Making Sex: Body and Gender from the Greeks to Freud.* Cambridge, MA: Harvard University Press, 1990.
Langford, Paul. *A Polite and Commercial People, England 1727–1783.* Oxford: Clarendon, 1989.
'The Uses of Eighteenth-Century Politeness'. *Transactions of the RHS*, 12 (2002), 311–31.
Levine, Joseph M. *The Battle of the Books: History and Literature in the Augustan Age.* Ithaca, NY: Cornell University Press, 1991.
Linch, Kevin, and Matthew McCormack, eds. *Britain's Soldiers: Rethinking War and Society, 1715–1815.* Liverpool: Liverpool University Press, 2014.
Lincoln, Andrew. 'The Culture of War and Civil Society in the Reins of William III and Anne'. *Eighteenth-Century Studies*, 44.4 (2011), 455–74.
'War and the Culture of Politeness: The Case of *The Tatler* and *The Spectator*'. *Eighteenth-Century Life*, 36.2. 2012., 60–79
Lincoln, Margarette. *Representing the Royal Navy: British Sea Power, 1750–1815.* Aldershot: Ashgate, 2002.
Loar, Christopher F. 'How to Say Things with Guns: Military Technology and the Politics of Robinson Crusoe'. *Eighteenth-Century Fiction*, 19.1&2 (2006–7), 1–20.
Loxley, James. *Performativity.* London: Routledge, 2007.
Luckhurst, Mary, and Jane Moody, eds. *Theatre and Celebrity in Britain, 1600–2000.* Basingstoke: Palgrave Macmillan, 2005.

Luff, P. A. 'Mathews v. Lestock: Parliament, Politics and the Navy in Mid-Eighteenth-Century England'. *Parliamentary History*, 10.1 (1991), 45–62.
Mackay, Ruddock, and Michael Duffy. *Hawke, Nelson and British Naval Leadership, 1747–1805*. Woodbridge: Boydell, 2009.
Mackesy, Piers. *The War for America, 1775–1783*. Lincoln: University of Nebraska Press, 1964; repr. 1993.
Mackie, Erin. *Market à la Mode: Fashion, Commodity and Gender in* The Tatler *and* The Spectator. Baltimore: Johns Hopkins University Press, 1997.
Macleod, Emma Vincent. *A War of Ideas: British Attitudes to the Wars Against Revolutionary France 1792–1802*. Aldershot: Ashgate, 1998.
Marcus, G. J. *Heart of Oak: A Survey of British Sea Power in the Georgian Era*. London: Oxford University Press, 1975.
Marshall, P. David. *Celebrity and Power: Fame in Contemporary Culture*. Minneapolis: University of Minnesota Press, 1997.
McCormack, Matthew. *The Independent Man: Citizenship and Gender Politics in Georgian England*. Manchester: Manchester University Press, 2005.
  'Citizenship, Nationhood, and Masculinity in the Affair of the Hanoverian Soldier, 1756'. *The Historical Journal*, 49.4 (2006), 971–93.
  'The New Militia: War, Politics and Gender in 1750s Britain'. *Gender and History*, 19.3 (2007), 483–500.
  ed. *Public Men: Masculinity and Politics in Modern Britain*. Basingstoke: Palgrave Macmillan, 2007.
  Embodying the Militia in Georgian England. Oxford: Oxford University Press, 2015.
McCormack, Matthew and Catriona Kennedy. *Soldiering in Britain and Ireland, 1750–1850: Men at Arms*. Basingstoke: Palgrave Macmillan, 2012.
McDaniel, Iain. *Adam Ferguson in the Scottish Enlightenment: The Roman Past and Europe's Future*. Cambridge, MA: Harvard University Press, 2013.
McGann, Jerome. *The Poetics of Sensibility: A Revolution in Literary Style*. Oxford: Clarendon, 1996.
McKendrick, N. 'Josiah Wedgwood: An Eighteenth-Century Entrepreneur in Salesmanship and Marketing Techniques'. *The Economic History Review*, New Series 12.3 (1960), 408–33.
McKeon, Michael. 'Historicizing Patriarchy: The Emergence of Gender Difference in England, 1660–1760'. *Eighteenth-Century Studies*, 28.3 (1995), 295–322.
McNairn, Alain. *Behold the Hero: General Wolfe and the Arts in the Eighteenth Century*. Liverpool: Liverpool University Press, 1997.
McNeil, David. *The Grotesque Depiction of War and the Military in Eighteenth-Century English Fiction*. London: Associated University Presses, 1990.
McWhorter, Ladelle. 'Culture of Nature? The Function of the Term 'Body' in the Work of Michel Foucault'. *The Journal of Philosophy*, 86.11 (1989), 608–14.
Meehan, Johanna, ed. *Feminists Read Habermas: Gendering the Subject of Discourse*. New York: Routledge, 1995.

Middleton, Richard. *The Bells of Victory: The Pitt-Newcastle Ministry and the Conduct of the Seven Years War, 1752–1762.* Cambridge: Cambridge University Press, 1985.
The War of American Independence, 1775–1783. Harlow: Pearson, 2012.
Miller, Amy. *Dressed to Kill: British Naval Uniform, Masculinity and Contemporary Fashions 1748–1857.* Greenwich: National Maritime Museum, 2007.
Mole, Tom. *Byron's Romantic Celebrity: Industrial Culture and the Hermeneutic of Intimacy.* Basingstoke: Palgrave Macmillan, 2007.
 ed. *Romanticism and Celebrity Culture, 1750–1850.* Basingstoke: Palgrave Macmillan, 2007.
Moore, James. 'Hume's Political Science and the Classical Republican Tradition'. *Canadian Journal of Political Science*, 10.4 (1977), 809–39.
Moore, Stephen. "A Nation of Harlequins'? Politics and Masculinity in Mid-Eighteenth-Century England'. *Journal of British Studies*, 49.3 (2010), 514–39.
Mosse, George L. *The Images of Man: The Creation of Modern Masculinity.* Oxford: Oxford University Press, 1996.
Mossner, Ernest Campbell. 'David Hume's "An Historical Essay on Chivalry and Modern Honour"'. *Modern Philology*, 45.1(1947), 54–60.
Mullan, John. *Sentiment and Sociability: The Language of Feeling in the Eighteenth Century.* Oxford: Clarendon Press, 1988.
Muthu, Sankar. *Enlightenment Against Empire.* Princeton, NJ: Princeton University Press.
Myrone, Martin. *Bodybuilding: Reforming Masculinities in British Art, 1750–1810.* New Haven, CT: Yale University Press, 2005.
Nagle, Christopher. *Sexuality and the Culture of Sensibility in the British Romantic Era.* New York: Palgrave Macmillan, 2007.
Newman, Gerald. *The Rise of English Nationalism: A Cultural History, 1740–1830.* London: Weidenfeld and Nicolson, 1987.
Newman, Steve. *Ballad Collection, Lyric and the Canon: The Call of the Popular from the Restoration to the New Criticism.* Philadelphia: University of Pennsylvania Press, 2007.
Novak, Maximillian E., and Anne Mellor, eds. *Passionate Encounters in a Time of Sensibility.* London: Associated University Presses, 2000.
Nussbaum, Felicity A. *The Limits of the Human: Fictions of Anomaly, Race and Gender in the Long Eighteenth Century.* Cambridge: Cambridge University Press, 2003.
Nussbaum, Felicity, and Laura Brown, eds. *The New Eighteenth Century.* New York: Methuen, 1987.
Nye, Robert A. 'Western Masculinities in War and Peace'. *The American Historical Review*, 112.2 (2007), 417–38.
O'Brien, Karen. *Narratives of Enlightenment: Cosmopolitan History from Voltaire to Gibbon.* Cambridge: Cambridge University Press, 1997.
Okie, Laird. *Augustan Historical Writing: Histories of England in the English Enlightenment.* Lanham, MD: University Press of America, 1991.

Padfield, Peter. *Maritime Supremacy and the Opening of the Western Mind: Naval Campaigns That Shaped the Modern World, 1588–1782*. London: John Murray, 1999.
Palmer, Michael A. '"The Soul's Right Hand": Command and Control in the Age of Fighting Sail, 1652–1827'. *The Journal of Military History*, 61.4 (1997), 679–705.
Parker, Geoffrey. *The Military Revolution: Military Innovation and the Rise of the West, 1500–1800*. Cambridge: Cambridge University Press, 1988.
Peck, John. *Maritime Fiction: Sailors and the Sea in British and American Novels, 1719–1917*. Basingstoke: Palgrave, 2001.
Perry, Gill, and Michael Rossington, eds. *Femininity and Masculinity in Eighteenth-Century Art and Culture*. Manchester: Manchester University Press, 1994.
Peters, Marie. *Pitt and Popularity: The Patriot Minister and London Opinion during the Seven Years' War*. Oxford: Clarendon, 1980.
Phillipson, Nicholas, *Hume*. London: Weidenfeld & Nicholson, 1989.
Philp, Mark, ed. *Resisting Napoleon: The British Response to the Threat of Invasion, 1797–1815*. Aldershot: Ashgate, 2006.
Reforming Ideas in Britain: Politics and Language in the Shadow of the French Revolution 1789–1815. Cambridge: Cambridge University Press, 2014.
Pinch, Adele. *Strange Fits of Passion: Epistemologies of Emotion, Hume to Austen*. Stanford, CA: Stanford University Press, 1996.
Pocock, J. G. A. *The Ancient Constitution and the Feudal Law: A Study of English Historical Thought in the Seventeenth Century*. Cambridge: Cambridge University Press, 1957.
The Machiavellian Moment: Florentine Political Thought and the Atlantic Republican Tradition, 2nd ed., Princeton, NJ: Princeton University Press, 1975, repr. 2003.
Virtue, Commerce, and History: Essays on Political Thought, Chiefly in the Eighteenth Century. Cambridge: Cambridge University Press, 1985.
Pocock, Tom. *Battle for Empire: The Very First World War, 1756–63*. London: Caxton, 1998; repr. 2002.
Pollard, Sidney. *The Idea of Progress: History and Society*. London: Watts, 1968.
Poovey, Margaret *The Proper Lady and the Woman Writer: Ideology as Style in the Works of Mary Wollstonecraft, Mary Shelley and Jane Austen*. Chicago: University of Chicago, 1984.
Pope, Dudley. *At 12 Mr Byng was Shot*. London: Weidenfeld and Nicolson, 1962.
Postle, Martin, ed. *Joshua Reynolds: The Creation of Celebrity*. London: Tate Publishing, 2005.
Punday, Daniel. 'Foucault's Body Tropes'. *New Literary History*, 31.3 (2000), 509–28.
Punter, David, ed. *A Companion to the Gothic*. Oxford: Blackwell, 2000.
Reeder, John, ed. *On Moral Sentiments: Contemporary Responses to Adam Smith*. Bristol: Thoemmes Press, 1997.
Richardson, John. 'Modern Warfare in Early Eighteenth-Century Poetry'. *Studies in English Literature*, 45.3 (2005), 557–77.

'Imagining Military Conflict During the Seven Years War'. *SEL*, 48.3 (2008), 585–611.
Richter, Simon. 'The Ins and Outs: Gender, Epistolary Culture, and the Public Sphere'. *The German Quarterly*, 69.2 (1996), 111–24.
Robertson, John. *The Scottish Enlightenment and the Militia Issue*. Edinburgh: John Donald Publishers, 1985.
Rodger, N. A. M. *Articles of War: The Statutes which Governed Our Fighting Navies, 1661, 1749, 1866*. Havant: Kenneth Mason, 1982.
—— *The Command of the Ocean: A Naval History of Britain, 1649–1815*. London: Penguin 2004; repr. 2006.
—— *The Wooden World: An Anatomy of the Georgian Navy*. London: Fontana Press, 1988.
Rogers, Clifford J., ed. *The Military Revolution Debate: Readings on the Military Transformation of Early Modern Europe*. Boulder, CO: Westview Press, 1995.
Rogers, Nicholas. *Crowds, Culture, and Politics in Georgian Britain*. Oxford: Clarendon Press, 1998.
Rogers, Nicholas. 'The Dynamic of News in Britain During the American War: The Case of Admiral Keppel', *Parliamentary History*, 25.1 (2006), 49–67.
Rojek, Chris. *Celebrity*. London: Reaktion, 2001.
Rose, Craig. *England in the 1690s: Revolution, Religion and War*. Oxford: Blackwell, 1999.
Rothschild, Emma. *Economic Sentiments: Adam Smith, Condorcet, and the Enlightenment*. Cambridge, MA: Harvard University Press, 2001.
Royle, Edward. *Revolutionary Britannia? Reflections on the Threat of Revolution in Britain, 1789–1848*. Manchester: Manchester University Press, 2000.
Runge, Laura L. 'Beauty and Gallantry: A Model of Polite Conversation Revisited'. *Eighteenth-Century Life*, 25.1 (2001), 43–63.
Sales, Rogers. *Jane Austen and Representations of Regency England*. New York: Routledge, 1994.
Schumann, Matt, and Karl Schweizer. *The Seven Years War: A Transatlantic History*. Routledge: Abingdon, 2008.
Schwoerer, Lois G. *"No Standing Armies!": The Antimilitary Ideology in Seventeenth-Century England*. Baltimore: Johns Hopkins University Press, 1974.
Scott, Joan W. 'Gender: A Useful Category of Historical Analysis'. *The American Historical Review*, 91.5 (1986), 1053–75.
Sedgwick, Eve Kosofsky. *Between Men: English Literature and Male Homosocial Desire*. New York: Columbia University Press, 1985.
Sekora, John. *Luxury: The Concept in Western Thought, Eden to Smollett*. Baltimore: Johns Hopkins University Press, 1977.
Shaw, Philip, ed. *Romantic Wars: Studies in Culture and Conflict, 1793–1822*. Aldershot: Ashgate, 2000.
—— *Waterloo and the Romantic Imagination*. Basingstoke: Palgrave Macmillan, 2002.
—— 'Dead Soldiers: Suffering in British Military Art, 1783–89'. *Romanticism*, 11.1 (2005), 55–69.
—— *Suffering and Sentiment in Romantic Military Art*. Aldershot: Ashgate, 2013.

Shepard, Alexandra. *Meanings of Manhood in Early Modern England*. Oxford: Oxford University Press, 2003.
Sher, Richard B. *The Enlightenment and the Book: Scottish Authors and their Publishers in Eighteenth-Century Britain, Ireland and America*. Chicago: University of Chicago Press, 2006.
Shoemaker, Robert B. *Gender in English Society, 1650–1850: The Emergence of Separate Spheres?*. London: Longman, 1998.
Siebert, Donald T. 'Chivalry and Romance in the Age of Hume'. *Eighteenth-Century Life*, 21.1 (1997), 62–79.
Silver, Sean R. 'Visiting Strawberry Hill: Horace Walpole's Gothic Historiography'. *Eighteenth-Century Fiction*, 21.4 (2009), 535–64.
Simons, Clare A., ed. *Medievalism and the Quest for the. "Real" Middle Ages*. London: Frank Cass, 2001.
Smith, R. J. *The Gothic Bequest: Medieval Institutions in British Thought, 1688–1863*. Cambridge: Cambridge University Press, 1987.
Snyder, R. Claire *Citizen Soldiers and Manly Warriors: Military Service and Gender in the Civic Republican Tradition*. Lanham, MD: Rowman & Littlefield, 1999.
Solkin, David H. 'Great Pictures of Great Men? Reynolds, Male Portraiture and the Power of Art'. *The Oxford Art Journal*, 9.2 (1986), 42–9.
  Painting for Money: The Visual Arts and the Public Sphere in Eighteenth-Century England. New Haven, CT: Yale University Press, 1992.
Sorensen, Janet. *The Grammar of Empire in Eighteenth-Century British Writing*. Cambridge: Cambridge University Press, 2000.
Southam, Brian. *Jane Austen and the Navy*. London: Hambledon and London, 2000.
Spadafora, David. *The Idea of Progress in Eighteenth-Century Britain*. New Haven, CT: Yale University Press, 1990.
Stephens, H. M. 'Blakeney, William, Baron Blakeney. 1671/2–1761.', rev. Richard Harding, *Oxford Dictionary of National Biography*. Oxford : Oxford University Press, 2004; online ed., January 2008.
Storey, Mark. *Southey: A Life*. Oxford: Oxford University Press, 1997.
Susato, Ryu. 'The Idea of Chivalry in the Scottish Enlightenment: The Case of David Hume'. *Hume Studies*, 33.1 (2007), 155–78.
Tanner, Tony. *Jane Austen*. London: Macmillan, 1986.
Terry, Richard. 'Literature, Aesthetics, and Canonicity in the Eighteenth Century', *Eighteenth-Century Life*, 21.1 (1997), 80–101.
Thompson, E. P. 'Eighteenth-Century English Society: Class Struggle Without Class?'. *Social History*, 3.2 (1978), 133–65.
Todd, Janet. *Sensibility: An Introduction*. London: Methuen, 1986.
Tosh, John. 'What Should Historians Do with Masculinity? Reflections on Nineteenth-Century Britain'. *History Workshop Journal*, 38 (1994), 179–202.
  A Man's Place: Masculinity and the Middle Class Home in Victorian England. New Haven, CT: Yale University Press, 1999.

Manliness and Masculinities in Nineteenth-Century Britain: Essays on Gender, Family and Empire. Harrow: Pearson Longman, 2005.
Tracy, Nicholas. *Navies, Deterrence and American Independence: Britain and Seapower in the 1760s and 1770s*. Vancouver: University of British Columbia, 1988.
Trim, D. J. B., ed. *The Chivalric Ethos and the Development of Military Professionalism*. Leiden: Brill, 2003.
Trumbach, Randolph. *Sex and the Gender Revolution:* Vol. 1: *Heterosexuality and the Third Gender in Enlightenment London*. Chicago: University of Chicago Press, 1998.
Tunstall, Brian. *Admiral Byng and the Loss of Minorca*. London: Philip Allan, 1928.
Turner, Graeme. *Understanding Celebrity*. London: Sage, 2004.
van Creveld, Martin. *Technology and War, from 2000BC to the Present*. New York: Macmillan, 1989.
Vickers, Daniel. 'Beyond Jack Tar'. *William and Mary Quarterly*, 50.2 (1993), 418–24.
Vickery, Amanda. 'Golden Age to Separate Spheres? A Review of the Categories and Chronology of English Women's History'. *The Historical Journal*, 36.2 (1993), 383–414.
Wahrman, Dror. *The Making of the Modern Self: Identity and Culture in Eighteenth-Century England*. New Haven, CT: Yale University Press, 2004.
Walker, Eric C. *Marriage, Writing and Romanticism: Wordsworth and Austen After War*. Stanford, CA: Stanford University Press, 2009.
Wanko, Cheryl. 'Celebrity Studies in the Long Eighteenth Century: An Interdisciplinary Overview'. *Literature Compass*, 8.6 (2011), 351–62.
Watt, James. *Contesting the Gothic: Fiction, Genre and Cultural Conflict, 1764–1832*. Cambridge: Cambridge University Press, 1999.
Watts, Carol. *The Cultural Work of Empire: The Seven Years' War and the Imagining of the Shandean State*. Edinburgh: Edinburgh University Press, 2007.
Weed, David M. 'Sexual Positions: Men of Pleasure, Economy, and Dignity in Boswell's London Journal'. *Eighteenth-Century Studies*, 31.2 (1997), 215–34.
Wein, Tony. *British Identities, Heroic Nationalisms, and the Gothic Novel, 1746–1824*. Basingstoke: Palgrave Macmillan, 2002.
Wells, David Franklin. *The Keppel–Palliser Dispute, 1778–9: A Case Study in Eighteenth-Century English Politics*, unpublished manuscript, British Library, DSC qX22/9349.
Western, J. R. *The English Militia in the Eighteenth Century: The Story of a Political Issue, 1660–1802*. London: Routledge, 1965.
Whitehead, Stephen M. *Men and Masculinities: Key Themes and New Directions*. Cambridge: Polity Press, 2002.
Wilkinson, Clive. *The British Navy and the State in the Eighteenth Century*. Woodbridge: Boydell, 2004.
Wilson, Kathleen. *The Sense of the People: Politics, Culture, and Imperialism in England, 1715–1785*. Cambridge: Cambridge University Press, 1998; repr. 1995.

The Island Race: Englishness, Empire and Gender in the Eighteenth Century. London: Routledge, 2003.
Wind, Edgar. *Hume and the Heroic Portrait*, ed. by Jaynie Anderson. Oxford: Clarendon Press, 1986.
Winton, Calhoun. *Captain Steele: The Early Career of Richard Steele*. Baltimore: Johns Hopkins University Press, 1964.
Wishon, Mark. *German Forces and the British Army: Interactions and Perceptions, 1742–1815*. Basingstoke: Palgrave Macmillan, 2013.
Wolper, Roy S. 'The Rhetoric of Gunpowder and the Idea of Progress'. *Journal of the History of Ideas*, 31.4 (1970), 589–98.
Woodfine, Philip. *Britannia's Glories: The Walpole Ministry and the 1739 War with Spain*. Woodbridge: Boydell, 1998.
Woodworth, Megan A. *Eighteenth-Century Women Writers and the Gentleman's Liberation Movement: Independence, War, Masculinity and the Novel 1778–1818*. Aldershot: Ashgate, 2011.
Wright, Angela. *Britain, France and the Gothic, 1764–1820: The Import of Terror*. Cambridge: Cambridge University Press, 2013.

Index

Addison, Joseph, 28, 31–33, 36–37, 45, 106, 222
Admiralty, *See also Articles of War*
 Admiralty Instructions, 50
 as authority, 50–52, 56–58, 60, 84, 86–87, 91, 154, 169, 178, 198, 202
 correspondence with, 48, 53, 65, 182
 criticism of, 53, 58–59, 68–70, 160, 168, 194
 reform of navy, 54, 56–58, 68–70, 222
Almon, John, 46
American Independence, War of, 151, 177, 219. *See also* Ushant, battle off
 party politics, 154–55, 177–79
American, native, 137–40, 143. *See also* Savage, savagery
Anson, George, 57, 76
Army, *See also* Military
 clothing, uniform, 31, 42, 84, 137
 corruption, 30–31, 193
 development of, 14–15. *See also* Standing Army Debate
 Disbanding Bill, 26
 Guards, Royal, 14, 28, 37–38, 42
 impressment, 146
 ordinary soldiers, 29–30, 146–48
 patronage, 29, 39
 purchase system, 29
 recruitment, shortages, 93–94, 225
 volunteering, 225
Articles of War, 50, 54, 69–70, 76, 87, 156, 157
Atkinson, William, 218–19
Austen, Charles, 198–99, 202
Austen, Frank, 198–200, 201
Austen, Henry, 198
Austen, James Edward, 185, 186
Austen, Jane, 185–88, 196–205, 211–17, 224
 the body, 211–15
 brothers' naval careers, 197–202
 courage, 199–204
 heroism, 187, 198–205, 211–17
 military celebrity, 203–4

military service and money, 198–204
proto-feminism, 205, 211–17
Austrian Succession, War of, 44, 46–47. *See also* Toulon, battle of
 Cape Finisterre, battle of, 90
 Culloden, battle of, 47
 Dettingen, battle of, 46, 87
 Fontenoy, battle of, 47
 Jenkin's Ear, 46
 Treaty of Aix-la-Chapelle, 74

Ballad Revival, 97–99, 108–11, 117–18
Bedford, John Russell, Duke of, 57
Berkenhout, John, 72–73, 77, 84
Blakeney, William, 75, 89–93, 152
Body. *See also Corpus rasa*
 disease, injury, 23, 38–39, 41, 147, 186, 203, 207–8, 212–15
 mental health, 208, 214–15
 sexed, female, 9, 32–33, 63, 88–89, 94, 112–14, 120, 123–25, 180, 205–7, 209–11
 sexed, male, 4–8, 9, 18–21, 32–33, 35–36, 40–42, 63, 70–71, 84–95, 112–17, 118–21, 123–25, 132–35, 138–39, 141–43, 157–59, 174–75, 179–80, 205–12, 220–21, 223–24
 torture, 139
Boscawen, Edward, 75
Boswell, James, 1–2, 36–42, 127, 222
 militarism, 37–42
 politeness, 36–42
 sexuality, 41–42
Braddock, Edward, 75
British Empire, 74. *See also* Imperialism
Britishness, 12, 60–62, 89, 114–15, 206–7. *See also* Standing Army Debate
Brown, John, 87–89, 94, 104, 128, 134, 151, 223
Budgell, Eustace, 40
Burke, Edmund, 124, 125, 177
Butler, Judith, 8, 64. *See also* Performativity
Byng, George, 116–17

253

Byng, John, 73–98, 115–17, 123, 128, 152, 157, 181, 222
 councils of war, 84–85
 courage, lack of, 80–87, 92, 115–17
 courage, view of, 79–80
 discipline, 77–78
 duty, 76, 77–80
 execution, 111
 heroism, 87–93
 international identity, 78–79
 professionalization, 77–80

Canning, George, 203
Carey, Henry, 114–15
Castlereagh, Robert Stewart, Viscount, 203
Celebrity. *See also* Performativity: and celebrity
 and class, 151–53, 171–72
 and commerce, commercialization, 171–77
 and militarism, 147–48, 151–53, 160, 172–77, 180, 195–96, 203–4, 223–24
 and women, 286
Chatham, William Pitt, Earl of, 80, 94
Chivalry, 97–99, 100–2, 106–14, 179, 223
 knight as unnatural, 112–14, 118–21
 and women, 111–13
Christian, Robert, 166
Civic humanism, 3–7, 9, 16–21, 26–27, 33–34, 87–96, 99–102, 103–6, 138–50, 177–80, 185–86, 189–90, 191–96, 218–26. *See also* Standing Army Debate
Clarke, James Stanier, 187–90, 205–7
 the body, 205–7
 courage, 189–90, 205–7
 heroism, 190, 224
 as naval chaplain, 189–90
 Naval Chronicle, 188, 200
 naval professionalization, 189–90
 The Life of Nelson, 190
Collingwood, Cuthbert, 198
Corbett, Thomas, 65
Corpus rasa, 21–26, 29–30, 32–33, 34–36, 63–65, 79–80, 105–6, 112–14, 118–21, 126–31, 139–41, 213–17, 224
 criticism of, 62–63, 65–68, 84–89, 92–95, 138–41, 174–75, 178–79, 205–11
Courage, 18–27, 29–31, 37–39, 47–49, 64–65, 69, 76–80, 82–96, 105–6, 115–17, 119–20, 128–31, 133–35, 139–43, 157–59, 174–75, 181–83, 189–90, 199–204, 220–22
Courts Martial, 47, 54, 69, 155–56, 199. *See also* case studies by officer
 commerce, commercialization, 171–77
 judges, behaviour and comments during proceedings, 174
 log books, status of, 169–71, 174

 mob violence, 85–86, 168
 private letters, status of, 164–65
 public interest in, 11, 44–45, 47–48, 62, 70–71, 80–87, 115–17, 160–77
 publication of, 91, 172–76
 women's interest in, 167
Cruttwell, Richard, 173–74
Cruttwell, William, 173

Defoe, Daniel, 21–26, 45, 101–2, 221
Digges, West, 37
Duke of York, corruption scandal, 193

Fame, *See* Celebrity
Femininity
 frivolity, 167, 180
 masculinization, 32–33, 88–89, 112–14
 vulnerability, 63, 94, 179, 212
Ferguson, Adam, 131–35, 141–43, 223
 the body, 134–35
 courage, 133–35
 heroism, 135
 militarism, 133–35
 military service and money, 193
 militia, support for, 133–34
 politeness, 133
 progress, 131, 141–43
 savage, savagery, 141–43
 sympathy, 132–35, 141–43
Feuquières, Antoine de Pas de, 78
Fletcher, Andrew, 16–21, 94, 101, 107, 178, 221
Forfar, William, 170–71
Foucault, Michel, 7–8, 36, 64, 85, 220
Fowkes, Thomas, 76
Fox, Henry, 80
France
 as ally, 138
 hostility towards, 15, 26–27, 58, 115, 191.
  See also war: invasion, fear of
 military superiority, 47, 60–61, 225
 politeness. *See* Politeness: French
French Revolutionary and Napoleonic Wars, 74, 185
 Copenhagen, battle of, 191, 192
 First of June, battle, 189
 Nile, battle of, 191
 Santa Cruz, battle of, 191
 St Domingo, battle of, 200
 St Vincent, battle of, 191
 Trafalgar, battle of, 191, 197, 198
 Walcheron Expedition, 203
 Waterloo, battle of, 186–87, 196–97

Gambier, James, 198
Gardiner, Arthur, 77

Garrick, David, 44
Gascoigne, John, 58, 63, 67
Gothic, *See also* Chivalry; Supernatural
   as historical period, 99–114
Griffin, Thomas, 69
Guthrie, William, 120

Habermas, Jürgen, 11, 27–28, 36, 44, 161
Hamilton, Emma, 209–11
Harland, Robert, 158–59
Harrington, James, 99–100
Hawke, Edward, 75, 90, 160
Heroism, 12, 5, 72–74, 83, 84, 87–99, 103, 113–23, 125, 130–31, 135, 137–41, 145–50, 151–53, 155–59, 166–67, 169, 177–87, 190–204, 205–17, 222–24
Hervey, Frederick, 62
Higgins, Godfrey, 218–19
Hood, Alexander, 169–71
Horsley, William, 63, 71
Hume, David, 102–6, 107–8, 112–14, 118–20, 125, 129–30, 137
   the body, 112–14
   chivalry, 107–8, 112–14, 119
   courage, 105–6, 129–30
   feudalism, 102–3
   heroism, 113–14, 119–20
   militarism, 104–6
   militia, 103–4
   progress, 104–8
   women, 112–14
Hurd, Richard, 110–14, 117–19

Imperialism, 146–50, *See also* Savage, savagery
India, *See* Imperialism

Jacobinism, 185
Jacobitism, 46–47, 47n. 8
Johnson, Samuel (1649–1703), 18–19, 27, 99–100
Johnson, Samuel (1709–84), 1–2

Keppel, Augustus, 153–84, 223–24
   as consumer product, 172–77
   courage, 157–59, 182
   court martial for loss of ship, 155–56
   discipline, 156–57
   duty, 157–59
   heroism, 157–59, 166
   political alliances, 154–55
   public information, 162–65, 182–83
   rivalry with Palliser, 154
   sensibility, 177, 182–83
   view of inferiors, 166
Keppel, William, 160

Lacqueur, Thomas, 5–6
Lestock, Richard, 44–55, 58–71, 72–74, 76–83, 87, 89, 95, 155–60, 184, 192
   discipline, 50–51, 58–62, 63–67
   duty, 49–51, 59
   international identity, 61–62
   political alliances, 49
   professionalization, 55, 58–62, 63–67
Lewis, Joseph (Lancelot Poverty-Struck), 89
Luxury, 4, 40, 84–85, 87–89, 101, 106, 115

Mackenzie, Henry, 143–50, 223
   heroism, 145–50
   militarism, 144–50
   savage, savagery, 146–50
Macpherson, James, 108, 178–79
Magna Carta, 99–100
Masculinity, *See also* Body: sexed, male
   age, ageing, 36–37, 92–93, 145–48, 212, 214
   effeminacy, 5, 41, 85, 87–89, 107, 115, 133, 140, 142, 149–50, 180
   father-daughter relationship, 118, 121, 144–45, 212
   father-son relationship, 36, 91, 116–17, 121, 146, 148–50, 156
   feminization, 4, 40–42, 87–89, 113, 131, 140–41
   gallantry, 111–13, 131
   hegemony, 3
   infertility, 121, 150, 213
   marriage, domesticity, 121, 150, 206–7, 209–17, 224
   modesty, 150
   patriarchal, 42, 93–94, 118–19, 121, 144–50, 179, 185–87, 205–17, 223–24
Mathews, Thomas, 44–55, 58, 62–71, 73, 76–78, 79–80, 83, 89, 95, 155, 160, 222
   discipline, resistance to, 51–54, 62–63, 66
   duty, 48, 52–53, 65–66
   political alliances, 49
   professionalization, resistance to, 62–63
McArthur, James, *See* Clarke, James Stanier: *The Life of Nelson*
Military, *See also* Army; Navy
   career, hardship, 22–23, 38–40, 203–4, 207–8
   career, payment, 18–19, 24–25, 27, 31, 40, 68, 104–5, 133–34, 147–48, 152, 156, 180, 204
   clothing, uniform, 31, 42, 57–58, 84, 137, 192
   discipline, training, 16–27, 29–30, 37–39, 49–63, 68–71, 77–79, 105–6, 127–30, 133–34, 156–57, 206, 222
   disease, injury, 23, 203, 207–8, 214
   literature on warfare, 78, 79
   officers and sexual desire, 40–42, 111–13, 145, 209, 212
   officers as authors, anxiety about, 67–68, 83

Index

Military (*cont.*)
  officers, international identity, 56, 61–62, 78–79, 138, 192
  professionalization, 16–27, 29–31, 37–39, 45–46, 49–71, 77–80, 82–87, 104–6, 127–31, 133–35, 144–48, 155–56, 189–90, 191–204, 222
  willingness to serve as duty, 94–95, 179, 189, 206–7, *See also* Standing Army Debate
Military Revolution, 7, *See also* Standing Army Debate
Military service
  levée en masse, 225
  as natural, 4–5, 16–21, 42, 65–68, 85–95, 114–17, 133–35, 138–39, 141–50, 174–75, 179, 189–90, 192–96, 205–12, 220–21, 222–23
  as performance, 7–8, 20–26, 29–33, 37–42, 49–62, 63–71, 77–80, 84–87, 104–6, 111–14, 118–21, 127–31, 139–41, 156–59, 162–68, 171–72, 196–204, 212–17, 221–24
Militia
  classical, 3–5, 17–18
  debate about, 22l, 21–26, 103–6, 127–28, 133–34, 178–79
  feudal, 100–2
  Militia Act, 94
  new militia, 5, 93–95, 151, 198, 226
  riots, 95
Minorca, battle of, 75–78, 80–85, 89–93, 116, 128
  councils of war, 84–85
  party politcs, 80–81
Monarchs
  Charles II, 14
  George II, 87
  George IV as Prince Regent, 189
  James II, 14
  William III, 15
  William IV as Duke of Clarence, 192
Monckton, Robert, 75
Mostyn, Savage, 69
Mulgrave, Constantine Phipps, Baron, 157, 165–66

Napoleon Bonaparte, 197
Nature, *See* Body
Navy, *See also* Military
  clothing, uniform, 57–58, 84, 192
  education, 55–56, 60–61
  escort duty, freight-money, 200
  Fighting Instructions, 51, 52, 78
  flag-titles, 65
  half-pay, 69–70, 199, 204
  homosexuality, 207
  impressment, 93, 95
  medals, rewards, 189, 195, 200
  midshipmen, 56, 85
  mutinies at Spithead and Nore, 189, 206–7
  Navigation Act, 195
  Navy Board, 50
  ordinary sailors, 62, 85, 203
  patronage, 56, 154–55, 198
  privateers, 201
  prizes, prize-money, 155–56, 194–95
  promotion, 198–200
  recruitment, shortages, 93–94, 225
  religion, 189–90, 205–7
  signalling, 50–54
  unemployment, 198–99
  warrant officers, 85, 166, 170–71
Nelson, Frances, 209
Nelson, Horatio, 90, 190–96, 207–11
  depression, 208
  duty, 194–95, 209
  heroism, 191–96
  illness, 207–8
  interest in celebrity, 195–96
  marriage, adultery, 209–11
  medals, rewards, 195
  politeness, 192
  prizes, lack of interest in, 194–95
  view of allies, 193–94
Newcastle, Thomas Pelham Holles, Duke of, 75, 80–81
Newspapers, 47–48, 81, 154, 161–65, 169–70, 172–73, 182–83, 204
Norris, John, 53
Nugent, Robert Craggs, Earl, 179–80

Opie, John, 54
Orme, Thomas, 100

Painting, grand manner, 73, 137–39
Palliser, Hugh, 153–59, 161–65, 169–71, 174–75, 177–84, 223
  courage, 158–59, 174–75, 181
  duty, 158–59
  log book scandal, 169–71
  political alliances, 154–55
  public information, 162–65
  rivalry with Keppel, 154
  sensibility, 181–83
Parry, Joshua, 137
Payne, John Willet, 189
Penny, Edward, 137
Percy, Thomas, 108–10
Performativity, 8, 9–6, 33–42, 63–68, 85–87, 104–6, 125–31, 163–66, 211–17. *See also* Military Service: as performance; Politeness: as performance
  celebrity, 171–72
  historicizing, 20–21

Index

Philips, Baker, 69
Pocock, J. G. A., 3–5, 99, 101, 219–20
Politeness
  defence of, 29–33, 44–45, 103, 104–14, 125–31, 140–41, 167–68
  as discipline, 34–42, 125–31
  and feminization, 40–42, 111, 131
  French, 26–27, 61–62, 115
  hostility towards, 5, 26–27, 33–34, 60–62, 66, 73–74, 84–85, 87–89, 133, 141–43, 180, 190, 192, 222
  as performance, 34–42, 61–62, 84–85, 104–6, 125–31
  and sensibility. *See* Sensibility: and politeness
  and women, 33, 40–42, 111–14, 131, 167
Politics, *See also* Standing Army Debate
  Bill of Rights, 15
  Disbanding Bill, 26
  extra-parliamentary politics, 12, 71, 81–82, 86, 160–61
  Militia Act, 94
  Parliament, history of, 99–103
  party politics, 15, 49, 80–81, 99–100, 114, 154–55, 161–62, 177–79
Portsmouth Naval Academy, 56
Progress, theory of, 21, 32–33, 103–14, 117–21, 130–31, 139–50
Public opinion, 46, 49, 62, 71, 81–82, 125, 160, 185–87, 223–24, *See also* Courts Martial: public interest in; Newspapers; War: public interest in
  mob violence, 85–86, 168
  rumour, status of, 169–71
Public sphere, 27, 36, 44–45, 98, 125, 160, 161–62, 185–87, 214–15, 223–24, *See also* Habermas, Jürgen; Newspapers
  commerce, commercialization, 116, 171–77

Reynolds, Joshua, 146, 168
Robinson, Thomas, 167–68
Rowley, William, 47, 48, 52
Russane, Henry, 47
Russell, Edward, 58

Sandwich, John Montagu, Earl of, 57, 154–55, 162, 165
Santa Cruz de Marcenado, Marquess, 78
Savage, savagery, 138–43, 146–50, 223
Sensibility
  and the body, 123–25, 126–31, 132–35, 138–43
  as conservative, 123–25, 148–50, 177, 223
  and humanitarianism, 148–50
  and imperialism, 146–50

  and politeness, 123–31, 133, 136–37, 181–83
  as sympathy. *See* Ferguson, Adam: sympathy; Smith, Adam: sympathy
Seven Years War, 74–75, 123, 125, 132, *See also* Minorca, battle of
  Quebec, battle of, 75, 136
  Quiberon Bay, battle of, 75
  recruitment, shortages, 93–94
Sexuality
  heterosexuality, 40–42, 111–13, 120–21, 140, 150, 209–12
  homosexuality, 95, 120, 207
Shaftesbury, Anthony Ashley Cooper, Earl of, 34–36, 106
Shenstone, William, 44
Sheridan, Thomas, 37–38
Smith, Adam, 35, 125–35, 139–41, 223
  the body, 126–31, 139–41
  courage, 128–31
  duty, 126–31
  heroism, 130–31, 139–41
  militarism, 127–31
  politeness, 126–27, 128
  savage, savagery, 139–41
  sympathy, 125–31, 136–38, 139–41
  women, 131
Smollet, Tobias, 48–49, 144
Somers, John, 21–26, 34–35, 221
Southey, Robert, 186, 190–96, 207–11
  the body, 207–9
  heroism, 191–96
  military service and money, 193–95
  naval professionalizaton, 193
  republicanism, 192
Spanish Succession, War of, 14
Spectator, 28–33, 37, 40
Standing Army Debate, 14–27, 33–34, 45, 55, 58, 61, 100–2, 104, 128, 134, 138, 142, 144, 152, 178, 184, 185, 189, 218–24
Steele, Richard, 28–32, 37, 40, 45, 128
Supernatural, 115–21, 210–11, 181, 223

Tindall, Nicholas, 70
Toland, John, 16–21, 26, 34, 94, 152, 221
Toulon, battle of, 46–49, 72–73
  parliamentary inquiry, 49, 155
Trenchard, John, 15–21, 22, 23, 24–25, 26, 33, 45, 100, 102, 104, 134

Ushant, battle off, 153–54, 156
  mob violence, 168
  parliamentary debate, 154–55

Vernon, Edward, 58–59

Walpole, Horace, 115–22, 223
   the body, 119–22
   chivalry, 119–20
   heroism, 119–20
   militarism, 115–16
Walpole, Robert, 46, 57, 115
War, *See also* battles by name; wars by name
   battlefield tourism, 186–87
   casualties, 22, 38–39, 123, 136–37, 191, 203–4
   debate about, 16–26, 32, 100–4, 142, 147–48, 187
   finance, 24, 104–5, 133–34, *See also* Military: career, payment
   intelligence, use of, 75, 162
   invasion, fear of, 17, 47, 75, 151, 178, 179, 185
   public interest in, 11, 44, 46–47, 75, 136, 154, 185–87, 197, 202–4. *See also* Courts Martial: public interest in; Public opinion

Warton, Thomas, 109
Wedgwood, Josiah, 176–77
Wellington, Arthur Wellesley, Duke of, 197
West, Benjamin, 137–39, 146
West, Temple, 81
Whistler, Anthony, 44–45
Winchilsea, Daniel Finch, Earl of, 57
Wolfe, James, 123, 136–39, 146, 176
Women. *See also* Celebrity: and women; Chivalry: and women; Politeness: and women
   impressed by militarism, 201, 215–17
   intelligence, 210, 213–14, 215
   military capacity, 32–33, 114, 213–14
   in need of protection, 94, 111–13, 179, 206–7, 212
   prostitution, 41–42, 144–45
   proto-feminism, 205, 211–17